This question of names deserves the closest attention for it seems full of pitfalls. Almost every day some well-intentioned chef or cook will either give a new name to a dish which is already known to everyone as something else or he will introduce under a well-known name a preparation different from that which the name normally implies. These are bad practices which all chefs and cooks conscious of their professional responsibility should do their best to stamp out. If allowed to continue, such practices will debase the culinary art beyond redemption.

Since this book is particularly for practitioners, it is in their mutual interest to keep the Author and Publishers informed of details of new creations or local recipes which have not so far been included so that every new edition of " *Le Répertoire* " may be made even more comprehensive than the last.

To The Master of Modern Cookery
AUGUSTE ESCOFFIER
OUR RESPECTFUL ADMIRATION
Louis Saulnier and Edouard Brunet

The Menu

WHETHER for a great banquet or just a family meal, the menu should be perfectly balanced and it should be short.

In composing the menu, the aim should be to express as far as possible the spirit of the occasion for which it is intended and to reflect, so to speak, the nature of the guests invited. Particular care is needed with the menu for an official meal in ensuring that it does not include dishes with names that might cause offence to any of those attending.

Pompous words such as *Cryptogamia* instead of *Mushroom* should not be used although, if employed with extreme moderation, a bold euphemism such as " Black Pearls " for truffles is occasionally permissible. On no account should new terms or names be created. Misuse of " à la " is a common fault, as for example "Omelette *à la* Masséna," "Sole *à la* Carmen," "Pêche *à la* Melba," when the name of the dish is meant as a dedication. These words mean "in the manner of" or " after the style of " and should be used only in a dedicatory sense.

The rule for the sequence of dishes on the menu is summed up in a sentence by Brillat Savarin: " The order of the eatables is from the substantial to the lighter ones." An exception to the rule will be the " hors d'oeuvre," which must not be heavy. There is a tendency nowadays to make them too complicated and important.

Never should the menu include the same form of vegetable twice, two dishes of the same kind of meat, fowl or game; two sauces of the same make or same colour; or, except for hunting dinners, two kinds of game.

The various cheeses should not be mentioned individually, except on certain rare occasions; they should always be served with the fruit.

Because the obvious is so frequently overlooked, it is worth remembering that when compiling a menu care must be taken to ascertain that the produce called for is in season and that nothing in the menu will obstruct any of the services in the kitchen.

It may not be out of place to add that neither a fine frame nor an artistic mount makes a menu a masterpiece; it is the skill with which it is conceived and thought out by the chef. The menu should, therefore, always be signed by him.

La bonne cuisine est la base du véritable bonheur.—

A. ESCOFFIER

The Wines

Of all the countries in the world, there is none that provides such really good wine as France. In the kitchen French wine is essential. The finest recipes may prove disappointing unless prepared with the best wine obtainable.

Where "White Wine" or "Red Wine" is mentioned in the following pages without reference to a particular wine, either wine from Bordeaux or Burgundy may be used. If these are not obtainable we would emphasise that only the very best quality of American, Australian or South African wine should be used.

This point is emphasised because it is of such great importance. The best practitioner in the world can obtain good results only if he has at his disposal products known to be authentic and of perfect quality.

TO THE SOCIETY HOST OR HOSTESS

Le Répertoire de la Cuisine is invaluable. Its limited edition and discriminative distribution ensures the possessor of invaluable knowledge for the production of the best menus. Therefore *Le Répertoire de la Cuisine* is a book treasured the world over.

Explanation of French Culinary Terms

Abats	-	Includes: heads, hearts, livers, kidneys, feet, etc.
Aiguillette	-	Any meats, cut thin and long.
Animelles	-	Delicate part of the lamb, also known as Criadillas.
Appareil	-	Mixture of different elements for preparation of a dish.
Aromates	-	All herbs and roots with a tasty flavour.
Barder	-	The wrapping of poultry, game or fish, with thin slices of fat bacon.
Blanchir	-	Ingredients gradually brought to the boil in order to remove the scum.
Bouquet garni		A faggot made of parsley, thyme, bay leaf, and celery.
Braiser -	-	Cook slowly and with little moistening under cover.
Brunoise	-	Vegetables cut in small dice.
Chapelure	-	Brown bread crumbs.
Chaufroiter	-	Coated with a chaudfroid sauce.
Chemiser	-	The clothing, or lining, of a mould with aspic, or ice cream, etc.
Chiffonnade	-	Lettuces or Sorrel, ciseled and cooked in butter for soup garnish.
Ciseler -	-	To cut a vegetable after the manner of a chaffcutter.
Concasser	-	To chop roughly.
Contiser	-	To incise meat or fish and insert slices of truffles, or other substance.
Crépinette	-	Sheet of cow's or calf's udder.
Crépin	-	Pig's caul.
Croustadines	-	Flat bouchées of different shapes made with puff paste.
Dépouiller	-	To cook slowly in order to remove scum and fat when it comes to the surface.
Ebarber	-	To remove the border part of oysters, mussels, or fish.
Emincer	-	To cut in thin slices.
Escaloper	-	To cut in thin slices, sideways.
Etouffer	-	To cook under cover and with very little moistening.
Farcir	-	To stuff the interior of poultry, fish, etc., with forcemeat, rice, etc.
Fleurons	-	Lozenges, crescents or other shapes made with puff paste.

Glacer -	-	To colour a dish under the salamander.
Gratiner	-	To pass in oven or salamander a prepared dish, sprinkled with bread crumbs or cheese in order to give it a golden colour.
Julienne	-	Vegetables cut into match-shaped rods.
Larder -	-	To insert with special larding needles some thin strips of fat bacon into meats or poultry, etc.
Macédoine	-	Vegetables or fruits of different kinds cut into dice and mixed.
Macérer	-	To keep for some time fruits in liquor, in order to flavour it.
Mariner -	-	To keep meat in marinade to give it more tenderness and flavour.
Marmite	-	Firstly is the stockpot. Secondly, French pot with lid similar to casserole with two fingergrips on each side.
Mijoter	-	To simmer for a long time.
Mirepoix	-	Is composed of carrots, onions, fresh bacon and ham cut into dice, and is used as base for sauces.
Mortifier	-	To hang meat, poultry or game, in order to make it more tender.
Mouiller	-	To moisten with water, stock or consommé, the ingredients to be cooked.
Napper	-	To coat or cover with sauce or aspic the prepared dishes.
Paner -	-	To egg and crumb any ingredients before frying.
Panade -	-	See page 5.
Parer -	-	To trim and remove all superfluous matters from any articles.
Peluche	-	Shreds of chervil.
Pincer -	-	To colour slightly in oven, vegetables, bones or chicken, before moistening.
Piquer -	-	To insert in meats or poultry some large Julienne of fat bacon, ham, or truffle, etc.
Plat à Sauter -		A flat-bottomed pan with low sides.
Pilaw-Pilaff	-	Fish or meat made with rice or barley and seasoning.
Réduire -	-	To boil a sauce or stock in order to give it thicker consistency and more richness when reduced.
Repère -	-	Flour mixed with water or white of egg, and used to seal lids of cocottes or pans when cooking.
Revenir	-	To toss quickly in hot fat any meats or vegetables in order to colour them before moistening.

Rissoler	-	To toss in hot fat or butter in order to give colour.
Salamandre	-	A gas apparatus to gratin or glaze the prepared dishes.
Salpicon	-	A mixture of various products, cut into dices and covered with sauce.
Sangler -	-	To place the ice-mould in a recipient with crushed ice and freezing salt.
Saucer -	-	To pour sauce over or round a prepared article.
Sauté -	-	Browned quickly in fat or butter.
Sauteuse	-	A sauté pan.
Singer -	-	To sprinkle with flour.
Suer -	-	To place meats, fish, etc., in a pan with fat and heat slowly under cover.
Suprêmes	-	A name given to the fillet or breast of fowl, fish, or game.
Tomated	-	The addition of tomato purée to any preparation in
Tomber des		order to give a distinct shade and flavour to it.
Tomber des		To cook vegetables with water and butter until water is
Légumes	-	completely evaporated.
Tourner	-	To give vegetables a regular shape.
Tronçons	-	Thick slices of fish or ox-tail.
Vésiga -	-	The dried spine-marrow of the sturgeon.
Voiler -	-	To cover or surround certain pieces of confectionery with spun sugar.
Zeste -	-	The yellow, glossy film of the rind of an orange or lemon.

THE COOKERY REPERTORY

FUNDAMENTAL ELEMENTS OF COOKING
FONDS DE CUISINE

The Foundations, Sauces and Stocks are of primary importance in Cookery and their value cannot be over-emphasised.

It is impossible for the chef or cook to do excellent cooking if the " fonds de cuisine " are not made with the best ingredients obtainable. The better the ingredients employed, the better will be the final result. It is therefore false economy to neglect this very important part of the Culinary Art.

Appareils à Cromesquis et à Croquettes.—(See Chapter on Entrées Volantes).

Appareil Maintenon.—Two parts of onion sauce and one part mushroom puree cohered with yolks of eggs; add minced mushrooms.

Appareil Montglas.—Julienne thick and short of tongue, foie gras, cooked mushrooms, truffles. Cohered with reduced Madeira sauce, and cooked on buttered dish.

Appareil à Mousse chaude et Mousseline.—(See Farce à Quenelles). With the addition of cream in order to have the preparation lighter.

Appareil à Mousse froide et Mousseline.—Purée of the cooked principal element mixed with melted aspic seasoned and mixed with whipped cream.

Appareil à Pommes Dauphine, Duchesse et Marquise.—(See Chapter on Vegetables).

Aspic.—Mould lined with aspic jelly, decorated to taste, place in the interior the ingredients required for the making of the aspic and cover with jelly. Let the first layer set if another one or more is necessary to fill the mould.

Bordures (Borders).—Borders are made with forcemeat or white paste, or noodle paste, or fried croûtons. Those made with forcemeat may be decorated with truffles, tongue, pistachios, white of eggs, etc. Those made with paste are shaped with fancy cutters dried and stuck together with yolk of eggs; when made of fried croûtons they are stuck together with meat glaze and dried.

Chaudfroid.—To coat with chaudfroid sauce the pieces laid on a wire stand, decorated and glazed with aspic.

Consommé Blanc (White Consommé).—Shin of beef, veal knuckles. water, carrots, turnips, leeks, parsnips, celery-stick, onion with clove stuck in it, cook 5 hours, strain.

Consommé Clarifié (Clarified Consommé).—Lean beef chopped or passed through mincing machine, and put in a pan with white of eggs previously beaten with water, add to the above White Consommé, minced carrots and leeks, and bring quickly to the boil; simmer gently for two or three hours.

Consommé de Volaille, de Gibier, etc. (Chicken or Game Consommé).—Same process as before, with less meat and the addition of an old fowl, or game, slightly coloured in the oven.

Coulis d'Ecrevisses, de Homard (Crayfish or Lobster cullis).—Same as Nantua sauce and Américaine sauce, but thicker.

Coulis de Tomates (Tomato Cullis).—Thick tomato sauce.

Court-Bouillon (A).—White wine or red wine, fish stock and aromatic herbs, for matelotes.
(B).—Salt water, milk, lemon juice, for sea fishes with white flesh.
(C).—Salt water, vinegar and aromatic herbs, for shellfish, salmon, trout, and various river fish.

Croûtons.—Are made with bread, cut different shapes, and fried in butter.

Duxelles à la Bonne Femme.—Dried duxelles mixed with same quantity of Pâté forcemeat.

Duxelles (dried).—Chopped onions lightly coloured in butter, add chopped mushrooms, cook until complete evaporation.

Duxelles for Stuffed Vegetables.—Reduction of white wine mixed with dried duxelles, add tomated half glaze, garlic, bread crumbs and chopped parsley.

Essence.—Juice of the ingredient reduced to a concentrated degree.

Farce à l'Américaine (American Stuffing).—Chopped onions tossed with smoked bacon, add bread crumbs, salt and pepper.

Farce à Gibier (Game Forcemeat).—$\frac{1}{2}$ pork meat, $\frac{1}{4}$ game meat, $\frac{1}{4}$ fat of fresh pork, seasoned, brandy, pounded and passed through the sieve.

Farce à Gratin pour Croûtons.—Chicken livers seasoned with salt and black pepper, tossed with fat bacon, pounded and passed through the sieve.

Farce à Gratin pour Gibier (Gratin Forcemeat for Game).—Chicken and game livers tossed with fat bacon, and game flesh, thyme, bay leaf, pounded and passed through sieve.

Farce à Gratin pour Pâtés Chauds (Gratin Forcemeat for Raised Pies).—Chicken livers tossed with fat bacon, seasoned with salt, pepper, spices, pounded and passed through sieve.

Farce à Pâté (Raised pie Forcemeat).—$\frac{1}{4}$ lean pork, $\frac{1}{4}$ veal, $\frac{1}{2}$ fresh pork fat, seasoned, add a small glass of brandy, pounded and passed through the sieve.

Farce à quenelles, etc. (Forcemeat for Veal, Chicken, Game, Fish, Quenelles, etc.).—Pound the raw meats in the mortar, pass through the sieve, seasoned, add cream gradually, and white of eggs for the fish forcemeat.

Farce de Canard à la Rouennaise (Stuffing for Duckling à la Rouennaise). Chopped onions tossed in butter, add the ducks' livers, salt, pepper, spices.

Farce de Canard (Stuffing for Duck à l'Anglaise).—Chopped onions cooked in butter, mixed with bread crumbs, salt, pepper, nutmeg and chopped sage.

Farce de Poisson (Fish Forcemeat).—Fillets of sea fish or river fish, pounded in mortar with white of eggs, seasoning, passed through the sieve and gradually add cream until the proper consistency.

Fonds Blanc (White Stock).—Veal bones and shin of veal, fowls' carcasses, carrots, onions stuck with clove, leeks, celery, faggot of herbs, water, salt. Allow to boil 3 to 5 hours, skim carefully, strain, and put aside until wanted.

Fonds Brun ou Estouffade (Brown Stock or Estouffade).—Shin of beef (flesh and bone), shin of veal, raw ham, fresh pork rind, carrots and minced onions, browned in butter. Break the bones, and colour in oven in saucepan, moisten with water, add the vegetables and a faggot, (see **Bouquet garni,** under "Culinary Terms"), cook slowly for 8 hours, strain.

Fonds Blanc de Volaille (White Chicken Stock).—Same preparation as ordinary white stock, with the addition of old chicken and carcasses.

Fonds de Gibier (Brown Game Stock).—Game trimmings, old birds, pheasants or partridges, browned in oven, add carrots, thyme, bay leaves, sage, onions, leeks, celery, moistened with white wine and water, cook slowly for 5 hours.

Fonds Plat, Tampons et Croustades.—Are made with bread or with rice. The bread ones are cut different shapes and fried in clarified butter.

Preparation of rice for cushion.—Wash the Patna rice, blanch for 5 minutes, drain, and wash again in hot water. Place it in a pan lined with fat bacon, add some alum, cover with more slices of fat pork, and cook slowly for 5 hours. Pound and work in a greased serviette and moulded in a greased recipient. When cold, shape to taste and keep in alum water.

Fondue de Tomates (Concassées Tomatoes).—Chopped onions, slowly cooked in butter, add dice of tomatoes, garlic, salt, pepper. Cooked until completely evaporated.

Fumet de Poisson (Fish Stock).—Minced onions and trimmings of soles and whiting, moistened with water and white wine, add parsley roots and stalks, mushroom parings, pepper, lemon juice and salt, cook 30 minutes, strain.

Fish Stock with Red Wine.—Same preparation as above with red wine instead of white.

Garnishes of Cod Dishes.—The following are mostly used:—

Hard-boiled eggs stuffed and cut in halves or quarters.
Small garnished tomatoes.
Quarters of large, stuffed tomatoes.
Tartlets filled with Russian salad.
Small cold soufflés.
Barquettes filled with vegetable purée.
Lettuce hearts in quarters or ciselled.
Olives, stoned or stuffed.
Anchovy fillets.
New vegetables, glazed with aspic.

Gelée Ordinaire (Ordinary Meat Jelly).—Operate as for White Stock, adding pieces of beef, calves' feet and pork rind, clarify the next day.

Gelée de Volaille (Chicken Jelly).—Same preparation as above, with old fowl instead of beef.

Gelée de Gibier (Game Jelly).—Same preparation with trimmings and carcases of game.

Gelée de Poisson (Fish Jelly).—Clarified fish stock reduced to the required consistency.

Meat Glaze, Chicken or Game Glaze.—Are made by reducing the brown stock, chicken stock and game stock.

Godiveau (Veal Quenelles).—Veal and beef kidney fat pounded together with salt, pepper, nutmeg, add eggs one at a time, passed through the sieve, finished with cream.

Godiveau Lyonnais.—½ pike flesh, ¼ beef kidney fat, ¼ marrow, pounded in mortar with Panade (C), white of eggs and seasoning, passed through the sieve and finished with cream.

Jus lié (Thickened Gravy).—Brown veal stock boiled and thickened with arrow-root, diluted with a little cold water and poured in the boiling gravy.

Kache de Sarrasin pour Potages (Kasha for Soups).—Moisten one pound of buckwheat with warm water to make a stiff paste; bake it in a large charlotte mould for 2 hours; remove the crust, and mix in butter while hot, spread on a buttered tray and let cool, cut into roundels, roll in flour, and fry in clarified butter.

Kache of Semolina for Coulibiac.—Coarse semolina mixed with egg, dried and poached in consommé, cooked 20 minutes and drained.

Marinade instantanée.—Minced shallots, parsley springs, salt, pepper, lemon juice, oil.

Marinade crue (Raw Marinade).—Carrots, onions, shallots, minced celery, garlic, parsley sprigs, thyme, bay leaves, black pepper, cloves, moistened with ½ white wine, ¼ vinegar, ¼ oil, place the meats to be marinaded in a terrine, and cover with the marinade.

Marinade with Red Wine (cooked).—Same as above. The vegetables partly cooked in oil, cooked 30 minutes, let cool before using.

Matignon.—Paysanne of carrots, onions, celery, raw ham, bay leaf, thyme, cooked in butter and Madeira wine.

Mirepoix.—Cubes of carrots, onions, raw ham, bay leaf and thyme, tossed in butter.

Mirepoix à la Bordelaise.—Fine Brunoise of carrots, onion and parsley roots, thyme and bay leaf, cooked in butter.

Pains froids.—Glaze of the principal element required, worked with yolk of eggs and butter as for **Hollandaise.** Mixed with dice of truffles and the treated element, and placed in a mould lined with aspic.

Panades—

(a) Bread crumbs soaked in milk and evaporated on the fire, let cool before using.

(b) Same as for **Pâte à Choux,** without eggs.

(c) Flour mixed with yolk of eggs, melted butter, salt, pepper and nutmeg, moistened with boiling milk (let cool before using).

(d) Rice moistened three times its volume with white consommé, add butter and cook 45 minutes. Work it to obtain a smooth paste.

(e) Cooked potatoes, minced and moistened with milk, seasoned with salt, pepper, nutmeg, reduced and worked with butter.

Provençale.—Reduced Béchamel sauce with little garlic. Cohered with yolk of eggs.

Pâte à Frire (Batter).—Flour, salt, oil, mixed with water into a thin paste, add white of eggs lightly beaten.

Riz à Farcir.—Rice and chopped onions partly fried in butter without colouration, moistened with double quantity of white consommé, cooked 17 minutes, cohered with cream Suprême sauce, or meat glaze.

Roux Brun (Brown Roux).—Clarified butter mixed with flour and cooked slowly in oven until a light brown colour is obtained.

Roux Blanc (White Roux).—Same as above but without colouring the preparation.

Saumure au Sel.—Salt and saltpetre, the pieces of meat must be pricked with a trussing needle and rubbed with powdered saltpetre, placed in a terrine and covered with the salt, thyme and bay leaves.

Saumure Liquide (Brine).—Saltpetre, grey salt, brown sugar. When the water boils throw in a peeled potato: if it floats add water until in begins to sink; if the potato sinks immediately reduce the liquid.

Twarogue for Pirogui.—In a terrine put some cream cheese, flour and butter, mix together, add egg, salt and pepper.

Beurres Composés—Compound Butters

Ail (Garlic).—Blanched garlic cloves, pounded in mortar with butter, pass through a fine sieve.

Amande (Almond).—Paste made with sweet almonds, pounded with a little water and butter, pass through sieve.

Anchois (Anchovy).—Anchovy fillets pounded in mortar with butter, pass through fine sieve.

Avelines.—Grilled avelines, pounded with a little water and butter, pass through sieve.

Bercy.—Reduction of white wine with chopped shallots, add dice of poached marrow, chopped parsley, salt, black pepper, lemon juice, and butter softened into a cream.

Beurre rouge (Red Butter).—Pound into fine powder some carcass of shellfish, add some butter. Melt the mixture in a saucepan in a bain-marie. Strain through muslin into a basin of iced water.

Beurre Vert (Green Butter).—Pound some raw spinach, and press it in a towel to extract the juice, put it in a pan and let it coagulate in a bain-marie, and pour it on to a serviette stretched over a bowl to drain the water. Collect the green colouring and mix it with butter, pass through a fine sieve.

Caviar.—Pound the caviar in mortar with butter and pass through the sieve.

Chivry or Ravigote Butter.—Parsley, shallots, tarragon, fresh pimpernel and chives, blanched and pounded in mortar with butter, passed through sieve.

Colbert.—Maître-d'hôtel butter mixed with meat glaze and chopped tarragon.

Crevettes (Shrimps).—Shrimps pounded with butter and passed through fine sieve.

Ecrevisses (Crayfish).—Carcass of crayfishes pounded with butter and passed through a tammy.

Escargots (Snails).—Chopped shallots, crushed garlic and chopped parsley, salt, pepper, mixed with butter and brandy.

Estragon (Tarragon).—Tarragon leaves blanched and pounded with butter, passed through sieve.

Hareng (Herring).—Fillets of smoked herrings pounded with butter and passed through sieve.

Homard (Lobster).—Creamy parts, eggs and coral of lobster pounded with butter and passed through sieve.

Laitance (Soft Roes).—Poached soft roes pounded with butter and mustard, passed through sieve.

Maître-d'hôtel.—Butter softened to a cream, mixed with chopped parsley, salt, black pepper, lemon juice.

Manié.—Butter in cream mixed with flour.

Marchand de Vins.—Reduction of red wine with chopped shallots, pepper, salt, mixed with meat glaze, lemon juice, chopped parsley and creamy butter.

Meunière.—Nut brown cooked butter mixed with lemon juice, chopped parsley.

Montpellier.—Watercress, parsley, chervil, chives, spinach, chopped shallots, boiled two minutes, drained and pressed, add gherkins, capers, garlic, anchovy fillets, pounded with butter, yolk of eggs raw and hard, add oil by degrees, cayenne pepper, and pass through fine sieve.
Note. If this preparation is for coating fish the oil and eggs are omitted.

Moutarde (Mustard).—Creamy butter mixed with French mustard.

Noir (Black).—Cook butter until black, strain, and add vinegar.

Noisette (Nut Brown).—Cook the butter until a nice light brown colour.

Paprika.—Chopped onions and paprika, tossed in butter, and mixed with creamy butter, passed through sieve.

Pimentos.—Pound the pimentoes with butter, and pass through sieve.

Pistaches.—(See **Beurre d'Amandes**) with pistachios instead of almonds.

Printanier.—Butter made with new vegetables such as carrots, French beans, peas, etc.

Raifort (Horseradish).—Scraped horseradish pounded with butter, and passed through sieve.

Tomates (de).—Tomatoes pounded with butter, passed through sieve.

Truffes.—Pounded with butter and Béchamel sauce, pass through sieve.

Garnitures—Garnishes

Africaine *(for large joints)*.—Mushrooms or cèpes, egg-plant, quarters of tomatoes, tossed in oil, château potatoes.

Algérienne *(for large joints)*.—Small tomatoes, peeled and cooked in oil, croquettes of sweet potatoes.

Allemande *(for large joints)*.—Noodles tosssed in butter, mashed potatoes.

Ambassadeur *(for large joints)*.—Duchesse potatoes, artichoke bottoms filled with mushroom purée, scraped horseradish.

Alsacienne—Tartlets garnished with braised Sauerkraut, and rondels of ham.

Américaine *(for Fish)*.—Slices of lobster tail and slices of truffles.

Ancienne *(for Chicken)*.—Small braised onions without colouring, and mushrooms.

Andalouse *(for large joints and Poultry)*.—Half capsicums stuffed with riz à la Grecque and sections of egg-plant cooked in oil, garnished with dice of tomatoes; chopped parsley on the tomatoes.

Anglaise *(for Chicken)*.—Carrots, turnips, cauliflowers, French beans, plain boiled potatoes. The lot cooked in salt water.

Anversoise *(for large joints)*.—Tartlets garnished with hop shoots mixed with cream, steamed potatoes.

Arlésienne *(for Tournedos and Noisettes)*.—Slices of egg-plant fried in oil, roundels of fried onions, and dice of tomatoes, cooked in oil.

Armenonville *(for large joints)*.—Quarters of artichoke bottoms, cocotte potatoes, tomatoes, French beans.

Aubergines *(for large joints)*.—Sections of egg-plant fried in oil and stuffed, château potatoes.

Badoise—

(a) *(for large joints).*—Braised red cabbages, lean bacon, purée of potatoes.

(b) *(for Tournedos and Noisettes).*—Stoned cherries.

Banquière *(for Tournedos and Noisettes).*—Boned and stuffed larks, quenelles and slices of truffles.

Batelière *(for Fish).*—Mushrooms, small glazed onions, fried eggs, and trussed crayfishes.

Beatrix *(for large joints).*—" Morels " tossed in butter, new carrots, artichoke bottoms, fondante new potatoes.

Beauharnais *(for Tournedos and Noisettes).*—Stuffed mushrooms and quarters of artichoke bottoms.

Belle-Hélène *(for large joints).*—Grilled mushrooms filled with con-cassed tomatoes, new peas, new carrot and potato croquettes.

Berrichonne *(for large joints).*—Balls of braised cabbage, small onions and chestnuts, slices of bacon.

Berny *(for Game).*—Croquettes of Berny potatoes, and tartlets filled with lentil purée, slice of truffle on top.

Bisontine.—Croustades made with duchesse potatoes, garnished with cauliflower purée, braised stuffed lettuces.

Bohémienne *(for Noisettes).*—Pilaw rice, concasséd tomatoes, roundels of fried onions.

Boitelle *(for Fish).*—Minced mushrooms, cooked with the treated fish.

Bordelaise.—Cépes á la Bordelaise Pommes Cocottes.

Boulangère *(for large joints).*—Onions and potatoes, salt and pepper, consommé, cooked same time as the joint in same roasting dish.

Bouquetière *(for large joints).*— Artichoke bottoms filled with carrot and turnip balls, dice of French beans, peas, and small heaps of cauli-flower coated with Hollandaise sauce, small château potatoes.

Bourgeoise *(for large joints).*—Shaped carrots, glazed onions, and dice of bacon.

Bourguignonne *(for large joints).*—Glazed onions, mushrooms tossed in butter, dice of bacon.

Brabançonne *(for Noisettes and Tournedos).*—Tartlets garnished with Brussels sprouts, coated with Mornay sauce and glazed, flat potato croquettes.

Bragance *(for Noisettes and Tournedos).*—Small tomatoes stuffed with Béarnaise sauce, potato croquettes.

Bréhan *(for large joints).*—Artichoke bottoms garnished with green broad beans purée, small heaps of cauliflower coated with Hollandaise sauce, parsley potatoes.

Bretonne *(for large joints).*—Haricot beans cohered with Bretonne sauce, chopped parsley.

Brillat-Savarin *(for Game).*—Small tartlets garnished with woodcock soufflé and truffles.

Bristol *(for large joints).*—Small rice croquettes, apricot shaped flageolets cohered with veloute, and large noisette potatoes rolled in meat glaze.

Bruxelloise *(for large joints).*—Braised chicory, Brussels sprouts and château potatoes.

Cancalaise *(for Fish).*—Poached oysters and shrimps, cohered with Normande sauce.

Cardinal *(for Fish).*—Collops of lobster and slices of truffles, Cardinal sauce mixed with dice of truffles and lobster.

Castillane *(for Tournedos and Noisettes).*—Concasséd tomatoes cooked in oil, small croquette potatoes and roundels of fried onions.

Catalane *(for Tournedos and Noisettes).*—Artichoke bottoms and grilled tomatoes.

Cavour *(for large joints).*—Croquettes of semolina, timbales of lasagne; ravioli.

Chambord *(for Fish).*—Large fish quenelles, mushroom heads, soft roes tossed in butter, crayfishes, slices of truffles. Fleurons.

Charolaise *(for large joints).*—Cauliflowers Villeroy, croustades filled with turnip purée.

Chartres—

    (a) *(for Tournedos and Noisettes).*—Small fondantes potatoes, decorate with tarragon leaves.

    (b) Stuffed mushrooms and braised lettuces.

    (c) Glazed new turnips, peas purée and mashed potatoes.

Chauchat *(for Fish).*—Border of roundels of cooked potatoes round fish.

Châtelaine—

    (a) *(for large joints).*—Quarters of artichoke bottoms, half tomatoes, braised celery and château potatoes.

    (b) Artichoke bottoms garnished with Soubise, whole chestnuts, noisette potatoes.

Chevreuse *(for Noisettes and Tournedos).*—Artichoke bottoms garnish with mushroom purée and sliced truffles, noisette potatoes.

Chipolata *(for large joints).*—Glazed onions, chipolata sausages, chestnuts cooked in consommé, dice of bacon.

Choisy *(for Tournedos and Noisettes).*—Braised lettuces, château potatoes.

Choron *(for Tournedos and Noisettes).*—Artichoke bottoms filled with peas, noisette potatoes.

Clamart *(for large joints).*—Tartlets or artichoke bottoms filled with peas à la Française or purée of peas, small château potatoes.

Clermont *(for Tournedos and Noisettes).*—Chestnuts mixed with Soubise sauce, cohered with yolk of eggs, poached in dariole moulds, roundels of fried onions.

Commodore *(for Fish).*—Croquettes of crayfish tails, large quenelles of fish, and mussels à la Villeroy.

Concorde *(for large joints).*—Peas, glazed carrots, mashed potatoes.

Compote *(for Pigeons).*—Dice of bacon, glazed onions, quarters of mushrooms tossed in butter.

Conti *(for large joints).*—Lentil purée and pieces of boiled bacon.

Cussy *(for Tournedos, Noisettes and Chicken).*—Large mushrooms grilled and garnished with chestnut purée, cocks' kidneys, and truffles cooked in Madeira.

Dartois *(for large joints).*—Turned carrots and turnips, braised celery and potatoes rissolées.

Daumont *(for Fish).*—Large mushroom heads cooked in butter, and garnished with crayfish tails cohered with Nantua sauce, fish quenelles, fried soft roes.

Dauphine *(for large joints).*—Croquettes of Dauphine potatoes (see Vegetable Chapter).

Derval *(for Tournedos and Noisettes).*—Quarters of artichokes tossed in butter.

Descar *(for large joints).*—Artichoke bottoms garnished with salpicon of chicken, croquette potatoes.

Dieppoise *(for Fish).*—Shrimps' tails, mussels and mushrooms.

Doria—Cucumber turned in clove of garlic shape, cooked slowly in butter.

Dubarry *(for large joints).*—Cauliflower moulded into balls with a serviette, coated with Mornay sauce, glazed, château potatoes.

Dubley *(for large joints).*—Croustades of duchesse potatoes filled with mushroom purée: grilled mushrooms.

Duchesse *(for large joints).*—Duchesse potatoes of different shapes.

Duse *(for large joints).*—French beans, tomatoes and Parmentier potatoes.

Excelsior *(for Tournedos and Noisettes).*—Braised lettuces and fondantes potatoes.

Favorite *(for Noisettes and Tournedos).*—Thick slices of foie gras, slices of truffles, asparagus heads.

Favorite *(for large joints).*—Quarters of artichoke bottoms, celery, small château potatoes.

Fédora *(for large joints).*—Tartlets filled with asparagus heads, carrots and turnips, quarters of oranges and glazed chestnuts.

Fermière *(for Chicken and large joints).*—Paysanne of carrots, turnips, onions and celery, cooked under cover in butter.

Ferval *(for Entrées).*—Artichoke bottoms, potato croquettes stuffed with ham salpicon.

Figaro.—Small nests of Duchesse potatoes panés Vermicelli fried garnish with small balls of carrots.

Financière *(for Chicken and Sweetbreads).*—Quenelles, cockscombs and kidneys, slices of truffles, mushroom heads and stoned olives.

Flamande *(for large joints).*—Balls of braised cabbage, carrots and turnips, rectangles of boiled bacon, roundels of saucisson, boiled potatoes.

Fleuriste *(for Tournedos and Noisettes).*—Tomatoes filled with jardinière, château potatoes.

Florentine *(for Fish and Sweetbreads).*—Spinach in leaves.

Florian *(for large joints).*—Braised lettuces, glazed onions, carrots, fondante potatoes.

Fontainebleau *(for Tournedos and Noisettes).*—Bouchées made with duchesse potatoes filled with jardinière.

Forestière—

   (a) *(for large joints).*—Morels tossed in butter, dice of bacon, Parmentier potatoes.

   (b) Cèpes tossed in butter, mushrooms and pommes cocotte.

THE COOKERY REPERTORY   11

Française *(for large joints).*—Spinach in leaves, Anna potatoes.

Frascati *(for Chickens and large joints).*—Thick slices of foie gras, mushroom heads, small truffles, asparagus heads, crescents of duchesse potatoes.

B

Gastronome *(for Chickens and Sweetbreads).*—Chestnuts cooked and glazed, small truffles, morels, and fowl kidneys rolled in chicken glaze.

Godard *(for Chickens and Sweetbreads).*—Small quenelles, mushroom heads, cockscombs and kidneys, lambs' sweetbread, truffles.

Grand-Duc *(for Fish).*—Asparagus heads, crayfish tails, slices of truffles.

Grand-Duc *(for Chicken).*—Asparagus heads, slices of truffles.

Grecque *(for Entrées).*—Rice à la Grecque.

Henri IV *(for Noisettes and Tournedos).*—Pont-Neuf potatoes and watercress.

Hongroise *(for large joints).*—Cauliflowers shaped into balls and coated with Mornay sauce and paprika mixed with chopped ham, glazed, potatoes à l'anglaise.

Hussarde *(for large joints).*—Stuffed potatoes and sections of egg-plant stuffed, scraped horseradish.

Impériale *(for Chicken).*—Collops of foie gras, truffled mushrooms and quenelles.

Indienne *(for Entrées).*—Rice cooked à l'Indienne.

Ismaïl Bayeldi *(for Tournedos and Noisettes).*—Slices of egg-plant fried in oil, half tomatoes, pilaw rice.

Italienne *(for large joints).*—Quarters of artichokes cooked à l'Italienne, and flat macaroni croquettes.

Japonaise *(for large joints).*—Croustades filled with Japanese artichokes and croquette potatoes.

Jardinière *(for Entrées).*—Carrots, turnips, French beans, flageolets, green peas and cauliflower coated with Hollandaise sauce.

Joinville *(for Fish).*—Salpicon of mushrooms and truffles, shrimps' tails cohered with Joinville sauce, mushroom heads stuck with prawns.

Judic *(for Entrées).*—Stuffed tomatoes, lettuces and château potatoes.

Jules Verne *(for large joints).*—Potatoes and turnips, stuffed and braised, quarters of mushrooms tossed in butter.

Jussière—

    (a) *(for Entrées).*—Onions and lettuces stuffed and braised, château potatoes.

    (b) Carrots, braised onions, lettuces, château potatoes.

Languedocienne *(for Entrées).*—Roundels of egg-plant fried, minced cèpes tossed in oil, concassed tomatoes, chopped parsley.

Lavallière *(for Chickens and Sweetbreads).*—Truffles à la Serviette, lambs' sweetbreads, crayfishes.

Ligurienne *(for large joints).*—Stuffed tomatoes, rizotto made with saffron, duchesse potatoes.

Lorette *(for Entrées).*—Chicken croquettes, asparagus heads, slices of truffles.

Lorraine *(for large joints).*—Braised red cabbage and fondante potatoes.

Louisiane *(for Chicken).*—Sweet corn à la crème, moulded rice on slices of fried sweet potato, roundels of fried bananas.

Lucullus *(for Chickens and Sweetbreads).*—Truffles cooked in mirepoix and madeira, scooped after having cut a slice to serve as cover, filled with cockscombs rolled in chicken glaze; seal the lid with chicken forcemeat, poached in oven, small quenelles made with chicken forcemeat and truffles passed through sieve, cockscombs.

Macédoine *(for large joints).*—(See **Jardinière**). Mixed and served in artichoke bottoms.

Madeleine *(for large joints).*—Artichoke bottoms filled with Soubise, and purée of haricot beans cohered with yolk of eggs, and moulded.

Maillot *(for Entrées).*—Carrots and turnips, glazed onions, braised lettuces, French beans and green peas.

Maraîchère *(for large joints).*—Salsify cohered with velouté, Brussels sprouts and château potatoes.

Maréchale *(for Entrées).*—
(a) Small quenelles with truffles, cockscombs, and truffles cohered with sauce Italienne.
(b) Asparagus heads, slices of truffles.

Marie-Louise *(for Entrées).*—
(a) Artichoke bottoms garnished with mushroom purée and Soubise, Noisette potatoes.
(b) Artichoke quarters, half tomatoes, château potatoes, braised lettuces.

Marie Stuart *(for Entrées).*—Tartlets filled with turnip purée, slices of marrow.

Marie-Jeanne *(for Noisettes and Tournedos).*—Tartlets filled with mushroom purée and slice of truffle, noisette potatoes.

Marigny *(for Entrées).*—Tartlets filled with green peas and French beans, fondante potatoes.

Marinière *(for Fish).*—Mussels, and shrimps' tails.

Marquise *(for Noisettes and Tournedos).*—Salpicon of amourettes, asparagus heads, julienne of truffles cohered with suprême sauce, small buns made with duchesse potatoes and stuffed with concasséd tomatoes.

Marseillaise *(for Tournedos and Noisettes).*—Small tomatoes scooped to contain a stuffed olive, poached in oven with oil and little garlic, surround the olive with an anchovy fillet, Copeaux potatoes.

Maryland.—Grilled slices of streaky bacon, small polenta galettes, and ½ bananas fried.

Mascotte *(for Chicken and large joints).*—Quarters of artichoke bottoms tossed in butter, cocotte potatoes, slices of truffles.

Masséna *(for Noisettes and Tournedos).*—Artichoke bottoms filled with Périgueux sauce, slices of poached marrow on the tournedos.

Massenet *(for Tournedos and Noisettes).*—Artichoke bottoms filled with marrow, French beans and Anna potatoes.

Matelote *(for Fish).*—Glazed onions, mushroom heads, heart-shaped croûtons, trussed crayfish.

Mazarine *(for Entrées)*.—Artichoke bottoms filled with jardinière, rice croquettes, decorated quenelles, mushrooms.

Médicis *(for Noisettes and Tournedos)*.—Artichoke bottoms garnished with green peas, carrots and turnip balls, noisette potatoes, Choron sauce on the tournedos or noisette.

Mentonnaise *(for large joints)*.—Stuffed vegetable marrow, small braised artichokes, potatoes rissolées.

Mercédès *(for large joints)*.—Grilled tomatoes, grilled mushrooms, braised lettuces, croquette potatoes.

Mexicaine *(for large joints)*.—Grilled mushrooms garnished with tomatoes concassees, grilled capsicums, half egg-plant cut lengthwise and grilled.

Mignon *(for Poultry and Sweetbreads)*.—Artichoke bottoms garnished with peas, round quenelles decorated with slices of truffles.

Milanaise *(for Escalopes)*.—Julienne of tongue, ham, mushrooms and truffles, sweat in butter, deglaze in Madeira. Add the spaghetti cohered with tomato sauce, grated cheese and butter.

Mirabeau *(for Grilled meats)*.—Anchovy fillets, stoned olives; anchovy butter (separate).

Mirette *(for Entrées)*.—Timbale of potatoes mirette.

Moderne *(for large joints)*.—Cauliflowers coated with Mornay sauce and glazed, stuffed tomatoes and duchesse potatoes.

Montbazon *(for Poultry)*.—Lambs' sweetbreads studded with truffles and cooked in butter, decorated quenelles, mushroom heads, slices of truffles.

Montmorency *(for Noisettes and Tournedos)*.—Artichoke bottoms garnished with carrot balls, noisette potatoes.

Montreuil *(for Noisettes and Tournedos)*.—Artichoke bottoms garnished half with peas and half with carrot balls same size of peas.

Montpensier *(for Noisettes, Sweetbreads)*.—Artichoke bottoms filled with asparagus heads, noisette potatoes, julienne of truffles.

Mozart *(for Entrées)*.—Artichoke bottoms filled with celery purée, copeaux potatoes.

Nantaise *(for large joints)*.—Glazed turnips, peas and mashed potatoes.

Nantua *(for Fish)*.—Crayfish tails covered with Nantua sauce, slices of truffles.

Napolitaine *(for Escalopes)*.—Spaghetti cohered with butter, tomato sauce and cheese; small heaps of tomatoes concassées.

Navets *(for large joints)*.—Turnips, shaped and tossed in butter and castor sugar; onions prepared same way, finish cooking with the meat.

Nemours *(for Entrées)*.—Green peas, carrots and duchesse potatoes.

Nemrod *(for Game)*.—Rissoles of marrow, croquette potatoes, small bouchées garnished with cranberries, grilled mushrooms garnished with chestnut purée, French beans.

Niçoise *(for Fish)*.—Tomatoes concassées tossed with garlic, capers and lemon slices, anchovy butter.
(for large joints and Poultry).—Small tomatoes cooked in oven with oil, French beans, château potatoes.

Nivernaise *(for Entrées)*.—Carrots and turnips shaped, cooked and glazed, braised lettuces, glazed onions, plain boiled potatoes.

Normande *(for Fish)*.—Oysters and mussels, mushroom heads, crayfish tails, fried fillets of sole en goujon, croûtons and slices of truffles.

Nouilles *(for Entrées)*.—Poached noodles tossed in butter.

Opéra *(for Noisettes, and Tournedos)*.—Tartlets garnished with collops of chicken livers tossed in butter and cohered with Madeira sauce. Croustades of duchesse potatoes filled with asparagus heads.

Orientale *(for large joints)*.—Half tomatoes garnished with rice à la grecque, croquettes of sweet potatoes.

Orleanaise *(for large joints)*.—(Separately): Braised chicory and maître-d'hôtel potatoes.

Orloff *(for large joints)*.—Dariole moulds lined with braised celery, filled with mousseline of celery, tomatoes, stuffed and braised lettuces, château potatoes.

Paloise *(for large joints)*.—New vegetables, and cauliflower coated with Hollandaise sauce, croquette potatoes.

Panachés *(for Entrées)*.—Flageolets mixed with French beans, cohered with butter.

Parisienne *(for Entrées)*.—
   (a) Braised lettuces surrounded with Parisienne potatoes.
   (b) Artichoke bottoms garnished with short julienne of tongue, mush-rooms and truffles cohered with velouté, glazed. Parisienne potatoes.

Parmentier *(for Entrées)*.—(See **Pommes Parmentier**).

Paysanne *(for Entrées)*.—(See Garnish **Fermière**). Add cocotte potatoes, carrots and dice of bacon.

Péruvienne *(for large joints)*.—Scooped oxalis filled with salpicon of ham and chicken mixed with the pulp of the oxalis, covered half-glaze sauce.

Petit-Duc *(for Entrées)*.—Tartlets filled with chicken purée mixed with cream, asparagus heads, slices of truffles.

Piémontaise *(for Entrées)*.—Rizotto with white truffles.

Portugaise *(for Entrées)*.—Small stuffed tomatoes and château potatoes.

Porte-Maillot *(for Entrées)*.—Large jardinière dressed in small heaps.

Primeurs *(for Entrées)*.-(See **Bouquetière**). Without artichoke bottoms.

Printanière *(for Entrées)*.—
   (a) Dice of vegetables treated same as jardinière, noisette potatoes.
   (b) Carrots and turnips glazed, braised onions, green peas, dice of French beans, asparagus heads (in cocotte).

Princesse *(for Noisettes, Tournedos, Sweetbreads)*.—Artichoke bottoms filled with asparagus heads, noisette potatoes.

Provençale *(for Entrées)*—
   (a) Small tomatoes, stuffed mushrooms with duxelles and garlic.
   (b) Tomatoes cooked with garlic, and stoned olives.

Rachel *(for Tournedos and Noisettes)*.—Artichoke bottoms garnished with slice of poached marrow, chopped parsley on the marrow.

Ravioles *(for Entrees)*.—(See **Ravioli** in **Pâtes alimentaires**).

Régence—
    (a) *(for Fish).*—Quenelles of fish with crayfish cullis, poached oysters, mushroom heads, poached soft roes, slices of truffles.
    (b) *(for Chicken and Sweetbreads).*—Quenelles of chicken and truffles, large quenelles decorated cockscombs, slice of foie gras, mushroom heads and truffles cohered with sauce Allemande.
    (c) *(for Game).*—(See **Garnish B).** The quenelles made with game forcemeat and smaller, cohered with Salmis sauce.

Renaissance *(for large joints).*—Artichoke bottoms garnished with carrots and turnips. French beans, green peas, asparagus heads, cauliflower coated with Hollandaise sauce, alternate the colours round the joint, new potatoes.

Richelieu *(for large joints).*—Stuffed tomatoes and mushrooms, braised lettuces, château potatoes.

Rochambeau *(for large joints).*—Croustades made with duchesse potatoes, filled with Vichy carrots, stuffed lettuces, cauliflower heads Polonaise, Anna potatoes.

Rohan *(for Chicken).*—Artichoke bottoms, the interior coated with meat glaze, garnished with slices of foie gras and slice of truffles, tartlets garnished with cocks' kidneys cohered with suprême sauce, a cockscomb between each tartlet and artichoke bottom.

Romaine *(for large joints).*—Tartlets garnished with gnocchi à la Romaine and gratinées. Small moulds of spinach cohered with chicken forcemeat and poached.

Romanoff *(for large joints).*—Stuffed cucumbers, croustade made with duchesse potatoes filled with salpicon of celeriac and mushrooms cohered with horse-radish sauce.

Rossini *(for Tournedos and Noisettes).*—Collops of foie gras tossed in butter, slices of truffles. Meat glaze.

Royale.—(Same as **Régence).**

Saint-Florentin *(for large joints).*—Collops of cèpes tossed à la Bordelaise, and Saint-Florentin potatoes.

Saint-Germain—
    (a) *(for Sweetbreads).*—Purée of new peas dressed dôme fashion in artichoke bottoms.
    (b) *(for large joints).*—Green peas purée cohered with yolk of eggs and finished with butter and cream, poached in dariole moulds, alternate with glazed carrots and fondantes potatoes.

Saint-Mandé *(for Entrées).*—Peas and French beans cohered with butter, small Macaire potatoes.

Samaritaine *(for large joints).*—Timbales of rice, Dauphine potatoes braised lettuces.

Sarladaise *(for large joints).*—Potatoes and truffles minced raw, and treated same as Boulangère garnish.

Sévigné *(for Entrées).*—Lettuces, grilled mushrooms, château potatoes.

Sarde *(for large joints).*—Ball-shaped croquettes made with Piémontaise rice, stuffed tomatoes, sections of cucumbers stuffed.

Sicilienne *(for Entrées)*.—Stuffed tomatoes, timbales of Piémontaise rice, croquette potatoes.

Soissonnaise *(for large joints)*.—Large haricot beans.

Strasbourgeoise *(for large joints)*.—Braised sauerkraut, pieces of boiled bacon, collops of foie gras.

Sultane *(for large joints)*.—Red cabbage, Duchesse potatoes crescent shaped.

Talleyrand *(for Sweetbreads and Poultry)*.—Macaroni cohered with butter and cheese, garnished with julienne of truffles and dice of foie gras.

Tivoli *(for Entrées)*.—Small faggots of asparagus heads, grilled mush-rooms filled with salpicon of cockscombs and kidneys cohered with Suprême sauce.

Tortue *(for Entrées)*.—Quenelles, mushroom heads, gherkins, garlic, collops of tongue and calves' brains, small fried eggs, heart-shaped croûtons, crayfish, slices of truffles.   Tortue sauce.

Toulousaine *(for Poultry, Sweetbreads)*.—Quenelles of chicken, collops of sweetbread, cockscombs and kidneys, mushroom heads cohered with Suprême sauce, slices of truffles.

Tourangelle *(for Entrées)*.—French beans and flagelots cohered with velouté.

Trouvillaise *(for Fish)*.—Shrimps, mussels and mushroom heads cohered with shrimp sauce.

Tzarine *(for Chicken suprême)*.—Shaped cucumbers prepared with cream.

Tyrolienne *(for Tournedos and Noisettes)*.—Roundels of fried onions and tomatoes concassées.

Vert-Pré—
(a) *(for Grilled meats)*.—Watercress and straw potatoes.
(b) *(for white Meats, Ducklings and Pintadeaux)*.—Green peas, French beans and asparagus heads cohered with butter.

Ventadour *(for Tournedos and Noisettes.)*.—Slices of marrow, artichoke purée and slices of truffles, cocotte potatoes.

Vernon *(for Entrees)*.—Artichoke bottoms filled with asparagus heads; cases made with turnips filled with mashed potatoes, and potato cases filled with peas purée.

Vichy *(for Entrées)*.—(See **Carottes à la Vichy**).

Victoria *(for large joints)*.—Macaroni, tomatoes, lettuces and mashed potatoes.

Viennoise *(for large joints)*.—Croustades of fried noodles filled with spinach in leaves, braised celery, plain boiled potatoes.

Viroflay *(for large joints)*.—Spinach balls à la Viroflay;   artichoke quarters tossed in butter and parsley, château potatoes.

Walewska *(for Fish)*.—Collops of lobster, slices of truffles.

Washington *(for Poultry)*.—Sweet corn reduced with cream.

Zingara *(for Escalopes)*.—Ham julienne, tongue, mushrooms and truffles cohered with tomated half-glaze, madeira and tarragon essence.

Sauces

B

Aïoli (Cold).—Garlic cloves pounded in mortar with a boiled potato, add yolk of eggs, salt, pepper, lemon juice, incorporate gradually some oil, wielding the pestle meanwhile so as to effect amalgamation.

Airelles (Cranberry sauce).—Cook the cranberries in water, drain, pass through fine sieve, add little sugar.

Albert.—Butter sauce mixed with horse radish scraped and poached in white consommé, add cream and bread crumbs, let it boil, pass through fine sieve, cohere with yolk of eggs, add mustard and vinegar.

Albuféra.—Suprême sauce mixed with meat glaze and pimented butter.

Allemande.—Ordinary velouté cohered with yolk of eggs.

Américaine.—Treat as for Homard Américaine, pound the shells and meats in the mortar and incorporate equal quantity of fish velouté, add butter.

Anchois.—Normande sauce mixed with anchovy butter, and garnished with dice of anchovy fillets.

Andalouse (Cold).—Mayonnaise sauce mixed with tomato purée, garnished with sweet capsicums.

Aromates (Aromatic sauce).—Pale velouté, mixed with an infusion of thyme, basil, marjoram, chives, chopped shallots and black peppercorns, garnished with chervil and blanched tarragon, lemon juice.

Aurore.—Suprême sauce lightly flavoured with tomato.

Aurore *(for Fish).*—Tomated fish velouté, butter.

Bâtarde.—White roux moistened with water, cohered with yolk of eggs, buttered and creamed lemon juice, pass through fine sieve.

Bavaroise.—Reduction of pepper-corns, scraped horse-radish, thyme, bay leaves, parsley stalks, vinegar. Add yolk of eggs and finish same as Hollandaise sauce, add crayfish, butter and cream. Garnished with crayfish tails.

Béarnaise.—Reduction of chopped shallots, mignonette pepper, tarragon, salt and vinegar. Add yolk of eggs and melted butter, whisk the sauce briskly on a slow fire so as to ensure the cooking of the yolks, pass through tammy cloth and add chopped tarragon and chervil.

Béchamel.—White roux moistened with milk, salt, onion stuck with clove, cook for 20 minutes.

Bercy (A).—Chopped shallots tossed lightly in melted butter, moistened with white wine for fish stock, reduced and mixed with fish velouté and chopped parsley, finished with butter. (Special for fish).

Bercy *(for Grilled meats).*—Chopped shallots, pepper, moistened with white wine, reduced, add liquid meat-glaze and butter, garnished with dice of marrow and chopped parsley.

Beurre à l'Anglaise (Butter sauce).—Bâtarde sauce without liaison.

Bigarade.—Duck's gravy reduced and mixed with orange juice and lemon; julienne of zest and butter, can be cohered with arrowroot.

Bohémienne (Cold).—Cold Béchamel sauce, cohered with yolk of eggs, seasoned with salt, pepper and vinegar; add oil gradually, same as for mayonnaise sauce, finished with tarragon vinegar.

Bonnefoy (See Sauce Moelle).—Velouté instead of half-glaze, and add chopped tarragon.

Bordelaise.—Chopped shallots, migonette pepper, thyme, bay leaves, red wine, reduced and mixed with half-glaze, strained.

Bourguignonne.—Chopped shallots, parsley stalks, thyme, bay leaves, mushroom parings, reduced with red wine, cohered with manié butter, cayenne pepper.

Bretonne—
   (a) Chopped onions partly fried in butter, moistened with white wine, reduced, add fresh tomatoes and tomato purée, garlic, strained, add butter and chopped parsley.
   (b) Julienne of leeks, celery, onions and mushrooms cooked slowly in butter, mixed with fish velouté.

Cambridge (Cold).—Pound in mortar hard yolk of eggs, anchovy fillets, capers, chervil, Tarragon, chives, mustard, vinegar, cayenne pepper. Add oil gradually as for mayonnaise, pass through sieve and finish with chopped parsley.

Canotière (See Sauce Bâtarde).

Câpres (Caper Sauce).—Bâtarde sauce without liaison and garnished with capers.

Cardinal.—Béchamel sauce with fish stock, truffles essence and lobster butter, cayenne pepper.

Céleri (Celery sauce).—Celery hearts cooked in white consommé with a faggot and onion stuck with clove, drain, pass through fine sieve, mix the purée with cream sauce.

Champignons—
   (a) Half-glaze garnished with small mushroom heads, buttered.
   (b) Allemande sauce garnished with mushroom heads.

Chantilly (Cold).—Mayonnaise sauce with lemon juice instead of vinegar, mixed with whipped cream.

Charcutière.—Robert sauce garnished with julienne of gherkins.

Chasseur.—Minced mushrooms tossed in butter, add chopped shallots, moistened with white wine, reduced, add half-glaze and butter, chopped parsley.

Chateaubriand.—Reduction of chopped shallots, thyme, bay leaves, mushroom parings and white wine. Add half-glaze and butter, finished with tarragon and chopped parsley.

Chaud-Froid (White).—Velouté made with jelly.

Chaud-Froid (Brown).—Half-glaze sauce made with aspic jelly, essence of truffles, madeira. (This sauce can be done with various game essences).

Chaud-Froid (Tomated).—Tomato sauce and aspic jelly.

Chevreuil.—Mirepoix of vegetables and game trimmings fried in butter, moistened with red wine, reduced and mixed with Poivrade sauce. Passed through sieve and strainer, finished with cayenne pepper and pinch of sugar.

Chevreuil (Roebuck Sauce).—Onion and ham cut in fine paysanne and coloured in butter, moistened with vinegar, add faggot and reduce, add half-glaze sauce, port and red currant jelly.

Chivry.—Chicken velouté mixed with an infusion of chervil, parsley, tarragon, chives, pimpernel, white wine, strained and finished with Chivry butter.

Choron.—Béarnaise sauce with tomato purée.

Colbert.—Chicken glaze worked with butter, chopped tarragon.

Crème.—Béchamel sauce with cream.

Crème à l'Anglaise (Cream Sauce).—Velouté with mushroom essence, flavoured with parsley and onion, add cream.

Crevettes.—Fish velouté with shrimp butter.

Crevettes à l'Anglaise (Shrimp Sauce).—Butter sauce mixed with anchovy sauce and garnished with shrimps, cayenne pepper.

Cumberland (Cold).—Red currant jelly dissolved with port, garnished with blanched, chopped shallots, julienne of orange zest and lemon juice, mustard, cayenne pepper and ginger.

Curry.—Dices of onions and apple lightly cooked in butter, add curry powder, moisten with cocoanut milk. Add velouté and pass through fine strainer, finish with cream.

Demi-Glace.—Espagnole sauce reduced to perfection (called half-glaze).

Diable.—Chopped shallots, mignonette pepper reduced with white wine and vinegar, add half-glaze, strained, chopped parsley.

Diable.—Chopped shallots, mignonnette pepper reduced with white wine tomated half-glaze, strained and finished with Harvey or Escoffier sauce, cayenne pepper.

Diane.—Poivrade sauce with cream.

Diplomate.—Normande sauce with lobster butter; garnished with dice of lobster and truffles.

Duxelles.—Onions and chopped shallots fried in butter, add white wine, reduce, add tomated half-glaze and dry duxelles (see **Fonds de Cuisine**), chopped parsley.

Ecossaise.—Normande sauce, garnished with large Brunoise of carrots, truffles and celery.

Ecossaise (Scotch Egg Sauce).—Thin Béchamel sauce garnished with white of eggs cut in strips and hard yolk of eggs passed through sieve.

Espagnole.—Foundation sauce made with brown roux, brown stock, fresh tomatoes, mushroom parings, mirepoix of carrots, onions, thyme, bay leaves (called brown sauce).

Estragon—
  (a) Thickened gravy with chopped tarragon.
  (b) Velouté with tarragon purée and chopped tarragon.

Fenouil (Fennel Sauce).—Butter sauce garnished with blanched, chopped fennel.

Financière.—Madeira sauce with truffle essence.

Fines Herbes—
(a) White wine and aromatic fines herbes, infused and mixed with half-glaze sauce, chopped fines herbes and lemon juice.

(b) White wine sauce with chopped herbs finished with shallot butter.

Foyot.—Bearnaise sauce and meat glaze.

Genevoise.—Mirepoix of vegetable and chopped salmon head, tossed in butter with mignonette pepper, thyme, bay leaves, faggot, moistened with red wine reduce by half, add half-glaze and cook 40 minutes. Strained and finished with butter and anchovy essence.

Génoise (Cold).—Purée of herbs, pistachios and almonds cohered with yolk of eggs. Seasoned with lemon juice, salt and pepper, and finished with oil, same as Mayonnaise.

Gloucester (Cold).—Mayonnaise sauce with sour cream, finished with Escoffier sauce and chopped fennel.

Godard.—Reduction of white wine with mirepoix of vegetable and chopped ham, add half-glaze and mushroom essence. Pass through tammy cloth or fine sieve.

Grand Veneur.—Poivrade sauce with venison flavour, mixed with red currant jelly and cream.

Gratin.—Reduction of white wine with chopped shallots, add dry duxelles and half-glaze made with fish stock, chopped parsley.

Gribiche (Cold).—Mayonnaise made with hard yolk of eggs and mustard. Garnished with gherkins, capers, chervil, tarragon and julienne of hard-boiled white of eggs.

Groseilles.—Green gooseberries, blanched and cooked with white wine and sugar; pass through fine sieve, mix with Bâtarde sauce.

Gooseberry Sauce.—Purée of green gooseberries with sugar.

Groseille au Raifort.—Red currant jelly with scraped horse-radish.

Hachée.—Chopped shallots and onions reduced with vinegar. Mixed with tomato half-glaze flavouring. Garnished with dice of ham, capers, dry duxelles and chopped parsley.

Hachée *(for Fish).*—Same as above with fish velouté and anchovy sauce instead of ham, butter.

Hollandaise.—Reduction of vinegar with mignonette pepper. Add yolk of eggs and whisk in gradually some melted butter and a little water or cream, strain and finish with lemon juice. (This sauce must not boil, and only requires regular heat to cook it).

Homard.—Diplomate sauce without garnish.

Homard à l'Anglaise (Lobster Sauce).—Bechamel sauce with anchovy essence, garnished with dice of lobster, cayenne pepper.

Hongroise.—Chopped onions partly fried in butter with paprika, moistened with white wine, faggot, reduced and mixed with Suprême sauce.

Huîtres.—Normande sauce with oyster juice, garnished with poached oysters.

Huîtres (Oyster Sauce).—Béchamel sauce with oyster juice and garnished with collops of poached oysters.

Huîtres à Brun (Brown Oyster Sauce).—Same as above with half-glaze sauce instead of Béchamel.

Hussarde.—Minced onions and shallots lightly fried in butter, moistened with white wine, reduced and mixed with half-glaze flavoured tomato, white stock, raw ham, garlic, faggot. Cook 25 minutes and pass through fine sieve or tammy cloth, garnished with Brunoise of ham, scraped horse-radish and chopped parsley.

B

Indienne.—(See **Curry Sauce**).

Italienne (Froide).—Mayonnaise sauce with lemon juice, garnished with dice of brains and chopped parsley.

Ivoire.—Suprême sauce with pale meat glaze.

Joinville.—Normande sauce with crayfish and shrimps cullis, garnished with julienne of truffles.

Jus Coloré (Brown Gravy)—
(a) (See **Fonds Brun** in Fundamental Element of Cooking).
(b) *(For Roast Veal).*—Butter sauce mixed with veal gravy, ketchup and Escoffier sauce.

Jus lié (Thickened Gravy).—Veal stock thickened with arrowroot.

Jus lié à l'Estragon.—Same as above with tarragon essence.

Jus lié Tomate.—Flavoured with tomato.

Laguipière.—Bâtarde sauce with fish glaze.

Livonienne.—Velouté with fish stock, garnished with julienne of truffles, and carrots, chopped parsley.

Lyonnaise.—Onions partly fried in butter, moistened with white wine and vinegar, reduced and mixed with half-glaze, pass through tammy cloth.

Madère.—Half-glaze with madeira.

Maltaise.—Hollandaise sauce with zest and juice of blood oranges.

Marinière.—Bercy sauce with mussels cooking liquor, garnished with mussels.

Matelote.—Reduction of fish stock, red wine, mushroom parings, add half-glaze, pass through tammy cloth, butter and cayenne pepper.

Matelote (White).—Reduction of fish stock and white wine, mushroom parings, add fish velouté, cayenne pepper. Pass through tammy cloth. Finished with butter and garnished with mushroom heads and small onions.

Mayonnaise.—Put some yolk of eggs in a basin. Season with salt, pepper, cayenne, pour some vinegar on the yolks while whisking briskly, add oil gradually, finish the sauce with lemon juice and a little boiling water to prevent turning.

Mayonnaise à la Russe.—Mayonnaise sauce with tarragon vinegar and horse-radish finely scraped, add some liquid aspic jelly, whisking gently until frothy. (This sauce is principally used for vegetable salads).

Mint (Cold).—Vinegar, sugar, salt, pepper, chopped mint.

Moelle.—Operate same as Bordelaise, using white wine instead of red. Add chopped parsley and slices of marrow.

Mornay.—Béchamel sauce mixed with butter, grated gruyère and parmesan.

Moscovite.—Poivrade sauce with infusion of juniper berries, garnished with grilled sliced almonds and currants swollen in warm water, glass of Marsala.

Mousquétaire.—Mayonnaise sauce with chopped shallots blanched in white wine and reduced, garnished with chives and cayenne pepper.

Mousseline ou Mousseuse.—Hollandaise sauce mixed with stifflly whipped cream.

Moutarde.—Hollandaise sauce with mustard.

Nantua.—Mirepoix of vegetables partly fried with crayfish butter, moistened with white wine and cognac, add fresh tomatoes and tomato purée, fish velouté, salt, cayenne pepper.

Newburg (with raw Lobster).—Divide lobster into four parts, remove the creamy parts and pound them with butter. Fry the pieces in butter until red, add burnt brandy and madeira, moisten with cream and fish stock, cook 25 minutes, remove the meat and cut into dice, finish the sauce by adding the creamy portions.

Newburg (with cooked Lobster).—Collops of lobster warmed with butter, seasoned with salt (cayenne pepper), moisten with madeira and cohere with yolk of eggs and cream, chopped parsley and coral.

Noisette.—Hollandaise sauce with nut brown cooked butter.

Normande.—Fish velouté with mushroom essence and oyster juice, cohered with yolk of eggs and cream. Reduced and finished with butter and cream.

Œufs à l'Anglaise (Egg Sauce).—Béchamel sauce garnished with dices of hard-boiled egg, nutmeg.

Œufs au Beurre Fondu (Egg and Butter Sauce).—Melted butter with dices of hard-boiled egg, salt, pepper, lemon juice, chopped parsley.

Oignons (Onion Sauce).—Minced onions cooked in milk, seasoned with salt, pepper, nutmeg. Strain and chop the onions, make a white sauce and add the chopped onions.

Orientale.—Sauce Américaine with curry and onions.

Oxford (Cold).—(See **Cumberland Sauce**).—With scraped zest instead of julienne.

Pain (Bread Sauce).—Boiled milk with onion stuck with a clove. Add breadcrumbs, butter and cream, salt, pepper.

Pain Frit (Fried Bread Sauce).—Consommé with dice of ham and chopped shallots, add brown crumbs fried in butter, finish with chopped parsley and lemon juice.

Paloise.—Same as Béarnaise, with mint instead of tarragon.

Périgueux.—Half-glaze with truffle essence, garnished with chopped truffles, madeira.

Périgourdine.—Half-glaze with foie gras purée, garnished with slices of truffle.

Persil (Parsley Sauce).—Butter sauce with blanched, chopped parsley.

Persil pour Poissons (Parsley Sauce for Fish).—Fish velouté with an infusion of parsley and garnished with chopped parsley.

Piquante.—Chopped shallots reduced with vinegar and white wine, add half-glaze, pass through tammy cloth. Garnished with gherkins, chervil, chopped tarragon, pepper.

Poivrade ordinaire.—Mirepoix of vegetables, partly fried in oil, with parsley stalks, thyme, bay leaves, moisten with marinade and vinegar, reduce. Add half-glaze, cook 30 minutes, pass through strainer.

Poivrade *(for Game)*.—Same as above, add game trimmings when frying the mirepoix, and moisten with game stock.

Pommes (Apple Sauce).—Marmalade of apples with a little cinnamon.

Porto.—Half-glaze with port when about to serve.

Porto (Port Wine Sauce).—Reduction of port, chopped shallots and thyme, add zest and juice of orange and lemon, salt, cayenne pepper. Strain and mix with good thickened veal gravy.

Portugaise.—Chopped onions partly fried in oil, add tomatoes concassées, salt, pepper, thin tomato sauce, meat glaze, little garlic, chopped parsley.

Poulette.—Allemande sauce with mushroom essence, lemon juice and chopped parsley.

Provençale—
  (a) Tomatoes concassées tossed in boiling oil, salt, pepper, pince of sugar, garlic, chopped parsley.
  (b) Sliced mushrooms, tossed in oil, mixed with the above preparations. Add thin tomato sauce.

Raifort Chaude (Horse-radish Sauce).—(See **Albert Sauce**).

Raifort (Cold).—Scraped horse-radish mixed with whipped cream, salt, pepper, vinegar or lemon juice.

Ravigote. —Reduction of white wine and vineagar, add velouté and shallot butter, garnished with chervil, chives and tarragon.

Ravigote (Cold).—Oil, vinegar, capers, parsley, chervil, tarragon, chopped onions, salt and pepper.

Réforme (Réforme Sauce).—One-half poivrade sauce and one half-glaze sauce, garnished with short julienne of white of eggs, gherkins, mushrooms, truffles and tongue.

Régence.—Mirepoix with truffles trimmings, moisten with Rhine wine, reduce, add half-glaze sauce. Pass through tammy cloth.

Régence *(for Fish)*.—Normande sauce with reduction of white wine, mushroom parings, and truffles, strained, finished with truffle essence.

Rémoulade.—Mayonnaise sauce with mustard, garnished with capers, parsley, gherkins, chervil and tarragon, and finished with anchovy essence.

Riche.—(See **Diplomate Sauce**).

Robert.—Chopped onions, cooked in butter, without colour. Moistened with white wine, vinegar, pepper; reduce, add half-glaze, and mustard to finish.

Romaine.—Pale caramel dissolved with vinegar, add half-glaze and game stock; reduce, pass through tammy cloth; garnish with grilled pignoli, sultanas and currants swelled in warm water.

Rouennaise.—Bordelaise sauce, very thin, mixed with purée of raw ducks' livers, cooked until cohered. Do not allow to boil. Pass through tammy cloth, add pepper, lemon juice; and reduction of red wine and shallots.

Rubens.—Reduction of white wine, fish stock and fine mirepoix. Strain, add yolk of eggs and finish with crayfish butter in the same way as with Hollandaise, and anchovy sauce.

Russe (Cold).—Mayonnaise sauce, mixed with the creamy parts of lobster, caviar purée, mustard and Escoffier sauce.

Saint-Malo.—White wine sauce with mustard and chopped shallots, cooked in white wine, finished with anchovy essence.

Salmis.—Mirepoix and game carcasses and trimmings, fried in butter. Moisten with red or white wine, reduce, add half-glaze and faggot. Strain and finish with butter.

Smitane.—Fried chopped onions in butter; add thin sour cream. Cook 20 minutes, strain, finish with Cabul sauce.

Solférino.—Meat glaze with shallots, butter Maître-d'hôtel, whisked together; add tomato essence, cayenne pepper and lemon juice.

Soubise—
    (a) Béchamel and cooked chopped onions, seasoned and strained.
    (b) Minced onions and rice, blanched, moistened with white stock. Cook 30 minutes, pound in mortar and pass through tammy cloth; finish with butter and cream.

Suchet.—White wine sauce garnished with Julienne of leeks, carrots and celery.

Suédoise (Cold).—Mayonnaise sauce with apple purée and scraped horse-radish.

Suprême.—Reduced Veloute. Cohere with cream.

Tartare (Cold).—Mayonnaise with hard yolk of eggs, garnished with onions and chives finely chopped.

Tortue.—Tomatoed half-glaze with an infusion of turtle herbs. (See Tortue Claire in **Potages** Chapter) maderia wine, truffle essence and cayenne.

Tyrolienne.—Choron sauce with oil instead of butter.

Valois—(See **Sauce Foyot**).

Velouté.—White " roux." Moisten with white stock.

Venaison.—(See **Sauce Grand Veneur**).

Vénitienne.—White wine sauce with a reduction of tarragon vinegar, chopped shallots and chervil. Strain and add green butter (see **Compound Butters**), chopped chervil and tarragon.

Véron.—Three parts Normande sauce mixed with one part Tyrolienne sauce, finished with pale meat glaze and anchovy essence.

Verte (Green) (Cold).—Mayonnaise sauce mixed with a purée of blanched herbs; spinach, water-cress, parsley, chervil, tarragon. Passed through hair sieve.

Victoria.—Lobster sauce with chopped truffles.

Villageoise.—Velouté mixed with Soubise sauce, veal stock and mushrooms, cooking liquor cohered with yolk of eggs and cream, butter.

Villeroy.—Allemande sauce, with ham fumet and truffle essence, well reduced.

Vincent.—Half Tartare sauce and half Green sauce, mixed together.

Vin Blanc—
- (a) Fish Velouté, thinned with fish stock, cohered with yolk of eggs and finished with butter, same as Hollandaise.
- (b) Reduced fish stock, cohered with yolks; add butter by degrees.
- (c) Yolk of eggs mixed with a little fish stock, and add butter by degrees, same as Hollandaise.
- (d) Fish stock reduced to glaze and mixed with butter, whisking it in gradually.

Vin Rouge.—Reduction of shallots and red wine; add fish glaze and whisk in butter by degrees. Finish with anchovy sauce and cayenne pepper.

Yorkshire.—Port wine sauce with red currant jelly; add Julienne of orange zest.

Zingara—
- (a) Tomated half-glaze, garnished with mushroom Julienne, truffles, ham and tongue, cayenne, Madeira.
- (b) Chopped shallots reduced with vinegar; add brown stock, brown crumbs; cook 5 minutes, chopped parsley and lemon juice.

Hors D'œuvre

SIDE DISHES, OR APPETISERS

Aceto-Dolce.—Italian produce.

Achards.—French produce.

Agoursis.—Russian cucumbers, salted, and dished up in slices.

Allumettes aux Anchois, aux farces de Poisson, etc.—Rectangles of puff paste, masked with fish purée, anchovy, etc.

Anchois frais marinés.—Salted for 2 hours, tossed in boiling oil, marinade and serve with the marinade.

Anchois (Filets d').—Filleted anchovies, cut in Julienne and marinaded in oil; dished and decorated to taste.

Anchois (Médaillons d').—Roundels of potatoes, surrounded with anchovy fillets, garnished to taste, with hard boiled eggs, caviar, etc.

Anchois (Paupiettes aux).—Filleted, stuffed and rolled in paupiettes, decorated with anchovy butter.

Anchois aux Poivrons.—Half pimentoes, half anchovy fillet, deocrated to taste.

Anchois des Tamarins.—Baked potato pulp, crushed with a fork, seasoned with oil, vinegar, salt, pepper; dish up with anchovy paupiettes round.

Anguilles Fumées.—Smoked eel fillets dressed on serviette.

Anguille Hongroise.—Sections of eels cooked as for matelote vin blanc, seasoned with paprika, cut in fillets, cool in the gelatinous cooking liquor.

Artichauts à la Grecque.—Small, tender artichokes. Cut the leaves short, parboil 10 minutes, and drain. Finish cooking in marinade of white wine, water, oil, salt, lemon juice, fennel and coriander seeds, pepper-corn, thyme, bay-leaf. Serve very cold upon hors-d'œuvre dish, with a little of the cooking liquor.

Artichauts Garnis.—Small artichoke bottoms, cooked and marinaded with oil and vinegar. Garnish to taste with fish purée, macédoine of vegetables, etc.

Barquettes.—Small croustades boat-shaped and garnished in any conceivable way, chicken, vegetables, oysters, fish mayonnaise, etc.

Betteraves.—Beetroots in oven and used for decorating purposes, or sliced with seasoning.

Betterave en Salade (with Cream).—Beetroot cut in Julienne, mixed with onions, salt, pepper, lemon juice, French mustard, and cream.

Beurre pour Hors-d'Œuvre.—(See **Beurres Composés**).

Bigarreaux Confits.—Hard cherries with stalks, marinaded in boiled vinegar, salt and tarragon, for 20 days.

Bœuf fumé de Hambourg.—Smoked Hamburg beef cut into very thin slices.

Canapés.—Toast, cut into various shapes, round, square, rectangular, oval, crescented, starlike, etc.

Canapés à l'Amiral.—Masked with shrimp butter, surrounded with shrimps' tails; centre garnished with lobster eggs.

Canapés aux Anchois.—Masked and decorated with anchovy butter, and filleted anchovies.

Canapés à l'Arlequine.—Decorated with various coloured butters.

Canapés au Caviar.—Decorated with butter, centre garnished with fresh caviar.

Canapés aux Crevettes.—Masked and decorated with pink shrimp butter, garnished with shrimp tails and a caper in centre.

Canapés City.—Masked with a preparation of butter, grated cheese and parmesan, cream. Decorated with half slice of Lyon saucisson, and half moon of Gruyère cheese.

Canapés Danoise.—Brown bread masked with horse-radish butter, garnished with slices of smoked salmon, herring fillets and caviar.

Canapés Ecarlate.—Masked with mustard butter; garnished with slice of tongue, star-shaped, a spot of mustard butter in centre.

Canapés Ecrevisses.—Masked with crayfish butter, garnished with half crayfish cut lengthwise.

Canapés Gibier.—Masked with cayenne butter, garnished with game purée.

Canapés Homard.—Masked with lobster butter, decorated with hard boiled eggs, chopped and cohered with mayonnaise; slice of lobster in the middle.

Canapés Lucile.—Masked with mustard butter, bordered with chopped tongue, centre garnished with chopped chicken mixed with mayonnaise sauce.

Canapés Poisson.—Masked with soft roe butter, decorated with crayfish butter, centre garnished with chopped fish, cohered with mayonnaise.

Canapés Printaniers.—Masked with Montpellier butter, bordered with chopped hard yolk of eggs. Centre garnished with mustard and cress.

Canapés Rochelais.—Masked with soft roe butter, decorated with crayfish butter; centre garnished with poached oyster.

Carolines Diverses (Various).—Small éclairs garnished with various kinds of mousse, coated with chaud-froid sauce and glazed with aspic jelly.

Caviar Glacé.—Hard roes of sturgeons or sterlets specially prepared and served with ice all round a dish.

Caviar on Blini (Hot).—Caviar served on hot buttered Blini.

Céleri Bonne Femme.—Celery and potatoes, minced and seasoned with cream custard sauce.

Céleri à la Grecque.—Celery prepared same way as artichoke bottoms.

Céleri Raves.—Julienne of celeriac seasoned with mustard and cream, or vinaigrette with mustard.

Cèpes Marinés.—Small cèpes marinaded in the following preparation: vinegar, oil, garlic, thyme, bay leaves, coriander, pepper-corns, parsley roots and brunoise of vegetables, boiled 10 minutes and marinaded for 8 days.

Cerises à l'Allemande.—Pour over some morello cherries some vinegar boiled with brown sugar, a few cloves, cinnamon, nutmeg, tarragon, cool, macerate for a fortnight.

Cerneaux au Verjus.—Inside of fresh walnuts sprinkled with verjuice; salt and chervil.

Cervelles Robert.—Collops of cooked brains, julienne of celery, cover with mustard cream sauce mixed with brain purée.

Choux-fleurs.—Blanched cauliflowers marinaded with oil and vinegar, coated with mustard cream sauce.

Choux-rouges.—Julienne of red cabbage mixed with apples, seasoned with oil, vinegar, salt, pepper.

Choux-verts en Paupiettes.—Blanched cabbage leaves cut in rectangles, garnished with blanched onions, rice, salad, seasoned and rolled in paupiettes, sprinkle with salad oil.

Concombres Danoise.—Cucumbers cut and shaped like cassolettes or barquettes, garnished with salpicon of smoked salmon, herrings, hard-boiled egg; sprinkled with scraped horse-radish.

Concombres Farcis.—Cucumbers cut as above and garnished to taste with various salads, vegetable macédoine, etc.

Concombres en salade.—Cucumbers, peeled and sliced, seasoned with salt, pepper, vinegar.

Cornets d'York.—York ham cut in thin slices and shaped like triangles, rolled into cones and garnished with any butter cream, or chopped aspic.

Duchesses Nantua.—Small choux of profiteroles, filled with crayfish purée and glazed with jelly.

Duchesses à la Reine.—Same as above, stuffed with chicken purée, glazed with jelly.

Duchesses Sultane.—Stuffed with chicken purée and pistachios, glazed with jelly, sprinkled with chopped pistachios.

Duchesses au Caviar.—Stuffed with caviar and glazed with jelly.

Duchesses à la Norvégienne.—Stuffed with a purée of kilkis and butter, glazed with jelly.

Duchesses au Saumon Fumé.—Stuffed with purée of smoked salmon, glazed with jelly.

Eclairs Karoly.—Small éclairs, stuffed with a purée made from the creamy parts of woodcock, with champagne, butter and seasoning. Cover the éclairs with Chaudfroid sauce and glaze with jelly, decorated with truffles.

Eperlans Marinés d'Escabèche.—Smelts partly fried in oil, and macerated for 24 hours with carrots, garlic, roundels of onion, bay leaves, parsley, pimentos, thyme and vinegar; boil the marinade 10 minutes.

Fenouil (Pieds de).—Fennel prepared same as artichokes à la Grecque.

Figues.—Figs served on vine leaves with crushed ice round.

Filets d'Anvers.—Same as cornets d'York.

Foie-Gras.—Served in shells on serviette.

Frivolités.—Hors-d'œuvre composed of moulded cream, barquettes, tartlets, etc.

Fruits de Mer.—All sorts of raw sea shell fish except oysters, served with bread and butter.

Goujons à la Russe.—Poached and coated with mayonnaise and aspic, sprinkled with chopped parsley.

Harengs Dieppoise.—Fresh herrings marinaded in white wine vinegar, roundels of carrots and onions, thyme, bay leaves, parsley stalks, minced shallots, cooked 10 minutes and, let the herrings cool in the marinade.

Harengs Saurs (Fillets of).—Soak the fillets in cold water and milk, drain and coat with mayonnaise sauce mixed with soft roes purée, add vinegar, chopped onions, parsley, chives, tarragon, chervil and celery.

Harengs aux Haricots Verts.—Holland Speciality. Are served skinned and with French beans.

Harengs à la Livonienne.—Smoked herring fillets cut into dice and mixed with dice of cold potatoes, russet apples, parsley, chervil, tarragon, seasoned with oil and vinegar. Dress in the shape of herrings and place the heads and tails, which should have been put aside to reshape the herrings.

Harengs Lucas.—Salted herrings, skinned and soaked in milk, cut in slices and coated with mayonnaise sauce made with hard yolk of eggs; mustard, shallots, chervil and gherkins, cayenne pepper.

Harengs à la Russe.—Fillets of herrings cut into thin slices, dish up and alternate with sliced boiled potatoes. Season with salt, pepper, vinegar, sprinkle with chopped chervil, fennel, tarragon and shallots.

Haricot Verts.—French beans, cooked rather underdone and seasoned while hot with oil and vinegar, add chervil and chives when serving.

Huîtres.—Oysters, served on crushed ice, with brown bread and butter, lemon quarters or shallots' sauce.

Huîtres Natives au Caviar.—Small tartlets, crusts garnished with caviare, and oyster on top, seasoned with pepper, lemon juice.

Kilkis or Anchois de Norvège.—Are found ready prepared in the market. Served with their liquor on hors-d'œuvre dishes.

Macédoine.—Small white onions, sections of cauliflower, French beans, collops of artichoke bottoms, small pimentoes. Place the lot in an earthenware pot and cover with boiling vinegar, mixed with mustard and salt; macerate before using.

Maquereaux Marinés.—Same preparation as **Harengs à la Dieppoise.**

Melon Cantaloup.—Served on crushed ice.

Melon Cocktail.—Cantaloup cut in large dice sprinkled with sugar, add maraschino, kirsch, cognac or white port. Served in glasses very cold.

Melon Frappé with Port, Marsala, etc.—Cantaloup or other melon of good quality just ripe. Make a round incision about the stalk and remove the pips, fill with madeira, port, marsala, etc. Replace the plug and keep the melon in ice-box surrounded with crushed ice. Serve with spoon.

Melons Confits.—Small melons treated same as gherkins.

Mortadelle.—Served cut very thin and rolled.

Moules.—Poached mussels, julienne of celery, seasoned with cream mustard sauce.

Museau et Palais de Bœuf.—Cooked in a blanc and finely sliced, seasoned with oil, vinegar, chopped onions and parsley.

Œufs Farcis et Garnis.—Hard-boiled eggs, garniture to taste.

Œufs de Pluviers ou Vanneaux.—Lapwing and plover's eggs, place in cold water and boil 8 minutes. Served in a nest of parsley or water-cress.

> N.B.—If the eggs float in cold water their freshness is doubtful and they should be discarded.

Olives.—Are served plain in hors-d'œuvres dishes.

Olives Farcies.—Large Spanish olives; remove the stones and garnish with anchovy butter, salmon, sardines, etc.

Pains à la Française.—Rolls open on the side, and garnished to taste.

Pains à la Varsovienne.—Same as above, garnished with Russian salad mixed with dice of herring fillets.

Pâté d'Alouettes.—Lark pâté cut into very small and thin slices.

Pimentos à l'Algérienne.—Grilled capsicums, skinned and cut lengthwise, cut in large julienne and season with oil and vinegar, dish up and surround with roundels of onions.

Poireaux à la Grecque.—Cut the leeks in short sectons, blanch and treat same as artichokes à la Grecque.

Poireaux Farcis.—Leeks cut in short sections, partly cooked in salt water marinaded with oil and vinegar, scooped and stuffed to taste.

Poitrines d'Oies Fumées.—Smoked goose fillets cut into thin slices.

Poivrons Doux.—(See **Pimentoes**).

Poutargue de Mulet.—Oriental produce, cut into thin slices oil and lemon juice.

Radis.—Radishes are served plain, with butter, they are used only for decorations and garnishes.

Radis Noir.—Black radishes peeled, sliced and sprinkled with salt, drained and seasoned with oil, vinegar and pepper.

American Relishes.—Various kinds of fruits, onions, gherkins, prepared with vinegar, seasoned with sugar and cinnamon, cayenne.

Rillettes de Tours.—Are found on the market and served in their pots.

Rillons de Blois.—Served on serviettes.

Rougets au Safran.—Small red mullet placed in oiled pan, add dice of tomatoes, parsley, fennel, thyme, bay, garlic, pepper-corns, coriander and saffron; cover the lot with white wine and poach 15 minutes. Leave to cool in the cooking liquor and serve with lemon slices.

Royans.—(See **Sardines**).

Salades.—Salads for hors-d'œuvres are endless, and should be made as light and as sightly as possible.

Salade de Pieds de Mouton.—Sheeps' feet, cooked and boned, cut into small fillets, seasoned white hot with oil and vinegar.

Salade de Pieds de Veau.—Calves' feet, prepared as above.

Salade de Pieds de Veau Clarence.—Calves' feet, cooked and boned, pressed and minced, marinaded with oil and vinegar, cohered with mayonnaise sauce, sprinkle with parsley. Surround with quarters of hard-boiled eggs.

Salade de Pieds de Veau à la Hongroise.—Same as above, but cut into julienne and seasoned with paprika. Dressed and surrounded with roundels of hard boiled eggs.

Salami de Gotha.—Cut into thin slices and dish up like a crown.

Salami de Milan.—Same preparation as above.

Salami à l'Hongroise.—Cut into thin slices.

Sauce Moutarde à la Crème.—Powdered mustard, lemon juice, salt, pepper, mix and incorporate some cream.

Saucisses de Francfort, Strasbourg, Vienne.—Poached for 10 minutes, served with scraped horse-radish.

Saucisson de Lyon, d'Arles, de Toulouse, de Bologne, etc.—Cut into thin roundels.

Saucisson de Foie Gras, Faisan, Poulet.—Cut in thin slices, dish up in a circle, chopped aspic in the centre.

Saumon Fumé.—Smoked salmon cut into triangular thin slices and rolled into cones.

Sigui Fumé.—Is served cut in thin strips.

Sprats.—Remove the heads and skin, sprinkle with shallots and chopped parsley, add oil and vinegar, leave to marinade for 6 hours.

Tartelettes et Barquettes.—Are garnished with mousses or compound butters, and finished according to taste and fancy.

Tartelettes de Thon.—Small croustades garnished tunny fish purée mixed with mayonnaise sauce. Place a round of tunny on too, and surround with hard-boiled white and yolk of eggs, chopped parsley.

Thon à l'Huile.—Tunny in oil is found on the market, and served as it stands.

Thon à la Marinette.—Slices of tunny fish, alternated with slices of tomatoes and spring onions, surrounded with a border of potatoes, seasoned with oil and vinegar, salt, pepper.

Tomate à la Génoise.—Tomatoes cut into slices, dish up and decorate with yellow and red capsicums, coat with anchovy vinaigrette, surround with slices of potatoes.

Tomates à la Monégasque.—Small tomatoes, cut the top and empty them, marinade the inside and garnish with a preparation of tunny, hard-boiled eggs, onions, parsley, chervil and chopped tarrgon, cohere with mayonnaise sauce.

Tomates au Naturel.—Small tomatoes, peeled and pressed in a piece of linen, seasoned with oil and vinegar. Stick a small piece of parsley stalk on top and imitate green leaves by means of small piping with green butter.

Tomates en Quartiers.—Tomatoes, peeled and emptied, stuffed with fish purée or macédoine of vegetables cohered with mayonnaise and aspic. Place on ice for a while, and cut into regular quarters.

Truites Marinées.—Trout poached in court-bouillon and white wine, add vinegar and leave to cool in the liquor, dish up with a few tablespoons· fuls of the latter, and decorate with slices of lemon.

Truites Marinées (Fillets).—Filleted trout; remove the skins when poached, and coat with mayonnaise; sprinkle with chopped coral, dish up on a bed of vegetable salad, decorate with roundels of hard-boiled eggs, radishes and cucumbers.

Variantes.—Assortment of blanched artichoke bottoms, French beans, cauliflowers, spring onions, pimentoes, gherkins, etc., marinaded in oil and vinegar, coriander and English mustard.

Zampino.—Boned pork trotter stuffed as a salami, cooked and served cold in slices.

Potages

CONSOMMES CLAIRS — CLEAR SOUPS

Ailerons.—Chicken consommé, garnished with fowls' wings, boned, stuffed and braised (boiled rice).

Albion.—Consommé, garnished with foie gras quenelles, asparagus heads, julienne of truffles, cocks combs.

Alexandra.—Chicken consommé thickened with tapioca, garnished with julienne of chicken, quenelles and shredded lettuces.

Allemande.—Consommé thickened with tapioca, flavoured with genièvre, garnished with julienne of red cabbage, roundels of Frankfort sausages, scraped horse-radish.

Alsacienne.—Consommé garnished with nouillettes and profiteroles stuffed with foie gras purée.

Ambassadeurs.—Chicken consommé, garnished with dice of royale with chopped truffles, mushrooms and white of chicken in dice.

Ambassadrice.—Chicken consommé, garnished with 3 royales chopped truffle (*black*), tomato (*red*), green peas (*green*); julienne of chicken and mushrooms.

Ancienne.—Petite marmite consommé, garnished with croûtes filled with vegetable purée and gratiné.

Andalouse.—Consommé blended with tomato purée, garnished with dice of Royale and dice of tomato, julienne of ham, boiled rice and vermicelli, threaded eggs.

Arenberg.—Chicken consommé, garnished with balls of carrots, turnips, truffles, peas, small round chicken quenelles, and roundels of asparagus royale.

Aurore.—Consommé thickened with tapioca and tomato purée, garnished with Julienne of chicken.

Béatrice.—Consommé garnished with semolina, roundels of chicken farce blended with tomato and royale.

Belle Fermière.—Consommé garnished with Julienne of cabbage, lozenges of French beans, Italian paste.

Belle Gabrielle.—Consommé thickened with tapioca, garnished with rectangles of chicken, mousseline and crayfish tails.

Berchoux.—Game consommé, garnished with dice of royale, blended with chestnut purée and quails' essence, Julienne of truffles and mushrooms.

Bergère—Oxtail consommé thickened with tapioca, garnished with asparagus tips, minced mushrooms or mousserons, tarragon leaves and chervil shreds.

Berny.—Consommé thickened with tapioca and garnished with small balls of Dauphine potatoes combined with chopped grilled almonds and chopped truffles, chervil shreds.

Blanc-Manger.—Chicken consommé garnished with green peas and chervil shreds. Serve separately some small tartlets filled with minced chicken.

Bohéminenne.—Chicken consommé thickened with tapioca and garnished with dice of royale blended with foie gras purée, profiteroles (Separately).

Boieldieu.—Consommé thickened with tapioca garnished with three sorts of quenelles, foie gras, chicken and truffles.

Bouchère.—Petite marmite consommé, garnished with small squares of cooked cabbage, and serve separately some marrow bones, cut thin and poached.

Bouquetière.—Chicken consommé thickened with tapioca, garnished with French beans, asparagus heads, green peas, etc.

Bourbon.—Consommé thickened with tapioca, garnished with sago and large quenelles, decorated with truffles representing fleurs-de-lis, chervil shreds.

Bourdaloue.—Consommé garnished with four different royales, tomato (*red*), ordinary (*white*), asparagus purée (*green*), carrot purée (*red*). Cut No. 1, into dice, No. 2, into lozenges, No. 3, into leaves, No. 4, into stars.

Bretonne.—Consommé garnished with Julienne of leeks, celery, onion, mushrooms and chervil shreds.

Brieux.—Consommé thickened with tapioca, garnished with Royale made with pistachios powder and cut into stars, dice of truffles and Japon perles.

Britannia.—Consommé thickened with tapioca, garnished with dice of royale, blended with lobster cullis and Julienne of truffles.

Brunoise.—Consommé garnished with small cubes of carrots, turnips, leeks, celery, peas and chervil: can be done with the addition of rice, barley, quenelles, etc.

Cancalaise.—Fish consommé thickened with tapioca, garnished with oysters, Julienne of fillets of soles, quenelles of whiting.

Carmélite.—Fish consommé thickened with arrowroot, garnished with roundels of fish forcemeat and plain boiled rice.

Carmen.—Consommé clarified with raw tomato purée and mild capsicums, garnished with lozenges of tomato, Julienne of capsicum, rice and chervil shreds.

Caroline.—Chicken consommé garnished with lozenges of Royale, rice and chervil shreds.

Castellane.—Game consommé flavoured with woodcock " fumet ", garnished with roundels of Royale made with woodcock purée and lentil purée, yolk of eggs chopped and thickened with the usual liaison, Julienne of woodcock fillets.

Célestine.—Consommé thickened with tapioca and garnished with Julienne of pannequets or pancakes, mixed with chopped truffles or fine herbs.

Chancelière.—Chicken consommé garnished with roundels of Royale with purée of fresh peas, Julienne of chicken, truffles and mushrooms.

Charolaise.—Petite marmite consommé, garnished with small glazed onions, carrot balls, roundels of braised cabbages and small sections of oxtail.

Chartreuse.—Consommé thickened with tapioca, garnished with three differently stuffed ravioli, one foie gras, one spinach and the other, chopped mushrooms; chervil shreds.

Chasseur.—Game consommé, garnished with Julienne of mushrooms and game quenelles, or (*Separately*): profiteroles stuffed with game purée.

Châtelaine.—Chicken consommé thickened with tapioca, garnished with dice of Royale made with three parts Soubise and one part artichoke purée; chicken quenelles stuffed with chestnut purée.

Cheveux d'Anges.—Chicken consommé garnished with very small vermicelli. (*Separately*): grated parmesan.

Chevreuse.—Chicken consommé garnished with large quenelles of chicken, stuffed with asparagus purée and Julienne of truffles.

Colbert.—Consommé garnished with printanier of vegetables and small poached eggs.

Colombine.—Chicken consommé garnished with vegetables, Julienne of pigeons and poached pigeons' eggs.

Comtesse.—Chicken consommé thickened with tapioca and garnished with lozenges of Royale and asparagus purée, roundels of stuffed lettuces, round quenelles decorated with truffles.

Crécy.—Chicken consommé thickened with tapioca, garnished with lozenges of Royale, blended with purée of carrots, Brunoise of carrots and chervil shreds.

Croûtes-au-Pot.—Petite marmite consommé ,garnished with dice of vegetables and (*Separately*): croûtes dried in the oven.

Cussy.—Game consommé flavoured with partridges garnished with roundels of Royale made with chestnut purée and partridges, quenelles, Julienne of truffles, half-glass of Madeira and brandy when about to serve.

Cyrano.—Consommé with duck fumet, garnished with large quenelles of duck, glazed and sprinkled with parmesan, and gratined.

Dame Blanche.—Chicken consommé thickened with tapioca, garnished with dice of Royale made with almond milk, stars of chicken and Japon perles.

Demidoff.—Chicken consommé garnished with printanier of vegetables, truffles, quenelles with fine herbs and chervil shreds.

Deslignac.—Chicken consommé thickened with tapioca, garnished with dice of Royale, roundels of stuffed lettuces and chervil shreds.

Diablotins.—Chicken consommé, garnished with slices of French bread cut one-quarter of an inch thick, buttered and coated with cheese and set to gratin.

Diane.—Game consommé garnished with julienne of game, dice of truffles, a glass of Madeira when serving.

Diplomate.—Chicken consommé thickened with tapioca and garnished with roundels of chicken forcemeat blended with crayfish butter, Julienne of truffles.

Doria.—Chicken consommé garnished with printanier and cucumber, large macaroni, filled with tomated chicken forcemeat, poached and cut into short lengths; profiteroles.

Douglas.—Consommé garnished with roundels of sweetbreads, artichoke bottoms, and asparagus heads.

Dubarry.—Consommé thickened with tapioca, garnished with roundels of Royale, small bouquets of cauliflower and chervil shreds.

Duchesse.—Chicken consommé, garnished with perles du Japon, dice of Royale and Julienne of lettuces.

Duse.—Consommé with tomato fumet, garnished with tomatoed quenelles, poached tortellini, small Gênes pastes.

Ecossaise.—Mutton broth garnished with dice of boiled mutton, pearl barley and large Brunoise of vegetables.

Ephémères.—Chicken consommé garnished with large Julienne of carrots, asparagus heads, peas and ephémères.
Preparation for Ephémères.—2 spoonfuls of grated parmesan, arrowroot, 3 yolk of eggs, ½ spoonful of cream, pepper, nutmeg, chicken glaze. Lay in the shape of buttons by means of piping bag, and poach in consommé.

Favorite.—Consommé thickened with tapioca, garnished with potato balls, Julienne of artichoke bottoms and mushrooms, chervil shreds.

Flamande.—Consommé garnished with dice of Royale blended with brussels sprouts purée, green peas and chervil shreds.

Floréal.—Chicken consommé garnished with carrots, turnips, peas, asparagus heads, small quenelles with pistachio powder and chervil shreds.

Francillon.—Chicken consommé garnished with poached eggs and chicken quenelles.

Garibaldi.—Chicken consommé garnished with perles du Japon and spaghetti.

Gauloise.—Chicken consommé thickened with yolk of eggs garnished with cocks combs and kidneys, and roundels of ham royale.

George Sand.—Fish consommé garnished with fish quenelles blended with crayfish butter and quarters of cooked morels. (*Separately*): serve slices of carp soft roe on roundels of French soup bread.

Germaine.—Consommé garnished with chicken quenelles, roundels of Royale blended with peas purée and mirepoix, chervil shreds.

Germinal.—Consommé with tarragon flavour, garnished with peas, dice of French beans, asparagus heads, quenelles and chervil shreds.

Girondine.—Consommé garnished with lozenges of Royale and chopped ham, Julienne of carrots.

Grande Duchesse.—Chicken consommé garnished with chicken quenelles, Julienne of chicken suprême, tongue, and asparagus heads.

Grenade.—Consommé with tomato flavour garnished with dice of Royale and vegetable purée with tomato, dice of tomatoes, chervil shreds.

Grimaldi.—Consommé clarified with fresh tomato purée, garnished with dice of royale and julienne of celery.

Hodge-Podge.—Mutton broth garnished with pearl barley, peas, Brunoise of vegetables and dice of cooked mutton.

Hongroise.—Consommé flavoured with tomato and paprika, garnished with roundels of chicken forcemeat and quenelles of calves' livers.

Impératrice (A).—Chicken consommé garnished with cocks' combs and kidneys, asparagus heads and roundels of Royale.

(B).—Chicken consommé garnished with roundels of chicken forcemeat made in the shape of a black pudding and inserted with French beans, sticks of truffles and carrots.

Impérial.—Chicken consommé thickened with tapioca, garnished with quenelles, cocks' combs and kidneys, green peas, chervil shreds.

Indienne.—Consommé flavoured with curry, garnished with dice of Royale made with coconut milk. (*Separately*): serve plain boiled rice.

Infante (A).—Chicken consommé thickened with tapioca, garnished with croûtons coated with vegetable purée and gratined.

(B).—Same as above, with profiteroles stuffed with foie gras and served separately.

Italienne.—Consommé garnished with dice of red Royale (*with tomato*) and green Royale (*with spinach*), spaghetti and grated cheese (*Separately*).

Jacobine.—Chicken consommé garnished with dice of potatoes. French beans, turnips, peas, Julienne of truffles.

Jockey Club.—Chicken consommé garnished with dice of Royale of carrots, of peas purée, and of chicken purée.

Joinville.—Chicken consommé garnished with quenelles of three different flavours and colours, green, red and white.

Jouvencel.—Consommé thickened with tapioca, garnished with stuffed lettuce leaves rolled cigarette shape and poached. (*Separately*): round croûtons coated with carrot purée sprinkled with cheese and set to gratin.

Juanita.—Chicken consommé, garnished with dice of tomatoed royale and hard yolks passed through the sieve.

Judic.—Chicken consommé garnished with braised lettuces, chicken quenelles and shreds of mushrooms.

Julienne.—Consommé garnished with carrots, leeks, turnips, celery, cabbage, cut into fillets 2 inches in length.—Stew the vegetables with a little butter, salt and pinch of sugar, moisten with the consommé and cook gently, removing the grease the while. Add green peas, sorrel chiffonade and chervil shreds.

Léopold.—Consommé with semolina and garnished with shreds of lettuce, sorrel and chervil.

Lorette.—Chicken consommé, flavoured with pimentoes, garnished with Julienne of truffles, asparagus heads, chervil. (*Separately*): Small balls of Lorette potatoes. (*See* Vegetable Chapter).

Macdonald.—Consommé, garnished with roundels of royale made with brain purée, dice of cucumber and small ravioli.

Madrilène.—Consomme with celery flavour, tomato and pimentoes. (*Can be served cold*) garnished with tomato Julienne, sorrel shreds and vermicelli (*Hot*).

Marguerite.—Chicken consommé, garnished with marguerites made with chicken forcemeat, poached and cut into thin roundels and stamped with fancy cutter to the shape of marguerite. Yolk of egg in the middle in imitation of the flower centre, asparagus heads.

Maria.—Chicken consommé thickened with tapioca, garnished with roundels of royale made with beans purée and printanier of vegetables.

Marquise (A).—Consommé with celery flavour, garnished with roundels of veal amourettes and quenelles of chicken mixed with chopped avelines.

(**B**).—Chicken consommé, garnished with tomato chicken quenelles, Julienne of lettuce and truffles.

Martinière.—Chicken consommé, garnished with roundels of stuffed cabbage, peas, chervil shreds.

Médicis.—Consommé, thickened with tapioca and garnished with cubes of green and red " royale " sorrel shreds.

Mégère.—Consommé, garnished with gnocchi made with potato, shredded lettuces large vermicelli.

Mercédès.—Consommé with Xérès wine, garnished with rings of red pimentoes and stars of cockscombs.

Messaline.—Chicken consommé flavoured with tomato, garnished with Julienne of sweet pimentoes, cocks kidneys and rice.

Metternich.—Game consommé with pheasant fumet, garnished with dice of Royale made with artichoke purée, Julienne of pheasant.

Mikado.—Chicken consommé with tomato flavour, garnished with dice of tomato and chicken.

Milanaise.—Chicken in consommé with tomato flavour garnished with mushrooms, ham, truffles in Julienne spaghetti. (*Separately*): grated cheese.

Mimosa (A).—Chicken consommé, garnished with pink, green and yellow royale (*carrots, green peas, hard yolks*).

(**B**).—Chicken consommé, garnished with hard boiled yolk of eggs pressed through a large sieve.

Mireille.—Chicken consommé, garnished with semolina and roundels of royale, and of tomato chicken forcemeat.

Mirette.—Petite marmite consommé, garnished with chicken quenelles, shredded lettuce, chervil. (*Separately*): serve some cheese croûtons.

Monaco.—Chicken consommé, garnished with pea-shaped truffles, carrots, turnips, and profiteroles.

Monte-Carlo.—Chicken consommé, garnished with roundels of carrots and turnips, stuffed pancakes, slices of truffles.

Montmorency.—Chicken consommé, thickened with tapioca, garnished with asparagus heads, white quenelles, rice and chervil shreds.

Montmort.—Consommé, garnished with roundels of chicken forcemeat, mixed with chopped truffles and tongue, dice of green royale (*peas purée*) carrots and turnips, crescent shaped, asparagus heads and chervil.

Mosaïque.—Consommé, garnished with various shapes of royale and chicken forcemeat of various flavours.

Moscovite.—Consommé of sterlet or sturgeon and cucumber essence, garnished with julienne of salted mushrooms and dice of vesiga poached in consommé.

Mousseline.—Chicken consommé, garnished with small chicken mousseline poached in grooved moulds.

Navarin.—Consommé, garnished with roundels of green royale (*green peas*), crayfish tails, blanched concassed parsley.

Neige de Florence.—Consommé, garnished with special Italian paste.

Nelson.—Fish consommé thickened with arrow-root, garnished with rice. (*Separately*): Serve small bouchées filled with dice of lobster Américaine.

Nemours.—Chicken consommé, thickened with tapioca, garnished with Crécy royale with dice of carrots, perles du Japon, julienne of truffles.

Nesselrode.—Game consommé prepared with hazel hen Fumet, garnished with roundels of royale made with chestnuts purée and game, cut with a grooved cutter, Julienne of hazel hen fillets and mushrooms.

Niçoise.—Consommé with tomato flavour, garnished with dice of tomatoes, French beans, potatoes, chervil shreds.

Nids d'Hirondelles.—Chicken consommé, garnished with swallow nests, thoroughly cleaned and poached.

Note.—The nests must be soaked in cold water for 24 hours in order to swell the mucilaginous elements and make them transparent; then place them in the boiling consommé and cook gently for 30 minutes, until the gummy portions are melted in the consommé.

Nilson.—Consommé thickened with tapioca, garnished with quenelles of chicken and ham, chopped truffles and chives, green peas, chervil.

Ninon.—Chicken consommé, garnished with small balls of carrots, turnips, truffles, chervil shreds. (*Separately*): Serve tartlets filled with minced chicken and yolk of eggs; decorate with a star made of truffle.

Olga.—Consommé with Port wine flavour, garnished with Julienne of leeks, celeriac, salted gherkins and carrots.

Orge Perlé.—Consommé, garnished with pearl barley.

Orientale.—Consommé, garnished with crescents of carrots, turnips and beetroots; rice with saffron.

Orléanaise.—Consommé, garnished with large cubes of royale made with purée of spinach, French beans, flageolets and chervil.

Orléans.—Consommé, thickened with tapioca, garnished with quenelles made in three different colours. (*White* with chicken, *red* with tomato, *green* with spinach).

Orsay.—Chicken consommé, garnished with poached yolk of eggs, quenelles of pigeons, Julienne of pigeons suprêmes, asparagus heads.

Parisienne.—Consommé with leek flavour, garnished with Julienne of potatoes and leeks.

Parmesane.—Consommé, garnished with Parmesan biscuits.

Pâtes diverses.—Consommé, garnished with vermicelli, Gênes paste, Italie alphabet, etc.

Petite Mariée.—Chicken consommé, very white, garnished with small roundels of royale made with chicken purée and almonds milk, chervil shreds.

Petite Marmite.—Strong consommé of beef and chicken, garnished with carrots and turnips, leeks and cabbage, Julienne of celery, roundels of marrow, dice of beef and chicken. Served in special marmite, (*Separately*) dry thin toast.

Petite Marmite Béarnaise.—Same as above with the addition of rice and Julienne of potatoes.

Princesse.—Chicken consommé, garnished with dice of green peas royale, pearl barley and thin slices of white chicken.

Printanier.—Consommé, garnished with balls of carrots, turnips, peas and chervil shreds.

Quenelles.—Consommé, garnished with quenelles to taste.

Quenelles à la Moelle.—Consommé thickened with tapioca, garnished with quenelles made with marrow.

Quenelles à la Viennoise.—Same as above with quenelles made with calf liver and fennel.

Queue de Bœuf (Ox-tail soup).—Consommé made with ox-tail cut into sections and browned with mirepoix in the oven. Moisten with stock and clarified in the ordinary manner. Garnish with carrots, turnips of the ox-tail. A glass of old Madeira when serving.

Rabelais.—Consommé, flavoured with lark and truffles essence, garnished with Julienne of celery, quenelles of truffled larks. A glass of Seuilly wine when serving.

Rachel.—Chicken consommé, thickened with tapioca, garnished with Julienne of artichoke bottoms. (*Separately*): croûtons fried in butter and filled with slices of poached marrow.

Ravioli.—Consommé, garnished with small ravioli.

Reine.—Chicken consommé, thickened with tapioca, garnished with dice of royale made with chicken purée, Julienne of chicken.

Réjane.—Chicken consommé with tapioca, garnished with shredded eggs, small roundels of Crécy royale made with avelines milk.

Renaissance.—Chicken consommé, garnished with balls of vegetables and royale cut into shapes, chervil shreds.

Richelieu.—Consommé, garnished with chicken quenelles stuffed with chicken jelly; stuffed lettuces rolled into paupiettes, Julienne of carrots and turnips; chervil shreds.

Riso a Fegatini.—Chicken or White consommé when boiling cook rice drop at the last minute small cubes of chicken liver just to be poached; (separately) grated Parmesan cheese.

Rossini.—Chicken consommé, thickened with tapioca and flavoured with truffles essence, garnished with profiteroles stuffed with foie gras purée and chopped truffles.

Rothschild.—Game consommé, garnished with roundels of royale made with purée of pheasant, chestnut purée and salmis sauce. When about to serve add a glass of Sauterne.

Royale.—Chicken consommé, garnished with cubes of royale, lozenges, etc.

Rubens.—Tomato chicken consommé, garnished with hop shoots.

Saint-Hubert.—Game consommé with white wine, garnished with royale of game purée and lentil purée. Julienne of game.

Sarah Bernhardt.—Consommé thickened with tapioca, flavoured with turtle herbs and Madeira wine. Garnished with tomato quenelles and roundels of marrow.

Sévigné.—Chicken consommé, garnished with white quenelles, Julienne of lettuces and asparagus heads.

Solange.—Consommé, garnished with pearl barley, squares of lettuce and chicken Julienne.

Soubrette.—Tomato chicken consommé, seasoned with cayenne pepper, garnished with round, flat quenelles decorated in the middle with a roundel of truffle in imitation of an eyepink shrimp's tail.

Souveraine.—Chicken consommé, garnished with large quenelles stuffed with vegetable Brunoise chervil shreds.

Surprise.—Same as above with quenelles stuffed with jelly mixed with beetroot juice.

Tapioca.—Consommé with Tapioca. Boil 10 minutes.

Théodora.—Chicken consommé, garnished with chicken Julienne and truffles, dice of royale and asparagus heads.

Tosca.—Chicken consommé, thickened with tapioca flavoured with turtle herbs and Madeira, garnished with Julienne of leeks, profiterolles.

Trévise or **Trois Filets.**—Consommé, garnished with chicken Julienne, tongue and truffles.

Tzarine.—Chicken consommé, flavoured with fennel; garnished with dice of vesiga.

Valois.—Consommé, garnished with tomato quenelles, pearl barley asparagus heads.

Vatel.—Fish consommé with sole fumet, garnished with roundels of royale made with crayfish, lozenges of fillets of sole.

Vénitienne.—Consommé, flavoured with chervil, tarragon and thyme; garnished with rice. (*Separately*): serve small gratined gnocchi.

Vermicelli.—Consommé with Vermicelli.

Véron.—Consommé, flavoured with truffles essence, garnished with dice of royale made with flageolets purée, julienne of capsicums. Glass of Port when serving.

Vert-Pré.—Consommé, thickened with tapioca, garnished with asparagus heads, peas, French beans, shredded lettuce and sorrel, chervil shreds.

Viennoise.—Consommé with pink paprika, garnished with julienne of cheese pancakes and gnocchi, seasoned with paprika.

Villeneuve.—Chicken consommé, garnished with dice of royale, and lozenges of lettuce coated with chicken forcemeat combined with chopped ham, poached in oven.

Viveurs.—Consommé duck flavour, celery and beetroot juice, cayenne pepper; garnished with julienne of celery, diablotins with paprika.

Xavier (A).—Consommé garnished with royale of chicken purée, peas, chervil.
(B).—Consommé, garnished with shredded eggs.

Windsor.—Consommé with calves foot and flavoured with turtle herbs; garnished with Julienne of calves foot-and-chicken quenelles with chopped yolk of eggs.

SPECIAL CONSOMMES FOR PARTIES OR SUPPERS

Consommé à l'essence de Cailles.	—	Quail flavour.
Consommé à l'essence de Céleri.	—	Celery flavour.
Consommé à l'essence d'Estragon.	—	Tarragon flavour.
Consommé à l'essence de Morilles.	—	Morrel flavour.
Consommé aux Piments doux.	—	With sweet pimentoes.
Consommé à l'essence de Truffes.	—	With truffle essence.
Consommé aux Paillettes d'Or.	—	With golden leaves.
Consommé à la Portugaise.	—	With tomato flavour.
Consommé au Fumet de Perdreau.	—	With partridge flavour.
Consommé aux Vins.	—	White wines.
Gelée de Volaille Napolitaine.	—	Chicken jelly with dice of tomato
Gelée de Volaille aux Tomates.	—	Tomato chicken jelly.
Velouté de Volaille Froid.	—	Cold chicken velouté.

D

SOUPES — SOUPS

All these soups are moistened with water, milk or thin white stock.

Ail (à l').—Thin slices of French bread sprinkled with grated cheese and gratined. Boil some garlic, sage, bay leaves, cloves, salt, pepper and pour over the toasted bread dressed in a soup bowl.

Aïgo à la Ménagère.—Onions and leeks fried in oil; add chopped tomatoes, crushed garlic, fennel, faggot, dried orange peel, pinch of saffron, minced potatoes and water; salt, pepper, boil 20 minutes. Poach some eggs in this broth and pour over some prepared toast, as above.

Aïgo Bouido.—Salt water boiled with crushed garlic, sage, oil, pepper, for 20 minutes, and pour over some prepared cheese toast. Sprinkle with herbs.

Aïgo Saou.—Slices of bread sprinkled with olive oil and black pepper, moistened with water. Add some sections of white fishes, quarters of potatoes, onions and tomatoes garlic, salt and pepper. Boil 20 minutes. Serve fish separately with aioli.

Albigeoise.—Marmite of beef, calves feet, ham, dry saucisson, preserve of goose, garnished with dice of carrots, turnips, cabbage, leeks, lettuce, broad beans.

Alénois.—Minced potatoes, watercress, milk, butter and chervil. Cook 20 minutes.

Alsacienne.—White consommé with sauerkraut, thickened with flour, garnished with potato quenelles.

Ardennaise.—Chicory, potatoes, white of leeks, moistened with milk, slices of French bread.

Aveyronnaise.—In a marmite; cabbage, potatoes, turnips, carrots. Add haricot beans, salted pork and ham, goose preserve, garlic. Cook 2 hours. Pour over slices of French bread.

Auvergnate.—In a marmite; head of salted pork, carrots, turnips, leeks, potatoes, cabbage, lentils; garnished with dice of pork head and slices of French bread.

Beaucaire.—Cabbage, leeks, celery, gizzards of chicken in Julienne, moistened with consommé, marjoram and thyme, garnished with pearl barley, collops of chicken livers; grated cheese.

Bonne Femme.—Minced leeks and potatoes fried in butter and moistened with white consommé; garnished with French bread, finished with butter and cream.

Brabançonne.—Carrots, leeks, turnips, onions, minced and tossed in butter; moistened with milk; garnished with Brussels biscottes.

Brésilienne.—Carrots, turnips, leeks, celery, minced onions tossed in butter, chopped tomatoes. Moistened with white consommé; cohered with purée of black haricot beans; garnished with rice.

Bûcheronne.—Cabbage, turnips and minced potatoes in a pan with fresh chopped lard, moistened with water. Add white haricot beans, garnished with dried slices of bread.

Cultivateur.—Vegetables paysanne tossed in butter with minced potatoes and salted pork. Moistened with white stock, garnished with dice of pork.

Dauphinoise.—Turnips, marrow and potatoes; moistened with milk and water; add leaves of beetroots, garnished with vermicelli and chervil shreds.

Estérel.—Chopped onion tossed in butter with dice of pumpkin, haricot beans. Moistened with consommé, strained and garnished with vermicelli.

Fermière.—Paysanne of vegetables and cabbage Julienne moistened with consommé. Slices of home made bread.

Flamande.—Brussels sprouts and minced potatoes, moistened with white stock, garnished with Brussels sprouts.

Franc-Comtoise.—Potatoes, turnips, lettuce and sorrel, moistened with water and milk, garnished with shredded sorrel, spinach, Italien paste, chervil.

Hochepot.—(*See* **Queue de Bœuf** in **Consommés Clairs**).

Jeannette.—Paysanne of vegetables with potatoes, moistened with white consommé. Add fresh peas, French beans in dice, sorrel, watercress and chervil, milk and butter when serving. Slices of French bread.

Julienne à la Russe.—Julienne of vegetables with salted mushrooms and parsley roots, moistened with consommé. Add fennel and sour cream when serving. (*Separately*): serve small stuffed rissoles.

Laboureur.—Marmite of salted pork and split peas with carrots, turnips, onions, leeks.

Maraîchère.—Same as Bonne-Femme with vermicelli, shredded lettuces, sorrel and spinach, chervil.

Mariage.—Marmite with beef, mutton and chicken, garnished with vegetables and rice with saffron.

Nevers.—Brussels sprouts and minced carrot, tossed in butter and moistened with consommé, garnished with vermicelli and chervil.

Normande.—Dice of carrots, potatoes and leeks, moistened with white consommé. Add fresh flageolets; butter and cream.

Palesto.—Consommé prepared with chicken abats, ham, lettuce, leeks, celery, chervil. Strain and thicken with arrowroot, garnished with vegetable Julienne, peas and rice.

Paysanne.—Dice of vegetables tossed in butter, moistened with consommé, garnished with peas, French beans, flageolets, chervil shreds.

Potée Bourguignonne.—Marmite with salted pork and knuckle, garnished with carrots, turnips, cabbage, leeks, potatoes, cervelas. Slices of brown bread.

Savoyarde.—Celery, leeks, onions, and minced potatoes, tossed in minced lard, moistened with water and milk. Slices of toasted bread sprinkled with cheese.

Thourins.—Minced onions, coloured in butter. Add flour; moistened with milk, cohere with yolk of eggs and cream. (*Separately*); serve thin toasted bread and grated cheese.

Thourins Roumanille.—Same as above. Garnished with vermicelli, grated cheese.

Viennoise.—Marmite with cubes of fresh beef, salt beef and smoked bacon. Garnished large dice of carrots and onions, haricot beans, split peas, rice, pearl barley.

Villageoise.—Minced leeks tossed in butter, moistened with white consommé, garnished with Julienne of cabbage, vermicelli, chervil shreds.

CREAMS OR VELOUTES — THICK SOUPS

Thick soups are named **CREAMS** *when the liaison is done with double cream; and* **VELOUTES** *when the liaison is done with yolk of eggs. Veloutés must not boil.*

Agnès Sorel.—Chicken velouté with mushrooms, garnished with Julienne of mushrooms, white of chicken, tongue, liaison with cream.

Algérienne.—Purée of sweet potatoes and grilled avelines. Cream.

Ambassadeur.—Purée of green peas garnished with rice, shredded lettuce and sorrel, chervil, butter and cream.

Américaine.—⅓ crayfish bisque, ⅓ tomato cream, ⅓tapioca; garnished with dice of crayfish, butter.

Andalouse.—Purée of tomato, rice and onions, mixed with cream and garnished with boiled rice and Julienne of capsicum.

Bagration (Gras).—Veal velouté garnished with macaroni; liaison with cream. (*Separately*): Grated cheese.

Bagration (Maigre).—Fish velouté with mushroom essence, garnished with Julienne of fillets of soles, quenelles of fish with crayfish, butter, small collops of crayfish. Liaison with yolk of eggs or cream.

Balvet.—(*See* Jubilée).

Bisque d'Ecrevisses.—Mirepoix of vegetables tossed in butter with crayfishes, peppercorns, moistened with white wine, fish stock, consommé and burnt brandy; add tomatoes, faggot, rice. Cook 30 minutes. Pound in mortar and pass through fine sieve; butter and cream. Garnish with crayfishes tails and stuffed carcasses.

Bisque d'Ecrevisses à l'Ancienne.—Same as above with fried croûtons instead of the rice.

Bisque de Crabes.—Same process as above with crabs instead of crayfish.

Bisque de Crevettes.—Same process with shrimps, garnished with shrimps' tails.

Bisque de Homards.—Same process, garnished with collops of lobster.

Boieldieu.—Chicken velouté, garnished with quenelles of chicken stuffed with foie gras, dice of chicken and truffles. Liaison with cream or yolk of eggs.

Bonvalet.—Purée of turnips and potatoes, garnished with dice of French beans royale, peas, haricot beans, Julienne of leeks, chervill. Liaison with cream or eggs.

Borely.—Fish velouté, garnished with quenelles, mussels. Liaison with cream or eggs.

Bourdaloue.—Velouté with cream of rice, garnished with tomato royale (*red*), chicken royale (*white*), haricot beans (*yellow*), asparagus royale (*green*), carrot oryale (*pink*). Liaison with cream.

Bressanne.—Purée of Pumpkin, garnished with Italian pastes poached in milk. Cream.

Bretonne.—Haricot beans purée with onions and leeks. Add tomato purée, butter and cream.

Cambacérès.—One part of pigeon velouté and one part of crayfish bisque, garnished with pigeon quenelles stuffed with crayfish salpicon. Butter and cream.

Camélia.—Purée of green peas, thickened with tapioca, garnished with Julienne of chicken and white of leeks. Butter and cream.

Cardinal.—Fish velouté with lobster cullis, garnished with lobster royale shaped into crosses.

Carmélite.—Fish velouté garnished with quenelles of whiting. Julienne of fillets of soles. Liaison with cream or yolk of eggs.

Carmen.—Velouté with tomated cream of rice, garnished with dice of tomatoes, Julienne of sweet capsicums. Butter and cream.

Caroline.—Velouté with cream of rice, garnished with royale made with almonds milk, rice, cream or yolk of eggs.

Céleri.—Velouté with celery purée. Cream.

Cérès.—Velouté with green wheat purée. Cream.

Clermont.—Velouté of celery with chestnut purée, garnished with roundels of fried onions and small balls of chestnut purée. Cream.

Chabrillan.—Tomato purée, garnished with chicken quenelles flavoured with tarragon, vermicelli, butter.

Champenoise.—½ Parmentier cream, ½ celeriac cream, garnished with brunoise of carrots and celeriac.

Chanoinesse.—Fish velouté with crayfish cullis, garnished with collops of soft roes. Butter.

Chantilly.—Purée of lentils. Cream. Garnished with chicken quenelles.

Chartreuse.—Velouté of chicken, garnished with dice of tomato, small ravioli stuffed with spinach, foie gras and chopped mushrooms; chervil. Liaison with cream or yolk of eggs.

Cherville.—Velouté of rabbit, garnished with minced morels, collops of rabbit fillets. Cream. Madeira.

Chevreuse.—Chicken velouté, garnished with Julienne of truffles and chicken, semolina, cream.

Chevrière.—Potatoes, white of leeks, lettuces, sorrel, chervil, fresh pimpernel minced and cooked together, strained and garnished with fried potato croûtons. Butter and cream.

Chicorée.—Velouté with endives, garnished with dice of fried bread, chervil. Butter and cream.

Choiseul.—Lentil purée, garnished with sorrel, and rice. Liaison with cream or yolk of eggs.

Choisy.—Velouté with lettuces, garnished with croûtons, chervil. Liaison with cream.

Colombine.—Pigeon velouté, flavoured with caraway seeds, garnished with Julienne of pigeon fillets and quenelles.

Compiègne.—Purée of haricot beans, garnished with sorrel, chervil shreds. Butter.

Comtesse (A).—Asparagus velouté, garnished with shredded sorrel, white asparagus heads. Cream.

(B).—Haricot beans purée, garnished with fried croûtons, chervil. Butter and cream.

Condé.—Purée of red haricot beans with red wine. Butter.

Conti.—Lentils purée, garnished with dice of fried bacon, chervil. Butter.

Conti à la Brunoise.—Same as above with Brunoise of vegetables.

Conti à la Clermont.—Same with Clermont garnish.

Cormeilles.—Potato purée with French beans, garnished with dice of French beans cream or yolk of eggs.

Crécy.—Carrots purée with rice. Butter and cream.

Crécy à l'Ancienne.—Same as above, garnished with fried croûtons.

Crécy à la Briarde.—Carrots and potato purée, garnished with fried croûtons, chervil shreds. Cream.

Cressonnière.—Purée of potatoes and watercress, garnished with blanched watercress leaves. Cream or yolk of eggs.

Crevettes à la Mignon.—Fish velouté with shrimps and oyster juice, garnished with fish quenelles, ½ white and ½ pink, green peas and balls of truffles. Butter and cream.

Crevettes à la Normande.—Fish velouté with shrimps, garnished with shrimp tails, poached oysters, butter and cream.

Dame Blanche.—Chicken velouté, garnished with dice of chicken, white quenelles, Japon pearls. Cream.

Danoise.—Velouté with artichokes and duck, garnished with quenelles of duck, julienne of mushrooms, butter and cream, glass of Marsala wine when serving.

Dartoise.—Purée of haricot beans, garnished with brunoise of vegetables, butter and cream.

Dieppoise.—Fish velouté with mussel juice, white of leeks and mushroom parings, garnished with shrimp tails, mussels. Cream.

Derby.—Velouté with Soubise cream of rice, flavoured with curry, garnished with chicken quenelles, stuffed with foie gras, truffle balls, rice and cream.

Diane.—Velouté with partridge essence, garnished with quenelles and Julienne of truffles. Butter and cream. Madeira.

Divette.—Fish velouté garnished with quenelles of smelt, truffle balls, dice of crayfish. Butter and cream.

Doria.—Cucumber velouté, garnished with cucumber balls and rice. Cream or yolk of eggs.

Dubarry.—Cauliflower velouté, garnished with small branch of cauliflower, chervil. Cream.

Ecrevisses à la Joinville.—Fish velouté with crayfish, garnished with crayfish tails, Julienne of truffles and mushrooms. Butter and cream. Fine champagne when serving.

Ecrevisses à la Lucullus.—Fish velouté with sole fumet mixed with crayfish bisque garnished with crayfishes' tails and stuffed carcasses. Butter and cream. Cognac.

Ecrevisses Princesse.—Velouté with crayfish cullis, garnished with whiting quenelles, asparagus heads. Cream. Butter. "Fine" champagne.

Egyptienne.—Purée of yellow " Egyptian " peas. Butter and cream.

Elisa—Chicken velouté, garnished with sorrel and chervil. Cream and butter.

Endives.—Potato purée with chicory. Cream.

Eperlans à la Dieppoise.—Fish velouté with smelt, garnished with shrimps, mussels. Cream or yolk of eggs.

Eperlans Lucullus.—Same as above with crayfish tails and carcasses filled with truffled fish quenelles of smelt with chopped truffles.

Esaü.—Lentils purée with rice. Butter and cream.

Excelsior.—Velouté with barley flour and green asparagus, garnished with pearl barley. Cream and yolks.

Fanchette.—Chicken velouté mixed with asparagus velouté, garnished with stuffed lettuce leaves, rolled, poached and cut into roundels, peas. Cream or yolk of eggs.

Faubonne.—Purée of green peas, garnished with Julienne of vegetables, chervil. Butter and cream.

Favori.—$\frac{1}{3}$ chicken velouté, $\frac{1}{3}$ lettuces velouté, $\frac{1}{3}$ asparagus velouté, garnished with green asparagus heads, shredded sorrel, cream.

Fèves à la Pythagore.—Broad beans purée with butter and cream.

Flamande.—Potato purée and Brussels sprouts. Cream or yolk of eggs.

Fontanges.—Green peas purée, garnished with shredded sorrel, chervil. Butter and cream.

Freneuse.—Turnip and potato purée. Cream and butter.

Garbure.—Vegetable purée, butter and cream. (*Separately*). Fried croûtons

Garbure Béarnaise.—Marmite with salted pork, goose preserve, turnips, cabbage, minced potatoes, white haricot beans, French beans. (*Separately*): Slices of French bread sprinkled with cheese and gratined.

Garbure Crécy.—Purée of carrots thickened with tapioca. Butter and cream. (*Separately*): Slices of bread gratined with cheese.

Garbure Dauphinoise.—Potatoes, marrow, beetroots, chopped onions fried in butter, moistened with white consommé. Slices of gratined bread.

Garbure Fermière.—Julienne of cabbages moistened with consommé. (*Separately*): Slices of bread coated with vegetable purée, sprinkled with cheese and gratined.

Garbure Freneuse.—Consommé. Serve separately croûtons coated with turnip purée and gratined with cheese.

Garbure Maraîchère.—Consommé. (*Separately*): Croûtons coated with purée of salsifis, celery, potatoes and whites of leeks, gratined with cheese.

Garbure Paysanne.—Same as Fermière.

Garbure Savoyarde.—Same as Maraîchère, with purée of onions instead of salsifis.

Gasconne.—Tomato velouté with onions, garnished with dice of goose legs, Butter.

Génin.—Purée with carrots, leeks, tomatoes, mushrooms and rice, garnished with shredded sorrel, chervil. Butter and cream.

Gentilhomme.—Lentils purée with game flavour, garnished with dice of ham, fried croûtons. Butter and Madeira.

Georgette (A).—Artichoke bottoms velouté, garnished with Perles du Japon or sago. Cream.

(B).—Velouté of tomatoes and carrots, thickened with tapioca. Butter.

Germinal.—Chicken velouté with tarragon flavour, garnished with asparagus heads, chervils. Cream or yolk of eggs.

Germiny.—Yolk of eggs mixed with cream and butter, moistened with boiling white consommé, garnished with shredded sorrel. (*Separately*): Cheese straws.

Gosford.—Velouté of green asparagus, thickened with tapioca. Cream.

Gounod.—Purée of green peas, garnished with dice of chicken, croûtons, chervil. Butter and cream.

Grecque (A).—Green peas purée, with mutton stock, garnished with Julienne of carrots, leeks, cabbages. Butter.

(B).—Velouté of tomatoes with pumpkin, fried croûtons. Butter.

Grenouilles.—(*See* **Nymphes**).

Grives à l'Ancienne.—Velouté with grives flavour, garnished Julienne of fillet of grives. Cream and brandy when serving.

Haricots verts or Favorite.—Velouté with French beans, garnished with French beans, chervil. Butter.

Herbes.—Potato purée with sorrel and watercress, pimpernel and chervil. Butter.

Homard à la Cleveland.—Velouté with cullis of American lobster, garnished with dice of lobster and dice of tomatoes. Butter; and brandy when serving.

Homard à l'Indienne.—Same as above, with curry, garnished with rice.

Homard au Paprika.—Same as above, with paprika, and dice of pimentoes.

Hugo.—Velouté with artichokes purée, thickened with tapioca, chervil. Cream or yolk of eggs.

Huîtres (A).—Fish velouté with oyster juice, garnished with poached oysters, cayenne pepper.

(B).—Crushed dried biscuits, mositened with milk, oyster juice, garnished with oysters.

Imperator.—Lentil purée with pheasant flavour, garnished with quenelles of pheasant, Julienne of truffles, dice of royale, small ravioli stuffed with foie gras purée. Butter. Marsala.

Impérial.—Tapioca cohered with yolk of eggs and cream, passed through tammy, garnished with large sago.

Indienne.—Chicken velouté with cocoanut milk, flavoured with curry, garnished with rice. Cream.

Idma.—Chicken velouté, garnished with chicken quenelles flavoured with curry, asparagus heads. Cream.

Isoline.—Chicken purée with crayfish cullis, garnished with sago. Cream.

Jackson.—Purée of potatoes and flageolet beans, thickened with tapioca, garnished with Julienne of leeks. Cream.

Jacqueline.—Fish velouté, garnished with carrots, peas, asparagus heads, rice. Cream.

Japonaise.—Velouté with Japanese artichokes, garnished with small croûtons. Cream.

Jean Bart.—Fish velouté, garnished with fish quenelles, dice of tomatoes, macaroni cut into sections, Julienne of leeks. Cream.

Jeannette.—Salsifis velouté, garnished with rice and dice of chicken. Cream.

Joinville.—Fish velouté with crayfish cullis, dice of truffles and mushrooms. Butter, cream.

Juanita.—Velouté with cream of rice, garnished with chicken quenelles, with hard yolk of eggs, dice of tomatoes. Cream.

Jubilée.—Petite marmite consommé and Saint-Germain purée, garnished with croûtes-au-pot vegetables.

Laitue.—Lettuce velouté, garnished with fried croûtons, chervil. Cream.

Lamballe.—½ fresh peas purée and ½ tapioca. Butter.

La Vallière.—½chicken velouté, ½ celery, garnished with royale and dice of celery. (*Separately*): Profiteroles stuffed with chicken purée. Cream or yolk of eggs.

Lison.—Velouté with cream of rice and celery, garnished with perles du Japon, or sago. Cream.

Longchamps.—Purée of fresh peas, garnished with vermicelli, shredded sorrel and chervil. Butter.

Longueville.—Same as above. Spaghetti instead of vermicelli.

Madeleine.—½ purée of haricot beans with onions, ½ velouté of artichoke bottoms, garnished with sago. Butter and cream.

Maïs.—Velouté with sweet corn, garnished with grains of sweet corn. Cream.

Malakoff.—Purée of tomatoes and potatoes, garnished with Julienne of spinach.

Mancelle.—½ game purée, ½ chestnut purée with celery, garnished with small collops of partridge fillets. Butter and cream. Madeira when serving.

Marcilly.—Chicken velouté and purée of fresh peas, garnished with sago and chicken quenelles. Butter and cream.

Maria.—Purée of haricot beans, garnished with vegetable printanier. Butter and cream.

Marianne.—Purée of potatoes and pumpkin, garnished with shredded lettuces and sorrel. Slices of bread gratined with cheese.

Marie-Louise.—Velouté of chicken with barley flour, garnished with printanier of vegetables and dice of macaroni. Cream.

Marie-Stuart.—Chicken velouté with barley flour, garnished with carrot balls. Cream.

Marigny.—Purée of fresh green peas, garnished with peas, French beans, shredded sorrel, chervil. Butter and cream.

Martha.—Chicken velouté with onion purée, garnished with chicken quenelles stuffed with brunoise; green peas, chervil. Cream.

Mathurine.—Fish velouté with sole fumet, garnished with salmon quenelles. Cream or eggs for liaison.

Médicis.—Carrots purée and green peas purée, butter and cream, chervil.

Milanaise.—Tomato chicken velouté, garnished with dice of macaroni, Julienne of white truffles, ham and mushrooms. Cream or eggs liaison.

Mogador.—Chicken velouté with foie gras purée, garnished with chicken julienne, tongue and truffles, cream or eggs liaison.

Montespan.—Asparagus velouté, garnished with tapioca, green peas. Cream or eggs.

Montorgueil.—Chicken velouté, garnished with vegetable printanier, shredded sorrel, chervil. Cream.

Morilles.—Morels velouté, garnished with slices of morels. Cream or eggs.

Musard.—Flageolet purée, garnished with small flageolets, fried croûtons. Butter and cream.

Navarin.—Purée of fresh green peas, garnished with crayfish tails, peas, chopped parsley. Butter.

Nelusko.—Chicken velouté with grilled nuts flavour, garnished with chicken quenelles. Cream or eggs.

Nivernaise.—1⅔ Crécy purée, ⅓ Freneuse purée, garnished with vegetable Brunoise. Cream.

Norvégienne.—Purée of swedes, garnished with julienne of beetroots. Liaison with cream or eggs.

Nymphes.—Fish velouté, garnished with royale and dice of frogs' legs. Cream or yolk of eggs.

Orge.—Velouté with barley flour, garnished with pearl barley. Liaison with cream.

Orléans.—Purée of chicken, garnished with quenelles of chicken (*white*) crayfishes' cullis (*pink*) and herb essence (*green*).

Orties.—Velouté with stinging nettles, garnished with fried croûtons, liaison with cream.

Oseille à l'Avoine.—Velouté with oats and sorrel. Cream.

Oxalis.—Velouté with oxalis, garnished with minced oxalis. Cream.

Palestine.—Purée of Jerusalem artichokes. Liaison with cream or eggs.

Parmentier.—Purée of potatoes with minced leeks, coloured in butter, garnished with fried croûtons, chervil. Cream or yolk of eggs.

Pastourelle.—Purée Parmentier with " mousserons ", garnished with small mousserons and small sauté potatoes. Liaison with cream or yolk of eggs.

Petit-Duc.—Velouté with woodcock flavour, garnished with collops of woodcock fillet, dice of royale with game essence. Butter and cream. Glass of brandy when serving.

Pierre-le-Grand (A).—Velouté with hazel hen flavour and mushrooms, garnished with julienne of carrots and celery. Butter and cream. Glass of vodka when serving.

(B).—Velouté with celeriac, garnished with dice of celeriac. Liaison with cream or yolk of eggs.

Poireaux.—Velouté with leeks, garnished with fried croutons. Liaison with cream or eggs.

Pois frais.—Purée of green peas, garnished with peas, chervil shreds, butter and cream.

Pois Frais à la Menthe.—Same as above, with the addition of blanched chopped mint.

Pompadour.—Tomato purée, garnished with sago and julienne of lettuces.

Portugaise.—Purée of tomatoes, garnished with rice. Butter.

Potiron.—Purée of pumpkin, garnished with vermicelli, butter and cream.

Potiron Maraîchère.—$\frac{1}{2}$ purée of pumpkin, $\frac{1}{2}$ purée of potatoes, garnished with julienne of leeks, lettuces, sorrel, spinach, peas, rice, chervil. Butter cream.

Pourpier.—Purée of potatoes with purslain, garnished with blanched purslain leaves. Liaison with cream or yolk of eggs.

Princesse.—$\frac{1}{2}$ chicken purée, $\frac{1}{2}$ asparagus cream, garnished with dice of chicken, asparagus heads, chervil. Cream.

Purée d'Oseille et Vermicelle à la Crème.—Shredded, sorrel, cooked in butter and moistened with milk and consommé, garnished with vermicelli. Cream and yolk of eggs.

Québec.—(*See* **Maria**).

Régence.—Velouté with barley flour and crayfish cullis, garnished with cocks combs, pearl barley and chicken quenelles. Butter and cream.

Reine.—Chicken purée with rice, garnished with dice of chicken. Cream.

Reine-Margot.—Chicken purée with almond milk, garnished with chicken quenelles with pistachio powder.

Riz.—Velouté with cream of rice, garnished with rice. Liaison with cream or eggs.

Rossini.—Purée of chicken, garnished with chicken quenelles, stuffed with foie gras, julienne of truffles.

Saint-Cloud.—Purée of fresh peas with lettuces, garnished with julienne of lettuces, fried croûtons, chervil shreds, butter and cream.

Saint-Germain.—Purée of fresh peas, garnished with green peas, fried croûtons, butter and cream.

Saint-Hubert.—Velouté with game flavour, garnished with dice of game and truffles, cream, red currant jelly, brandy.

Saint-Marceaux.—Purée of fresh peas, garnished with julienne of leeks, chervil, butter and cream.

Santé.—Parmentier purée with shredded sorrel cooked in butter, chervil, cream or yolks. (*Separatly*): Serve pieces of dried French bread.

Sévigné.—½ chicken cream, ½ chicken lettuces, garnished with julienne of lettuces and chicken quenelles.

Sicilienne.—½ tapioca and ½ tomato cream, garnished with " perles des Roches "

Soissonnaise.—Purée of haricot beans, butter and cream. Fried croûtons.

Solférino.—½ Parmentier, ½ tomato cream, garnished with carrot balls and potatoes.

Sport.—Potage Santé with vermicelli.

Sultane.—Chicken velouté with aveline milk and pistachio butter, garnished with chicken forcemeat, crescent-shaped and decorated with truffles cut star-like.

Suzon.—Saint-Germain purée with cream, garnished with small poached eggs.

Tourangelle.—½ purée of white haricot beans, ½ purée of flageolets, garnished with dice of French beans and small flageolets. Butter and cream.

Velours.—Purée of carrots with tapioca.

Verneuil.—½ fresh peas purée, ½ barley flour cream, garnished with dice of carrots, mushrooms, roundels of royale.

Vigneronne.—½ cream of pumpkins, ½ Condé purée with onions and leeks, garnished with slices of brown bread.

Villars.—½ artichoke purée, ½ flageolets purée with onions, garnished with fried croûtons, butter and cream.

Viviane.—Chicken cream, garnished with dice of artichoke bottoms, truffles and carrots.

Vuillemot.—Haricot beans purée, garnished with shredded sorrel and rice, fried croûtons, butter and cream.

Waldèze.—½ tapioca, ½ cream of tomatoes. (*Grated Cheese*).

Washington.—Cream of maize, with whisky and port when serving, garnished with grains of maize.

Windsor.—Strong cream of rice velouté made with calves feet and turtle herbs, garnished with chicken quenelles made with hard yolk of eggs and julienne of feet. Liaison with yolk of eggs and cream.

Xavier.—Velouté with cream of rice, garnished with dice of royale and chicken.

POTAGES ETRANGERS — FOREIGN SOUPS

Abatis à l'Allemande.—Chicken abats tossed in butter, moistened with white consommé, garnished with pearl barley, poached chicken livers, abats. Liaison with yolks and cream. Butter. (*German*).

Abatis à l'Anglaise.—Same as above, but brown, and garnished with rice and julienne of celery. Black pepper. (*English*).

Barzey Pomidory.—Consommé with tomato flavour, garnished with celery Julienne. (*Separately*): Serve small pies, shaped like a marquis hat and stuffed with chicken forcemeat. (*Italian*).

Batwinia.—Purée of spinach, sorrel and beetroot leaves, shallots and white wine, garnished with dice of "agoursis", chervil, Tarragon. (*Separately*): Serve small cubes of rice. (*Russian*).

Bennet Soup.—Beef consommé with pearl barley, garnished with dice of carrots, turnips, celery, onions, cabbage. Pepper corns and cloves. (*American*).

Bière.——Velouté with beer, salt, sugar, pepper, cinnamon, garnished with toast. (*German*).

Bortsch Koop.—Julienne of leeks, carrots, onions, celery, beef, moistened with water. The consommé garnished with minced beetroots. (*Separately*): Serve small pies in puff paste stuffed with chicken forcemeat beetroot juice. (*Russian*).

Bortsch Polonais.—Consommé with ducks fumet, strongly flavoured with parsley roots, celery, fennel, marjoram, peppercorns: add scraped beetroot, strain and remove fat. Garnish with julienne of leeks, carrots, beetroot, cubes of beef and duck. (*Separately*): Sour cream and beetroot juice, small pies stuffed with duck forcemeat. (*Polish*).

Boulettes de Foie (Leberknödeln).—Beef or chicken consommé, garnished with prunes and chicken. (*Scottish*).

Camaro à la Brésilienne.—Marmite with whole fowl, Faggot, chervil, onions, garnished with rice. (*Brazilian*).

Cerises.—Broth made with Bordeaux wine or Port, purée and juice of cherries cooked with lemon zest and cinnamon, garnished with stoned cherries and finger biscuits. (*German*).

Clam Chowder.—Chopped onions fried with fresh pork fat, parsley and tomatoes, dice of potatoes, clams and juice of clams, pepper, thyme, moistened with water, thickened with crushed biscuits. (*American*).

Cocky-Leeky.—Chicken and veal consommé, garnished with julienne of leeks, prunes and chicken. (*Scottish*).

Foies de Volaille à l'Anglaise.—Thin half-glaze with chicken liver purée, garnished with collops of sauté chicken livers. (*English*).

Hochepot à la Flamande.—Marmite made with pig-tail, ears and pork feet, salted pork, beef, shoulder of mutton, moistened with water, garnished with carrots, onions, cabbage, potatoes, minced leeks. Serve the meat and vegetables separately. (*Belgian*).

Hongrois.—Dice of beef seasoned with paprika, tossed in butter with onions, add flour and moisten with consommé, garnish with dice of potatoes, pinch of Kümmel, crushed garlic, fried croûtons. (*Hungarian*).

Kroupnick.—Barley, chicken gizzard, chicken necks tossed in butter, moistened with chicken broth, and cook for an hour, cream. (*Separately*): Serve small pies stuffed with salpicon of chicken. (*Russian*).

Lièvre.—Thin half-glaze with hare flavour, add turtle herbs, cayenne, garnished with dice of hare. Glass of port when serving. (*English*).

Lithuanien.—Thin potato purée with julienne of celery, shredded sorrel, sour cream, garnished with small lardons, poached chipolatas and fried yolk of eggs. (*Russian*).

Livonien aux kloskis.—Velouté with spinach and sorrel purée, butter and cream, garnished with kloskis and chervil. The kloskis are made, with pâte à choux mixed with chopped shallots and ham, small fried croûtons, shaped into balls and poached. (*Russian*).

Mille-Fanti.—Consommé garnished with a preparation of bread crumbs, parmesan, eggs, pepper, nutmeg, poached in the consommé. (*Italian*).

Minestra.—Chopped onions and all sorts of vegetables, tossed in chopped fat pork moistened with water and white consommé, garnished with tomatoes, dice of French beans, spaghetti, rice, peas, garlic and parsley. (*Italian*).

Miss Betsy.—Consommé with pearl barley, parsley, chervil, celery; add tomato purée; garnished with dice of apple. (*English*).

Mock Turtle.—Thin half-glaze with celery and mushrooms flavour, infusion of turtle herbs, cayenne papper, garnished with roundels of calf-head's skin, quenelles of chicken with hard-boiled yolk of eggs. Madeira wine when serving. (*English*)

Moelle (Marschknödeln).—Strong beef consommé, garnished with balls of marrow wrapped in a preparation of bread crumbs, eggs, parsley, nutmeg, salt and pepper, shaped the size of a pigeon egg and poached. (*German*).

Mouton à la Grecque.—Peas purée with mutton broth, garnished with julienne of mutton and brunoise of vegetables. (*Greek*).

Mulligatawny.—Chopped onions and apples fried in butter with curry flour and tomato purée, moistened with chicken consommé, cream, garnished with dice of chicken and rice. (*Indian*).

Mutton Broth.—Mutton stock with pearl barley, garnished with brunoise of vegetable and dice of boiled mutton, chopped parsley. (*English*).

Noques.—Chicken velouté, garnished with noques.
Preparation for Noques.—Butter in cream with yolk of eggs, flour, and beaten white of eggs, shaped into quenelles and poached. (*Italian*).

Okra.—Consommé with tomato and celery flavour, garnished with Okra or Gombos, dice of tomatoes and julienne of celery. (*Portuguese*).

Olla Podrida (*See* **Hochepot à la Flamande**).—With raw ham, partridge, ½ chicken, garbanzos or pois chiche, lettuce and chorizos. (*Spanish*).

Orge au Céleri.—White consommé with celery flavour, garnished with pearl barley and Julienne of celery. (*American*).

Orloff (*See* **Bortsch**).—With mutton broth instead of beef consommé, dice of mutton. (*Russian*).

Ouka.—Fish broth prepared with sturgeon and fish parings, water, white wine, parsley, celery, fennel, mushrooms clarified with whiting and caviar, garnished with paupiettes of Sigui, julienne of leeks. (*Separately*): Serve kasha of sarrasin and rastegaïs dished on serviette. (*Russian*).

Oxtail Clair.—Sections of oxtail browned in oven with vegetables and veal bones, moistened with white consommé, cook slowly. Clarified and garnished with dice of vegetables and small pieces of oxtail. Madeira wine.

Oxtail Lié.—Same as above, with a brown roux as liaison. (*English*).

Oyster with Okra.—Consommé with tomato and Soubise fumet, pimentoes, garnished with dice of tomatoes, gombos or okra. Oyster. Liaison with arrow-root. (*American*).

Pistou.—French beans, potatoes, tomatoes, salt, cooked in water, garnished with vermicelli, flavoured at the last moment with a paste made of garlic, basil, tomato, oil, gruyère cheese. (*Italian*).

Puchéro (*See* **Olla Podrida**).—With less garnish. (*Spanish*).

Purée de Foie.—Thin half-glaze with calves liver purée and white wine, fried croûtons. (*German*).

Purée de Jambon.—Tomato purée with onions and ham purée thinned with white consommé, cayenne, butter. Garnished with fried croûtons. Madeira wine when serving. (*Russian*).

Rahm Suppe.—Velouté with milk and veal stock, flavoured with parsley, peppercorn, onion stuck with clove, nutmeg, cumin, sour cream for liaison, fried croûtons. (*Russian*).

Rizzo Figatini—Chicken consommé with celery flavour, liaison with yolk of eggs and cream, garnished with collops of chicken livers tossed in butter. (Grated cheese). (*Italian*).

Rognons de Veau.—Chicken velouté, thickened with yolk of eggs, cream and argousis juice, garnished with collops of veal kidneys tossed in butter, arousis, mushrooms, stuffed olives, parsley. (*Russian*).

Rognons à l'Anglaise (*See* **Foie de Volaille à l'Anclaise**).—With veal kidneys instead of livers. (*English*).

Rossolnick.—Thin chicken velouté with agoursis juice, garnished with parsley celery, agoursis. (*Separately*): Small bouchées filled with chicken and agoursis, cohered with Suprême sauce. (*Russian*).

Selianka.—Consommé with ham fumet, garnished with sauerkraut and blanched parsley. (*Russian*).

Stchy.—Consommé of Bortsch, garnished with sauerkraut, julienne of leeks and carrots. (*Separately*): Serve beetroot juice and sour cream, (*Russian*).

Terrapènes.—Turtle, clear or thick, garnished with dice of terrapins. (*Separately*): Serve slices of lemon, chopped blanched parsley, hard-boiled eggs. (*American*).

Tortue Claire.—Consommé of beef, chicken and turtle, flavoured with turtle herbs, thickened with arrow-root, garnished with dice of turtle, collops of turtle fat. Madeira wine. (*English*).

Turtle herbs.—Basil, marjoram, sage, rosemary, thyme, coriander, peppercorns, bay leaves *in infusion*.

Milk Punch—Syrup at 17° with juice and zest of oranges and lemons, rum, kirsch, milk, strained and served very cold.

Tortue Liée.—Same as tortue claire, thickened with a pale roux.

Tortue Sèche.—Dried turtle, soaked for 24 hours, and operate same as for Tortue claire.

Tortue Verte de Conserve.—Chicken and veal consommé, flavoured with parsley roots, mushroom parings, leeks, celery, thyme, bay leaves, marjoram, basil, thickened with arrow-root, garnished with pieces of green turtle, cayenne pepper. Xérès when serving.

Œufs — Eggs

BROUILLES — SCRAMBLED

Cooking Process

Eggs in a pan with salt, pepper; whisk and cook them in bain-marie. Finish with cream and butter.

Archiduchesse.—Mixed with dice of ham mushrooms, asparagus heads on top.

Aumale.—Mixed with tomatoes, dice of kidneys sautés with Madeira.

Balzac.—Garnished with dice of truffles and tongue, surround with croûtons coated with soubise (or onion purée), a thread of tomato, half-glaze.

Batelière.—Mixed with chopped parsley, surround with a thread of sole purée with cream.

Cannelons.—Horns made with puff paste and filled with scrambled eggs to taste.

Carême.—Mixed with foie gras, chicken and truffle salpicon, collops of foie gras and truffle in the centre.

Champignons.—Garnished with dice of mushrooms.

Châtillon.—Garnished in the centre with sautés minced mushrooms and fried parsley, surround with fleurons.

Croûtons.—Garnished with dice of fried bread, surround with croûtons.

Divette.—Mixed with dice or crayfish tails and asparagus heads, surround with a thread of Nantua sauce.

Espagnole.—In half tomatoes cooked in oil, julienne of pimentoes on top.

Fines-Herbes.—With the addition of chopped chive, chervil, tarragon and parsley.

Foies de Volaille.—Garnished in the centre with collops of chicken liver tossed in butter, Madeira sauce round.

Forestière.—Garnished with collops of sauté morels and dice of bacon.

Georgette.—In baked potatoes, scooped, and fill with the eggs mixed with crayfish, butter and crayfish tails.

Grand'Mère.—Garnished with dice of fried bread; finished with chopped parsley.

Leuchtemberg.—Mixed with blanched chives, caviar in the centre.

Magda.—Mixed with chopped parsley, grated cheese and mustard, surround with croûtons.

Marivaux.—Mixed with chopped truffles, mushroom heads in the middle, surrounded with slices of mushrooms, and a thread of meat glaze.

Nantua.—Mixed with salpicon of crayfish and truffles, surround with slices of truffles and thread of Nantua sauce.

Normande.—Garnished in the middle with poached oysters, coated with Normande sauce.

Orloff.—In cocottes; garnished with crayfish tails, slice of truffle on top.

Parmesan.—Mixed with Parmesan cheese.

Pointes d'Asperges.—Mixed with asparagus heads and a bouquet of heads on top.

Portugaise.—Mixed with dice of tomatoes.

Princesse Marie.—Small timbales garnished with scrambled eggs and parmesan cheese, and dice of truffles.

Rachel.—Mixed with asparagus heads and dice of truffles, a bouquet of heads on top, surrounded with slices of truffles.

Reine Margot.—In tartlets, surrounded with a thread of velouté with pistachio butter.

Rothschild.—With crayfish cullis, a bouquet of asparagus heads in the middle surrounded with crayfish tails, slices of truffles and Nantua sauce.

Sultane.—Dressed in potato croustades, finished with pistachio butter.

Sylvette.—Mixed with paysanne of carrots and minced morels, slices of truffles.

Truffes.—Mixed with dice of truffles, decorated with large slices of truffles, a thread of meat glaze.

Yvette.—Garnished with asparagus heads and dice of crayfish tails, dressed in tartlets, slice of truffle on top, a thread of Nantua sauce.

EN COCOTTE — IN COCOTTE

Preparation and Cooking Process

Butter the cocotte and break the eggs in, season and place them in a pan or tin with water, steam under cover, or bake in oven.

Bergère.—Interior garnished with minced mutton and mushrooms a thread of meat glaze round.

Bordelaise.—The bottom garnished with slices of poached marrow, a thread of Bordelaise sauce when the egg is done.

Crème.—A thread of thick cream when done.

Diane.—Interior coated with game purée, a thread of a salmis sauce; slice of truffle on top.

Diplomate.—The bottom garnished with a slice of foie gras, a thread of tomato sauce when the egg is done.

Forestière.—The bottom garnished with dice of fried bacon, mushroom purée round, chopped parsley when egg is done.

Jeannette.—Interior coated with chicken forcemeat and foie gras purée, a thread of Suprême sauce.

Jus (au).—A thread of reduced gravy when the egg is done.

Léontine.—Interior coated with fish forcemeat mixed with salpicon of crayfish and truffles, a thread of tomato sauce.

Parisienne.—Interior coated with chicken forcemeat mixed with tongue, mushrooms and truffles, a thread of half-glaze.

Périgourdine.—Slices of foie gras in the bottom, a thread of Périgueux sauce when done.

Périgueux.—A slice of truffle and a thread of Périgueux sauce when the egg is done.

Petit Duc.—Asparagus heads in the bottom, a thread of Périgueux sauce.

Portugaise.—Dice of tomatoes tossed in butter with shallots, in the bottom a thread of tomato sauce.

Reine.—Mince chicken cohered with cream, in the bottom, a thread of thick cream.

Ribaucourt.—When done, a border of Zingara in dice.

Rouennaise.—Interior coated with Rouennaise forcemeat, a thread of half-glaze round.

Saint-Hubert.—Interior coated with game purée, a thread of poivrade sauce, decorate with a cross made with truffle.

Soubise.—Interior coated with soubise, a thread of meat glaze.

Valentine.—A border of dice of tomatoes and mushrooms, cohered with meat glaze and veal gravy.

Zingara.—When done a thread of Zingara sauce round.

DURS — HARD BOILED

Cooking Process

Place the eggs in boiling water and cook 8 minutes, plunge in cold water.

Aurore (*See* Œufs Chimay).—Coated with tomatoed Béchamel, grated cheese, glaze.

Belloy.—Cut in halves lengthwise, pass the yolk through the sieve and mix with dice of lobster, truffles and mushrooms, cohere with Mornay sauce, coat with same, glaze.

Boulangère.—Small roll cut in half and scooped, filled with dice of egg cohered with Béchamel sauce sprinkled with cheese and chopped hard yolk of egg, chopped parsley.

Bretonne.—Béchamel sauce mixed with mushrooms, chopped onions and leeks cooked in butter, coat the bottom of a dish with the sauce, place the eggs cut in halves and cover with the rest of the sauce.

Carême.—In timbale, place the eggs cut into roundels, collops of artichoke bottoms, slices of truffles, cohered and coated with Nantua sauce, decorate with slices of truffles.

Chimay.—Cut in halves, remove the yolk and pass through the sieve, mix with dry duxelles and chopped parsley, add cream, salt, pepper. Stuff the whites and coat with Mornay sauce, glazed.

Côtelettes d'Œufs.—Dice of eggs mixed with Béchamel and yolk of raw eggs reduced when cold, shaped into cutlets, egg and crumb and fry deep fat. Tomato sauce.

Côtelettes Manon.—Same preparation as above with the whites only, and stuffed with a preparation of chopped ham, hard yolks, cohered with reduced Soubise sauce in egg crumb and fried. (*Separately*): Thin onion sauce.

Cromesquis d'Œufs.—Dice of eggs, mushrooms and truffles, cohered with Allemande sauce, let cool and shape into round pellets, dip in batter and fry deep fat. Tomato sauce.

Croquettes d'Œufs.—Same preparation as above, egg shaped, egg and crumb fry deep fat. Cream sauce.

Gourmet.—Cut in halves lengthwise; the yolks crushed and mixed with dice of salmon, crayfish tails and truffles cohered with Mornay sauce. Stuff the whites and set to gratin.

Granville.—Cut into quarters and mixed with Bordelaise sauce.

Hongroise.—Cut into roundels and dressed in a dish with slices of tomatoes coated with paprika sauce containing cooked minced onions.

Percheronne.—Roundels of eggs alternated with slices of potatoes, coated with Béchamel sauce

Portugaise.—In half tomatoes cooked in oil, coated with tomato sauce.

Poulette.—Roundels of egg and minced mushrooms, coated with poulette sauce, chopped parsley.

Rissoles d'Œufs.—Preparation of egg croquettes wrapped in up puff paste, the shape of a turnover. Fry deep fat.

Tripe (à la).—Cut into roundels and mix with onion sauce, chopped parsley.

Vol-au-Vent d'Œufs.—Croûte of Puff-paste garnished with roundels of eggs, mushrooms, slices of truffles. Cohered with Béchamel sauce.

FRITS — FRIED

Cooking Process

Break the egg on a plate, season with salt and pepper, heat some oil in an omelet pan, let the egg slide into the oil and with a wooden spoon cover up the yolk with the solidified portions of the white, one egg at a time.

E

Andalouse.—Dressed in a crown, alternated with slices of fried egg plant.

Anglaise.—Same as à la Poêle.

Américaine (A).—Dressed on rashers of grilled bacon, fried parsley. Tomato sauce.

(B).—Same with half a grilled tomato.

Bordelaise.—Dressed on half grilled tomatoes stuffed with chopped cèpes à la Bordelaise.

Bûcheronne.—Sprinkle the yolk with chopped chives before frying, dressed round Macaire potatoes.

Diable.—Cooked in butter, both sides, pour over some nut-brown butter and vinegar.

Fermière.—Dressed in a circle round a dome of vegetables macédoine, grilled bacon, and noisettes potatoes.

Lard (au).—Fried with grilled bacon.

Moissonneurs.—Dressed in a circle, alternated with large slices of bacon; the centre filled with peas à la paysanne.

Pastourelle.—Dressed in a circle with slices of grilled bacon, the centre garnished with sautés mushrooms with shallots, chopped parsley, on each egg place half a grilled kidney.

Poêle.—Break the eggs on a plate, season and cook in a small frying pan with hot butter, finish in the oven.

Romaine.—Dressed on a bed of spinach, mixed with anchovy fillets.

Villeroy.—Poach egg, coated with Villeroy sauce, egg and crumb, fry deep fat, tomato sauce.

Yorkshire.—Dressed in a circle alternated with slices of fried York ham and toasts. tomato sauce.

FROIDS — COLD

Alexandra.—Poached egg, coated with chaud-froid sauce decorated with truffles and glazed with aspic, dressed on tartlets half filled with lobster mousse, surround the egg with caviar.

Andalouse.—Poached egg coated with tomated Soubise sauce mixed with aspic, decorated with strips of pimentoes, lattice way, and dressed on prepared tomato and aspic shapes, dish up in a circle, and garnished with rings of onions, centre, garnished with chopped aspic jelly.

Argenteuil.—Soft boiled eggs or poached eggs coated with chaud-froid sauce combine with asparagus purée and glazed with aspic, dressed round a heap of asparagus heads salad surrounded with slices of cold potatoes neatly cut with fancy cutter.

Balzac.—Poached eggs coated with celery chaud-froid sauce, decorated with truffles and glazed with aspic, placed on tartlet crusts half filled with celery mousse, dish up in a circle, chopped aspic.

Carême.—Cook the egg on the dish, trim with oval fancy cutter and place on tartlet crust filled with dice of cooked salmon cohered with mayonnaise sauce, surround with caviare and decorate with truffles.

Chartres.—Poached egg decorated with tarragon and glazed with aspic jelly, dressed on a chicken mousse, decorated round with tarragon butter.

Colinette.—Oval moulds lined with aspic, and decorated with eggs and truffles to imitate a draught-board; place a small poached egg and fill with aspic, dish up round a Rachel salad encircled with rings of sliced potatoes, border the dish with crescents of aspic.

Dreux.—Baba moulds coated inside with aspic and decorated with truffles and asparagus heads, filled with a poached egg, and covered with jelly, dressed on toast in a circle, chopped aspic in middle.

Frou-Frou.—Poached eggs coated with chaud-froid sauce combined with chopped hard yolk of eggs, decorated with a ring of truffle, and bordered with chopped truffle, dressed round a vegetable salad cohered with mayonnaise, chopped aspic round.

Hojos.—Poached egg sprinkled with ham julienne and sweet pimentos, glazed with jelly, and dished on a bed of sweet corn with cream.

Jeannette.—Slices of ham and collops of whites of chicken set in aspic, and cut with a heart-shaped cutter when cold, set a poached egg sprinkled with ham and chopped truffles on each heart, dressed in a circle and chopped aspic in the middle.

Maupassant.—Poached egg coated with red wine sauce with fish jelly, glazed with fish jelly, dished in a circle and chopped aspic in middle.

Mosaïque.—In oval moulds, lined with aspic and decorated mosaic fashion with tongue, white of egg, truffles. French beans, place the poached egg, and fill with aspic, dish up round a Russian salad, chopped aspic.

Moscovite.—Hard boiled eggs cut both ends to imitate small barrels, surround the top and base with anchovy fillets to imitate the iron hoops, and a bit of truffle to imitate the bung, empty the eggs with a cutter and garnish them with caviar, dress on artichoke bottoms, surround with chopped jelly.

Nantua.—Same as above, fill the cavity with crayfish tails cohered with mayonnaise, decorate with truffles and crayfish tails, glazed with jelly.

Niçoise.—Poached egg coated with tomato mayonnaise and dished up on tartlet fillets with dice of French beans, tomatoes and potatoes cohered with mayonnaise, glazed with aspic.

Polignac (*Cold*)—**(Œufs Polignac A or B).**—Select some moulds a little larger and coat the insides with aspic, place the egg in and fill with jelly, dish up in a circle with chopped aspic in the middle.

Printanière.—Poached egg glazed with aspic and placed on tartlets garnished with dice of vegetable cohered with mayonnaise sauce.

Ravigote.—In oval moulds lined with aspic and decorated with tarragon leaves, gherkins and capers; half fill with rémoulade sauce mixed with aspic, and place the poached egg, when set, dish up on a bed of aspic jelly.

Reine.—Poached egg, coated with mayonnaise sauce and dressed on brioche croustades, garnished with dice of chicken cohered with mayonnaise, decorated with truffles and glazed with aspic.

Rosita.—Poached egg coated with white chaud-froid sauce with lobster coral, decorated with crescents of truffles, glazed with aspic, dish up in a circle and surround with small tomatoes stuffed with fish purée.

Rubens.—Poached eggs coated with white chaud-froid sauce, decorated with tarragon leaves and glazed with jelly, placed on tartlet shapes made with hop shoots, chopped parsley, chervil tomato purée and jelly, dish up in a circle, alternating with aspic cut into the shape of a cock's comb.

Viveurs (des).—Soft-boiled egg, cut at the base and coated with Américaine sauce mixed with aspic. dressed on a lobster collop coated with mayonnaise sauce and aspic, dish up round a potato salad à la Parisienne, slices of potatoes alternated with slices of beetroots.

Skabeloff.—In tartlets garnished with shrimps cohered with mayonnaise, place the egg coated with tomated mayonnaise, decorate with strips of smoked salmon.

COQUE, MOLLETS, MOULES ET POCHES
BOILED, SOFT-BOILED, MOULDED AND POACHED

Cooking Process

Coque (à la).—*Plunge the egg in boiling water and cook two to three minutes.*

Mollets.—*Boil five and half minutes, cool and shelled.*

Moulés.—*Break the eggs in buttered moulds, cook five and half minutes, let stand a while and unmould.*

Pochés.—*Break the eggs in boiling water and poach two minutes and a half, when done dip them into cold water.*

Nota.—*Add salt and vinegar before poaching the eggs.*

Africaine.—On toasts garnished with grilled ham, pilaw rice, and dice of tomatoes.

Alsacienne.—Place the eggs on tartlets garnished with sauerkraut and a slice of ham.

Américaine.—On half tomatoes cooked in butter, coated with Américaine sauce, slices of truffles.

Anglaise.—On toast, sprinkled with Cheshire cheese and cayenne, and melted butter, set to gratin.

Anversoise.—In tartlets garnished with hop shoots and cream, coated with cream sauce.

Archiduc (A).—In croustadines, coated with Archiduc sauce.

(B).—Collops of chicken liver and slices of truffles tossed in butter, fill some tartlet crusts and place the egg on top, coat with Hongroise sauce.

Argenteuil.—In tartlet crusts garnished with asparagus heads, coated with cream sauce mixed with green asparagus purée.

Armenonville.—Dish upon brioche croûtons, coat with suprême sauce with Xérès, garnish with asparagus heads and carrots with cream.

Aurore.—In croustadines, coated with Aurore sauce.

Beauregard.—In oval tartlet crusts garnished with egg-plant purée, coated with tomatoed half-glaze, slices of truffles.

Belle-Hélène.—Croquettes of asparagus heads oval shaped, place the egg on the croquettes and coat with suprême sauce.

Bénédictine (A).—In tartlets garnished with brandade of salt codfish with truffles, coated with cream sauce.

(B).—On muffin toasted, with a slice of tongue and the egg on it, coated with Hollandaise sauce.

Berceau.—Baked potatoes cut lengthwise and emptied to imitate small cradles, coat the interior with chicken mincemeat mixed with cream, and place an egg coated with Aurore sauce in each.

Bergère.—Dish the eggs on minced lamb mixed with mushrooms, and white sauce, coated with Mornay sauce and glazed.

Bignon.—On tampon of chicken forcemeat, coat the egg with tarragon velouté and decorate with tarragon leaves.

Bohémienne.—On croûtons coated with Mornay sauce and sprinkled half with ham julienne and half with truffles, the eggs coated with Mornay sauce and glazed.

Boïeldieu.—In tartlets garnished with salpicon of white of chicken, truffles and foie gras cohered with velouté, coated with thickened gravy.

Boitelle.—Butter some moulds and line them with minced mushrooms tossed in butter, break the eggs in and poach, dish up on oval toast and coat with mushroom sauce.

Bombay.—In timbales, coated with Curry sauce.

Bonvalet.—On croûtons, the egg coated with suprême sauce, a thread of tomatoed Béarnaise sauce round, slices of truffles.

Bourguignonne.—Poached in red wine, dressed on croûtons, coated with red wine sauce mixed with half-glaze.

Bragance.—On half tomatoes cooked in oil, coated with Béarnaise sauce, a thread of thickened gravy.

Bretonne.—In tartlets garnished with Bretonne purée, coated with thickened gravy, chopped parsley on top.

Bruxelloise.—In tartlets garnished with braised chicory cohered with cream sauce, the egg coated with cream sauce, sprinkled with biscottes powder, and glazed.

Cambridge.—In boat shaped vegetable marrow, garnished with chicken purée and coated with Vénitienne sauce.

Cardinal.—In tartlets garnished with dice of lobster cohered with Cardinal sauce, decorated with lobster eggs.

Carignan.—Line some moulds with chicken forcemeat, break the egg in, poach, and dish up on toast, coat with Colbert sauce.

Cendrillon.—In scooped baked potatoes, the eggs coated with Mornay sauce and glazed, slice of truffles.

Chantilly.—In croustades garnished with lentil purée, the eggs coated with Chantilly sauce.

Chartres.—On croûtons, decorate the eggs with tarragon leaves and coat with tarragon, thickened gravy.

Chabaisienne.—In croustades garnished with French bean purée, coated with cream sauce, dice of tomatoes on top.

Chasseur.—In tartlets garnished with chicken livers and mushrooms tossed in butter and cohered with Chasseur sauce, the egg coated with same sauce.

Châtelaine.—In tartlets garnished with dice of chestnuts cohered with meat glaze, the egg coated with soubise suprême sauce, slices of truffles.

Chivry.—In tartlets garnished with herb purée, the eggs coated with Chivry sauce.

Cingalaise.—(*See* Œufs Bombay).—With plain boiled rice.

Clamart.—In tartlet crusts garnished with green pea purée, coated with suprême sauce, slice of truffle on the egg.

Colbert.—In tartlets garnished with dice of vegetables cohered with Hollandaise sauce. (*Separately*): Colbert sauce.

Condé.—On toast, dressed in a circle, centre garnished with purée of red haricot beans, coated with thickened gravy, chopped parsley on the egg.

Comtesse.—In tartlets garnished with purée of fresh peas and asparagus heads, place the eggs, and coat with suprême sauce, chopped truffles on top.

Continental.—On collops of foie gras, coated with Périgueux sauce, slice of truffles.

Crécy.—On brioche croûtons stuffed with carrot purée, coat the egg with cream sauce, decorate with slices of carrots cut with fancy cutter.

Dalmont.—On croûtons garnished with collops of foie gras, coat with tomatoed Madeira sauce.

Daumont.—On large grilled mushrooms, garnished with crayfish tails cohered with Nantua sauce, coated with same sauce, decorated with truffles.

Diane.—In timbales filled with game purée and minced mushrooms, coated with Madeira sauce, decorated with truffles.

Doriac.—On slices of tongue, coated with suprême sauce, sprinkled with chopped truffles.

Dino.—On croûtons, coated with Curry sauce sprinkled with julienne of chicken and mushrooms.

Duchesse.—On croûtons of duchesse potatoes, coated with thickened gravy.

Estragon.—(*See* Œufs Chartres).

Flamande.—In tartlets garnished with Flamande purée coated with cream sauce, small Brussels sprout on top of the egg.

Fédora.—In croustades garnished with foie gras and truffles cohered with suprême sauce, coated with same sauce.

Flora.—In croustades, the egg coated half with tomato sauce and half with suprême, chopped parsley on the tomato side, and chopped truffle on the other.

Floréal.—In croustades, the egg coated with suprême sauce, containing chopped parsley, the base surrounded with green peas purée, decorated with chervil.

Florentine.—In croustades garnished with spinach in leaves tossed in butter, coated with Mornay sauce and glazed.

Forestière.—In duchesse potato croustades, the interior garnished with morels, tossed in butter, coated with thickened gravy, dressed in a circle, centre garnished with morels, chopped parsley.

Galli-Marié.—Buttered moulds filled with half scrambled eggs and half beaten egg, poached, and dressed on artichokes, bottoms filled with rice à la Grecque, coated with Mornay sauce and glazed.

Gambetta.—On croûtons stuffed with truffled soubise purée, one poached egg on a croûton, and a fried egg cut round on another, serve two by two, surround the base with Mornay sauce, slice of truffle on one egg and chopped parsley on the other.

Georgette.—In scooped baked potatoes, half filled with dice of lobster cohered with Américaine sauce, coated with Mornay sauce, glazed, slice of truffles.

Grand-Duc.—In croustades garnished with asparagus heads, coated with Mornay sauce and glazed, slice of truffles and asparagus heads to finish.

Gratin.—In croustades, coated with Mornay sauce, glazed.

Gribouis.—In croustades garnished with mushroom purée, coated with thickened gravy.

Grillés Diable.—Rolled in melted butter, crumbed and grilled, devil sauce.

Halévy.—In tartlets garnished with half tomato and half chicken purée, the egg coated with half tomato sauce and half suprême sauce, separate the colours with a thread of meat glaze.

Héloïse.—On fried croûtons, the egg coated with Allemande sauce, containing dice of tongue, chicken and truffles, the base surrounded with tomato purée.

Henri IV.—In croustades, coated with Béarnaise.

Hollandaise.—In croustades garnished with salmon purée, coated with Hollandaise sauce.

Hussarde.—In half tomatoes, cooked in the oven, garnished with chopped onions tossed in butter with dice of ham cohered with half-glaze, the eggs coated with suprême sauce, cayenne pepper.

Indienne.—On a bed of rice with curry, and coated with Curry sauce.

Infante.—In tartlets garnished with truffled mushroom purée, coated with Mornay sauce, glazed, slice of truffle on the eggs.

Italienne.—On spaghetti à l'Italienne, coated with tomato sauce.

Lapérouse.—In croustades garnished with purée of artichokes' bottoms, coated with suprême sauce, slices of truffles.

La Vallière.—In tartlets garnished with sorrel purée with cream, coated with suprême sauce, decorated with asparagus heads.

Lili (*Moulded*).—Buttered moulds, sprinkled with chopped coral or lobster eggs, filled with scrambled eggs and beaten egg, mixed with shrimp tails and truffles, dished and coated with shrimp sauce.

Lithuanienne.—In croustades garnished with mushroom purée, coated with Périgueux sauce.

Lorette.—In croustades of Dauphine potatoes garnished with asparagus heads, slice of truffle. (*Separately*): Thickened gravy.

Madras.—In tartlets garnished with rice, the egg coated with Curry sauce.

Maintenon.—In croustades garnished with mushroom purée, coated with Soubise sauce, glazed.

Malmaison.—In tartlets garnished with peas, lozenges of French beans, asparagus heads, cohered with cream, the base of the egg surrounded with Béarnaise sauce, a pinch of chervil and tarragon on top.

Marivaux.—In timbale half filled with sweet corn with cream, coated with Marivaux sauce.

Masséna.—On artichoke bottoms, garnished with Béarnaise sauce, the egg coated with tomato sauce, roundels of marrow, and chopped parsley on top.

Massenet.—On artichoke bottoms, garnished with a small Anna potato, place the egg on the potato, coat with cream sauce mixed with French beans purée.

Mentonnaise.—In croustades, coat the egg with cream sauce mixed with leeks julienne, glazed.

Metternich.—On artichoke bottoms garnished with julienne of tongue cohered with velouté coated with Mornay sauce, glazed.

Mignon.—On artichokes bottoms garnished with green peas and shrimp tails cohered with butter, the egg coated with shrimp sauce, slice of truffles on top.

Milanaise.—In tartlets garnished with macaroni and coated with Mornay sauce glazed.

Mireille.—On a bed of rice with saffron, the egg coated with cream sauce and saffron surrounded with croûtons fried in oil and garnished with dice of tomato tossed in butter.

Mirepoix.—On croûtons garnished with a slice of ham, coat the egg with Madeira sauce mixed with Mirepoix of vegetables.

Mogador.—On croûtons made with Marquise potatoes, coat the eggs with suprême sauce mixed with foie gras purée, decorated with slices of tongues and truffles.

Monselet.—In croustadines, coated with tomatoed Madeira sauce, sprinkled with julienne of artichokes' bottoms and truffles.

Montglas.—In tartlets garnished with ham, foie gras and truffles cohered with Madeira sauce, coated with tomatoed half-glaze.

Montmorency.—On toast, the egg coated with tomatoed Suprême sauce, garnished with artichoke bottoms filled with asparagus heads à la crème.

Mornay.—(*See* Œufs Pochés au Gratin).

Montpensier.—In croustades garnished with scrambled eggs mixed with shrimps, coated with shrimp sauce.

Mortemart (*Moulded*).—Scrambled eggs and beaten eggs mixed together, placed in buttered moulds and poached. Dish up on tartlets filled with mushroom purée, decorated with slice of truffle. Colbert sauce.

Montrouge.—On grilled mushrooms, the egg coated with suprême sauce mixed mushroom purée.

Nantua.—In tartlets filled with dice of crayfish tails cohered with Nantua sauce, the egg coated with Nantua sauce, decorated with crayfish tails.

Napolitaine. (*Moulded*).—Scrambled egg and beaten egg, mixed and poached in brioche moulds. Dish up on a buttered gratin dish, coated with tomatoed half-glaze, sprinkled with cheese, glazed.

Niçoise.—In potatoes shaped like artichoke bottoms and cooked same as château potatoes; garnished with French beans, the egg on top and dice of tomatoes to finish, thickened gravy, round.

Ninon.—On croûtons or tartlets garnished with asparagus heads. Coat the egg with suprême sauce, decorate with truffles dressed in a circle alternating with asparagus heads, the centre garnished with same.

Normande.—In tartlets garnished with poached oysters cohered with Normande sauce, the egg coated with same sauce.

Orléans (A).—In tartlets garnished with dice of chicken cohered with tomato sauce, the egg coated with suprême sauce blended with pistachio butter.

(B).—In tartlets garnished with dice of marrow and truffles, cohered with half-glaze sauce, coated with Colbert sauce.

Orsay.—On buttered toasts, coat the egg with Chateaubriand sauce.

Ostendaise.—In croustades garnished with salpicon of shrimps, mushrooms, truffles, cohered with Nantua sauce, coat the egg with same sauce, slice of truffle.

Otéro.—Same as above but in scooped baked potatoes coated with Mornay sauce, glazed.

Pacha.—On a bed of rice à la Turque, coat the egg with Mornay sauce, glazed.

Païva—In croustades garnished with mushroom purée, coat the egg with Mornay sauce, glazed, slice of truffle.

Palermitaine (*Moulded*).—In buttered baba moulds, the bottom decorated with truffles, the sides sprinkled with chopped tongue, poached and dished on tartlet crusts half filled with macaroni and cream.

Parisienne.—In croustades the egg coated half with Mornay and half with Nantua sauce, separate the sauces with small noisette potatoes, glazed, sprinkled with chopped truffles.

Patti.—In tartlets garnished with artichoke purée, coat the eggs with suprême sauce, sprinkled with chopped yolk of eggs.

Périgourdine.—The egg coated with Périgueux sauce and dished up on large slices of truffles.

Petit-Duc.—On large grilled mushrooms, the egg coated with Chateaubriand sauce.

Piémontaise.—Coat the eggs with tomato sauce, dished on minced lamb. Rice à la Piémontaise in the centre.

Polignac (*Moulded*) **(A).**—In baba moulds buttered and decorated with truffles, poached, and dressed on croûtons coated with meat glaze mixed with butter.

(B).—In mould buttered and sprinkled with chopped ham and parsley, poached and dressed on croûtons. Périgueux sauce round.

Polonaise.—The eggs dished on minced mutton cohered with half-glaze, Polonaise butter on the eggs.

Pont-Biquet.—In croustades garnished with turbot purée, coated with Vénitienne sauce, slice of truffles.

Portugaise.—In half tomatoes cooked in oven, coated with Portugaise sauce.

Princesse.—In croustades garnished with asparagus heads cohered with butter, dressed in a circle, alternated with asparagus heads, the eggs coated with cream sauce decorated with slices of truffles.

(*Moulded*).—Dariole moulds, buttered and the bottom decorated with slice of truffle, the sides coated with a thin layer of chicken forcemeat, filled with scrambled eggs mixed with beaten egg, and finished with a layer of chicken forcemeat; poached seven minutes in bain-marie, dressed in a circle, surrounded with thin suprême sauce.

Printanière (*Moulded*).—Butter some hexagonal moulds and garnish them chartreuse-fashion with cut up cooked vegetables, varying the shades, break the egg in, and poach, dish up on croûtons and coat with cream sauce finished with printanier butter.

Rachel.—(*See* Œufs Sans-Gêne).

Régina.—In croustades garnished with fillet of sole in dice, shrimps and mushrooms, cohered with shrimp sauce, coat the egg with Normande sauce, sprinkle with julienne of truffles.

Reine.—In croustades garnished with dice of chicken cohered with suprême sauce, the egg coated same sauce.

Roland.—In croustades garnished with minced chicken cohered with cream, coat the egg with suprême sauce containing truffles and white of chicken in dice, glazed.

Rossini.—In tartlets garnished with a foie gras collop, the egg coated with Madeira sauce, slice of truffle on top.

Rougemont.—The egg coated with Mornay sauce, glazed and dished up on a bed of rice à la Milanaise, surround the base with tomato sauce.

Royale.—In tartlets garnished with dice of cockscombs, truffles and mushroom cohered with suprême sauce, coated with same sauce.

Saint-Hubert.—In tartlets garnished with game purée, the eggs coated with Poivrade sauce, slice of truffle.

Sans-Gêne.—On artichoke bottoms, the eggs coated with Bordelaise sauce, slice of poached marrow on top, chopped parsley.

Sarde.—In tomatoes skinned and scooped, place the raw egg in, replace the lid, egg and crumb and fry deep fat, half-glaze sauce with parsley.

Savoyarde.—On a bed of Savoyarde potatoes the eggs coated with Mornay sauce and glazed.

Sévigné.—On croûtons garnished with purée of braised lettuces, the eggs coated with suprême sauce, decorated with a ring of truffle.

Soubise.—In croustades garnished with soubise purée, coated with soubise sauce.

Souveraine.—In croustades garnished with purée of green asparagus, coat the eggs with suprême sauce, slice of truffles.

Stanley.—In tartlets garnished with curried soubise sauce, coat the egg with Curry sauce with cream.

Sultane.—In tartlets garnished with scrambled eggs with truffles, decorated with a crescent made of truffle.

Suzette.—In scooped baked potatoes garnished with Mornay sauce, the egg coated with same, glazed, decorated with truffles.

Toupinel.—Same as above, with celery purée instead of Mornay sauce.

Tourangelle (A).—(*See* Œufs Bourguignonne).

    (B).—In tartlets garnished with purée of green flageolets, coat the egg with cream sauce blended with French beans butter.

Toussenel.—On flat game croquettes, coat the eggs with salmis sauce mixed with chestnut purée, sprinkled with chopped truffles.

Tyrolienne.—On croûtons, the eggs coated with tomatoed suprême sauce, dressed in a circle, centre garnished with roundels of fried onions.

Velidoff.—In croustades garnished with asparagus heads with cream, coated with shrimp sauce, decorated with asparagus heads and slices of truffles.

Verdi.—In buttered dariole moulds decorated with truffles and filled with scrambled eggs mixed with Parmesan, chopped truffles and beaten eggs, poached, dressed on croûtons, surround base with half-glaze.

Victoria.—In tartlets garnished with dice of lobster and truffles cohered with lobster sauce, coat the egg with Victoria sauce, glazed.

Viroflay.—In croustades garnished with spinach tossed in butter, coated with suprême sauce.

(*Moulded*).—In buttered baba moulds, lined with spinach leaves, break the egg in and poach, dish up on croûtons and coat with suprême sauce.

Wywern.—In croustades, coated with fish velouté and sprinkled with " Bombay Duck " in powder.

OMELETTES — OMELETS

Cooking Process

Omelet making is at once very simple and very difficult, for tastes differ regarding their preparation. Some like them well done, some just done, and others almost liquid.

The eggs are beaten, seasoned and poured in an omelet-pan containing very hot butter, stir briskly with a fork in order to heat the whole evenly, and if the omelet is to be garnished it should be done before rolling it up. The whole process should be done speedily, and requires long practice to attain perfection.

Agnès Sorel.—Stuff the omelet with minced mushrooms tossed in butter and cohered with thin chicken purée, lay some roundels of tongue on the top, surround with a thread of thickened gravy.

Américaine.—Stuffed with dice of tomatoes tossed in butter, and dish up on rashers of grilled bacon.

Andalouse.—Stuffed with pimentoes and tomatoes, surrounded with roundels of fried onions.

Archiduc.—Stuffed with collops of chicken livers tossed in butter, and cohered with half-glaze sauce, a thread of Archiduc sauce round, slices of truffles on top.

Bénédictine.—Stuffed with Brandade of morue and truffles, a thread of surpême sauce round.

Bonne-Femme.—Mix with the beaten eggs, some dice of bacon, minced mushrooms and slices of onion tossed in butter.

Bouchère.—Stuffed with dice of poached marrow, cohered with meat glaze, decorated with slices of marrow, surround with a thread of strong gravy.

Boulonnaise.—Stuffed with poached soft roes mixed with maître d'hôtel butter.

Bourguignonne.—Stuffed with prepared snails and chopped walnuts, chopped parsley.

Bretonne.—Mix with the eggs some white of leeks, mince onions and mushrooms, the lot previously cooked in butter.

Brillat-Savarin.—Stuffed with dice of woodcock and truffles cohered with woodcock cullis, decorated with slices of truffles, surrounded with strong game gravy.

Bruxelloise.—Stuffed with braised chicory, cohered with cream, surround with a thread of suprême sauce.

Champignons.—Mix with the eggs some minced mushrooms tossed in butter, decorate with slices of mushrooms.

Chartres.—Mix with the eggs some chopped tarragon, decorate with blanched tarragon leaves, a thread of gravy.

Chasseur.—Stuffed with collops of chicken livers and minced mushrooms tossed in butter and cohered with half-glaze sauce and Madeira, the omelet split in the middle and garnished with some of the liver preparation, sauce around.

Châtelaine (A).—Stuffed with cooked chestnuts cohered with meat glaze, surrounded with a thread of soubised suprême sauce.

(B).—Mix with the eggs some dice of truffles and artichoke bottoms, slices of truffles and minced artichoke bottoms on top.

Chevreuse.—Mix with the eggs some dice of truffles, artichokes bottoms and asparagus heads, decorate with slices of truffles and artichoke bottoms.

Choisy.—Stuffed with braised lettuces, cohered with suprême sauce, a thread of same sauce round.

Clamart.—Stuffed with peas à la Française. The omelet split and cavity filled with peas.

Crécy.—Stuffed with carrot purée, decorated with slices of carrots, suprême sauce round.

Crevettes.—Stuffed with shrimps tails cohered with shrimp sauce, split the omelet and fill cavity with shrimps.

Durand.—Mix with the eggs some minced mushrooms and artichoke bottoms tossed in butter, stuffed with julienne of truffles and asparagus heads cohered with suprême sauce, surround with a thread of tomatoed half-glaze.

Espagnole.—Mix with the eggs some dice of tomatoes, julienne of sweet capsicums and minced onions cooked in butter, the omelet is made flat like a pancake.

Fermière.—Mix with the eggs some dice of ham and chopped parsley, must be flat.

Fines-Herbes.—Mix with the eggs chopped parsley, chives, tarragon leaves, chervil.

Fleurs de Courge.—Add to the eggs some calices of freshly plucked young vegetable marrow flowers, ciseled and tossed in butter, chopped parsley.

Florentine.—Mix with the eggs some blanched spinach leaves, tossed in butter.

Fonds d'Artichauts.—Mix with the eggs some minced artichoke bottoms tossed in butter, decorate with slice of artichoke bottoms, thickened gravy round.

Forestière.—Stuff the omelet with morels and cèpes, minced and tossed in butter, cohered with meat glaze, thickened gravy round.

Grand'Mère.—Mix with the eggs some chopped parsley and dice of fried bread.

Hollandaise.—Mix with the eggs some thin collops of smoked salmon tossed in butter, surround with Hollandaise sauce.

Hongroise.—Stuffed with dice of tomatoes and minced onions tossed in butter with paprika, surround with Hongroise sauce.

Jambon.—Mix with the eggs some dice of ham tossed in butter, decorate with lozenges of ham.

Japonaise.—Mix with the eggs some chopped parsley, and stuff with Japanese artichokes blanched and tossed in butter, cream sauce.

Jessica.—Stuffed with minced morels and asparagus heads with cream, a thread of Chateaubriand sauce round.

Jets de Houblon.—Stuff the omelet with young shoots of hops cohered with cream, split and garnish cavity same shoots, a thread of cream sauce round.

Joinville.—Stuffed with shrimps tails, mushrooms and truffles, a thread of shrimp sauce.

Jurassienne.—Mix with the eggs some dice of cooked bacon and chopped chives, stuffed with sorrel, ciseled and tossed in butter.

Lard.—Mix some dice of bacon with the eggs and dish up on rashers of fried bacon.

Limousine.—Mix with the eggs some dice of potatoes and ham tossed in butter.

Lorraine.—Mix with the eggs some dice of fried bacon, thin slices of Gruyère cheese, cream and chopped chives.

Lyonnaise.—Mix with the eggs some minced onions tossed in butter.

Maria.—Same as above, with chopped parsley.

Masséna.—Stuffed with collops of artichoke bottoms tossed in butter, cohered with tomato sauce, decorate with slices of marrow coated with meat glaze, surround with a thread of Béarnaise sauce.

Mascotte.—Mix with the eggs some dice of artichoke bottoms, truffles and potatoes tossed in butter, thickened gravy round.

Maxim.—Decorate the omelet with a row of crayfish tails and slices of truffle, surround with a border of frogs legs tossed in butter until cooked and well gilded.

Mexicaine.—Mix with the eggs some minced mushrooms tossed in butter, julienne of sweet capsicums, stuff with dice of tomatoes, surround with tomated half-glaze.

Mireille.—Stuffed with tomatoes tossed in butter with a little garlic, make the omelet with oil, surround with a thread of cream sauce with saffron.

Monselet.—Stuffed with julienne or truffles and mushrooms, asparagus heads cohered with foie gras purée, decorated with mushrooms, asparagus heads, and slices of truffles.

Morilles.—Stuffed with minced morels tossed in butter and cohered with half-glaze sauce.

Moules.—Stuffed with mussels, poached and cohered with Marinière sauce.

Mousseline.—Separate the yolk from the white, beat the yolk with salt and cream, add the whites beaten to a stiff froth and cook in the ordinary way, serve immediately.

Mousserons.—Same as Morels, with " Mousserons ".

Nantua.—Stuffed with crayfish tails cohered with Nantua sauce, decorated with slices of truffles and crayfish tails, a thread of Nantua sauce round.

Nature.—Plain omelet.

Nonats.—Mix with the eggs some " Nonats " tossed in butter.

Normande.—Stuffed with poached oysters, cohered with Normande sauce.

Oseille.—Mix with the eggs some shredded sorrel tossed in butter.

Ostendaise.—Stuffed with mussels, mushrooms and truffles cohered with Nantua sauce, surrounded with thread of same sauce.

Parisienne.—Mix with the eggs some dice of truffles and potatoes tossed in butter.

Parmentier.—Mix the eggs with sauté potatoes.

Parmesan.—Mix the eggs with Parmesan cheese.

Patti.—(*See* **à la Chevreuse**).

Paysanne.—Mix the eggs with dice of cooked bacon, potatoes tossed in butter, sorrel stewed in butter, pinch of chervil, make the omelet flat, same as pancake.

Périgord.—Mix with the eggs some dice of truffles, surround with Périgueux sauce.

Pointes d'Asperges.—Mix with the eggs some asparagus heads cooked in butter, decorate with small faggots of asparagus heads.

Portugaise.—Stuffed with concassed tomatoes, tomato sauce round.

Prélats.—Stuffed with saplicon of poached soft roes, shrimps tails and truffle julienne cohered with Normande sauce with crayfish butter, coat the omelet with same sauce, sprinkle with chopped truffles.

Princesse.—Mix the eggs with dice of chicken and asparagus heads, decorate with slices of truffles and small faggot of asparagus, surround with thread of suprême sauce.

Provençale.—Stuffed with dice of tomatoes tossed in butter with a little garlic, surround with a thread of Provençale sauce.

Réforme.—stuffed with dice of tongue, truffles, gherkins and white of egg cohered with poivrade sauce and red currant jelly, a thread of same sauce round.

Reine.—Stuffed with chicken purée, surround with a thread of suprême sauce.

Richemont.—Decorate the omelet with half morels and slices of truffles, Madeira sauce round.

Rognons.—Stuffed with dice of kidneys tossed in butter and cohered with Madeira sauce.

Rossini.—Mix with the eggs some dice of foie gras and truffles, decorate with collops

Salvator.—Mix with the eggs some truffles, ham and mushrooms in julienne.

Savoyarde.—Mix with the eggs some potatoe: tossed in butter and slices of Gruyère cheese, must be flat same as pancake.

Soubise.—Stuffed with soubise purée, surround with a thread of soubise sauce.

Suissesse.—Mix with the eggs some grated Gruyère cheese, sprinkle the omelet with cheese and glaze.

Thon.—Mix with the eggs some dice of tunny-fish with oil, sprinkle the omelet with melted anchovy butter.

Tomates.—(*See* **Omelette Portugaise**).

Truffes.—Mix with the eggs some dice of truffles, decorate with glazed slices of truffles, a thread of meat glaze round.

Turque.—Stuffed with chicken livers, sliced and tossed in butter, cohered with Madeira sauce, split the omelet and fill cavity with the livers. Madeira sauce round.

Vichy.—Stuffed with Vichy carrots.

Victoria.—Stuffed with dice of lobster and truffles cohered with lobster sauce, the top decorated with slices of lobster and truffles, surrounded with sauce.

ŒUFS SUR LE PLAT — EGGS ON THE DISH

Cooking Process

Butter the egg dish, season the bottom and break the egg in, start cooking on the stove and finish in the oven, in a tin containing water.

Américaine (A).—Break the egg on a slice of grilled ham, when cooked surround with thread of tomato sauce.

(B).—Garnish the bottom of the dish with collops of lobster, break the egg in and cook, surround with Américaine sauce.

Anchois.—The bottom of dish garnished with anchovy fillets in dice, when the egg is cooked surround the yolk with anchovy fillets.

Anversoise.—The bottom of dish garnished with hops shoots with cream, cook the egg and surround with thick cream.

Bacon.—The bottom of dish garnished with rashers of bacon, break the egg on top and cook.

Bercy.—When cooked, garnish with small grilled sausage, and a thread of tomato sauce.

Beurre Noir.—Seasoned, cooked in a frying-pan, slide it on an egg dish and pour over some black butter with vinegar.

Bruxelloise.—The bottom of dish garnished with braised chicory and cream, break the egg in and cook.

Catherinette.—Chopped onions, dice of tomatoes, slices of egg-plant, garlic, tossed in oil; dressed in egg dish and break the egg on the preparation, cook in oven.

Chasseur.—When cooked, garnished with chicken livers and minced mushrooms tossed in butter and cohered with Madeira sauce.

Clamart.—Break the egg on a bed of peas à la française, cook in oven.

Cluny.—When cooked garnished with small chicken croquettes and a thread of tomato sauce.

Condé.—The bottom of dish garnished with purée of red haricot beans and rashers of fried bacon. Break the egg in, cook and surround with a thread of red wine sauce.

Conti.—The bottom of dish garnished with lentil purée and grilled bacon.

Crécy.—The bottom garnished with purée of carrots.

Crevettes.—When the egg is cooked garnish round with shrimps' tails and shrimp sauce.

Diable.—Cook in frying-pan, both sides, slide the egg on the dish and pour over some nut brown butter with vinegar.

Duchesse.—Make the figure 8 with potato Duchesse on the bottom of the dish, brown in oven, break an egg in each hole, coat with cream and cook in oven, decorate with truffles.

Egyptienne.—The bottom of dish garnished with white of leeks and mince onions tossed in butter and cohered with cream sauce.

Espagnole.—In half grilled tomatoes, the egg cooked in frying-pan and shaped with round cutter the size of the tomatoes, dressed in a circle, centre garnished with fried onions.

Estragon.—Break the egg in a buttered dish, add a spoonful of thickened tarragon gravy, and cook in oven, decorate with blanched tarragon leaves.

Florentine.—Break the egg on a layer of blanched spinach leaves tossed in butter, and sprinkled with grated cheese, coat the egg with Mornay sauce and cook in hot oven.

Forestière.—Bottom of dish garnished with minced morels tossed in butter with small dice of bacon and chopped shallots. Break the egg in and cook.

Granier.—The bottom of dish garnished with asparagus heads and slices of truffles, break the egg in and cook, decorate the yolk with a slice of truffle and the white with asparagus heads.

Gratin.—The bottom of dish coated with Mornay sauce, break the egg in, cover with same sauce and cook in oven.

Isoline.—When the egg is cooked garnish with half tomato à la Provençale stuffed with chicken livers tossed in butter and covered with Madeira sauce, chopped parsley.

Jessica.—When the egg is cooked, garnish with minced morels and asparagus heads, a thread of thickened gravy.

Jockey-Club.—Cook the egg in an omelet pan and trim with round cutter, dress in a circle on round toasts coated with foie gras purée, the centre garnished with veal kidneys tossed in butter; dice of truffles covered with Madeira half-glaze sauce.

Lilloise.—The bottom of dish garnished with small Brussels sprouts, break the egg in and cook, cream sauce round.

Lorraine.—The bottom of dish garnished with rashers of grilled bacon and slices of gruyère cheese, break the egg in, coat with thick cream, cook in oven.

Lully.—Cook the egg in omelet pan, trim with round cutter and dish up on slices of ham same shape dressed in a circle, centre garnished with macaroni Napolitaine.

Lyonnaise.—The bottom of dish garnished with onions tossed in butter, break the egg in, cook and surround with Lyonnaise sauce.

Maraichére.—The bottom of dish garnished with shredded lettuce, sorrel, chervil, break the egg in and cook, small pieces of bacon on each side of the egg.

Matelote.—The bottom of dish, coated with mariniére matelote sauce, break the egg in, cook, a thread of sauce round.

Maximilienne.—Break the eggs in half tomatoes fried in oil, the inside sprinkled with chopped parsley and garlic, grated cheese and brown crumbs on the egg, cook in hot oven.

Metternich.—The bottom of dish garnished with minced mushrooms tossed in butter, the egg sprinkled with grated cheese, glazed.

Meyerbeer.—When the egg is done, garnish with grilled lambs' kidneys, coated with Périgueux sauce.

Mirabeau.—The bottom of dish buttered with anchovy butter, break the eggs and cook them, surround each yolk with anchovy fillets and garnish with olives stuffed with tarragon butter, decorate with tarragon leaves.

Miroir.—Break the egg in the dish and coat with thick cream, cook in hot oven.

Montargis.—In tartlets garnished with julienne of chicken livers tossed in butter, tongue and mushrooms covered with Béchamel sauce and meat glaze, coated with Mornay sauce and glazed, cook the egg in frying pan, trim with round cutter the size of the tartlet and place the egg on it, decorate with roundel or tongue.

Montmorency.—The bottom of dish garnished with asparagus heads à la crème, break the egg in, cook and garnished one side with asparagus heads and the other with artichoke bottoms tossed in butter.

Monégasque.—The bottom of dish garnished with tomato and chopped tarragon. When the egg is done, decorate with anchovy fillets, tomato sauce round.

Nantua.—The bottom of dish garnished with crayfish tails, break the egg in, cook, decorate with truffles and crayfish tails. A thread of Nantua sauce round.

Négus.—When the egg is cooked garnish with small game croquettes, a thread of Périgueux sauce.

Néron.—(*See* **Œufs sur le Plat à la Cluny**).

Normande.—The bottom of dish garnished with cream, raw oysters with their liquor and a little fish glaze break the egg in and cook in oven; surround with Normande sauce.

Omer Pacha.—The bottom of dish garnished with chopped onions cooked in butter, break the egg in and sprinkle with grated cheese, cook in hot oven, surround with tomato sauce.

Opéra.—When the egg is cooked, garnish one side with asparagus heads and the other with chicken livers tossed in butter and cohered with Madeira sauce.

Orléans.—The tartlet crusts garnished with dice of marrow and truffles cohered with Madeira sauce, the egg cooked in frying pan, and trimmed with round cutter the size of the tartlet, dish up in an egg dish and surround with Chateaubriand sauce.

Orléanaise.—Cook the egg on a layer of endive purée à la crème, surround with thick cream.

Parmentier.—In scooped baked potatoes half filled with a purée made with the pulp, break the egg in, coat with cream and cook.

Parmesan.—Sprinkle the egg with grated cheese and cook in hot oven.

Périgourdine.—The bottom of dish buttered and sprinkled with truffle juice, break the egg in, cook and garnish with dice of truffles, surround with a thread of Périgueux sauce.

Petit-Duc.—When the egg is done, garnish with grilled mushroom filled with scraped horse-radish, surround with Chateaubriand sauce.

Piémontaise.—The egg cooked with grated cheese and surrounded with rizotto.

Portugaise.—When cooked surround with dice of tomatoes tossed in butter, tomato sauce.

Provençale.—In half tomatoes fried in oil, the inside sprinkled with chopped parsley, and garlic, break the egg in and cook.

Rachel.—The egg cooked in omelet pan, trimmed with round cutter and dressed on croûtons same shape, a slice of marrow on the egg, and finish with slice of truffle, surround with thickened gravy.

Richemont.—When the egg is done garnish with minced morels tossed in butter and decorate with slice of truffle. Madeira sauce.

Rossini.—The egg cooked in frying pan, trimmed with round cutter and dressed on collops of foie gras tossed in butter and cut same shape, slice of truffle, surround with thread of Périgueux sauce.

Rothomago.—The bottom of dish garnished with rashers of fried bacon or grilled ham. Break the egg in and cook, garnish with grilled chipolatas, surround with a thread of tomato sauce.

Sagan.—The egg sprinkled with cheese and glazed, garnished with slice of brain coated with cream sauce, surround with thread of same sauce.

Savoyarde.—The bottom of dish garnished with potatoes, tossed raw in butter and sprinkled with grated cheese, break the egg in and coat with thick cream, cook in oven.

Sicilienne.—When the egg is done, garnish with half tomatoes cooked in oven and filled with Italienne sauce, a thread of same sauce round.

Turque.—When the egg is done garnish with dice of chicken livers, tossed in butter and cohered with half-glaze and tomato purée.

Vaucourt.—Rings made with Duchesse potatoes, half filled with scrambled eggs, asparagus heads and truffles, break the egg in and cook in oven. Decorate with slice of truffles.

Victoria.—When the egg is done, garnish with dice of lobster and truffles cohered with lobster sauce. A thread of same sauce round.

Villars.—The bottom of dish garnished with minced artichoke bottoms cohered with soubise sauce, break the egg in, cook. Garnished with rashers of bacon, surround with haricot beans purée.

Wladimir.—When done, decorate the yolk with slice of truffle, and asparagus heads on each side, surround with a thread of Périgueux sauce.

ŒUFS DE PLUVIER — PLOVERS' EGGS

Aspic (*Cold*).—In border mould lined with aspic, place the boiled shelled eggs and fill with jelly.

Danoise.—Poached and dished on tartlet crusts garnished with salmon purée.

Gabrielle (*Cold*).—In tartlet crusts filled with purée of soles, place the eggs soft boiled and moulded in dariole moulds with jelly, decorate with lobster eggs, finish with aspic.

Jeannette (*Cold*).—In tartlet crusts filled with ham mousse, the egg poached and glazed with aspic, dress in a circle, decorate with ham mousse.

Moderne (*Cold*).—Place the egg in dariole moulds, lined with aspic and decorated " chartreuse " fashion, fill the mould with aspic jelly, dish up round a dôme of vegetable macédoine cohered with mayonnaise and aspic.

Moscovite (*Cold*).—In tartlets garnished with caviar.

Nid (au).—Imitate a nest with Montpellier butter, place the soft boiled eggs in the nest and fill centre with aspic jelly, surround with mustard and cress.

Omelette.—Same as ordinary omelet in the proportion of one chicken egg to six plovers'.

Petite Reine (*Cold*).—In dariole moulds lined with aspic, decorated with truffles and white of eggs, place the egg, hard boiled, fill with aspic, and dish up in a circle round a heap of asparagus heads salad, decorate with aspic.

Royale (*Hot*).—In tartlet shapes made with chicken purée cohered with eggs and poached, scoop the top and place the soft boiled egg in the cavity, coat with mushroom purée mixed with cream, sprinkle with chopped truffles.

Troubadours.—Place the soft boiled egg in a cooked scooped morel, and set the morels in tartlet crusts garnished with foie gras purée.

E

Poissons — Fish

AIGREFIN — FRESH HADDOCK

Beurre Fondu.—Poach in salt water, dress on a serviette, garnish with parsley and plain boiled potatoes. (*Separately*): melted butter.

Fines Herbes.—In a buttered gratin dish, sprinkled with mushrooms, onions and chopped parsley, season the fish, moisten with white wine, cover with crumbs and small pieces of butter, cook in oven.

Flamande.—Poach in white wine in a buttered dish, garnish with onions and mushrooms, dress, reduce the cooking liquor, add parsley and coat the fish.

Maître d'Hôtel.—In fillets fried, poached or grilled, served with maître-d'hôtel butter.

ALOSE — SHAD

Bercy.—Season, oil, cook in oven, Bercy sauce.

Farcie.—Stuff with fish forcemeat, season and wrap in oiled paper, cook in oven, Bercy sauce.

Gratin.—In a buttered gratin dish, garnish bottom with fish Duxelles sauce. The fish coated with same sauce, sprinkle with breadcrumbs, add small pieces of butter and glass of white wine, cook in oven.

Grillée.—Season, marinade with oil, lemon juice, parsley, thyme and bay leaf, grill. (*Separately*): Serve maître-d'hôtel butter, anchovy butter, etc. Slices of lemon.

Grillée à l'Oseille.—Same as above with braised sorrel, served in timbale. *Separately*): melted butter.

Hollandaise.—Boil in salt water and vinegar, pepper, parsley, dress on serviette with plain boiled potatoes. Hollandaise sauce.

Provençale.—Stuff with fish forcemeat flavoured with garlic, braise with chopped tomatoes, white wine, salt, pepper and oil. Dress on a dish ,coat with the reduced cooking liquor, chopped parsley.

Oseille.—Crumb, grill, add melted butter and lemon juice, serve with sorrel. purée

ANCHOIS — ANCHOVY

(*Are mostly used salted, but if fresh, can be grilled or fried*).

ANGUILLES — EELS

Anglaise (Boiled à l').—Cut in sections, poach, parsley sauce.

Beaucaire.—Bone, stuff with whiting forcemeat, combined with chopped mushroom, braise with chopped shallots, brandy, white wine, butter mushrooms and onions.

Benoîton.—In fillets, flour, fry, dress with fried parsley. (*Separately*): pass a sauce made with eel trimmings, shallots, parsley, reduced with red wine, through the sieve and finish with butter.

Coulibiac.—Pie made with brioche paste, stuffed with collops of poached eels, créole rice, hard boiled eggs, mushrooms and chopped onions, cooked vesiga, cook in oven 35 mintues.

Durand.—Cut in sections, boned and stuffed with fish forcemeat, wrap in muslin and poach with water and white Pouilly wine, reduced cooking liquor mixed with butter, add cayenne pepper.

Eel Pie.—(*See* **Pâté à l'Anglaise**).

Frite.—In sections, flour and fry.

Frite à l'Anglaise.—In fillets, season ,oil and lemon juice, egg and crumb, fry deep fat, serve with Anchovy sauce.

Gourmets.—In sections ,poach in Chablis, coat with fish velouté, combined with crayfish cutlets, garnish with crayfish tails.

Mâconnaise (Matelote).—Cook with red wine, small onions, mushrooms crayfish, croûtons.

Matelote.—Cut in sections, poach with red wine with aromates, reduce the liquor and cohere with flour and butter. Garnish with small glazed onions, mushrooms and fleurons.

Ménagère.—In sections, season, grill, dress with gherkins, sauce, mustard maître-d'hôtel.

Meunière.—In sections, flour, cook in butter, finish with nut brown butter, lemon juice, chopped parsley.

Normande.—Same as matelote, moisten with cider, garnish with oysters.

Orly.—In fillets, season, egg and crumb and fry deep fat. Tomato sauce.

Pâté Chaud d'Anguille.—Pâté mould, line with paste, coat the sides and bottom with fish forcemeat well truffled, alternate with layers of eel collops studded with truffles, marinaded in brandy, oil, white wine and stiffen in butter with shallots and parsley, cook in oven for 2 hours, serve with sauce demi-glace maigre.

Pâté Chaud d'Anguilles à l'Anglaise.—In a pie dish, layers of collops of eels blanched in salt water, seasoned with pepper, salt, nutmeg, chopped parsley, add hard-boiled eggs, moisten with white wine, cover with puff paste, cook in oven. When serving add half-glaze sauce flavoured with fish essence.

Pompadour.—In rings, cook in court-bouillon with white wine, cool, drain, coat with Villeroy sauce, egg and crumb, fry deep fat, dress on serviette with fried parsley and small Dauphine croquettes, tomatoed Béarnaise sauce.

Poulette (A).—In sections, partly fried in butter with chopped onions, flour, moisten with water, season, add faggot, dish in timbale with cooked mushrooms. Cohere sauce with flour and butter and yolk of eggs.

(**B**).—Sections cooked in fish stock and served in Poulette sauce.

Romaine.—Cut in sections, season, stiffen in butter, add peas, minced lettuces, butter, white wine, cook slowly, dish in timbale, coat with the reduced sauce cohered with flour and butter.

Rouennaise.—Poach in red wine and mirepoix, glaze in oven, dress on a round dish, garnish with mushrooms, oysters and collops of poached soft roes, coat with the reduced liquor cohered with Espagnole sauce, surround with smelts cooked in butter.

Sainte Menehould.—Cut in sections, poach in white wine, drain, dip in melted butter and roll in breadcrumbs mixed with chopped mushrooms, grill, dress in a dish decorated with gherkins, sauce Hachée and dice of anchovy fillets.

Soleil.—Roll in spiral, egg and crumb, grill, serve tomato sauce.

Suffren.—Sections, stud with anchovy fillets, poach in white wine, dress in timbale, coat with reduced cooking liquor, cohered with tomato purée, finish with butter, anchovy essence and cayenne pepper.

Tartare.—In sections, poach in white wine, court-bouillon, drain. Egg and crumb, fry, decorate with gherkins, Tartare sauce.

Vénitienne.—Sections, poach in white wine, glaze in oven, garnish with cooked mushrooms and dice soft roes, coat with Vénitienne sauce.

Verte (A) (*Cold*).—Sections, stiffen with sorrel, stinging nettles, parsley, sage, sarriette and tarragon, moisten with white wine, season, cohere with yolk of eggs ,add lemon juice, dress in terrine.

Verte à la Flamande (B).—Sections, stiffen in butter, moisten with beer, season, add herbs as above, dress in terrine.

Villeroy.—Poach in court-bouillon, allow to cool with Villeroy sauce, egg and crumb, fry, tomato sauce.

BARBEAU ET BARBUE — BRILL

*(See preparation of turbotin when served whole and see filets
de sole or brill in fillets.)*

BLOATERS

(Are served grilled with maître-d'hôtel butter.)

BOUILLABAISSE

Marseillaise.—Fish to employ: rascasses, John Dory, whitings, conger-eels, red mullets, frelas, rouquiers, boudreuil, langoustines (all fish from Mediterranean sea), large fishes cut, others whole.

Preparation.—Fried in oil, minced onions, leek, add crushed garlic, bay leaf, fennel, dice of tomato, the fishes, season, moisten with water and white wine cook 15 minutes. Set some fried slices of bread in a deep dish pour over cooking liquor, serve fish in another dish.

Parisienne.—Can be done with other fish using same process.

BROCHET — PIKE

Anglaise.—Fillets of pike, seasoned, bread crumbed baked in oven in a gratin dish, serve in the dish.

Benoîton.—Fillets seasoned, fried, serve with wine sauce.

Bleu.—(*See* **Truite au Bleu**).

Bordelaise.—Cut into sections, cook in red wine with mirepoix, coat the pieces with the sauce cohered with butter and flour.

Côtelettes.—Pike forcemeat in cutlet moulds, garnish interior with salpicon of truffles and mushrooms, cohered with Allemande sauce, poach, unmould, egg and crumb, fry in clarified butter, dress in a circle. Soubise sauce.

Court-Bouillon.—(*See* **Truite** same name).

Filets Régence.—Cut oval shape, stud with truffles, poach with white wine and fish stock, reduce the cooking liquor, dress in a circle, coat with sauce Régence, garnish in centre.

Grenadins à l'Oseille.—Cut as above, stud with gherkins and blanched carrots in strips, stiffen in clarified butter, moisten with fish stock, reduce, add butter, dress in circle, coat with sauce, glaze. Serve purée of Sorrel separately.

Grillé.—Small size fish, marinaded with aromates, white wine, oil season, grill slowly, basting with oil. Serve Mayonnaise sauce combined with chopped walnuts.

Matelote.—(*See* **Matelotes**).

Matelote Rémoise.—(*See* **Matelote Marinière**). Champagne instead of white wine.

Meunier (du).—Cut the fillets in sections, season and flour, cook in butter, and chopped shallots, swill with white wine and white consommé cohere sauce with cream and yolk of eggs, chopped parsley.

Meunière.—In fillets, operate same as in all Meunière preparations.

Montebello.—Skin one side, stuff inside with fish forcemeat, spread the skinned side with forcemeat, place on it small fillets of sole, studded with truffles, braise with white wine and aromates, dress on a rice tampon, coat with white wine sauce and anchovy, garnish with croquettes of shrimps, soft roes and oysters, trussed crayfish.

Normande.—Stuff with fish forcemeat, braise in white wine, remove skin, coat and garnish with Normande sauce.

Orly.—(*See* **Filets Merlans Orly**).

Pain.—In dome moulds well buttered, poach, dress and garnish with grooved mushrooms, slices of truffles. Bâtarde sauce.

Persil.—Cut in thick slices, poach in salt water, dress, decorate with lemon quarters. Nut brown butter and parsley.

Pompadour.—Soused fillets, egg and crumb, fry deep fat, dish in a circle, garnish with potato croquettes, fried parsley. Tartare sauce.

Provençale.—Fillets, poach, dish and coat with a reduction of tomatoes, parsley, garlic, shallots, mushrooms and cooking liquor.

Quenelles à la Morland.—Large quenelles stuffed with a poached soft roe, rolled in egg and chopped truffles, cook in clarified butter, dress in a circle, garnish centre with mushroom purée.

Valvins.—Skin one side, stud with anchovy fillets, wrap in oiled paper, roast. Serve separately a Ravigote sauce, combined with mustard maître-d'hôtel.

CABILLAUD OU MORUE FRAICHE — FRESH COD FISH

Boulangère.—Cut in large sections, season, bake in a dish with butter, surround with raw potatoes, cook for 30 minutes, when nearly done sprinkle with garlic, chopped parsley and crumbs.

Flamande.—In thick slices, poach with white wine, parsley, shallots. Dish and set a slice of lemon on each piece of cod. Coat with the reduced cooking liquor.

Portugaise.—Cut in slices, poach with white wine, chopped onions, garlic, parsley and dice of tomatoes, dress, coat with sauce.

CARPE — CARP

Alsacienne.—Stuff with fish forcemeat, poach in white wine and fish stock, dish on sauerkraut, serve plain boiled potatoes and the thickened reduced cooking stock.

Bière.—Braise with onions and celery, dice of spiced bread, faggot, moisten with beer, dish and coat with the reduced stock passed through the sieve, garnish with collops of poached roes.

Bleu.—(*See* **Truites au Bleu**).

Canotière.—Sprinkle a gratin dish with chopped shallots, add butter, place the carp stuffed with fish forcemeat, surround with raw mushrooms. Treat as for Bercy, sprinkle with crumbs and bits of butter, cook in oven, decorate with cooked crayfish, fried goujons and fleurons.

Chambord.—Stuff with fish forcemeat, skin the back, and stud with truffle, braise with red wine and fish stock, dish on a rice cushion, surround with quenelles decorated with truffles, fried soft roes, fillets of sole en goujon, grooved mushrooms, trussed crayfish, coat with the reduced stock.

Juive.—Cut the carp in sections, poach with a sauce made of chopped onions, shallots, white wine, fish stock, garlic, cayenne and faggot. When cooked, take out the sections and reshape the fish on a dish, reduce the cooking stock, finish the sauce with oil and coat the fish. Sprinkle with chopped parsley.

Juive à l'Orientale.—Same as above with the addition of saffron and chopped almonds to the sauce.

Juive aux Raisins.—Same as **Juive** with the addition of castor sugar, raisins, sultanas and currants soaked in warm water and vinegar and mixed with the sauce.

Polonaise.—Stuff, cook with red wine, onions, chopped shallots, faggot, large dice of spiced bread, reduce the stock, pass through the sieve and add pale caramel dissolved with vinegar, finish sauce with butter, cayenne pepper and sliced almonds, coat with sauce.

Quenelles de Carpe Morland.—(*See* **Quenelles de Brochet Morland**).

Royale.—In fillets, skin, cut in collops, poach in white wine and fish stock, dress in a circle, fill centre with Royale, garnish, coat with Normande sauce, decorate with slices of truffles.

COQUILLES SAINT-JACQUES — SCALLOPS

Curry.—Blanch, slice and toss in butter, chopped onions and tomato purée, finish cooking in fish Curry sauce. Serve with plain boiled rice and chutney.

Gratin.—Blanch, slice, braise in white wine and mushrooms cooking liquor, place in the shells and coat with gratin sauce, sprinkle with breadcrumbs and set in oven to gratin.

Mornay.—Same as above with Mornay sauce, glaze.

Nantaise.—Same as above, surround the scallops with bearded and poached oysters and mussels, coat with glazing white wine sauce—glazed.

Ostendaise.—Same treatment, garnish with shrimps, dice of mushrooms, oysters, coat with Nantua sauce, decorate with slices of truffles.

Parisienne.—Same treatment, border the shell with Duchesse potato, coat with white wine sauce and chopped truffles, glaze.

CRABES — CRABS

Are cooked in salt water and dressed in the shell, seasoned and mixed with mayonnaise sauce, decorated with hard yolk and white of eggs and chopped parsley.

CREVETTES — SHRIMPS OR PRAWNS

Aspic (en).—(*See* **Aspic** in **Fonds de Cuisine**).
Coquilles (en) (A).—In silver shells, border with Duchesse potato, coat the shrimps with white wine sauce combined with chopped truffles, glaze.
(B).—In shells bordered with Duchesse potato, the bottom garnished with asparagus heads and julienne of truffles cohered with butter, coat with Mornay sauce sprinkled with grated cheese, glaze.
Frites.—Alive, toss the shrimps in clarified butter or oil, cayenne pepper.
Mayonnaise.—(*See* **Mayonnaise de Saumon**).
Mousse.—Same preparation as all mousses. (*See* in **Entrées Volantes**).
Nature.—Poach in salt water, let cool, dress round a lemon or on crushed ice.

ECREVISSES — CRAYFISH

Aspic (en).—(*See* **Aspic**, in **Fonds de Cuisine**).
Bordelaise.—Tossed alive in butter with salt and cayenne pepper, add mirepoix à la Bordelaise, brandy, white wine and fish velouté, cook 10 minutes, dress in timbale, reduce the sauce, add fish glaze, coat the crayfish, chopped parsley.
Buisson (en).—Cook in court-bouillon, let cool in their own juice, serve hung by the tail on special tier stand, garnish with parsley.
Coquilles Cardinal.—In silver shells bordered with mashed potatoes, coated with Cardinal sauce and decorated with slices of truffles.
Liégeoise.—Same as **à la Nage.** Add some butter to the reduced cooking liquor.
Magenta.—Same as **Bordelaise,** add dice of tomatoes tossed in oil, finish the sauce with butter and add little basilic.
Soufflé Florentine.—(*See* **Soufflé Parmesan**, in **Savouries**). Add crayfish cullis to the preparation, dress the soufflé in layers alternating with truffles and crayfish tails.
Soufflés Froids (Petits).—Mousses of crayfish in small cocottes.
Soufflé Léopold de Rothschild.—Same preparation as Florentine, with the addition of asparagus heads.
Suprême au Champagne (*Cold*).—Cook in champagne Bordelaise fashion, let cool, shell the tails, make a mousse with the shells and cooking juice, decorate with the tails, truffles and chervil, glaze with aspic.
Timbale Marinière.—Cook in white wine with thyme and bay leaf powder, dress in timbale, reduce the juice and cohere with fish velouté, finish with butter, coat the crayfish, chopped parsley.
Timbale Nantua.—Same as **Bordelaise,** shell the tails, dress in timbale with a garnish of fish quenelles and mushrooms, coat with Nantua sauce, decorate with truffles.

Timbale Parisienne.—Dress in timbale on macaroni à l'Italienne, cohere the crayfish tails with sauce Nantua decorate with slices of truffles and raw mushrooms tossed in butter.

EPERLANS — SMELTS

Anglaise.—Split and bone, egg and crumb, cook in butter, maître-d'hôtel butter.

Bercy.—(*See* **Merlans Bercy**).

Buisson.—Egg and crumb, fry deep fat, serve on a napkin in a bushy way with parsley sprigs and lemon quarters.

Brochette.—Thread on a wooden skewer through the head, dip in milk, flour and fry.

Colbert.—(*See* **à l'Anglaise**). Fry and Colbert sauce.

Gratin.—(*See* **Merlans au Gratin**).

Grillés.—Split up the back, bone, flour, dip in melted butter and grill, lemon and fried parsley.

Meunière.—(*See* **Truite Meunière**).

Mousseline Alexandra.—(*See* **Mousseline de Saumon Alexandra**).

Mousse Royale.—Decorate the buttered inside of a charlotte mould with truffles, alternate with smelt fillets. Fill the mould with mousse and layers of truffles and fillets, poach, dish and decorate with grooved mushrooms, coat with mousseline, sauce combined with crayfish cullis.

Orly.—Egg and crumb, fry deep fat, Tomato sauce.

Richelieu.—Same as **à l'Anglaise** with slices of truffles on the maître-d'hôtel butter.

ESCARGOTS — SNAILS

Bourguignonne.—Cook in salt water and aromates for 3 hours, let cool in their own juice, remove the snails from the shells and trim the end. Boil the shells with carbonate of soda for 30 minutes, wash in cold water and dry. In each shell place a little **Beurre d'Escargots.** (*See* **Beurres Composés**) and the snail, and finish with the butter, serve very hot.

Chablaisienne.—The prepared shells are garnished with a reduction of white wine and chopped shallots cohered with meat glaze, finish same as above.

Dijonnaise.—Reduced wine and shallots as above mixed with marrow, salt, pepper, spices, garlic and chopped truffles, treat same as Bourguignonne with this preparation.

Mode de l'Abbaye.—Chopped onions partly fried in butter, add the cooked snails, season, flour, moisten with cream, simmer 15 minutes and cohere with yolks of eggs and butter.

Omelette.—(*See* **Omelette Bourguignonne**).

Vigneronne.—Toss the snails in butter with chopped shallots, garlic, salt and pepper, dip them in batter and fry in walnut oil.

Villebernier.—Mix the snails previously cleaned and cooked, with a reduction of shallots, red wine, vinegar and pepper, finished with butter, serve very hot.

ESTURGEON — STURGEON

(These fish are very rare, and are treated the same way as veal.)

FERA

Very scarce in England, comes from Swiss Lakes, and are treated Meunière, gratin, etc.

GOUJONS — GUDGEONS

(Are served fried and Meunière.)

GRENOUILLES — FROGS

Were not popular before the Great War, but now epicures generally appreciate them.

Fines Herbes (A).—Season, toss in butter, chopped parsley and lemon juice.
    (B).—Poach in white stock, the cooking liquor reduced, cohered with flour, butter and yolk of eggs, serve in timbale with chopped parsley.
Frites.—Dip in butter, fry and serve on a napkin with fried parsley and lemon.
Gratin.—(*See* **Sole au Gratin**).
Meunière.—Same preparation as for **Soles Meunière.**
Nymphes.—Poach in white wine, let cool, coat with Paprika chaud-froid sauce, dress and decorate with tarragon leaves and sprigs of chervil, glaze with aspic jelly.
Poulette.—Poach in white wine and mushroom stock, serve in timbale, coat with Poulette sauce.

HADDOCKS

(Are served grilled or poached with milk).

HARENGS — FRESH HERRINGS

Calaisienne.—Split and boned, stuff with the roes, shallots, parsley and mushrooms, all mixed with maître-d'hôtel butter, cook in papillotes.
Diable.—Spread with mustard, sprinkle with bread crumbs, grill. Ravigote sauce.
Farcis.—Split up the back and boiled, stuffed with chicken forcemeat and fine herbs, cook in papillotes.
Grillés.—Oiled and grilled, serve mustard sauce.
Meunière.—Season, flour and toss in butter, sprinkled with chopped parsley and lemon juice.

Nantaise.—Season roll in flour, egg and crumb, fry in clarified butter, coat with a sauce made with purée of roes, mustard and finished with butter.

Paramé.—Season, partly cook in butter, finish in papillotes with duxelles, cook in oven.

Portière.—Same as Meunière. When cooked spread with mustard and sprinkle with chopped parsely, nut brown butter.

HOMARDS — LOBSTERS

LANGOUSTES — CRAWFISH

Américaine.—Cut into sections, season with salt and cayenne pepper (*put aside the creamy parts and coral*) fry in butter and oil with chopped onions, add chopped shallots at the last moment, moisten with burnt brandy and white wine and fish stock, add chopped tomatoes and purée of tomatoes, cook 20 minutes dress in timbale, reduce the cooking sauce, and cohere with the creamy parts and chopped coral, together with a piece of butter, pass through a strainer and coat the pieces.

Bicard.—Cut into sections, season with salt, paprika and curry powder moisten with curry and paprika sauce.

Bordelaise.—Same as **Américaine,** but split lengthwise in two and add to the reduced sauce a Mirepoix Bordelaise.

Brunetière.—Cook in court-bouillon, border the carcase with duchesse potatoes, garnish the bottom with oysters, mushrooms, truffles, cohere with Victoria sauce, set the collops of lobster on it, and coat with same sauce added with mushroom purée, glaze.

Cardinal.—Cook in court-bouillon, split lengthwise, remove the flesh and cut into slices, coat the bottom of carcasses with Mornay and Américaine sauce mixed together, set the collops on it, cover with same sauce, sprinkle with grated cheese, glaze.

Carnot (*Cold*).—Decorate the collops with truffles and glaze with aspic, dress on a border of lobster mousse, decorate with aspic, sauce Russe.

Chantecler.—Split in halves, season and sprinkle with curry, toss in butter, remove the flesh, cut in collops, rice in the shell, dress the collops on the rice, coat with Nantua and curry sauce combined together, glaze, garnish with mushrooms, shrimps and cocks combs.

Chevreuse (*Cold*).—Cook in court-bouillon, remove the flesh cut in collops and glaze with aspic, dress on the carcass, alternating with large slices of truffles, garnish with asparagus heads and decorate with aspic. (*Separately*): Sauce mayonnaise.

Clarence.—(*See* **Homard Chantecler).** Cook in court-bouillon, Mornay sauce instead of Nantua, glaze, decorate with truffles.

Coquilles Mornay, Vin Blanc, Parisienne, Cardinal.—In silver shells bordered with mashed potatoes and coloured in oven, coat bottom with sauce of the name, place the collops of lobster and cover with same sauce, glaze.

Côtelettes.—Minced lobster, truffles and mushrooms, cohered with fish velouté, lobster butter and yolk of eggs, let cool, shape, like cutlets, egg and crumb, fry deep fat. Fried parsley, sauce required.

Côtelettes Arkangel (*Cold*).—Salpicon of lobster mixed with caviar and lobster mousse, dress in oiled cutlet moulds, let cool, unmould and coat with fish Chaud-froid sauce, dress round a Russian salad, decorate with aspic and truffles.

Crème.—Cut as for Américaine, toss in clarified butter, swill with brandy, add slices of truffles and cream, season, cook, remove the flesh, dress in timbale, coat with the reduced sauce mixed with fish glaze and lemon juice.

Croquettes.—Same as côtelettes, but in the shape of croquettes.

Curry.—Cut the flesh in large dice and add to a good curry sauce, serve plain boiled rice separately.

Dumas.—Cook in court-bouillon, remove the flesh, cut in collops, toss in butter, swill with white wine, add tomatoed half-glaze, dress in timbale. Fleurons.

Française.—Cut in sections, season with salt, pepper ,cayenne, toss in clarified butter, moisten with brandy and white wine, add carrots and onions partly cooked in butter, parsley and fish stock, cook, dress in timbale, coat with the reduced cooking juice cohered with fish velouté and butter.

Grammont. (*Cold*).—Glaze the collops with aspic, decorate with truffles and oysters, dress on half shells filled with lobster mousse, garnish with lettuces. and parsley sprigs.

Grillé.—Split alive in halves, season with salt and cayenne pepper, grill and baste with oil. (*Separately*): Diable sauce and melted butter.

Hollandaise.—Cook in court-bouillon, split in halves, serve with Hollandaise sauce and plain boiled potatoes.

Hongroise.—Operate same as for **Newburg à Cru,** but add chopped onions and pink paprika tossed in butter.

Majestic.—Same as **Bordelaise.** coat with Nantua sauce, decorate with truffles.

Mayonnaise (à la Sauce).—Cook in court-bouillon, split in halves, decorate with parsley sprigs, mayonnaise sauce.

Mayonnaise.—Place the collops on a bed of lettuce in a salad bowl, coat with mayonnaise sauce, decorate with anchovy fillets, capers and coral, etc.

Mornay au Gratin.— (Same as for **Cardinal** with Mornay sauce only).

Newburg (*With raw lobster*).—Cut up the live lobster, season and toss in butter and oil, swill with brandy and marsala, reduce, add cream and fish stock, cook 15 minutes, dish the fillets in timbale, thicken the sauce with the creamy parts and coral, finish with butter, strain and coat.

Newburg (*With cooked lobster*).—Cook in court-bouillon remove the meat from the shells, cut into regular slices, heat the slices in butter, moisten with brandy and madeira, dress in timbale and coat with a liaison of cream, yolk of eggs and brandy.

Palestine.—Cut the live lobster in pieces, toss in butter with mirepoix, moisten with burnt brandy, white wine and fish stock. withdraw the meat from the carapaces, pound the shells and remains of lobster, fry in oil with mirepoix, moisten with cooking liquor of the lobster, cook 15 minutes, reduce the liquid, thicken with the creamy parts and fish velouté, finish the sauce with curry butter. Set the pieces in a border of rice pilaw and coat with the sauce.

Parisienne (*Cold*).—Collops decorated and glazed with aspic, dress on the carapace, decorate with artichoke bottoms garnished with Russian salad and hard-boiled eggs, garnish same, decorate with truffles and coat with aspic.

Phocéenne.—Same as **Bordelaise,** add garlic, quarters of pimento, dice of red pimento, saffron rice, fish stock, dress in a circle, with rice in the middle.

Pompadour.—Cut as for **Américaine,** toss in butter and oil with mirepoix of carrots, onions, shallots, thyme, bay leaves, season, moisten with burnt brandy, cream and fish stock, finish cooking, remove the meat from the shells and dress in timbale, reduce the sauce and cohere with the creamy parts; mixed with butter, coat.

Russe.—Same as **Parisienne,** the collops of lobster are coated with mayonnaise combined with aspic.

Suédoise.—Soufflé, garnish with collops of lobster, poach, dish and coat with melted anchovy butter.

Suchet.—Collops warmed in white wine and julienne of vegetables, replace in the shells, reduce the juice with white wine sauce and Mornay ,coat the collops and glaze.

Thermidor.—Dress the collops in halved carapaces and coat with Bercy reduction and mustard cohered with Mornay sauce, glaze.

Trouville.—In a rizotto border, the centre garnished with collops of lobster, minced mushrooms tossed in butter, oysters mussels and slices of truffles, cohered with Normande sauce, coat with Mornay sauce, sprinkle with cheese and glaze.

Turque.—Same as **Américaine** remove the meat from the shells and dress in a border of pilaw rice.

Valençay.—Cook and cut the lobster in halves, cut the flesh in dice, replace in the carapaces and coat with a sauce made of red pimento, tomatoes, shallots and chopped parsley, tossed in butter, add tomato purée, meat glaze and English mustard, finish with butter, sprinkle with bread crumbs, set to gratin.

Vanderbilt.—Cook as **Bordelaise,** remove the flesh from the carapace, cut in collops, garnish the bottom of shell with a salpicon of crayfish tails, truffles and mushrooms, cohered with Américaine sauce, place the collops alternating with slices of truffles, coat with sauce and glaze.

Victoria.—Garnish the bottom of the carapaces with a salpicon of lobster, truffles, mushrooms, cohered with Victoria sauce. Place the collops and coat with sauce, glaze.

Washington.—Same as **Homard à l'Américaine.**

Winterthur.—Same as **Victoria,** with shrimps and shrimp sauce instead of the lobster salpicon, sprinkle with chopped truffles, glaze.

HUITRES — OYSTERS

Américaine (à l') (A).—Poach and serve in the shell with Américaine sauce.

(B).—Poach. Set in shell covered with bread crumb mixed with lemon juice, butter and cayenne pepper. Glaze.

Anglaise.—Set the oysters on a skewer alternating with a piece of bacon, cayenne and grill.

Bercy.—Poach and serve in the shell, coat with Bercy sauce, glaze.

Bretonne.—Reduction same as for Bercy sauce, add brown bread crumbs and cover the oysters.

Favorite.—Poach, put back in the shell with Mornay sauce, slice of truffle on the oyster and coat with Mornay, sprinkle with grated cheese, glaze.

Florentine.—Same as **Favorite,** with the shell bottoms garnished with spinach in leaves tossed in butter, no truffles.

Frites.—Egg and crumb and fry deep fat.

Mornay.—Same as **Favorite** without truffles.

Nature.—Are served plain on the flat shell, brown bread and butter, lemon or vinegar sauce combined with chopped shallots and pepper.

Stewed.—Poach in milk and cream, season with salt, pepper and nutmeg.

Villeroy.—Poach and trim, dip in Villeroy sauce, let cool, egg and crumb fry deep fat, fried parsley and lemon.

Vladimir.—Poach, set in shells, coat with Suprême sauce, sprinkle with brown crumbs and cheese, glaze.

LAITANCES — SOFT ROES

Aspic.—(*See* treatment of aspics).

Barquettes.—In boat shaped tartlet crusts garnished Ostendaise, Florentine or Mornay. (*See* **Garnitures**).

Beignets.—Dip in batter, fry deep fat.

LAMPROIE — LAMPREY

(*Same preparation as for Eels.*)

MAQUEREAU — MACKEREL

Anglaise.—Poach in court-bouillon with fennel, serve with boiled potatoes and purée of green gooseberries.

Batelière.—In fillets, grill, serve with sauce verte.

Beurre Noir.—In fillets, season, cook in butter, sprinkle with parmesan, capers and cover with black butter.

Bonnefoy.—In fillets, Meunière, Bonnefoy Bordelaise sauce, serve plain boiled potatoes.

Boulonnaise.—Cut into sections, poach in court-bouillon, dish and garnish with mussels, coat with Bâtarde sauce.

Calaisienne.—(*See* **Harengs Calaisienne**).

Chanoine.—In fillets, Meunière, decorate with fish forcemeat, forming the figure 8 on the skin side, poach in oven and garnish the 8 with a salpicon of shrimps, cohered with shrimp sauce.

Crème.—In fillets, coat with cream sauce.

Crème d'Anchois.—In fillets, cook in butter, coat with anchovy sauce.

Dieppoise.—In fillets, poach in white wine and mushrooms cooking liquor. Dieppoise garnish. White wine sauce.

Eau de Sel (à l').—In sections, poach, serve with butter sauce, capers and chopped green fennel.

Fines Herbes.—Poach whole or in fillets and coat with parsley sauce.

Flamande.—In fillets, poach and serve coated with fish velouté mixed with mustard.

Francillon.—Fillets, grill and dress on fried croûtons coated with anchovy butter, surround with straw potatoes, Tomato sauce.

Grillé.—Season and grill, serve with melted butter, Tartare or Ravigote sauce.

Indienne.—In fillets, poach, coat with curry sauce, serve plain boiled rice.

Meunière.—Season, flour and saute in butter, parsley and lemon juice.

Papillotes.—(*See* **Rougets en Papillotes).**

Persil.—In fillets, poach, coat with parsley sauce, plain boiled potatoes.

Printanière.—In fillets, poach, coat with Bâtarde sauce, mixed with Printanière butter, garnish with peas on one side and roundels of potatoes on the other.

Provençale.—(*See* preparation in **Rougets).**

Rosalie.—In fillets, sauté in walnut oil, coat with chopped onions, shallots and chopped garlic tossed in oil, add vinegar.

Vénitienne.—In fillets, poach in stock, coat with Vénitienne sauce.

MATELOTES

Canotière.—Different kinds of fish, moisten with white wine and burnt brandy, reduce the cooking juice, cohere with flour and butter, garnish with mushrooms, small glazed onions and crayfish.

Marinière.—Same as above with the addition of fish velouté and heart shaped croûtons.

Meunière.—Moisten with red wine, burnt brandy, cohere with flour and butter, garnish with crayfish and croûtons.

Meurette (*Rose*).—Different kinds of fish, moisten with red wine and burnt eau-de-vie, cohere with flour and butter, garnish with dry croûtons rubbed with garlic.

Normande (*Blanche*).—' me as above, with white wine, moisten with dry cider and burnt calvados, reduce and add fish velouté and cream, garnish with mushrooms, oysters, crayfish and heart-shaped croûtons.

Pochouse.—Different kinds of fish, moisten with red wine and burnt brandy, cohere with butter and flour, garnish with dice of bacon, glazed onions, mushrooms and croûtons.

Waterzoï.—Eel, carp, pike; cook in court-bouillon with salt, pepper, faggot, sage, celery and butter, garnish with slices of bread and butter.

MERLAN — WHITING

Anglaise.—Egg and crumb and fry deep fat.

Bercy.—Split up the back and bone, bake with butter, shallots, white wine and lemon juice, serve with the reduced stock.

Boîtelle.—Same as **Bonne-Femme** without the potato border.

Bonne Femme.—Cook in white wine with shallots, mushrooms and parsley, serve with the reduced stock. Potato border.

Cancalaise.—Poach, garnish with mussels, oysters an shrimps, coat with Normande sauce.

Cécilia.—Filleted, sauté in butter, garnished with asparagus heads, sprinkled with grated cheese, brown in butter.

Colbert.—(*See* **Eperlans Colbert).**

Colère (en).—Skin, the tail in the mouth, egg and crumb, fry deep fat, tomato sauce.

Diplomate.—Split up the back, remove the bone, stuff with chasseur, well reduced and tomatoed, poach, coat with Mornay sauce and glaze.

Doria.—Filleted, seasoned and fried in butter, garnished with cucumbers cooked in butter.

Duguesclin.—Poach, garnish with artichoke bottoms filled with shrimps, coat with shrimp sauce.

Fines Herbes.—Poach, drain, coat with parsley sauce.

Française.—Filleted dipped in milk, floured and fried, Tomato sauce.

Frits.—Filleted, egg and crumb, fry deep fat, serve with lemon, or Tartare sauce, etc.

Gratin.—In gratin dish with chopped shallots, mushrooms, white wine, bread crumbs, butter and lemon juice, cook in oven.

Hôtelière.—Split up the back, remove the bone, season, egg and crumb, fry deep fat, serve with maître-d'hôtel sauce and chopped mushrooms, mixed with half-glaze.

Jackson.—Same as **Sur le Plat** with onion sauce and parsley, garnish with small onions, coat with the reduced stock finished with butter, glaze.

Juive.—Filleted, marinaded, dipped in batter and fried, Tartare sauce.

Lorgnette.—Separate the fillets from the bones, proceeding from tail to head, remove the spine near the head, roll into scrolls with tail-ends inside, skewer through egg and crumb, fry deep fat.

Lorgnette au Gratin.—Same as above, but cover the fillets with fish forcemeat, before rolling and proceed as for gratin instead of frying.

Maître-d'Hôtel.—Remove the bone, egg and crumb, fry, serve with Maître-d'hôtel.

Marchand de Vins.—Poach in red wine with chopped shallots and fish stock, reduce the cooking liquor, add butter and coat the whiting.

Medicis.—Same as **à l'Anglaise** garnish with small grilled tomatoes, stuffed with Béarnaise sauce.

Meunière.—(*See* **Sole Meunière**).

Montreuil.—(*See* **Sole Montreuil**).

Mousse et Mousseline.—(*See* preparation in **Entrées Volantes**).

Niçoise.—(*See* **Rougets Niçoise**).

Orly.—(*See* **Sole Orly**).

Paupiettes.—(*See* **Paupiettes de Filets de Sole**).

Quenelles.—(*See* preparation in **Fonds de Cuisine**).

Richelieu.—(*See* **Eperlans**, same name).

Tabellion.—Prepare as for **Lorgnette**, poach, coat with white wine sauce, slices of truffles.

Verdi.—Filleted, poached and coated with Choron sauce, sprinkled with chopped truffles.

Vin Blanc.—(*See* **Soles Vin Blanc**).

MORUE SALEE — SALT CODFISH

Anglaise.—Poach, parsley, plain boiled potatoes and quarters of parsnips, egg sauce.

Bénédictine.—Poach, drain, cut in small pieces, remove skin and bones, pound it while hot and add cooked potatoes and oil, finish with milk, serve in buttered gratin dish, sprinkle with melted butter and set to colour in oven.

Benoîton.—Chopped onions tossed in oil and butter, add flour, moisten with red wine and fish stock, add crushed garlic, slices of cooked potato and flaked morue, cook 15 minutes, serve in gratin dish, sprinkle with crumbs and set to gratin.

Beurre fondu, Noisette, Noir.—Poach and serve with plain boiled potatoes and the required butter on top of the morue, chopped parsley.

Biscaïenne.—Poach and cut in dice, partly fried in olive oil with pounded garlic, chopped onions and tomatoes, dress in layers in a timbale, alternating with Spanish pimento, surround with heart shaped croûtons.

Brandade.—Same as **Bénédictine** with less potatoes and the addition of garlic, highly seasoned, dress in timbale, croûtons.

Brandade à la Crème.—Same preparation with cream instead of milk.

Brandade truffée.—Add chopped truffles and decorate with truffle in slices.

Crème.—Poached and flaked, coat with cream sauce, chopped parsley.

Créole.—Poach, drain and flake, dress in a gratin dish, the bottom garnished with cooked chopped onions and tomatoes à la Provençale, sprinkle with lemon juice and lightly brown butter, serve very hot.

Epinards.—Poached and flaked, and mixed with cooked spinach seasoned with salt, pepper, nutmeg, add anchovy fillets, cohere with Béchamel sauce, in a buttered gratin dish, sprinkle with crumbs, set to gratin.

Espagnole.—Same as **Biscaïenne**, add some potatoes in slices and coat the layers with tomato sauce. Serve in the timbale.

Fish balls.—One part of morue mixed with same quantity of potato Duchesse and shaped into balls, flatten, egg and crumb, cook in clarified butter, tomato sauce.

Gratin.—Poached and flaked, coat with Mornay sauce, glaze.

Hollandaise.—Poach and serve with plain boiled potatoes and Hollandaise sauce.

Indienne.—Coat with Curry sauce, serve with plain boiled rice.

Italienne.—Cut in dice, roll in flour, fry in oil, tomato sauce.

Lyonnaise.—Poached and flaked and mixed with Lyonnaise potatoes, add vinegar, dress in timbale, chopped parsley.

Provençale.—Poached and flaked and mixed with chopped onions and tomatoes, tossed in olive oil, add capers, black olives, parsley and crushed garlic, dress in timbale.

Soufflé.—Treat as all soufflés.

Valencia.—Dress in timbale, a layer of rice pilaff, alternate with flaked morue, tomatoes and roundels of fried onions, finish with rice, surround with hard boiled eggs cut in quarters, sprinkle with nut brown butter and crumbs, finish in oven, serve very hot.

MOSTELE — ROCKLING

(Same preparation as **Merlans**).

Côte-d'Azur.—In a buttered gratin dish, cut the mostèle lengthwise on the back, season with salt and pepper, cover with chopped tomatoes, julienne of lettuces and blanched celery, chopped shallots, minced mushrooms, thyme, bay leaves, crushed garlic, moisten with white wine and fish stock, lemon juice, add meat glaze and butter, cook in oven, remove the fish on another dish, reduce the cooking liquor, finish with butter and cream, coat with the sauce, sprinkle with drops of Hollandaise, glaze chopped parsley.

Lerina.—Split, remove the bones, cook in a gratin dish with mushrooms, chopped shallots, white wine and fish stock, surround the fish with tomatoes in dice and chopped parsley, sprinkle with lemon juice, cook in slow oven, basting occasionally.

MOULES — MUSSELS

Américaine.—Poached mussels, dress in silver shells, coat with Américaine sauce and bake in oven.

Bonne-Femme.—Same as **Marinière,** add julienne of mushrooms and celery.

Catalane.—Poach with chopped onions, parsley, pepper, remove one shell, make a sauce with the cooking liquor, add lemon juice, dress and coat with sauce.

Frites.—Poach, marinaded with lemon juice, oil and chopped parsley, drain, dip in batter and fry deep fat.

Marinière.—Stewed in their shells with shallots and white wine, cohere with beurre manié, add lemon juice, serve in timbale, chopped parsley.

Marseillaise.—Poach, remove one shell, dress and coat with Marseillaise sauce.

Poulette.—Dress in timbale, coat with Poulette sauce, chopped parsley.

Rizotto Toulonnaise.—Poach, remove the shells, cohere with white wine sauce, dress in a rizotto border.

Rochelaise.—Poach, remove one shell, stuff with prepared butter containing thyme, parsley, chopped shallots and lemon juice, set to gratin.

Villeroy.—Poach, remove the shells, drain, dip in Villeroy sauce, egg and crumb, fry deep fat.

MULETS — GREY MULLET

(Are served grilled with maître-d'hôtel butter.)

NONATS

(Same preparation as **Whitebait.**)

OMBRE CHEVALIER — CHAR

(Same preparation as **Trout.**)

Potted Char.—Poach in white wine with mirepoix, remove the fillets and lay them in an earthen pot, cover with clarified butter, cook in oven 15 minutes, keep in cool place.

PERCHE — PERCH

(Same preparation as **Alose.**)

POULPE — OCTOPUS

Ménagère.—Boil and trim, prepare same as for Bouillabaisse, add rice and cook.

RAIE — SKATE

Beurre Noir.—(*See* **Morue Beurre Noir**).

Foie de Raie en Coquilles.—Poach in court-bouillon, cut in slices, dress in shells bordered with mashed potatoes, lemon juice, chopped parsley, coat with Polonaise butter.

Fritot.—Cut in slices, marinade, dip in thin batter, fry deep fat, dish on serviette with fried onions and parsley.

Gelée.—Poach, dress in deep dish, cover with jelly made from the stock.

Gratin.—(*See* **Merlan Gratin**).

Provençale.—Cut in slices, dress in a gratin dish, cover with dice of tomatoes, add fish stock, anchovy essence and lemon juice, simmer 15 minutes, chopped parsley.

ROUGETS — RED MULLET

Baron Brisse.—Season, flour, grill, dress on dish with noisette potatoes, maître-d'hôtel butter.

Beurre fondu.—Grill, serve with melted butter flavoured with lemon juice.

Bordelaise.—Cook in clarified butter and serve with Bordelaise sauce.

Caisses à l'Italienne.—Fried or grilled, placed in paper cases with duxelles and tomatoe in dice, coated with Italienne sauce, sprinkled with brown crumbs and set to brown.

Caisses à l'Américaine.—In paper cases with pilaw rice, the mullet coated with Américaine sauce and slices of truffles.

Danicheff.—Poached with julienne of truffles, chopped shallots and fish stock, reduce, add butter and glaze.

Epicurienne.—Cook in butter, coat with cooked tomatoes, cohered with thickened gravy, Meunière butter on top.

Fenouil.—Seasoned and marinaded with oil, lemon juice, fennel, chopped parsley, mix the marinade with chopped fat bacon and cook in buttered paper.

Francillon.—Grilled and serve on toast same length, spread with anchovy butter, garnish with straw potatoes, tomato sauce, blended with anchovy butter.

Gratin.—(*See* **Merlans au Gratin**).

Grenobloise.—Flour and cook in butter, lemon slices, capers and chopped parsley on top, coat with Meunière butter.

Grillé.—Seasoned, floured, grilled, serve with maître-d'hôtel or anchovy butter.

Italienne.—Poached and coat with Italienne sauce.

Juive.—(*See* **Truite à la Juive**).

Livournaise.—Poached and coat with a reduction of shallots, dice of tomato, julienne of truffles and fish stock, finished with butter and glaze.

Maréchale.—In fillets, seasoned, dipped in melted butter and rolled in chopped truffles, cook in butter.

Marseillaise.—(*See* **Bouillabaisse**).

Montesquieu.—In fillets, seasoned, dipped in melted butter, rolled in chopped onions and parsley, cook in butter, lemon juice.

Nantaise.—Grilled and dish on a reduction of shallots, white wine and half-glaze, surround with lemon slices.

Niçoise.—Oiled and grilled, serve with chopped tomato tossed in butter, decorate with anchovy fillets, and black olives.

Papillotes.—Oiled and grilled, place on thick slice of ham and a layer of chopped mushrooms, mixed with brown sauce, wrapped in oiled paper and set in oven to swell when required.

Plat.—Baked in oven with white wine, oil, chopped onions and parsley, sprinkled with crumbs, lemon juice when serving.

Polonaise.—Cook in butter, coat with a reduction of fish stock cohered with yolk of eggs and cream, Polonaise butter when serving.

Portugaise.—Poached and coated with Portugaise sauce.

Provençale.—Cook in oil with chopped tomatoes, parsley, shallots and garlic, decorate with capers, black olives and anchovy fillets, Meunière butter.

Théodore.—Stuffed with chopped mushrooms and poached in white wine, coat with white wine sauce.

Trouvillaise.—Remove the bones, stuff and poach in white wine, dress and surround with lemon slices, Colbert sauce.

Vénitienne.—In fillets, cook in oil, garnish with stuffed olives and mushroom heads, coat with Vénitienne sauce.

Villeroy.—Filleted and marinaded, coated with Villeroy sauce, egg and crumb, fry deep fat, parsley, lemon.

SAINT-PIERRE — JOHN DORY

(*See preparation of* **Turbotin** *and* **Soles.**)

SARDINES AND ROYANS

Antiboise.—Remove bone, egg and crumb, fry in oil, dish round a heap of cooked tomatoes à la Provençale.

Basque.—Same as above, dress in a circle, fill centre with Béarnaise and capers.

Bonne Femme.—Cook the sardines in a gratin dish with chopped onions, tomatoes and white wine, sprinkle with bread crumbs and fennel, set to gratin.

Coulibiac.—(*See* **Coulibiac de Saumon**). With rice instead of semolina and Poutargue instead of vésiga.

Courtisane.—Stuffed with duxelles, poached in white wine, dress in a circle on toast, coat with vin blanc sauce, combined with spinach purée, glaze, surround with small potato croquettes.

Dartois.—(*See* **Dartois de Filets de Soles**).

Frites à l'Italienne.—Dipped in batter and fried in oil, tomato sauce.

Grillées.—Oiled and grilled, serve with maître-d'hôtel or Bercy sauce.

Havraise.—Same as **Courtisane,** without duxelles coat with white wine sauce, garnish with fried mussels, meat glaze.

Hyéroise.—Leeks par fried in butter, moistened with white wine and mushroons, cooking liquor, poach the stuffed sardines in this stock, dress on croûtons, reduce and cohere with yolk of eggs and butter, cayenne, chopped parsley, coat the sardines.

Ménagère.—Stuffed same as **Havraise,** cook in gratin dish, with chopped shallots, minced mushrooms and white wine, melted butter, when serving add lemon juice and parsley.

Niçoise (A).—Fillets stuffed with duxelles and rolled in paupiettes, wrapped in vegetable marrow blossoms and poached with consommé, coat with the reduced juice cohered with flour, butter and anchovy essence.

(**B**).—Boned and seasoned, stuffed with the following stuffing, chopped onion, fried in oil, fresh spinach cooked until completely evaporated, moisten with mussel cooking liquor, add the poached mussels, garlic and eggs, reshape the sardines, arrange them in gratin dish, sprinkle with crumbs and oil, set to gratin.

Pisane.—Stuffed fillets rolled in paupiettes, poached in wine and mushroom essence, dress in the centre of a spinach border, surround with quarters of hard-boiled egg, coat with cooking liquor mixed with tomatoes and Béchamel sauce, sprinkle with crumbs and grated cheese, set to gratin.

Provençale.—Prepare as for **Meunière,** cook in oil, flavoured with garlic, thyme, bay leaves. When serving add drop of vinegar and chopped parsley.

Saint-Honorat.—Same as **Colbert,** dress in a circle, garnish centre with tomatoes tossed in butter, surround with Paloise sauce.

Sicilienne.—Cook in butter, dress on lemon slices, sprinkle with chopped hard-boiled egg and capers, decorate with anchovy fillets, nut brown butter on top when serving.

Toulonnaise.—Boned and stuffed, poached, dressed in a circle, garnish centre with mussels, coat with white wine sauce.

Vivandière.—Paupiettes prepared as for **Niçoise** and placed in blanched cucumbers shaped to contain them, moisten with mushroom cooking liquor, cook in oven, dish and coat with thin tomato sauce, chopped parsley.

SAUMON — SALMON

Amiral.—Braised and coat with lobster sauce, garnished with collops of lobster, mushrooms, fried oysters, crayfish and slices of truffles.

Amiral Courbet.—Remove the skin when raw, mask with fish forcemeat, decorate with crescents of truffles, braise with champagne, garnish with quenelles, mushrooms, large truffles, fried smelts and crayfish, coat with Normande sauce.

Anglaise.—Suprême, egg and crumb and grilled, serve with melted butter and plain boiled potatoes.

Artois (à la d').—Cut the salmon in thick slices (known as " Darnes ") poach in fish stock, trim and dress on toasts, mask with shrimp sauce and decorate with fish forcemeat, poach in oven, garnish with quenelles, alternating with tartlets containing mushroom heads, truffles and prawns.

Beurre de Montpellier (*Cold*).—Darnes poached and cooled, trimmed and masked with Montpellier butter, decorate with truffles, hard-boiled eggs, anchovy fillets, olives, capers, tarragon leaves, glaze with aspic, surround with chopped aspic.

Brillat-Savarin.—Darnes poached in fish stock with white wine, onion, celery, leeks, carrots, trim and reduce the cooking liquor, adding butter and cream, coat with sauce and garnish with mushroom heads, olive-shaped truffles and stuffed crayfish.

Cadgery.—Cooked salmon trimmed and tossed in butter, mixed with pilaw rice and dice of hard-boiled egg, seasoned, dress in timbale.

Chambord.—Darnes poached in red wine, garnished with braised onions, mushrooms, fish quenelles, slices of truffles and fried soft roes, coat with Chambord sauce.

Condorcet.—In suprêmes, poach, sliced tomatoes and cooked cucumbers on each suprême, coat with white wine sauce, chopped parsley.

Coquilles Edward VII.—In shells, coated with Curry sauce, sliced truffles.

Coquilles Mornay.—In shells bordered with Duchesse potatoes, coated with Mornay sauce, glaze.

Coquilles Victoria.—Same as above with lobster collops and truffles and coated with Nantua sauce.

Côtelettes (en).—Cooked salmon, mushrooms and truffles, cohered with reduced Béchamel and yolk of eggs, let cool, shape, egg and crumb, fry deep fat, garnish to taste.

Côtelettes d'Artois.—Collops of salmon, cut the shape of a cutlet, mask with fish forcemeat, decorate with truffles, cook in butter, finish in oven. Coat with oyster sauce.

Côtelettes Clarence.—Place some thin slices of salmon in well buttered cutlet moulds, fill with salmon and lobster forcemeat, poach and dress in a circle on a forcemeat cushion. Place a mushroom head with a prawn stuck on it on each cutlet, serve with Newburg sauce.

Côtelettes Italienne.—Prepare as for **d'Artois,** coat with mushrooms purée, cohered with yolk of eggs, dip in egg and breadcrumbs mixed with grated cheese, fry deep fat, anchovy sauce.

Côtelettes Maréchale.—Same preparation as **d'Artois,** mask with fish forcemeat, decorate with truffles, cook in oven with clarified butter, dress on toasts, garnish with mushroom heads and crayfish, coat with Nantua sauce, sliced truffles, trussed crayfish and fleurons.

Côtelettes Pojarsky.—Three parts of raw salmon, one part of bread crumbs soaked in milk, seasoned and worked together to form a paste, shape like a cutlet, egg and crumb, fry in clarified butter.

Côtelettes Soubise.—(*See* **Côtelettes de Brochet**), with salmon for the forcemeat.

Coulibiac.—Roll some brioche paste into rectangles, spread in successive layers some kache or pilaw rice, collops of salmon, chopped vésiga, mushrooms, quarters of hard-boiled egg, onions and chopped parsley, finish with a layer of kache or pilaw rice, moisten the edges of the paste and join the two rectangles of paste together, make a slit on top, set to rise for 30 minutes and cook in oven, fill with melted butter when about to serve. The Coulibiac can be done with puff paste or in small turnover.

Note.—Vésiga must be soaked 3 or 4 hours and cooking process about 6 hours, it swells 5 times its size.

Court-bouillon.—Poach in court-bouillon dress on serviette, plain boiled potatoes and parsley sprigs, sauce to taste.

Darne Danoise.—Poached and garnished with potatoes, sauce Bâtarde finished with anchovy butter.

Darne Daumont.—Braise in white wine, trim and dress on toast, garnish with round quenelles, decorated with truffles, mushroom heads, crayfish and fried soft roes, coat with Nantua sauce.

Darne Dieppoise.—Poach, garnish and Dieppoise sauce.

Darne Ecossaise.—Poach, coat with white wine sauce, garnish with large Brunoise of vegetables and truffles.

Darne Grillée.—Oiled and grilled, serve with maître-d'hôtel butter.

Darne Lucullus.—Stud with truffles, braise in champagne, garnish with patties of crayfish tails, tartlets of soft roes, oyster mousseline, coat with the reduced liquor finished with crayfish butter.

Darne Nesselrode.—Remove the spine, stuff with lobster mousse and pike force-meat, cook in a raised pie paste, serve with Américaine sauce, finished with cream and garnished with oysters.

Darne Radziwill.—Large darne, poach, garnish the interior with a salpicon of shrimps and truffles cohered with shrimp sauce, decorate with slices of truffles, surround with cucumbers, cooked in butter, coat with white wine sauce.

Darne Régence.—Braise with white wine, garnish with large quenelles of fish forcemeat, prepared with crayfish butter, oysters, mushrooms and poached soft roes, coat with Normande sauce finished with truffle essence.

Darne Royale.—Braise with white wine, garnish with tartlets stuffed with crayfish tails, cohered with Nantua sauce, fish quenelles, mushroom heads, truffles and noisettes potatoes boiled à l'anglaise, coat with Normande sauce.

Darne Suzette.—Braise, dress on toast, make a border with forcemeat, poach in oven, garnish with Joinville garnish and sauce, surround with lobster sauce, truffles, julienne and mushrooms.

Darne Valois.—Poach, garnish with large noisettes potatoes cooked à l'anglaise, poached soft roes, trussed crayfish, coat with sauce Valois.

Darne Vernet.—Poach, trim, coat with white wine sauce, finished with anchovy butter and julienne of truffles ,mushrooms and hard white of eggs.

Darne Victoria (A).—Poach, dress on serviette, surround with shells containing salpicon of lobster and truffles cohered with lobster sauce.

(B).—Braise, trim, garnish the top with slices of lobster, coat with Victoria sauce, decorate with slices of truffles, fleurons.

Escalopes, Médaillons ou Suprêmes.—Are slices cut sideways from the fillet of salmon, or any other large fish, same preparation as for fillets of sole.

Froid en Darnes (*Cold*).—Dress on serviette with parsley sprigs at each end, serve with mayonnaise sauce or tartare, etc.

Froid Bellevue.—Skinned and trimmed, decorate the back and sides with truffles, white of eggs, tarragon leaves, chervil and yolk of eggs, etc., glaze with aspic.

Froid Chambertin.—Poach with Chambertin wine, let cool, decorate and coat with aspic, dish in a glass dish, filled with jelly made with the stock.

Froid Champagne.—Same as above with champagne instead of Chambertin.

Froid en Côtelettes à l'Alaska.—Cut the collops of salmon the shape of a cutlet, poach, drain and cool, coat with chaud-froid sauce and glaze with aspic, dress in a circle round a pyramide of Russian salad. Serve with mayonnaise.

Froid en Côtelettes Arkangel.—Same preparation as **Homard Arkangel**, with salmon instead of lobster.

Froid en Côtelettes Suédoises.—Same as **Alaska,** without the chaud-froid sauce.

Marcel Prévost.—Poached and braised, dress in timbale on a bed of spinach, surrounded with poached mussels, Marinière sauce.

Mayonnaise de Saumon.—(*See* **Mayonnaise Homard).**

Médaillons Médicis.—Egg and crumb, grill, garnish with small poached tomatoes filled with Béarnaise sauce.

Médaillons Metternich.—Poached with Madeira and chopped truffles, dress on a rice cushion, coat with the reduced stock, mixed with Génevoise sauce, and finished with butter and cream, garnish with large truffles scooped and filled with salpicon of truffles cohered with cream, glaze, Fleurons.

Médaillons Parisienne.—Poach in red wine, garnish with crayfish tails, mushroom heads, poached oysters, small fish croquettes coat with Génevoise sauce mixed with the reduced cooking liquor.

Médaillons Turenne.—Poach, garnish with slices of cucumber and tomato, coat with white wine sauce finished with anchovy essence.

Mousse et Mousselines.—(*See* preparation in **Fonds de Cuisine).**

Moscovite (*Cold*).—Same as for **Belle-Vue,** coat with mayonnaise mixed with aspic, decorate and dress on a bed of salade Russe, garnish with artichoke bottoms, filled with salade Russe and half eggs filled with caviar, glaze with aspic.

Norvégienne (*Cold*).—Same as for **Belle-Vue,** dress on dish, the bottoms previously coated with aspic jelly, place a semolina cushion on the aspic and set the salmon on it, decorate with shrimps, small cucumber timbales, filled with purée of smoked salmon, half eggs stuffed with shrimps mousseline, small tomatoes, beetroot barquettes garnished with shrimps cohered with mayonnaise sauce, serve with Russian sauce.

Parisienne (*Cold*).—Trim the middle of the salmon, poach, remove the skin in such way as to make a rectangle, coat the bare part with mayonnaise sauce mixed with aspic, make a border with Montpellier butter, decorate, place the salmon on a rice cushion, coat the bottom of dish with aspic, garnish with artichoke bottoms filled with Macédoine of vegetables, cohered with mayonnaise sauce.

Riga (*Cold*).—Prepare as for **Parisienne,** garnish with cucumber, timbales stuffed with macédoine of vegetables cohered with mayonnaise, tartlets garnished with same; place on each a carcase of crayfish filled with crayfish mousseline, alternate with half eggs filled with caviar.

Royale (*Cold*).—Operate same as **Moscovite,** mask the fish with cold mousse of salmon before coating with the mayonnaise, a crown for decoration.

Salade (en) (*Cold*).—Same as for **Mayonnaise.** but the ordinary salad seasoning instead of the mayonnaise sauce.

Santos- Dumont (*Hot*).—Same process as for **Marcel Prévost,** dress in papillotes with poached oysters, giving the shape of a dirigible balloon to the papillotes.

Sévigné (*Cold*).—Darne poached and trimmed, dress on a dish, garnish cavity with a mousse of crayfish, decorate with tarragon leaves and crayfish tails, surround with cucumber timbales filled with crayfish tails cohered with mayonnaise and small tomatoes scooped and filled with crayfish mousse, glaze with aspic.

F

SOLES AND FILLETS OF SOLES

Adrienne.—Fillets, folded and poached coated with Polignac sauce, garnished with soft roes and tartlets filled with crayfish tails cohered with Nantua sauce. Fleurons.

Aiglon.—Poached and dressed on mushrooms purée, coat with white wine sauce mixed with Soubise, a thread of meat glaze. Fleurons.

Alexandra (A).—Fillets, poach in fish stock, coat with Nantua sauce, sliced truffles on each fillet, glaze. Fleurons.

(B).—Fillets, poach, decorate with tomatoes, mushrooms and truffles, dress in a circle, garnish with collops of lobster and noisettes potatoes cooked à l'anglaise, asparagus heads between each fillet, coat with white wine sauce and glaze.

Alice.—Poach in buttered fish dice, with fish stock, send as it is to the dining room, (*Separately*): Send raw oysters, chopped onions, powdered thyme, powdered salted biscuits and finish in the dining room.

Alphonse XIII.—Fillets, cook in butter, dress on half egg plant fried in oil, serve with tomato sauce mixed with julienne of pimento.

Alsacienne.—Filleted and poached, dressed on sauerkraut, coated with Mornay sauce and glazed.

Ambassade.—Filleted and poached, garnished with slices of truffles and lobster collops, coat with the reduced stock mixed with cream and lobster butter, glaze.

Ambassadrice.—Fillets rolled round stuffed crayfish, dress in timbale, garnish and sauce Normande.

Amélie.—Poached, border with sliced truffles and potatoes, coat with Nantua sauce.

Américaine.—Filleted and poached, garnished with lobster collops and coat with Américaine sauce.

Amiral.—Poached and garnished with small onions and mushroom heads, coat with white wine sauce.

Andalouse.—Filleted, masked with fish forcemeat and julienne of capsicums rolled in paupiettes, poached and dressed on half tomatoes, filled with rizotto and poivrons and placed on slices of egg plant, fried in oil, nut brown butter.

Anglaise.—Fillets, egg and crumb, cook in clarified butter, maître-d'hôtel butter.

Archiduc.—Poached with madeira, whisky, port wine and fish stock, reduce the cooking liquor, add butter and cream and brunoise of vegetables and truffles, coat with sauce. Fleurons.

Archiduc en Paupiettes.—Filleted and coated with fish cream, rolled and poached, placed in timbale, partly filled with salpicon of lobster, truffles and mushroom cohered with Normande sauce, coat fillets with thin Nantua sauce, slices of truffles, oysters Villeroy and fish quenelles.

Argenteuil.—Poached and coated with white wine sauce, garnished with white asparagus heads.

Arlésienne.—Poached with chopped onions, dice of tomatoes, crushed garlic, parsley and fish stock, garnished with shaped vegetable marrow and crisp fried onions, coat fish with the reduced cooking liquor.

Armenonville.—Filleted, folded and egged and crumbed, fried deep fat, dish up in a circle, garnish the centre with cucumber à la crème, Nantua sauce round the base, a crayfish claw at each end of fillet.

Armoricaine.—Filleted and poached, dish up and place a poached soft roe on the fillets and a poached oyster on the roe, garnish with collops of lobster, coat with Américaine sauce, finished with cream. Fleurons.

Aspic (*Cold*).—(*See* preparation in **Fonds de Cuisine).**

Bagration (*Hot*).—Poached and coated with Mornay sauce and julienne of truffles, glazed.

Bagration (*Cold*).—Poached folded fillets, dressed on collops of lobster, and dished up round a Russian salad, chopped aspic.

Baron Brisse.—Filleted and stuffed with fish forcemeat, rolled in paupiettes, poached and dressed on a hollow border made of fish forcemeat. Centre garnished with crayfish tails coated with American sauce, the paupiettes coated with white wine sauce, slices of truffles.

Batelière.—Filleted, stuffed, folded and poached; placed on barquettes filled with salpicon of shrimps and mussels cohered with Vin blanc sauce, a fillet of sole en goujon at each end of barquette, coat fillets with parsley sauce.

Béatrice.—Rolled in paupiettes and poached, dressed on large mushrooms, the fillet encircled with poached roe, a slice of truffle and prawns stuck in top of each fillet. Coat with white sauce blended with shrimp butter.

Beaumanoir.—Poached and coated with half white wine sauce and half American sauce; garnished with oysters Villeroy and slice truffles.

Bedfort.—Grilled sole, dress on maître-d'hôtel butter, surround with rounds of toast masked with mushroom purée and half with spinach, and coat with Mornay sauce, glaze the toast.

Belles de Nuit.—Filleted and stuffed with fish forcemeat mixed with prawn butter and poached oyster, folded and poached. Dressed in a circle, garnished with noisette potatoes, coated with Normande sauce, finished with shrimp butter.

Bénédictine.—Filleted, poached and dressed in a circle round a heap of brandade of morue, coated with white wine sauce.

Bercy.—Poached with shallots and chopped parsley, white wine and fish stock. Reduce the stock, add butter, and coat the fish, glaze.

Biron.—Poached and coated with Génevoise sauce and chopped truffles. Fleurons.

Boïeldieu.—Filleted and stuffed with fish forcemeat mixed with shrimps, truffles and crayfish tails, rolled in paupiettes, dressed on flat lobster croquettes, coated with Nantua sauce, slices of truffles.

Boitelle.—Same as **Bercy,** with the addition of sliced mushrooms.

Bolivar.—Boned and stuffed with fish forcemeat combined with soubise and tomato purée, poached and coated with white wine sauce mixed with soubise sauce.

Bonaparte.—Poached and coated with the reduced liquor mixed with butter and cream, glazed and garnished with small potatoes, chopped parsley.

Bonne-Femme.—Same as **Boitelle,** with a border of slices of steamed potatoes.

Bordelaise.—Poached in red wine with chopped shallots, coated with the reduced stock mixed with Bordelaise sauce.

Bosniaque.—Poached and coated with white wine sauce mixed with julienne of truffles, carrots, mushrooms, seasoned with paprika.

Bouillard.—Skinned both sides, cooked in cream, seasoned, dressed and garnished with crayfish tails. Coat with the reduced liquor, decorate with truffles.

Bourguignonne.—Poached in red wine, garnished with small onions and mushroom heads, coat with red wine sauce made with the cooking stock.

F

Breteuil.—Poached in court-bouillon, garnished with barquettes filled with soft roes. Serve with melted butter and plain boiled potatoes.

Bretonne.—Poached and garnished with mushroom heads, coated with Bretonne sauce, glazed. Fleurons.

Bréval.—Same as **Bonne-Femme,** with chopped tomatoes.

Café-de-Paris.—Same as **Au-Plat,** with julienne of truffles, garnished with asparagus heads and mushrooms, with prawns stuck on it, oysters on each side of mushrooms. Victoria sauce all round.

Calypso (*Cold*).—Rolled in paupiettes and poached, scooped and filled with crayfish mousseline and salpicon of crayfish tails. Place in half tomatoes, dress in a circle, decorate with soft roes and crayfish tails, chopped aspic.

Campanoff.—Poached and coated with half white wine sauce and half red wine sauce, a thread of Victoria sauce to finish.

Cancalaise.—Filleted, folded and poached in oyster cooking liquor and butter. Dress in a circle, centre garnished with shrimps and poached oysters, coated with Normande sauce.

Caprice.—Filleted, dipped in butter and crumbs, grilled. Dressed on half bananas, cooked in butter. Robert sauce.

Cardinal.—Filleted, stuffed with fish forcemeat mixed with lobster butter, folded and poached. Dressed in a circle garnished with lobster collops, coated with Cardinal sauce, sprinkled with coral.

Carême.—Poached, garnished with poached soft roes, mushroom heads and oysters. Coated with white wine sauce combined with celery purée. Slices of truffles.

Carlier.—Filleted, cut in goujons, tossed in butter, meunière fashion. Dressed on creamy macaroni. Coated with Boitelle sauce flavoured with port wine, glazed.

Carmen.—Filleted and poached, garnished with slices of tomatoes. Coat with a Béarnaise reduction mixed with white wine sauce, tarragon leaves placed crosswise on the tomatoes.

Casanova.—Poached, decorated with sliced truffles, surrounded with oysters and mussels, coated with white wine sauce. Fleurons.

Castiglione.—Filleted and poached, bordered with sliced, steamed potatoes, collops of lobster and mushrooms on each fillet. Coated with white wine sauce blended with cream sauce, glazed.

Catalane.—Filleted and rolled in paupiettes, poached and arranged in half tomatoes filled with cooked minced onions. Coated with white wine sauce and glazed.

Cecil Rhodes.—Filleted, folded and poached in oyster cooking liquor; garnished with asparagus heads and truffles olive-shaped, poached oysters in middle. Coated with the reduced stock mixed with butter and glazed.

Cécilia.—Filleted, cooked in butter, garnished with asparagus heads, sprinkled with cheese, and glazed.

Chambertin.—Poached in red wine, drained and trimmed. Coat with the reduced liquor mixed with red wine sauce. Glazed, garnished with fillets of sole en goujons.

Chambord.—(*See* **Carpe à la Chambord**).

Champagne.—Poached in champagne, garnished same as **Chambertin,** and coated with champagne sauce.

Champignons.—Poached with minced mushrooms, coated with white wine sauce mixed with the reduced cooking liquor. Fleurons.

Charlotte (*Cold*).—Filleted, folded and poached, dressed round a mousse of soft roes and   horse-radish, decorated with chervil and coral, glazed with aspic.

Chauchat.—Poached, bordered with sliced steamed potatoes. Coated with white wine sauce and glazed. Fleurons.

Chauchart.—Filleted, folded and poached, garnished with collops of lobster and mushroom heads. Coat with white wine sauce and glazed. Sliced truffles and thread of meat-glaze.

Cherbourg.—Rolled in paupiettes and poached, dressed in a circle, centre garnished with shrimps, oysters and mussels. Coated with shrimp sauce.

Chérubin.—Filleted, folded and poached, dressed in croustades, garnished with mushrooms and cream. Coat one fillet with white wine sauce, and alternate with others coated same sauce with the addition of smoked salmon purée.

Chevalière.—Filleted and folded, inserted in crayfish shells, poached and dressed in a circle on a border of fish forcemeat. Centre garnished with truffles, oysters, mushrooms and crayfish tails cohered with American sauce. Surround with a thread of white wine sauce.

Chivry.—Filleted, folded and poached, dressed in a circle, and coated with Chivry sauce. Fleurons.

Choiseul.—Poached and coated with white wine sauce added with julienne of white truffles.

Choisy.—Poached and coated with white wine sauce, with julienne of lettuces and truffles added.

Cingalaise.—Filleted and poached, dressed in a circle, centre garnished with pilaw rice mixed with julienne of green and red pimentoes. Coat the fillets with curried white wine sauce.

Clara-Wart.—Filleted and cut in goujons, cooked in butter with celeriac and dice of artichoke bottoms. Meunière butter.

Claremont.—Poached and coated with white wine sauce mixed with dice of tomatoes and chopped parsley. Croûtons.

Clarence.—Filleted and poached, garnished with poached soft roes and shrimps. Coated with white wine sauce mixed with anchovy essence.

Claudinette.—Filleted, folded and poached with mirepoix, white wine, tomatoes, chopped parsley, reduced and mixed with lobster cullis. Dressed in paper cases on a Joinville garnish, coat with sauce, cover with another paper case, and put in oven before serving.

Cléopâtre.—Boned and stuffed with truffled fish forcemeat, poached and coated with white wine sauce mixed with truffles, julienne and the reduced stock, glazed.

Colbert.—Sole opened along the back, bread-crumbed and fried. Remove part of the bone and fill bare place with maître-d'hôtel butter.

Condé.—Filleted, poached and coated with white wine sauce, a thread of tomato purée all round and in the middle of the dish glaze.

Condorcet.—(*See* **Suprême de Saumon Condorcet).**

Coquelin.—Rolled in paupiettes with oysters in the middle, the fillets previously coated with tomatoed fish forcemeat, poached and dressed in timbale on half tomatoes cooked in oven. Coat with white wine sauce and glazed. Sliced truffle and lobster collops on each paupiette.

Cooch Bihar.—Filleted, cooked in butter, dressed in half egg-plants fried in oil and stuffed with gratin forcemeat made with the egg plant, tomatoes, duxelles, chopped onions and shallots, garlic. Sprinkle with crumbs and set to gratin. Meunière butter.

Cornelain.—Poached and coated with white wine sauce, sprinkled with chopped truffles and lobster eggs. Fleurons.

Courgettes.—Filleted and cooked in gratin dish, with slices of vegetable marrow, dice of tomatoes, thyme, lemon juice. Sprinkled with bread crumbs and set to gratin. Serve in the dish.

Court-Bouillon.—Poached in court-bouillon, with vegetables à la Russe and white wine. Serve with the vegetables and the cooking liquor, chopped parsley, Hollandaise sauce and melted butter.

Crécy.—Filleted and folded, stuffed with fish forcemeat mixed with Crécy purée. Poached and coated with the reduced stock, garnished with artichoke bottoms, filled with carrot balls.

Crevettes.—Poached and garnished with shrimp tails, coated with shrimp sauce.

Cubat.—Poached and dressed on mushroom purée. Coated with Mornay sauce and glazed. Slices of truffles on top.

Czarine.—Filleted, folded and poached. Coated with white wine sauce, mixed with cream and grated horse-radish. Garnished with rounds of toast masked with caviar.

Dartois.—Puff paste rolled flat and cut into rectangles, masked with forcemeat. Place thin slices of fillets on it and cover with the puff paste, glazed and cooked in oven.

Daumont (A).—Boned and stuffed with fish forcemeat, poached and coat with Nantua sauce, Daumont garnish.

(B).—Rolled in paupiettes, coated with Normande sauce, large mushrooms filled with crayfish tails cohered with Nantua sauce on each paupiette, dress in a circle, alternating with stuffed crayfish and fried soft roes.

Dauphine.—Filleted, stuffed and folded, poached. When cold, masked with reduced Normande sauce, finished same as Villeroy. Serve with Tartare sauce mixed with dice of tomatoes.

Deauvillaise.—Poached with cream and chopped onions. Coat with the reduced stock mixed with butter, surround with small puff paste shapes.

Déjazet.—(*See* **Filets de Sole à l'Anglaise**). Dress on tarragon butter, and decorate with tarragon leaves.

Demi-Deuil.—Filleted, poached and coated with white wine sauce and cream. Slices of truffles in the middle, a thread of meat glaze round. Fleurons.

Desmoulins.—Poached with chopped shallots, dice of tomatoes, minced mushrooms, parsley, white wine and fish stock. Reduce, add butter and coat the fish.

Dieppoise.—Poached and coated with white wine sauce mixed with the reduced stock, Dieppoise garnish.

Diplomate.—Poached and coated with Diplomate sauce. Slices of truffles.

Dominos (*Cold*).—Poached fillets of soles cut the size of a domino, coated with chaud-froid sauce and decorated same as dominoes. Placed on rectangles of fish mousse and caviar same size and glazed with aspic. Dressed on a pyramid of chopped aspic.

Donia.—Filleted, stuffed and folded, poached and dressed in a circle on a rice border. Centre garnished with crayfish tails, truffles and mushrooms cohered with Nantua sauce. Coated with white wine sauce.

Dorée.—Cooked in butter, and served with slices of lemon on top.

Doria.—Cooked in butter and garnished with cooked, shaped cucumbers.

Dragomiroff.—Poached and coated with Mornay sauce, glazed and surrounded with mussels in half shells.

Dubois.—Filleted and cut in goujons, cooked in butter and coated with white wine sauce mixed with meat glaze and butter, and finished with lemon juice.

Dugléré (*Hot*).—(*See* **Turbotin** same name).

Dugléré (*Cold*).—Filleted, poached in white wine with tomatoes in dice, chopped onions, parsley, reduce the cooking liquor, cool, and mix with mayonnaise sauce, coat the fillets, serve very cold.

Duguesclin.—Poached and coated with shrimp sauce, garnished with artichoke bottoms filled with shrimps.

Duse.—Filleted, stuffed, folded, poached, dressed in a savarin mould lined with rizotto, dished and coated with Mornay sauce, set to gratin. Centre garnished with salpicon of shrimps cohered with white wine sauce, sprinkled with chopped truffles.

Eléonore.—Filleted, poached and dressed on julienne of lettuces. Coated with white wine sauce and paprika.

Emmanuel II.—Cooked in butter, swill pan with fish stock and Xérès wine, reduced and mixed with cream and butter, coated and garnished with artichoke bottoms filled with truffles and mushrooms cohered with cream.

Epigramme.—Filleted, stuffed, folded, egged and crumbed. Grilled.

Escoffier (*Cold*).—Rolled in paupiettes, half stuffed with fish forcemeat mixed with lobster butter, and the other half with forcemeat mixed with chopped truffles, poached. When cold cut in four, and dress in a mould lined with aspic, alternating the colours. The mould filled with crayfish mousse. Dish up on serviette.

Espagnole.—Cooked in butter, dressed on tomatoes cooked in oil. Garnished with fried onions and julienne of capsicums.

Etouffé.—Cut in sections, partly cooked in butter and finished in cocotte with lemon juice, chopped parsley.

Excelsior.—Rolled in paupiettes and poached, dressed in a circle on a cushion. Centre garnished with salpicon of lobster à la Newburg, the paupiettes coated with Normande sauce mixed with julienne of musrooms. Slice truffles on each paupiette.

Favorite.—In buttered dariole moulds, lined with strips of fillets of sole and filled with fish mousse. Poached, dished up and coated with white wine sauce, a thread of Nantua sauce round and sliced truffles on each.

Fécampoise.—Filleted and poached, garnished with mussels and shrimps. Coated with shrimp sauce.

Fermière.—Poached with vegetables, white wine and fish stock, reduced and mixed with cream and butter. Fleurons.

Fines Herbes.—Poached and coated with white wine sauce. Sprinkled with chopped parsley.

Flaubert.—Poached and garnished with mushrooms and shrimps. Coated with white wine sauce containing paysanne of vegetables. Glazed.

Floréal.—Rolled in paupiettes, dressed in cocotte containing asparagus heads à la crème, coated with white wine sauce blended with Printanier butter, decorated with carrots and chervil.

Florentine.—Poached and dressed in a gratin dish on a bed of spinach, coated with Mornay sauce and glazed.

Foyot.—Same as **Bercy** with the additions of meat glaze.

François. (I*er*).—Filleted and poached in white wine, with butter, chopped onions, dice of tomatoes, minced mushrooms, parsley, coated with the reduced stock.

Frite (A).—Skinned and trimmed, dipped in milk and floured, fried deep fat, fried parsley and lemon.

(B).—Egged and crumbed, fried deep fat, parsley and lemon.

Gallia.—Poached with white wine, fish stock, julienne of fresh truffles and lettuces, lemon juice, coated with the reduced stock mixed with meat glaze and cream. Fleurons.

Galliéra.—Poached with same garnish as above, with the addition of julienne of mushrooms and not meat glaze. Coated and glazed.

Georges Sand.—Poached and dressed; place in middle of a row of quenelles, and garnish on each side with crayfish tails. Coated with Normande sauce blended with crayfish butter.

Georgette.—Filleted, folded and poached, Placed in baked potatoes scooped and garnished with crayfish tails and mushrooms. Coated with Nantua sauce. Slices of truffles.

Gillet.—Poached dressed and bordered with Duchesse potatoes. Coated with white wine sauce sprinkled with cheese. Set to gratin.

Giselle.—(*See* **Sole Crevette**). With the addition of asparagus heads.

Gismonde.—Poached and coated half white wine sauce and half Archiduc sauce.

Goujons (A).—Filleted and cut the size of gudgeons. Seasoned floured after having been dipped in milk, and fried deep fat. Fried parsley and lemon.

(B).—Cut same way. Egged and crumbed and fried deep fat. Serve with diable or horse-radish sauce, etc.

Gourmets.—Poached with fish stock, mushrooms cooking liquor, and port wine.

Grand-Duc.—Filleted, folded and poached, dressed in a circle. Coated with Mornay sauce and glazed. Garnished with asparagus heads and crayfish tails. Slices of truffles.

Granville.—Poached and garnished with shrimps, mushrooms and truffles. Coated with white wine sauce.

Gratin.—(*See* **Merlan au Gratin**).

Grecque.—Filleted and fried in oil, dressed on pilaw rice and coated with tomato sauce mixed with dice of pimentoes.

Grenobloise.—(*See* **Truite** same name).

Grillée.—Floured, oiled and grilled, sauce to taste.

Grimaldi.—Rolled in paupiettes or folded, poached and dressed in timbale on a spaghetti bed, coated with Nantua sauce, sliced truffles.

Gringoire.—Filleted, poached and dressed, garnished with poached soft roes and collops of lobster. Coated with American sauce finished with cream.

Havraise.—Poached, coated with Bercy sauce, garnished with stuffed mussels, egged and crumbed and fried.

Hélène.—Poached, dressed on a bed of fresh noodles. Coated with Mornay sauce and glazed.

Héliopolis.—Filleted, folded and poached, dressed on half lobster shell garnished with salpicon of lobster, mushrooms and truffles cohered with white wine sauce, place a collop of lobster on the fillet and coat with Normande sauce mixed with julienne of truffles and mushrooms, glazed.

Héloïse.—(*See* **Sole Bercy**). chopped mushrooms instead of shallots.

Henriette.—Filleted and cut in gudgeons, poached and cohered with white wine sauce and paprika, dressed in baked potatoes, coated with Mornay sauce, sprinkled with chopped walnut, glazed.

Hollandaise.—Poached in water, milk and salt, dressed on serviette with plain boiled potatoes, served with Hollandaise sauce.

Hongroise.—Filleted, folded and poached with chopped onions and paprika, dice of tomatoes, white wine and fish stock, coat with the reduced stock and glaze.

Horley.—Filleted, marinaded and dipped in batter, fried and dressed on serviette with fried parsley, Remoulade sauce.

Hôtelière.—Cooked in butter, dressed on maître-d'hôtel butter, mixed with duxelles, bordered with lemon slices.

Huîtres.—Same as **Sole Vin Blanc,** garnished with poached oysters. Fleurons.

Impératrice.—Filleted, folded and poached, dressed in a circle on toasts, the centre garnished with oysters, coated with Normande sauce, slices of truffles.

Impériale.—Poached and garnished with crayfish tails and poached soft roes, coated with white wine sauce mixed with julienne of truffles. Fleurons.

Indienne.—Filleted, folded and poached, dressed in a circle, centre garnished with pilaw rice, coated with Curry sauce.

Infante.—Same as **Mornay** with mushroom purée underneath.

Ismaïl (A).—Filleted and poached with minced mushrooms, Curry and fish stock, add white grapes, coated with the reduced cooking liquor, mixed with butter and glazed.

(**B**).—Filleted, folded and poached, dressed in the centre of pilaw rice border, adding green peas and dice of red pimento, coated with the reduced stock mixed with butter.

Italienne (*Cold*).—Filleted and cut in strips poached with red capsicums, dressed in a border mould, lined with aspic jelly, fill the mould with aspic, and dish up, on a semolina cushion, centre garnished with Italienne salad, Mayonnaise sauce.

Ivanhoë.—Rolled in paupiettes, stuffed with haddock forcemeat, placed in cocotte on a bed of artichoke bottoms, grilled mushrooms on the paupiette, moistened with whisky and lemon juice, poached in oven and serve.

Jean-Bart.—Filleted and poached and dressed round a dôme of shrimps, mussels and mushrooms cohered with reduced Béchamel sauce. Coated with Normande sauce, surrounded with half mussels, coated with Mornay sauce and glazed.

Jeannette.—Filleted, stuffed with fish forcemeat mixed with foie gras purée, rolled in paupiettes and poached, coated with white wine sauce, mixed with cream, slice of truffles on each paupiette. Can be served cold with aspic jelly.

Jeovah.—Filleted and poached, dressed on salpicon of asparagus heads and shrimps cohered with white wine sauce, coated with Mornay sauce and glazed.

Jetée Promenade.—Filleted and placed in a gratin dish alternating with hearts of braised celery cut lengthwise, collops of mushrooms and truffles, moistened with half white wine and half fish stock, cooked in oven basting occasionally.

Joinville.—Filleted and folded, place a crayfish claw at the end of each fillet, poached, dressed in timbale in a circle. The centre garnished with Joinville, slices of truffles on each fillet, coated with Joinville sauce.

Jouffroy.—Poached in white wine with sliced mushrooms, coated with white wine sauce, garnished with small bouchées filled with asparagus heads, sliced truffles on each.

Judic.—Filleted, folded and poached, garnished in the middle with small braised lettuces, surrounded with fish quenelles, coated with Mornay sauce and glazed.

Jules Janin.—Poach whole and garnished with slices of truffles along the middle; coated with the reduced stock, mixed with tortue sauce and crayfish butter, surround with poached mussels and crayfish tails.

Julienne.—Cut the fillets in julienne and treat as gudgeons.

Killarney.—Rolled in paupiettes, dressed in a circle, centre garnished with salpicon of lobster, truffles and mushrooms, coated with Normande sauce.

Lacam.—Poached and garnished with dice of truffles, coated with white wine sauce, heart shaped croutons.

Lacharme.—Same as **Bercy**, without parsley, garnished with truffles à la crème.

Lady Egmont.—Filleted, folded, poached with fish stock and minced mushrooms, coated with the reduced stock mixed with cream and butter, garnished with asparagus heads, glazed.

Laguipière.—Filleted and poached, coated with white wine sauce, sprinkled with Brunoise of truffles.

Lapérouse.—Filleted and poached, garnished between each fillet with a row of mussels and shrimps, coated shrimp sauce, the fillets coated with white wine sauce.

La Vallière.—Filleted, stuffed, folded and poached, dressed in a circle on a forcemeat border, the centre garnished with oysters, quenelles, poached roes and mushroom heads, covered with Normande sauce mixed with crayfish butter, a slice of truffle on each fillet.

Léopold.—Filleted, folded and poached, dressed in a circle, coat one fillet with lobster sauce and chopped truffles, alternate with Génevoise sauce, sprinkled with lobster eggs, the centre garnished with salpicon of shrimps cohered with white wine sauce.

Livonienne.—Filleted and stuffed with fish forcemeat, mixed with truffles and minced mushrooms, folded and poached in fish stock with shallots, julienne of fennel and parsley, coated with the reduced stock mixed with butter and glazed.

Louis XIV.—Filleted and poached, coated with Nantua sauce, mixed with shrimp sauce, add brunoise of vegetable and glaze.

Louis XV.—Poached and coated with white wine sauce, sprinkled with lobster eggs, decorated with truffles.

Louisiane.—Filleted, cooked in butter, garnished with roundels of cooked bananas and dice of red pimento on each fillet, coat with Meunière butter mixed with dice of tomatoes.

Lutèce.—Cooked in butter, dressed on a bed of spinach, garnished round with cooked onion roundels, collops of artichoke bottoms and slices of plain boiled potatoes, chopped parsley and lemon.

Lydia.—Filleted and poached, coated with white wine sauce, garnished with shrimps and asparagus heads, glazed.

Mâconnaise.—Filleted and poached in red wine, garnished with small braised onions, mushroom heads and coated with red wine sauce, croûtons.

Magny.—Filleted, cooked in butter in china dish and served.

Manon.—Rolled in paupiettes and poached, dressed in a circle and bordered with Duchesse potatoes, coated with white wine sauce, centre garnished with asparagus heads, julienne of truffles and mushrooms cohered with butter.

Marcelle.—Filleted, folded and cooked with butter and lemon juice, placed on barquettes garnished with soft roe purée, decorated with slices of truffles.

Marchand de Vin.—Same as **Bercy** with red wine.

Maréchale.—Poached in white wine and fish stock, coated with the reduced cooking liquor mixed with butter and meat glaze, garnished with dice of mushrooms and tomatoes, chopped parsley.

Marguerites (aux).—Poached and coated, half with white wine sauce, sprinkled with julienne of truffles and half shrimp sauce sprinkled with julienne of white of egg, decorated with daisies made with cooked turnips, the centre of the flower made with yolk of egg.

Marguéry.—Poached and garnished with shrimps and mussels, coated with white wine sauce and glazed. Fleurons.

Marie-Louise.—Boned and stuffed with fish forcemeat mixed with Duxelles and chopped truffles, coated lengthwise, half white wine sauce and half Italienne, garnished with fillets of sole fried in gudgeons.

Marie-Stuart.—Filleted, folded and poached, coated with Newburg sauce, garnished on each fillet with a round flat quenelle, decorated with truffles.

Marinette (A).—Remove the fillets of the sole when still warm, stuff them two by two with a paste made with grated cheese, egg and Béchamel sauce, coat all round with Villeroy sauce, egg and crumb and fry in deep fat.

(B).—Filleted, folded and poached, dressed in half stuffed egg plant, coated with Mornay sauce, glazed.

Marinière.—Same as **Marguéry** with oysters, mushrooms and parsley, not glazed.

Marocaine.—Poached and dressed on sweet potato purée, coated with Américaine sauce. Fleurons.

Marquise (A).—Filleted, folded and poached, dressed in a circle on a border of potato Marquise, the centre garnished with saumon quenelles, shrimps and truffles, coated with shrimp sauce.

(B).—Poached with chopped shallots, minced mushrooms, dice of tomatoes, truffles juice and fish stock, glazed with the reduced stock, garnished with asparagus heads and slices of truffles.

Marseillaise.—Poached and coated with white wine sauce mixed with saffron.

Mascotte.—Rolled in paupiettes and poached, dressed in a circle with a border of Duchesse potatoes, centre garnished with salpicon of lobster and truffles, cohered with fish cream, coated with Mornay sauce and glazed, slices of truffles.

Mathilde.—Poached and coated with white wine sauce mixed with onion sauce, garnished with cooked cucumbers.

Maurice.— Same as **Fécampoise.** glazed.

Ménagère.—Poached with red wine and fish stock, coat with the reduced stock mixed with julienne of carrots and truffles.

Mercédès.—Poached with shallots and white wine sprinkled with bread crumbs, add meat glaze and butter to the cooking liquor, brown in oven, dish up and sauce round the fish.

Meunière.—Whole or filleted, floured and cooked in butter on each side, nut brown cooked butter, lemon juice, poured over and sprinkled with chopped parsley.

Metternich.—Filleted, poached, coated with white wine sauce, seasoned with paprika, slices of truffles.

Mexicaine.—Rolled in paupiettes and poached, dressed on grilled mushroms, containing dice of tomatoes, dressed in a circle, coated with tomatoes, white wine sauce, mixed with dice of capsicums.

Mignonnette.—Filleted and cooked in butter, dressed in timbale with a garnish of small noisette potatoes, slices of truffles, rolled in meat glaze, coat with meat glaze worked with butter.

Minute.—Filleted and floured, cooked in butter and served with the butter poured over the fillets.

Mirabeau.—Filleted, cooked in anchovy butter, served decorated with fillets of Anchovies and tarragon leaves.

Miramar (A).—Filleted and cut into lozenge shape, floured and cooked in butter, dressed on a layer of cooked rice, surrounded with fried egg plant.

(B).—Same as **Portugaise**, with julienne of lettuces.

Mireille (A).—Sole Colbert fried in oil, stuffed with Béarnaise sauce, surrounded with dice of tomatoes tossed in oil, crushed garlic, chopped parsley.

(B).—In a gratin dish, bordered with truffles, steamed potatoes artichoke bottoms in slices, the sole sprinkled with bread crumbs, moistened with white wine and fish stock, cooked in oven.

Montespan.—Filleted and poached in white wine with fish stock, white wine, mushrooms and parsley, coated with the reduced stock, mixed with butter.

Montgolfier.—Poached and coated with white wine sauce mixed with julienne of mushrooms, carrots and truffles. Fleurons.

Montmorency.—Rolled in paupiettes, poached and dressed in a circle, centre garnished with salpicon of shrimps, truffles and mushrooms, cohered with shrimp sauce. The paupiettes coated with white wine sauce, a large noisette potato, rolled in Béarnaise sauce between each paupiette.

Montreuil.—Poached and coated with white wine sauce, garnished with noisette potatoes, steamed and coated with shrimp sauce.

Montreux.—Filleted, poached and coated with Mornay sauce, bordered with truffles slices and steamed potatoes, glazed.

Montrouge.—Filleted, folded, poached and dressed in a circle, centre garnished with minced mushrooms à la crème, coated with white wine sauce, mixed with mushroom purée.

Mornay.—Poached and coated with Mornay sauce, glazed.

Moscovite (*Cold*).—Same as **Calypso**. The interior of paupiettes garnished with caviar, dressed in a circle, chopped aspic in centre, serve with Russe sauce.

Moules (aux).—Filleted and folded, poached with mussels cooking liquor, coat with Normande sauce, garnished with poached mussels.

Moulin d'Or.—Prepared as for **Colbert**, stuffed with foie gras purée mixed with truffles, treated same as gratin with cèpes instead of mushrooms, roundels of foie gras surmounted with sliced truffles on top of cèpes, lemon juice and chopped parsley.

Mourier.—Poached with Rhine wine and fish stock with celery and truffles, coated with the reduced stock mixed with butter, garnished with mushroom heads filled with asparagus and alternate with lobster croquettes.

Mousse et Mousseline.—(*See* preparation of **Mousses**).

Murat.—Filleted, cut in gudgeons, cooked in butter and mixed with dice of artichoke bottoms and potatoes previously tossed in butter.

Nantua.—Filleted, poached dressed in timbale with garnish and Nantua sauce.

National.—Poached and coat with three different coloured sauces, white wine with pistachios, white wine and Nantua.

Nelson.—Filleted, folded and poached, dressed in a circle, coated with white wine sauce and glazed, centre garnished with noisettes potatoes and surrounded with poached soft roes.

Nemours.—Filleted, stuffed, folded and poached, dressed in a circle, coated with shrimp sauce, sliced truffles on each fillet, centre garnished with quenelles, poached soft roes, mushroom heads, cohered with Normande sauce, surrounded with small croquettes of shrimps crumbed with chopped truffles.

Newburg.—Poached and garnished with collops of lobster, coated with Newburg sauce, slices of truffles.

Niçoise (A).—Grilled sole with fish Niçoise garnish.

(B).—Filleted, poached, garnished with small potatoes, coated with white wine sauce, fried nonats or whitebait on each side and stoned black olives.

Noilly.—Poached with Noilly Vermouth, fish stock, minced mushrooms, lemon juice coat with reduced stock and white wine sauce.

Normande.—Whole or filleted, poached and finished with Normande sauce and garnish.

Offémont (d').—Filleted, poached with fish stock and chopped shallots, coated with the reduced stock mixed with white wine sauce and cream, garnished with morels cohered with cream and olive shaped truffles.

Olga.—Same as **Georgette,** coated with white wine sauce and glazed.

Opéra.—Poached, coated with white wine sauce, garnished with balls of truffles and asparagus heads.

Orientale.—Poached, coated with curried Newburg sauce, served with plain boiled rice.

Orlanda.—Filleted, folded and poached, dressed in paper cases, garnished with clovisses and mushrooms, coated with curried Américaine sauce.

Orléans.—Stuffed, rolled in paupiettes and poached, dressed in small cocottes, garnished with a salpicon of shrimps, mushrooms and truffles cohered with white wine sauce, the paupiettes coated with shrimp sauce, crowned with a slice of truffle and a shrimp stuck on top.

Orly.—Filleted, dipped in batter, or egged and crumbed, fried deep fat, fried parsley, tomato sauce.

Ostendaise.—Filleted, stuffed and folded, poached with oysters cooking liquor, dressed in a circle, the centre garnished with poached oysters, coated with Normande sauce, mixed with the reduced stock, surround with small fish croquettes, slice of truffle on each fillet.

Otello.—Same as **Sole au Plat,**—with the addition of minced mushrooms and slices of truffles.

Otéro.—Same as **Georgette,** coated with Mornay sauce and glazed.

Pagani.—Filleted, poached in white wine and mushrooms cooking liquor, garnished with mushrooms, oysters and mussels, coated with white wine sauce, mixed with the reduced stock, sprinkled with cheese and glazed.

Paillard.—Same as **Bercy,** garnished with morels tossed in butter, trussed crayfish, heart shaped croûtons.

Palace.—Poached with shallots, chopped tarragon, brandy and white wine, garnished on top with slices of tomatoes and mushrooms coated and glazed.

Parisienne.—Filleted, poached and coated with three different sauces, white wine sauce in the middle. Nantua sauce and anchovy at either end, garnished with macédoine of vegetables and mushroom heads alternating with slices of truffles.

Parmentier.—Same as **Georgette,** without garnish, coated and glazed.

Paulette.—Rolled in paupiettes and poached, dressed in tartlets filled with morels and truffles, cohered with cream, coated with white wine sauce.

Paupiettes.—Paupiette is the French name for a fish rolled on itself beginning at the thick end, it is generally stuffed, if not, the thin end must be dipped in beaten egg in order to prevent unrolling.

Paysanne.—Poached with paysanne of vegetables, coated with the reduced stock mixed with butter.

Persane.—Same as **Newburg,** season with paprika, served with pilaw rice.

Petit-Duc.—Poached with minced mushrooms and fish stock, coated with the reduced stock mixed with white wine sauce, garnished with asparagus heads, and slices of truffles, glazed.

Picarde.—Same as **Marguéry,** with oysters and slices of truffles, but not glazed.

Piccadilly.—Poached with onions, shallots, chopped tarragon, and fish stock, sent in dining room with a sauceboat of cooking liquor and finished in front of customer, by the waiter, the fillets of the sole are removed and coated with the reduced stock mixed with butter, burnt brandy and whisky and Worcestershire sauce.

Pierre-le-Grand.—Filleted, poached and coated with white wine sauce, sprinkle half chopped ham and the other half with chopped truffles, glazed.

Plat.—Poached with fish stock, white wine and chopped shallots, coated with the reduced stock, mixed with butter and glazed.

Polignac.—Poached and coated with white wine sauce, mixed with cream and julienne of mushrooms and truffles. Fleurons.

Pompadour (A).—Poached, the middle garnished with dice of tomatoes, coated with white wine sauce, sprinkled with short julienne of truffles.

   (B).—Filleted, dipped in butter and crumbed, grilled and garnished with noisette potatoes and slices of truffles on each fillet, Béarnaise sauce.

Princesse.—Poached and coated with white wine sauce mixed with asparagus purée, garnished with croustades of Duchesse potatoes filled with asparagus heads and slices of truffles on top.

Princière.—Filleted, poached and coated with Nantua sauce, mixed with dice of truffles, glazed, slices of truffles.

Printanière.—Filleted, folded and poached, dressed in a circle, coated with white wine sauce mixed with Printanier butter, centre garnished with vegetables, surrounded with small steamed noisette potatoes.

Provençale.—Poached, coated with Provençale sauce, chopped parsley, garnished with tomatoes à la Provençale.

Quo Vadis.—Poached, coated with white wine sauce mixed with tarragon butter, garnished with trussed crayfish and slice of truffles.

Rabelais.—Same as **Normande,** sprinkled with lobster eggs.

Rachel (A).—Filleted, stuffed with sliced truffles, folded, poached and coated with shrimp sauce, mixed with dice of truffles, glazed.

   (B).—Same preparation, coated with white wine sauce and sprinkled with asparagus heads and dice of truffles.

Ravigote.—Filleted, poached and coated with Ravigote sauce.

Régence.—Poached and garnished with fish Régence sauce.

Reine Fiamette.—Rolled in paupiettes and dressed on croustadines, stuffed with Joinville salpicon, one coated with Nantua sauce and sprinkled with dice of lobster and the other coated with white wine sprinkled with lobster eggs.

Réjane.—Filleted and poached, coated with white wine sauce, mixed with watercress butter, garnished with Duchesse potatoes.

Renaissance.—Poached and coated with white wine sauce, garnished with small heaps of carrots, balls of turnips, green peas, cauliflowers, asparagus heads, noisette potatoes, alternate the colours.

Rhodésia.—Paupiettes, poached and dressed on lobster collops, coated with Américaine sauce.

Riche.—Poached, garnished with crayfish tails, and dice of truffles, coated with Nantua sauce, slices of truffles.

Richebourg.—Filleted and cooked in butter, coated with Américaine sauce, garnished with oysters à la Villeroy, sliced truffles.

Richelieu.—Same as **Colbert,** cooked in clarified butter, the open part filled with maître-d'hôtel butter and a row of sliced truffles.

Richepin.—Filleted, stuffed with fish forcemeat and duxelles, rolled in paupiettes, poached, dressed in a circle, the centre filled with stuffed ravioli, surrounded with crayfish tails and coated with Nantua sauce mixed with cream, sliced truffles.

Riviera.—Filleted, cooked in butter, dressed in cocotte with truffles, mushrooms, minced artichoke bottoms, finished like meunière.

Rochelaise (A).—Poached in red wine with chopped onions, garnished with oysters, mussels and poached soft roes, coated with the reduced stock mixed with butter and half-glaze.

(B).—Coated with shrimp sauce, Béarnaise sauce.

Rosine.—Poached, coated with tomatoed white wine sauce, garnished with small tomatoes filled with fish forcemeat and poached in oven.

Rossini.—Filleted, masked with fish forcemeat, mixed with foie gras, poached, dressed in a circle, coated with white wine sauce, sprinkled with chopped truffles, centre garnished with truffles cohered with half-glaze.

Rouennaise.—Poached with red wine and chopped shallots ,garnished with oysters and poached mussels, mushrooms head, shrimps, coated with the reduced stock, mixed with meat glaze and butter, surround with trussed crayfish, fried smelts and croûtons.

Rougemont.—Poached and coated with tomated white wine sauce.

Royale.—Poached, coated with white wine sauce, garnished with fish Royale garnish.

Russe.—Poached, coated with white wine sauce, mixed with vegetables à la Russe, chopped parsley.

Saint-Germain.—Dipped in butter and crumbed, grilled and garnished with noisette potatoes, serve with Béarnaise sauce.

Saint-Henry.—Grilled, served with Oursins purée.

Saint-Valéry.—Poached and garnished with shrimps and dice of mushrooms, coated with white wine sauce and glazed.

Salisbury.—Filleted, stuffed, folded and poached, dressed in a circle, coated with lobster sauce, slice of truffle on each fillet, centre garnished with pilaw rice, cohered with white wine sauce.

Salvator.—Filleted, seasoned with paprika, poached, coated with the reduced stock mixed with white sauce, garnished with minced mushrooms, crayfish tails, slices of tomatoes, lemon quarters, chopped parsley, glazed.

Sapho.—Poached with white wine, fish stock and truffle essence, coated with the reduced stock, mixed with butter, julienne of truffles and mushrooms, garnished with lobster croquettes, trussed crayfish and croustades filled with Joinville salpicon.

Sarah Bernhardt.—Poached and coated with Vénitienne sauce, mixed with julienne of carrots and truffles.

Sarcey.—Poached with fish stock, julienne of mushrooms, truffles, gherkins, coated with the reduced stock mixed with butter.

Savoy.—Poached with fish stock, white wine, mushrooms and truffles essence, parsley, dressed on a dish and garnished with dice of tomatoes and asparagus heads, sliced mushrooms over the sole, and row of truffles, glazed.

Schneider.—Same as **Bercy**, garnished with mussels, sprinkled with brown bread crumbs.

Ségovia.—Filleted, poached, dressed in barquettes of cucumbers, stuffed with fish mousseline, coated with white wine sauce mixed with crayfish butter, glazed.

Soufflée.—Boned and stuffed with fish forcemeat, poached with white wine and mushroom cooking liquor, finished same as **Au Plat.**

Sportive.—Filleted, poached with champagne, meat glaze, sliced mushrooms chopped shallots, Bordelaise mirepoix, crayfish tails, reduced and add butter and cream, lemon juice.

Suchet.—Filleted, poached, coated with white wine sauce, mixed with julienne of vegetables and truffles.

Sullivan.—Filleted, folded, poached and garnished with asparagus heads, coated with Mornay sauce and glazed, slices of truffles.

Sully.—Filleted, egged and crumbed, fried deep fat. Béarnaise sauce and anchovy butter.

Sultane.—Poached, coated with white wine sauce, mixed with pistachio butter, garnished with bouchées filled with shrimps, slice of truffle on each.

Suzanne.—Same as **Polignac**, garnished with crayfish tails and poached soft roes. Fleurons.

Sylvette.—Filleted, folded and poached with fish stock. Xérès wine, dice of truffles and mushrooms and large brunoise of vegetables, coated with the reduced liquor, mixed with butter and cream, garnished with small tomatoes, filled with sole purée and gratined in oven.

Sylvia.—Rolled in paupiettes masked with fish forcemeat, mixed with artichoke purée, poached and dressed on artichoke bottoms, coated with white wine sauce, slice of truffles.

Talleyrand.—Filleted and placed raw on a bed of spaghetti à la crème and julienne of truffles, coated with white wine sauce, cook in oven.

Théodora (A).—Filleted and poached with white wine sauce sprinkled with chopped truffles, alternating with Vénitienne sauce and plain white wine.

(B).—Same as **Bercy**, garnished with poached oysters, slices of truffles and Fleurons.

Thérèse (A).—Filleted and poached, garnished with steamed noisette potatoes, a row of sliced truffles in the middle of sole, coated with white wine sauce, sprinkled with chopped truffles.

(B).—Rolled in paupiettes, poached and coated with white wine sauce, sprinkled with lobster coral.

Thermidor.—Same as **Bercy**, not glazed, a thread of meat glaze.

Tivoli.—Filleted, poached, garnished with poached soft roes, oysters, and mushrooms, coated with Génevoise sauce, surround with noodles tossed raw in butter.

Tout-Paris.—Filleted, inserted in crayfish shells and poached, coated with half Nantua sauce and half white wine, garnished with crayfish tails rolled in Nantua sauce, slices of truffles.

Traviata.—Same as **Bercy**, surrounded with small tomatoes cooked in oven and filled Nantua garnish.

Trouvillaise.—Same as **Fécampoise.**—

Turenne.—(*See* **Saumon** same name).

Tzarine.—Poached, garnished with cucumbers, olive shaped and cooked in butter, coated with Mornay sauce, seasoned with paprika.

Urville (d').—Filleted, stuffed and folded, studded with truffles, poached and coated with Américaine sauce, garnished with barquettes filled with crayfish tails, cohere with same sauce.

Valentino.—Filleted, poached and coated with Mornay sauce, glazed and garnished with barquettes filled with Piémontaise rizotto.

Valois.—Poached and coated with white wine sauce made with a Béarnaise reduction.

Van den Berg.—Poached, coated with white wine sauce, mixed with dice of mushrooms and tomatoes.

Varsovienne.—Poached with fish stock, julienne of carrots, onions, celery and parsley, coated with the reduced stock mixed with butter, glazed.

Vatel.—Filleted, poached and coated with Chambord sauce, garnished with cucumber chunks, stuffed and cooked under cover, fillets of sole in goujons.

Vendôme.—Same as **Grimaldi,** glazed.

Vénitienne.—Poached and coated with Vénitienne sauce.

Verdi.—Filleted, poached, dressed on a bed of macaroni mixed with lobster and truffles, coated with Mornay sauce, glazed.

Véron.—Filleted, dipped in butter and crumbed, cooked in clarified butter, dressed on Véron sauce.

Véronique.—Poached with fish stock and curaçao, garnished with muscat grapes peeled and pipped, coated with the reduced stock mixed with butter. Glazed.

Villaret.—Filleted and placed in a savarin mould crosswise, the cavity filled with crayfish mousseline, poached, dressed and centre filled to taste.

Villeroy.—Filleted, stuffed folded and poached, rolled in Villeroy sauce, egged and crumbed, fried, tomato sauce.

Vin Blanc.—Poached with white wine, coated with the reduced cooking liquor mixed with white wine sauce.

Vin Rouge.—Same treatment with red wine and red wine sauce.

Walewska.—Filleted, poached, garnished with slices of truffles and lobster collops, coated with Mornay sauce glazed.

Washington.—Filleted, cooked in butter, garnished with lobster collops coated with Américaine sauce, sprinkled with short julienne of truffles.

Wilhelmine.—Same as **Georgette,** garnished with cucumbers à la crème, oysters on the fillets, coated with Mornay sauce, glazed.

Yvette.— **(A).**—Same as **Sole Fines Herbes,** garnished with small tomatoes stuffed with fish forcemeat.

(B).—(Same as **Sole Crevettes,**) glazed, slices of truffles.

STERLET

(Same preparation as **Esturgeon.**)

STOCKFISCH (see MORUE SALEE)

Brandade.—(*See* **Brandade of Morue**).

Niçoise.—(Same as **Bouillabaisse,**) with the addition of capsicums, black olives and new potatoes.

SUPIONS — SMALL SQUID

(*Are best-fried.*)

TANCHE — TENCH

(*Treated* **Meunière, au Bleu, Bercy, au Gratin,** *etc.*)

THON — TUNNY FISH

Grillé.—Same as **Grilled Saumon.**
Indienne.—Studded with anchovy fillets, marinaded, braised and coated with Curry sauce, serve with plain boiled rice.
Meunière.—Same as **Sole Meunière.**
Orly.—Cut in strips (treated as **Sole Orly.**)
Provençale.—Marinaded and tossed in oil with chopped tomatoes, garlic and onion, moistened with white wine and consommé, braised in oven, coated with the reduced stock, mixed with capers and chopped parsley.

TERRAPENES ET TORTUES — TURTLE

Baltimore.—Cooked pieces of turtle, tossed in nut brown cooked butter, dressed in cocotte, with the thickened gravy, and a glass of Xérès wine.
Maryland.—Same as above, cohered with butter and yolk of egg purée.
Nageoires de Tortue Américaine—Cook the fins in water and finish in Madeira, coat with Américaine sauce.
Nageoires de Tortue à la Tortue.—Braised, garnished and Tortue sauce.

TRUITE — TROUT

Américaine.—Filleted, poached and coated with Américaine sauce.
Belle-Vue.—(*See* **Saumon** froid).
Bleu.—Trout poached in boiling water with salt and vinegar, served on serviette with plain boiled potatoes and parsley sprigs, Hollandaise sauce and melted butter.
Bretonne.—Cooked in butter, garnished with shrimps and minced mushrooms.
Cambacérès.—Salmon trout, skinned on one side, studded with truffles and carrots, boned and stuffed with fish forcemeat, braised in fish stock mixed with white wine sauce, garnished with stoned olives, soft roes, morels and slices of truffles.
Caruso.—Filleted, masked with lobster forcemeat, decorated with crayfish tails and slices of truffles, poached, coated with white wine sauce, glazed, surrounded with small bouchées, garnished with caviar.
Chambertin.—(*See* **Saumon** same name).
Champagne.—(*See* **Saumon** same name).
Cléopâtre.—Same as **Meunière,** garnished with shrimps, capers and soft roes tossed in butter.

Coulibiac.—(*See* **Saumon**).

Coulis (au).—Poached trout, skinned and coated with fish cream blended with cray-fish paste.

Court-Bouillon.—Poached in boiling water, with salt, vinegar, pepper-corns, carrots, onions, and aromatic herbs, served with steamed potatoes and melted butter.

Doria.—River trout floured and cooked in butter, garnished with olive shaped cucumbers, chopped parsley.

Ecossaise.—(*See* **Saumon** same name).

Farcie.—River trout, boned and stuffed, wrapped in oiled paper and grilled, Marinière sauce, lemon.

Félix.—Fillets of Salmon trout, skinned, floured, cooked in butter, coated with Américaine sauce.

Frite.—Small trout egged and crumbed, fried deep fat, served with lemon quarters.

Gavarnie.—Small river trout, cooked and serve in papillotes, with maître-d'hôtel butter, and plain steamed potatoes.

Génevoise.—Large salmon trout, poached in court-bouillon, dressed on serviette, Génevoise sauce.

George Sand.—Filleted, poached, skinned, coated with shrimp sauce, garnished with quenelles and shrimps, slices of truffles.

Grenobloise.—Floured and cooked in butter, served with the butter poured over and garnished with peeled lemon quarters and capers.

Hollandaise.—Poached whole and served on a serviette with plain boiled potatoes, Hollandaise sauce.

Hôtelière.—(Same as **Merlan** same name).

Hussarde.—Boned and stuffed with fish forcemeat, mixed with chopped fried onions, poached and coated with soubise white wine sauce, glazed.

Impérial.—Salmon trout, skinned on one side, studded with truffles, braised in champagne, garnished with prawns and poached herring roes, coated with white wine sauce, sprinkled with julienne of truffles.

Ivanhoë.—Salmon trout filleted, baked in the oven in cocottes with peeled quarters of lemon, apples and sliced artichoke bottoms, served masked with fish velouté blended with lobster butter, glazed.

Juive (*Cold*).—Cooked in court-bouillon decorated with tarragon leaves, coated with aspic jelly.

Juive (*Hôt*).—Fried in oil and served with Tartare sauce.

Mantoue.—Boned and stuffed with truffled fish forcemeat, poached in stock, coated with Italienne sauce.

Médicis.—Same as **Saumon Médicis**.

Meunière.—Seasoned, floured, cooked in clarified butter, dressed, lemon juice, chopped parsley and nut brown cooked butter.

Montgolfier.—Salmon trout, boned and stuffed with fish forcemeat and truffles, poached in fish stock, skinned and garnished with lobster collops, mushroom heads and truffles, coated with white wine sauce.

Monseigneur.—Poached in red wine, garnished with mushroom heads, coated with red wine sauce, surrounded with barquettes filled with poached egg coated red wine sauce and alternated with barquette filled with soft roes coated white wine sauce, slices of truffles.

F

Nansen (*Cold*).—Poached, skinned, served on a " socle " of rice, glazed with aspic, surrounded by small timbales of aspic with julienne of vegetables, half tomatoes filled with Russian salad and cucumber shapes filled with caviare, Mayonnaise sauce.

Nantua.—(*See* **Sole** same name).

Norvégienne (*Cold*).—Salmon trout, served on a "socle" of rice, garnished round with barquettes containing Russian salad and prawns, lettuce hearts, slices of truffles and hard-boiled eggs in quarters, green sauce.

Ondines (*Cold*).—Oval mousse the size of an egg, garnished inside with shrimps, dressed in deep dish, prawns stuck on the mousse, covered with aspic containing chervil shreds.

Piémontaise.——Poached, skinned and coated with white wine sauce, sprinkled with julienne of truffles, served with Piémontaise rice.

Régence.—(*See* **Saumon** same name).

Rothschild.—Stuffed, poached and finished same as **Saumon Royale.**

Suchet.—(*See* **Filets de Sole** same name).

Vauclusienne.—Treated same as Meunière, oil instead of butter.

Vin Blanc, Vin Rouge.—(*See* **Filets de Sole** same name).

Yvette.—Poached fillets of trout, finished as **Filets de Sole,** same name.

TURBOT OR TURBOTIN — YOUNG TURBOT

Aïda.—Filleted, poached, dressed on a bed of spinach, seasoned with salt and paprika, coated with Mornay sauce, sprinkled with cheese and breadcrumbs, glazed.

Ambassade.—Braised, and garnished with collops of lobster and slices of truffles, coated with white wine sauce mixed with crayfish butter.

Américaine.—Braised, slices of lobster and coated with Américaine sauce.

Amiral.—Boned and stuffed with fish forcemeat mixed with crayfish butter, braised and coated with Nantua sauce, decorated with slices of truffles, garnished with oysters, fried mussels, fillets of sole in goujons, and trussed crayfish, Fleurons.

Andalouse.—Cook the turbotin in a fish dish with roundels of onions, dice of tomatoes, minced mushrooms, julienne of sweet pimento, sprinkled with crumbs and bits of butter, moistened with white wine and fish stock, cooked in oven.

Arlésienne.—Braised, coated with Bercy sauce, glazed, garnished with half tomatoes, cooked in oven and filled with roundels of fried onions.

Boitelle.—(*See* **Sole** same name).

Bonne-Femme.—(*See* **Sole** same name).

Cadgery.—(*See* **Cadgery de Saumon**).

Chambertin.—(Same as **Sole** same name).

Champagne.—(Same as **Sole** same name).

Chauchat.—(Same preparation as **Sole Chauchat**).

Commodore.—Poached, drained and garnished with noisette potatoes, quenelles, crayfish, oysters à la Villeroy, lobster croquettes, served with Normande sauce mixed with anchovy butter.

Coquilles (en).—(*See* **Saumon**).

Coumeig (*Cold*).—Braised, remove the fillets when warm and collop them, mask the carcase with fish mousseline and decorate all round making a border with the same mousseline, garnish the middle with the Russian salad, dress the decorated collops on it and glaze with aspic, Mayonnaise sauce.

Crème Gratin.—Border a dish with Duchesse potatoes, mask the bottom with Mornay sauce, place the collops of turbot, coat with sauce and glaze.

D'Antin.—Same as **Dugléré**, garnished with croûtons fried in butter.

Daumont.—(*See* **Saumon** same name).

Diplomate.—(*See* **Merlan** same name).

Dieppoise.—(*See* **Sole** same name).

Dugléré.—Cut in sections, poached with fish stock, tomatoes and parsley, onions and chopped shallots, coated with the reduced stock, mixed with butter.

Empire.—Poached, dressed and garnished with poached oysters, collops of lobster, mushroom heads, coated with Nantua sauce, slices of truffles, Fleurons.

Fermière.—(*See* **Sole** same name).

Feuillantine.—Boned and stuffed with fish forcemeat and lobster cullis, poached and dressed on a dish, coated with thin Nantua sauce, a row of sliced truffles in the middle of the fish, garnished with poached oysters and truffles. Béchamel sauce with cayenne pepper.

Française.—Braised, coated lengthwise with half white wine sauce and half same sauce mixed with tarragon butter, garnished with small bouchées filled with mussels, crayfish, slices of truffles, cohered with Poulette sauce.

Françoise Ier.—Same as **Dugléré** with the addition of minced mushrooms.

Gavarnie.—Poached, served with Hollandaise sauce mixed with dice of truffles.

Gratin.—(*See* **Merlan** same name).

Hollande (Mode de).—Braised, remove the fillets, fill carcase with Régence garnish, coat with Nantua sauce, serve with plain boiled potatoes and Hollandaise sauce.

Hollandaise.—Poached in salt water and milk, served with plain boiled potatoes and Hollandaise sauce.

Hongroise.—Poached and coated with white wine sauce seasoned with paprika, garnished with steamed potatoes.

Huîtres.—(Same preparation as **Sole** same name).

Impérial.—Poached, garnished with crayfish carcasses filled with Nantua salpicon, fried nonats, oysters and Villeroy mussels, served with Hollandaise, Génevoise or Victoria sauce, steamed potatoes.

Kléber.—Braised and garnished with dice of truffles, mushrooms and shrimps, coated with Bercy sauce mixed with meat glaze.

Laguipière.—Poached, coated with Normande sauce, sprinkled with dice of truffles, garnished with potato croquettes and oyster shells filled with Joinville salpicon.

Marquise.—(Same as **Sole Marquise**.)

Meunière.—Divided into slices, floured and tossed in butter, served sprinkled with chopped parsley, lemon juice, and brown cooked butter poured over.

Mirabeau.—Poached, coated with two sauces alternating the colours, white wine and Génevoise sauce, decorate with truffles and tarragon leaves.

Nelson.—Same as **Dugléré**, glazed and garnished with balls of Duchesse potatoes, egged and crumbed and fried.

Ostendaise.—(*See* **Sole** same name).

Parisienne.—(*See* **Sole** same name).

Prince de Galles.—Braised, and coated with white wine sauce mixed with Curry and crayfish cullis, garnished with oysters, garnished with oysters, Villeroy mussels, and croquette potatoes.

Rachel.—(*See* **Sole** same name).

Régence.—(*See* **Saumon** same name).

Reynière.—Boned, stuffed, poached, decorated with a row of mushroom heads in the middle, and each side with soft roes alternated with anchovy fillets, Soubised white wine sauce.

Richmond.—Same as **Chambord.** (*See* **Carpe Chambord).**

Rostand.—Poached in fish stock, truffle juice, minced cèpes, or mushrooms, julienne of truffles, garnished with bouchées filled with salpicon of lobster Américaine small heaps of fried nonats, or whitebaits, and tartlets filled with asparagus heads, coated with the reduced stock mixed with butter.

Royale.—(*See* **Saumon** same name).

Russe.—(*See* **Sole** same name).

Saint-Malo.—Seasoned and grilled, garnished with noisette potatoes, Saint-Malo sauce (*separately*).

Suédoise.—(*See* **Turbotin Mirabeau).**

Valentino.—(*See* **Filets de Sole** same name).

Vatel.—Filleted, poached, coated with Genevoise sauce, garnished with fried soles en goujons and stuffed shaped cucumbers cooked under cover.

Wladimir.—(Same as **Russe,**) with chopped tomatoes and poached cockles, glazed.

VIVE

(See preparation of **Merlan—Whitings.)**

BLANCHAILLE — WHITEBAIT

Floured, shaken in sieve and fried in very hot fat, seasoned, lemon and parsley, cayenne pepper if required.

ZANDRE — PIKE PERCH

(Prepared **Bercy, Dugléré, Gratin, White Wine,** *etc.*)

Entrées D'abats

Various preparations of fowl.

ABATIS

Bourguignonne.—Fry in butter with chopped onions, add little flour, moisten with red wine and white consommé. Add bunch of herbs, garnish with dice of bacon, mushrooms and small onions.

Chipolatas.—Same as above with white wine and garnish with chipolatas.

Giblets.—Fry the giblets in butter, place them in a pie dish, moisten with consommé, cover with puff paste, cook in oven.

Légumes Nouveaux (aux).—Toss in butter with chopped onion, add a little flour moisten with white consommé, cook with carrots and turnips previously tossed in butter, when nearly done add French beans and green peas.

AMOURETTES

(Or Marrow bones of Ox or Calves).
(Treat the Amourettes same as Cervelles) (Brains.)

ANDOUILLES ET ANDOUILLETTES

CHITTERLINGS

(Are served grilled.)

BOUDINS BLANCS ET NOIRS

BLACK AND WHITE PUDDINGS

(Are served grilled.)

BOUDINS DE VOLAILLE

Preparation

Large quenelles made with chicken forcemeat, stuffed with salpicon, poached, egg and bread crumbs tossed in clarified butter and fried in deep fat.

Corigneau.—Stuff with salpicon of mushrooms, mixed with Allemande sauce, fried in clarified butter, dress in a circle, garnish centre with cockscombs dipped in batter and fried, serve with tomato sauce.

Ecossaise.—Stuff with salpicon of tongues, mixed with half-glaze, fried in butter, dished up alternately with slices of tongue. serve Ecossaise sauce mixed with Mirepoix.

Estragon.—Stuff with chopped tarragon leaves, poached and covered with tarragon velouté.

Morland.—Dip the quenelles in egg and roll them in chopped truffles, fry in butter, . dish up and garnish centre with mushroom purée, serve with Suprême sauce.

Richelieu.—Stuff with salpicon of truffles, chicken and mushrooms, fry, and serve with Périgueux sauce.

Soubise.—Stuff with Soubise purée, prepare same way as Richelieu, serve with Soubise sauce.

Uzès.—Poach, cover with Aurore sauce, mixed with julienne of truffles.

CERVELLES — BRAINS

Beurre Noir ou Noisette.—Poach, and slice the brains, season, chopped parsley, drop of vinegar, cook the butter until slightly black or nut brown and pour over brains.

Bourguignonne.—Poach. Dress with garnish and Bourguignonne sauce.

Coquilles Gratin.—(*See* preparation in **Entrées Volantes**). Cover with Duxelles sauce and breadcrumbs, place in the oven to be browned.

Cromesquis à la Française.—(*See* preparation in **Entrées Volantes**). Salpicon made of truffles, brains and mushrooms, mixed with Allemande sauce, shaped in small squares, dip in batter and fry in deep fat, serve with Périguéux sauce.

Cromesquis à la Polonaise.—Salpicon of cèpes or mushrooms, truffles, brains, mixed with Espagnole sauce, shape them, wrap in a thin unsweetened pancake, dipped in batter and fried. Serve with herb sauce.

Cromesquis à la Russe.—Prepared same as above, wrapped in pig's caul, dip in batter and fried, served with Duxelle sauce.

Croquettes.—(*See* preparations in **Entrées Volantes**).

Croûtes.—Cut in scallops dressed in hollowed croûtons, sprinkled with grated cheese, then browned.

Fritot.—(*See* preparations in **Entrées Volantes**).

Frite à l'Anglaise.—Egg and bread crumb the brains, fry in deep fat, serve with tomato sauce.

Financière.—Poach, dress on toast, garnish with Financière, covered with Madeira sauce flavoured with essence of truffles.

Italienne.—Scalloped raw, floured, fried in oil and butter, dress in a circle, fill centre with Italian sauce.

Matelote (en).—Poached in red wine, garnish with Bourguignonne.

Mazagran (en).—Border made with Duchesse potatoes. Garnish with truffles, brains scalloped and mushroom heads, mixed with Suprême sauce, cover with a thin layer of potato Duchesse, egg wash and browned in oven. Serve surrounded with tomato sauce and grilled chipolatas.

Montrouge.—Scalloped. Dress in a thin crust, garnish with minced mushrooms, with a little cream, cover with Mornay sauce and glaze.

Mousseline.—(*See* preparation in **Entrées Volantes**).

Parisienne.—Cover with Suprême sauce, mixed with slices of mushrooms, decorate with truffle and mushrooms head.

Poulette.—Dress in timbale, cover with Poulette sauce.

Ravigote.—Scalloped, dress in timbale, cover with Ravigote sauce.

Soufflé.—Béchamel sauce, mixed with purée of brains and yolk of eggs, then whip white of eggs, to a stiff froth, mix altogether, cooked in a soufflé dish.

Subrics.—(*See* preparation in **Entrées Volantes**).

Timbale Ecossaise.—In dariole moulds, decorate the inside with tongues, then place forcemeat round the inside, fill the interior with salpicon of tongues and brains mixed with Suprême sauce, then cover with forcemeat, poached ,and dish up with Ecossaise sauce.

Timbale Napolitaine.—In dariole moulds, line the inside with cooked macaroni, garnish interior with salpicon of mushrooms and brains, mixed with tomato half-glaze, cover with forcemeat, poach, serve with sauce tomato and half-glaze.

Timbale Villeneuve.—In oval moulds, buttered and sprinkled with chopped parsley, coated with chicken forcemeat, garnish inside with salpicon of brains and truffles mixed with Suprême sauce, finish same as Ecossaise. Serve with Soubise sauce mixed with cream.

Villeroy.—In scallops, covered with Villeroy sauce, egg and bread crumbs, fry in deep fat, serve with Périgueux sauce.

FOIE — LIVER

Anglaise (à l').—Cut in slices, grilled, dressed alternately with grilled rashers of bacon.

Bercy.—Cut in slices, grilled, covered with Bercy sauce.

Bordelaise.—Whole, larded, fried in butter, wrapped in pig's caul with onions, shallots, mushrooms, moistened with white wine, and half-glaze, braise in the oven, garnish with sautéd cèpes à la Bordelaise.

Bourgeoise.—Whole, larded, braise same way as **Pièce de Bœuf Bourgeoise**.

Brochette (en).—(*See* preparation in **Entrées Volantes**). Made with liver cut in squares, mushrooms, and blanched salted pork, cover with a well thickened Duxelles, egg and bread crumbs, grilled, serve with either Duxelles, Italienne, or Maître-d'hôtel sauce.

Espagnole.—Cut in slices, grill, garnish with grilled tomatoes, rounds of onions fried in oil, fried parsley.

Fines-Herbes.—Cut in slices, fry in butter, serve with parsley sauce.

Frit.—Cut in thin slices, egg and bread crumbs, fry and dish up with fried parsley.

Italienne.—In slices fried in oil, served with Italienne sauce.

Lyonnaise.—Cut in slices, fry, dress in a circle, garnish centre with sliced onions cooked in butter, add a drop of vinegar.

Provençale.—(Same as **Italienne**). Served with Provençale sauce.

Quenelles Alsacienne.—½ chicken liver and ½ veal liver, chopped fine and mixed with a little cooked onion, chopped parsley, eggs, add salt pepper and nutmeg, shape with a soup spoon, poached. Served with Maître-d'Hôtel butter.

Quenelles Viennoise.—Prepare same way as above with chopped fennels.

Raisins (aux).—In slices, fry in butter, rinse pan with vinegar, add a little brown sugar and half-glaze, dish up the liver, sprinkle with currants and sultanas and cover with the sauce.

Rizotto.—(*See* preparation in **Entrées Volantes**).

Soufflé.—Same way as **Cervelles Soufflé** with liver purée instead of brains purée.

Sous la Cendre.—Larded, season same way as **Bœuf à la Mode**, cover wtih Duxelles, wrapped in a paste, same as **Coulibiac** (*see* Saumon) cook in the oven, basting with half-glaze, put through hole made in the paste, serve with Madeira sauce.

G

FRAISE

Cooking Process

(Cook in a Blanc, serve well done and very hot).

Frite.—Cut in pieces, egg and bread crumbs fry in deep fat, serve with Devil sauce·
Lyonnaise.—Toss in smoking oil, and finish same as **Veau à la Lyonnaise.**
Poulette.—Cut in shreds and mix with a Poulette sauce, dress in a timbale.
Ravigote.—Dress in timbale, serve Ravigote sauce.
Vinaigrette.—Dress in timbale, serve Vinaigrette sauce.

GAYETTES — CAILLETTES — FAGGOTS

(Are generally served grilled.)

MOU — LIGHTS

Civet (en).—Cut in cubes, season, toss with Mirepoix in butter, add little flour, moisten with red wine and half-glaze, add faggot of herbs and garlic, braze, garnish with dice of bacon, mushrooms and small glazed onions. Serve in timbale.

OREILLES — EARS

(Calves' and pigs')

Farcies.—Calves' ears, blanch, stuff with sausage meat, wrap in a cloth, poach in white stock. Serve with the reduced braising liquor.
Frites.—Calves' ears, blanch, braise in Madeira, cut in shreds, dip in batter and fry deep fat. Serve with tomato sauce.
Froides.—Calves' ears, blanch, braise, coat with clarified braising liquor. *(Serve cold).*
Grillees.—Calves' ears, blanch, braise, cut in halves lengthways, spread with mustard, butter and crumbs, grilled, serve with Diable sauce.
Italienne.—Calves' ears, blanch and braise, coat with Italienne sauce.
Naturel.—Pigs' ears, blanch. poach in salt water, garnish with braised cabbage or any vegetable purée.
Rouennaise *(Pork).*—Cook as above, remove the meat part, chop and simmer in Madeira sauce, cool, mix with sausage meat and chopped parsley, shape in small balls, place the balls on the other part of the ears, wrap in pig's caul and grill, serve with Madeira sauce.
Sainte-Menehould *(Pork).*—Cook as above, cut in halves, butter and crumbs, grill.
Tortue.—Calves' ears, blanch and braise, garnish and turtle sauce.
Toulousaine.—Same preparation as above with Toulousaine garnish.

PALAIS DE BŒUF — PALATE OF BEEF

Dunoise.—Cut in squares, butter and crumbs, grill ,serve with Rémoulade sauce.
Gratin.—Cut in large Julienne, dress in a border of Duchesse potatoes, cover with Duxelles sauce, set to gratin.
Italienne.—Cook in butter, dish up in a circle, coat with Italienne sauce.
Poulette.—Dress in timbale, coat with Poulette sauce.
Paysanne.—Cut in squares, cook in butter, garnish with vegetables, coat with Madeira sauce.

PIEDS — FEET

(Mutton, Pork, Veal.)

Cooking Process.

Are cooked in a blanc, with the exception of pork feet which are cooked in an Aromates stock.

Blanquette (en).—Same as **Blanquette de Veau.**
Custine.—Calvesfoot, blanch, braise, cut in small dice, mix with reduced Duxelles, cool, divide in squares, wrap in pigs caul, cook in oven ,serve with half-glaze.
Frits.—Blanch, cook in a blanc, bone, egg and bread crumbs, fry in deep fat, serve with tomato sauce.
Fritot (en).—With veal or mutton, (same process as **Fritot de Volaille.**)
Grillés.—Cook, roll in butter and crumbs, grill, serve with Diable sauce.
Poulette.—Cook, bone, dress in timbale, coat with Poulette sauce, chopped parsley.
Rouennaise.—(Same preparation as **Oreilles de Porc**).
Sainte-Menehould.—Pork feet, cook, bread crumbs and grill.
Tortue.—(*See* **Tête de Veau Tortue**).
Truffés.—Braise, bone, cut in small cubes, add truffles in dice, thicken with braising stock, cool, divide in small balls, wrap in pork forcemeat, mix with chopped truffles, and place in pig's caul. Cook in butter, dress in a circle, serve with Madeira sauce.
Tyrolienne.—Chopped onions cooked in butter, with dice of tomatoes, seasoned, add garlic and chopped parsley and Poivrade sauce, simmer for 10 minutes with boned calvesfoot, dress in a timbale.
Vinaigrette.—Blanch, cooked in a blanc, serve very hot, with Vinaigrette sauce separate.

QUEUE DE BŒUF — OXTAIL

Auvergnate.—Cut in sections, braised in white wine, garnish with large dice of bacon, braised chestnuts and glazed onions, cover with braising stock.
Cavour.—In sections, braise with brown stock and white wine, place in a cocotte, and add the braising stock, strain and thicken. Serve with chestnut purée.
Charolaise.—Same way as above, garnish with carrots and turnips shaped and cooked, also poached quenelles made of pork forcemeat, dressed in a Duchesse potato, bordered with lardons round the dish.

Chipolata.—Same process, with chipolata garnish.

Daube (en).—Same process, garnish with small onions, dice of bacon, and julienne of calves foot.

Farcie.—Large Ox-tail, boned without spoiling the meat, stuff with forcemeat made of lean beef and fat bacon, bread crumbs soaked in milk, then well pressed, eggs, chopped truffles, salt and spices, wrap same way as the galantine, cook 3 hours in salt water and finish in a braising stock, basting occasionally to glaze the meat, garnish with purée of vegetables.

Grillées.—Cut in sections, twice the usual length, cook in a stock pot for 4 or 5 hours, then cool, spread with mustard, buttered and bread crumbs, grilled, serve with Devil sauce.

Hochepot.—Cut in pieces, and cook with two feet and ears of pork, when half done, add shaped carrots and turnips, small onions and small cabbages, dish the pieces in a circle, and garnish centre with the vegetables, surround with chipolatas, and the ears cut in julienne.

Nohant.—Cut in pieces, same way as for **Cavour,** dressed in a circle, garnish centre with Macédoine of vegetables, surround with glazed lamb sweetbreads, alternately with slices of tongue.

Paysanne.—Cut in pieces, partly fry with vegetables, dice of pork rind, and raw ham, sprinkle a little flour, moisten with red wine and white stock, when nearly done, remove the pieces into another pan, add carrots, turnips and small onions fried in butter, also new potatoes. Strain the stock over the lot, and finish cooking, serve in casserole.

ROGNONS — KIDNEYS

(Lamb, Beef, Mutton, Veal and Pork.)

Américaine.—Grill, dress on a half grilled tomato, surrounded with grilled rashers of bacon, nut brown butter.

Bercy.—Cut in slices, tossed in butter, seasoned, dished in timbale, cover with Bercy sauce.

Berrichonne.—Cut in halves, toss in butter, add Bordelaise sauce, garnish with dice of bacon, small glazed onions, sliced mushrooms, dress on toast, cover with the sauce, surround with the garnish and chopped parsley.

Bonne-Femme.——Veal kidney in slices, cooked in a casserole with bacon glazed onions, potatoes, bunch of herbs, white wine, dish up and surround with the garnish.

Bordelaise.—Cut in slices, tossed in butter, add Bordelaise sauce, mixed with dice of marrow and minced mushrooms or cèpes. Dish in timbale, chopped parsley.

Brochette.—Slit the kidneys in halves without separating them, place them through a skewer, grill, serve maître-d'hôtel in the centre.

Brochette (en).—(*See* preparation in **Entrées Volantes).**

Bouchère.—In slices, tossed in butter, with chipolatas and squares of fillet of beef, add Madeira sauce, dish in timbale, and chopped parsley.

Carvalho.—Cut in halves, tossed in butter, add Madeira sauce, dress on toast, garnish with truffles and sliced mushrooms, cover with the sauce.

Casserole.—Veal kidney wrapped in its suet, cooked in a casserole, add thickened veal gravy, serve in a casserole.

Champignons.—Cut in slices, tossed in butter, add tomatoed half-glaze, mixed with mushrooms and chopped shallots.

Chasseur.—Cut in slices, tossed in butter, add Chasseur sauce, dished in timbale, chopped parsley.

Chipolata.—Same as Madeira, with chipolata garnish.

Chateaubriand.—Grill, garnish with watercress, and Château potatoes, served with Chateaubriand sauce.

Curry.—Tossed in butter, cover with Curry sauce, serve plain boiled rice.

Grillés.—(*See* **Brochette**).

Henri IV.—Grilled. Fill the centre with Béarnaise sauce, garnish with fried potatoes and water-cress.

Japonaise.—Grilled, fill one kidney with dice of tomatoes, and alternately fill another with the fried yolk of egg, garnish with straw potatoes and water-cress.

Liégeoise.—Same process as **Casserole**, set alight with gin.

Louis XIV.—Cook en brochette, dressed on grilled slices of ham, covered with tarragon, thickened gravy. Garnish with water-cress.

Madère.—Cut in slices, tossed in butter, add Madeira sauce, served in timbale. Can be done with Port wine, Xérès, white wine etc.

Marchand de Vin.—Tossed in butter, cohered with red wine Bercy sauce.

Montpensier.—Same as Madeira, garnish with asparagus tips, Noisette potatoes, decorated with slices of truffles.

Petit-Duc.—Grilled, fill centre with scraped horse-radish, dress on Anna potatoes surrounded with Château sauce.

Portugaise.—Cut in halves, tossed in butter, add tomatoed half-glaze, dress in a circle on half tomatoes cooked in oven, garnish centre with dice of tomatoes, cover kidneys with the sauce.

Présidence.—Grilled, fill centre with Villeroy sauce, egg and bread crumbs, finish cooking in clarified butter. Dressed in a circle with Jardinière garnish in the centre.

Robert.—Same as **en Casserole,** finish it in the dining-room in front **of** guests, rinse the casserole with Fine Champagne, set alight, add a little French mustard, lemon juice, chopped parsley butter, and add sliced kidneys. Mix the lot together and serve immediately.

Saint-Lazare.—Same as **à la Bordelaise.** Cut the kidneys in halves lengthways.

Turbigo.—Cut in halves, toss in butter, add tomatoed half-glaze, dress on toast, garnish chipolatas and mushroom heads, cover with the sauce.

Tyrolienne.—Grilled. Fill centre with tomatoes cut in dice, garnish with rounds of fried onions.

Vert-Pré.—Grilled, fill centre with Maître-d'hôtel butter, garnish with water-cress and straw potatoes.

G

SAUCISSES ET CREPINETTES
SAUSAGES AND CREPINETTE

Crépinette de Porc.—Sausage meat mixed with chopped truffles, wrapped in pig's caul, shaped like a flat rectangle, grilled gently, dressed in a circle pour **Périgueux** sauce in the centre, and serve with mashed potatoes.

Crépinettes Cendrillon.—Wrapped in an oval layer of paste, egg wash, and bake 20 minutes.

Crépinettes Liégeoise.—Cooked in clarified butter, covered with thickened gravy, flavoured with gin.

Saucisses Anglaises.—The most well known are those of Cambridge, Chesterfield and Melton serve grilled.

Saucisses aux Choux.—Poached or grilled, serve with braised cabbage.

Francfort bu Strasbourg.—Place the sausages in cold water and bring to a boil, garnish with braised sauerkraut.

Marmelade (à la).—Cooked and served with apple sauce.

Rizot (en).—Cook sausages, rinse pan with white wine and half-glaze sauce. Dressed on a pilaw rice border.

Vin Blanc.—Cooked in butter, rinse pan with a little white wine add half-glaze, dress on long toasts, pour sauce over.

TETES — HEADS

Tête de Porc.—Is used for the preparation of pork brawn.

Tête de Veau.—Boned and cut in pieces, cook in a blanc. The following garnishes may be served: Financière, Godard, Poulette, Tortue, Toulousaine. Suitable sauces may also be served such as : Tomato, Vinaigrette, Ravigote.

Anglaise.—Served with boiled bacon, parsley sauce, or brain sauce.

Froide.—Serve with Vinaigrette sauce, mixed with capers, chopped onions and parsley.

TRIPES ET GRAS DOUBLE — TRIPE

Gras Double.—Can be done in blanquette, Bourgeoise, fritot or grilled. (*See* the different preparations in **Pieds de Mouton et Veau**).

Mode de Caen (à la).—Lay on the bottom of a stewing pan ,carrots, onions, seasoned and ox feet cut in fair sized pieces, add the tripe which is comprised of: The paunch, the honey comb bay, the manyplies and the reed, place a bunch of herbs with it lay the bones of the feet and slices of beef fat on top, moisten with cider, white wine, and brandy, cook slowly for 10 hours.

Tripous ou Paupiettes.—Stuff with forcemeat made of fresh pork combined with dice of ham and chopped parsley, cook in special marmite with white wine brandy, and white consommé. Cook 6 hours.

ENTREES VOLANTES

BEEFSTEAKS, STEAKS, RUMPSTEAK, ENTRECOTE

(*Beef.*)

Américaine.—Grilled. Fried egg on top, serve with tomato sauce.

Béarnaise.—Grilled, garnish water-cress, serve with Béarnaise sauce.

Bercy.—Grilled. Coat with Bercy sauce.

Bordelaise.—Grilled, slices of poached marrow, coat with Bordelaise sauce.

Cécilia.—Cook in butter, garnish with large grilled mushrooms filled with asparagus heads, and surround with soufflées potatoes.

Champignons.—Fry in clarified butter, coat with mushrooms sauce, and mushrooms heads.

Cheval.—Grilled, place two fried eggs on top of steak.

Forestière.—Same as champignons, garnish with sautéd morels, dice of bacon and Parmentier potatoes.

Hambourg or **Bismark.**—Chopped raw, seasoned with salt, pepper, and nutmeg. add raw egg, chopped onion tossed in butter, mix together, divided and shape like a Tournedos, flour and cook in clarified butter.

Hongroise.—Cook in butter, coat with sauce Hongroise, garnish with bacon and potatoes à l'Anglaise.

Hôtelière.—Cook in butter, coat with Hôtelière butter.

Lyonnaise.—Cook in butter, garnish with sliced onions, coat with half-glaze.

Marchand de Vins.—Grilled, coat with red wine Bercy sauce.

Marseillaise.—Grilled, coat with tomatoed maître-d'hôtel, butter add garlic, garnish with copeaux potatoes.

Mexicaine.—Grilled, serve with Mexicaine garnish and tomatoed thickened gravy.

Mirabeau.—Grilled, decorate with tarragon leaves and anchovies fillets, garnish with stoned olives, serve with anchovies butter.

Tyrolienne.—Grilled, garnish with fried onions rounds, and dice of tomatoes.

Vert-Pré.—Grilled, garnish with straw potatoes and water-cress.

BITOKS, FRICADELLES, KEFTEDES

Bitoks à la Russe.—Chopped raw beef mixed with bread crumbs soaked in milk and pressed, cooked chopped onions and egg seasoned, shape like tournedos, cook in clarified butter, coat with Smitanne sauce.

Fricadelles.—Two parts of cooked meat mixed with one part of mashed potatoes, cooked chopped onions, chopped parsley, egg, season and mix together, shape and cook, serve with vegetable purée and highly seasoned sauces.

Keftédès.—Same preparation without onions can be done with veal or pork.

COTES, COTELETTES, CHOPS

(Lamb, Mutton.)

Agneau et Mouton.—Grilled, serve with vegetables or purée of vegetables.

Belle-Vue.—(*See* **Côtes de Veau Belle-Vue**).

Bergère.—Egg and bread crumbs, cook in clarified butter, dress in a circle alternately with slices of grilled ham, garnish centre with straw potatoes, surround with cooked morels or Mousserons and glazed onions (small).

Bouchère.—Cut without shaping or trimming.

Bretonne.—Egg and bread crumbs, cook, dish in the form of a crown, garnish cenrte with beans à la Bretonne, serve with thickened gravy.

Buloz.—Grill one side, coat it with reduced Mornay sauce, egg and bread crumbs with half crumbs and half parmesan, cook the other side in butter and glaze in the Salamander, dress on pilaw rice and truffles.

Carignan.—Egg and bread crumbs à la Milanaise, cook, dress in the form of a crown, garnish centre with fritots of cocks combs and kidneys, serve with tomato sauce.

Charleroi.—Cook one side, stuff it with Soubise purée, coat à l'Anglaise, cook the other side in butter, glaze in Salamander.

Champvalon.—Partly cook both sides, lay them in a stew pan on a bed of raw potatoes, onions rounds, garlic, faggot, season, cover the cutlets with another layer of vegetables, moisten with white stock, cook and dish up.

Châtillon.—Prepare same way as above, stuff with mushrooms mixed with reduced Béchamel sauce, finish similar to Charleroi, garnish with Favorite purée, surround with Colbert sauce.

Chaud-Froid.—(*See* Chaud-froid preparation in **Fonds de Cuisine**).

Choiseul.—Cook one side, stuff with veal forcemeat mixed with truffles and tongue, finish cooking in slow oven, dish up in form of a crown, garnish centre with turned mushrooms, sweetbreads, artichoke bottoms, mixed with Allemande sauce.

Cyrano.—Cook in butter, dish up in the form of a crown, alternately with heart shaped croûtons, garnish round with artichoke bottoms filled with Foie Gras purée and decorated with slices of truffles, served with Chateaubriand sauce.

Financière.—Stuff with forcemeat mixed with chopped truffles, partly fry each side and braise. Dress in a circle, garnish centre with Financière.

Henriot.—Grill, cool, then cover with Villeroy sauce, egg and bread crumbs, cook in butter, dress in a circle, garnish centre with cooked mushrooms with a little cream.

Italienne.—Crumbed à la Milanaise, cooked in butter, dress in a circle, garnish centre with artichoke bottoms, mixed with Italian sauce.

Laura.—Grill, wrapped in pig's caul with spaghetti and dice of tomatoes, sprinkle with bread crumbs and melted butter, brown under salamander, surround with tomatoed half-glaze.

Maintenon.—Cook one side, stuff with Maintenon preparation, cook the other side in butter and glaze under salamander, serve with Périgueux sauce.

Malmaison.—Egg and bread crumbs, cook in butter, dress in a circle on a cushion of Duchesse potatoes, surround with tartlets filled with lentil purée and green pea purée alternately, grilled stuffed tomatoes.

Maréchale.—Egg and bread crumbs, cook in butter, dress in a circle, slices of truffle on each, garnish centre with asparagus heads.

Marie-Louise.—Egg and bread crumbs, cooked in butter, garnish with artichoke bottoms filled with mushroom purée and Soubise mixed together, served with thickened gravy.

Minute.—Cut thin, fry quickly in butter, add chopped parsley and lemon juice to the cooking butter.

Mirecourt.—Cook one side. Stuff with forcemeat, then finish cooking in the oven in a closed pan, garnish with artichoke purée, serve with Suprême sauce, flavoured with essence of mushrooms.

Montglas.—Stuffed with Montglas preparation, sprinkle with brown bread crumbs, finish cooking, then brown in the oven. Serve with half-glaze sauce.

Morland.—Dip in egg and roll in chopped truffles, cooked in butter, garnish centre with mushroom purée, serve buttered meat glaze.

Mousquétaire.—Cook one side in oil, then cover with Godiveau forcemeat mixed with Duxelle and chopped parsley, finish cooking in oven, dress in a circle, garnish centre with mushrooms and artichoke bottoms mixed with Duxelle sauce.

Murillo.—Same way as **Châtillon,** surrounded with dice of tomatoes and grilled Poivrons.

Navarraise.—Cook one side, stuff with salpicon of ham, mushrooms, sweet poivrons, mixed with Béchamel sauce, cook the other side and glaze under the salamander, surround with tomatoes à la Navarraise.

Nelson.—Same as above with Soubise stuffing, sprinkle with brown bread crumbs, garnish with croquettes potatoes, serve with Madeira sauce.

Orsay.—Cook, dress in a circle, garnish centre with julienne of mushrooms, truffles, and tongue mixed with Velouté.

Parisienne.—Grill, Parisienne garnish.

Pompadour.—Cook in butter, garnish with artichoke bottoms, filled with lentil purée, alternately with round croquette potatoes.

Provençale.—Cook one side, stuff with Provençale preparation, finish cooking in the oven, garnish with grilled mushrooms, filled with stuffed olives.

Réforme.—Egg and bread crumbs, with chopped ham added to the bread crumbs serve with Réforme sauce.

Sévigné.—Cook one side, cover with a salpicon of mushrooms and artichoke bottoms, egg and bread crumbs finish cooking in the oven, garnish with braised lettuces, and grilled mushrooms, served with Colbert sauce.

Suédoise.—Buttered and bread crumbs, frilled, served with Suédoise sauce.

Valois.—Serve same as **Montglas,** garnish with stuffed olives serve Valois sauce.

Villeroy.—Same way as all Villeroy preparations.

COTES DE PORC — PORK CUTLETS AND CHOPS

Charcutière.—Grill or fry the cutlet, cover with Charcutière sauce, served with mashed potatoes.

Flamande.—Partly fry the cutlet, finish cooking with sliced apples, to be served just as it is.

Grand'Mère.—Chop the meat with onion, add egg, butter, little seasoning, reshape the cutlet, add the bone, wrapped in pigs caul, grill slowly, served with mashed potatoes.

Grillée.—Serve with Piquante or Robert sauce.

Milanaise.—(*See* **Côtes de Veau Milanaise**).

COTES DE VEAU — VEAL CUTLETS

Basilic.—Fry, rinse the pan with white wine, finish with meat glaze and Basilic butter.

Belle-Vue.—Braise. decorate with truffles and cooked vegetables, garnish with aspic.

Bonne-Femme.—Cooked in butter, garnish Bonne-Femme.

Casserole.—Cooked in casserole and served with a thickened gravy.

Cocotte.—Cooked and garnish with small glaze onions, mushrooms, and shaped potatoes, served in cocotte.

Dreux.—Studded with tongue, ham and truffles, cooked in butter, dress in a circle, garnish Financière.

Fermière.—In a cocotte with Fermiere garnish.

Fines-Herbes.—Cooked in butter, rinse pan with white wine, serve with thickened gravy. Add fines herbes.

Jus.—(*See* **Casserole**).

Maintenon.—(*See* **Cotelettes de Mouton Maintenon**).

Maraîchère.—Cooked in butter, garnish with sautéd salsify, french beans, Château potatoes, serve with thickened gravy.

Maréchale.—(*Same as* **Côtelettes de Mouton Maréchale**).

Marigny.—Cooked in butter, garnish with tartlets filled with peas and French beans alternately. Serve thickened gravy.

Milanaise.—(*See* **Escalopes of Veal**).

Montholon.—Cooked in butter, decorated with tongue and truffles, and turned mushrooms. Surround with Suprême sauce.

Napolitaine.—Egg and bread crumbs, cooked in butter, Napolitaine garnish and thickened gravy.

Orléanaise.—Cooked in butter, Orléanaise garnish and thickened gravy.

Orloff.—(*See* **Côtelettes Maintenon**). Add slices of truffles and Orloff garnish.

Papillote.—Cooked in butter first, then place cutlet in a paper bag same as **Rouget en Papillote.**

Périgourdine.—Cooked in butter, cover with pork forcemeat mixed with truffles and foie gras, wrapped in pig's caul, grilled slowly, serve with Périgueux sauce.

Pojarski.—Veal forcemeat, mixed with white bread crumbs soaked in milk and well pressed, a little butter, reshape the cutlet, add the bone, then egg and bread crumbs, cooked in clarified butter, garnish to taste.

Printanière.—Braise, Printanière garnish, with braising stock.

Provençale.—(*See* **Côtelette de Mouton Provençale**).

Rubens (*Cold*).—Braise, garnish with hop shoots, cover with tomato sauce and aspic.

Talleyrand.—Cooked in butter, cool, cover the two sides with chicken forcemeat, dip in egg, then roll in chopped truffles, finish cooking and dish up with Talleyrand garnish, Périgueux sauce.

Truffles.—Cooked in butter, garnish with slices of truffles, mixed with meat glaze and buttered sauce.

Véronaise.—Cooked in butter, dressed on a layer of Polenta, garnish with dice of tomatoes, and French beans, Cover with tomatoed thickened gravy.

Vert-Pré.—(*See* **Rognons Vert-Pré**).

Vichy.—Cooked in butter, Vichy garnish and thickened gravy.

Viennoise.—(*See* **Escalopes Viennoise**).

Zingara.—(*See* **Escalopes Zingara**).

ESCALOPES, GRENADINS ET MEDALLIONS

(*Veal.*)

Anglaise.—Egg and bread crumbs, cooked in butter, dish up alternately with slices of grilled ham, pour over some nut brown cooked butter.

Champignons.—Egg and bread crumbs, cooked in butter, serve with mushroom sauce.

Crème (à la).—Cooked in butter, rinse pan with cream, add lemon juice, and pour over sauce.

Fritti Quanti.—Small scallops fried quickly in butter, serve thickened gravy and croûtons.

Grenadins.—Scallops larded with fat bacon, cook in butter, any of the following garnishes can be served: Japanese artichokes, spinach, Financière, Jardinière, Orléanaise, Sorrel, Peas, Asparagus heads, Vichy, and vegetable purée.

Holstein.—Egg and bread crumbs cooked in butter, garnish with fried eggs and fillet of Anchovies.

Milanaise.—Egg and bread crumbs, cooked in butter, Milanaise garnish.

Paprika.—Sprinkle with paprika, cooked in butter, rinse pan with cream, cover with sauce.

Viennoise (A).—Egg and bread crumbs, fried, dish up, and place a slice of lemon and anchovy fillet on each scallop, decorate dish with hard yolks and white of eggs, and chopped parsley, serve thickened gravy.

(B).—Dip the scallop in butter and fry in deep fat.

(C).—(*Schnitzel*). Season, floured, egg and bread crumbed, fry in deep fat, dished up with lemon and parsley.

Yorkshire.—Same as à l'Anglaise with slices of ham and capers.

Zingara.—Egg and bread crumbs, cooked, Zingara sauce and garnish.

NOISETTES, TOURNEDOS, FILETS MIGNONS

(*Lamb, Mutton, and Beef*)

Alexandra.—Cook in butter, garnish with slices of truffles and artichoke bottoms.

Alsacienne.—Grilled, dish on croûtons, garnish with sauerkraut and bacon.

Ambassade.—Grilled, dish on croûtons, garnish with artichoke bottoms filled with cooked shaped cucumbers, Choron sauce.

Ambassadrice.—Cook in butter, rinse pan with Madeira and thickened gravy, garnish with chicken livers, mushrooms, cockscombs and kidneys, braised lettuce and Noisette potatoes.

Andalouse.—Cook in butter, garnish with chipolatas and stuffed capsicums, a slice of egg plant filled with tomatoes and chopped ham on each tournedos.

Arenberg (D').—Cook in butter, rinse with madeira and half-glaze, Béarnaise sauce and truffle slices on each tournedos, garnish with tartlets filled with spinach alternately with carrots cooked with cream.

Arlésienne.—Cook in butter, dress on croûtons, garnish with slices of fried egg plant, rounds of fried onions, and slices of tomatoes, Madeira sauce.

Armenonville.—Cook in butter, dress on Anna potatoes croûtons, garnish with morels, cocks combs and kidneys, Madeira sauce.

Baltimore.—Cook in butter, dress on tartlets filled with sweet corn, set round of tomato tossed in butter on each tartlet and a smaller round of green capsicum on the tomato, Chateaubriand sauce.

Banquière.—Cook in butter, dress on croûtons, Madeira half-glaze sauce, and Banquière garnish.

Baron Brisse.—Cooked in butter, dice of cooked tomato on each tournedos, garnish with soufflé potatoes and artichoke bottoms filled with truffle balls, half-glaze sauce.

Béarnaise.—(*See* **Entrecôte Béarnaise**).

Béatrice.—Cooked in butter, garnish with morels, shaped carrots, artichoke bottoms, new potatoes, half-glazed sauce.

Beaugency.—Cooked in butter, dress on croûtons, place artichoke bottoms filled with dice of tomatoes on each tournedos and a slice of marrowfat on each tomato, Madeira half-glaze sauce.

Beauharnais.—Cooked in butter, garnish with stuffed mushrooms, and quarters of artichoke, Périgueux sauce.

Belle-Hélène.—Grilled, garnish with straw potatoes, and artichoke bottoms filled with Béarnaise sauce and water-cress.

Benjamin.—Cook in butter, dress on croûtons, garnish with croquettes potatoes, stuffed mushrooms on the tournedos, Madeira half-glaze sauce.

Bercy.—(*See* **Entrecôte Bercy**).

Berny.—Fried in oil, dress on Berny potatoes, place a slice of truffle on each Tournedos, pour over thin Poivrade sauce.

Blanchette.—Cooked in butter, cover with Bordelaise sauce mixed with julienne of truffles ham and mushrooms, place a slice of marrowfat on the top. Madeira half-glaze.

Bohémienne.—Cooked in butter, dress on rizotto, place dice of cooked tomato on top, and rounds of fried onions.

Bordelaise.—(*See* **Entrecôte Bordelaise**).

Bouquetière.—Cooked in butter, Bouquetiere garnish, Madeira half-glaze sauce.

Brabançonne.—Cooked in butter, garnish with tartlets filled with brussels sprouts, cover with Mornay sauce and glazed, serve croquette potatoes Madeira half-glaze.

Brébant.—Grilled, garnish with straw potatoes and water-cress, place a thread of Béarnaise sauce on the border of the Tournedos and meat glaze in the centre.

Bréhan.—Cooked in butter, garnish with artichoke bottoms filled with broad beans purée, alternately with small bunches of cauliflower covered with Hollandaise sauce and parsley potatoes.

Bristol.—Cooked in butter, garnish with rizotto croquettes, flageolet beans and Château potatoes rolled in meat glaze.

Bruxelloise.—Cooked in butter, garnish with Brussels sprouts, braised chicory and Château potatoes, Madeira half-glaze sauce.

Byzantine.—Grilled, dress on croûtons, garnish with Duchesse potatoes, croustades filled with cauliflower purée, stuffed braised lettuces, Madeira sauce.

Carignan.—Cooked in butter, dressed on Pomme Anna croûtons garnish with artichoke bottoms, filled with asparagus tips, and potato croquettes egg-shaped, emptied and refilled with foie gras purée.

Castillane.—Cooked in butter, dressed on croûtons, garnished with tartlet crusts filled with dice of tomatoes surrounded with fried rounds of onions.

Catalane.—Grilled, dress on artichoke bottoms, surround with grilled tomatoes, served with thickened veal gravy.

Catherine.—Cooked in butter, dress on Pomme Macaire croûtons, slice of marrowfat on the tournedos, serve Bordelaise sauce made with white wine and tomato purée.

Cendrillon.—Cooked in butter, dress on artichoke bottoms filled with truffled Soubise sauce, glaze, thickened tomato gravy.

Champignons.—(*See* **Entrecôte** same name).

Chantecler.—Cooked in butter, cover with port wine sauce, mixed with julienne of truffles, garnish with lambs' kidneys slightly cut and cooked, insert a cockscomb in the kidney and place the kidney on the tournedos, surround with rest of cocks combs and tartlets filled with asparagus heads.

Chartres.—Cooked in butter, decorate with blanched tarragon leaves, garnish with Château potatoes, cover with thickened tarragon gravy.

Chasseur.—Cooked in butter, cover with Chasseur sauce.

Châtelaine.——Cooked in butter, garnish with noisette potatoes, and artichoke bottoms.

Chevreuil.—Marinade the tournedos, toss in oil, cover with thin Poivrade sauce serve with chestnut purée.

Chevreuse.—Cooked in butter, cover with Madeira half-glaze sauce, garnish with artichoke bottoms filled with mushroom purée, a slice of truffle on top.

Choisy.—Cooked in butter, dressed on croûtons cover with white wine half-glaze sauce, garnish with braised lettuces and Château potatoes.

Choron.—Grilled, covered with Choron sauce, garnish with artichoke bottoms filled with peas, and noisettes potatoes.

Clamart.—Cooked in butter, garnish with artichoke bottoms filled with green peas, serve thickened Madeira gravy sauce.

Claude.—Cooked in butter, garnish with potatoes, croustades filled with shaped carrots and braised lettuces.

Clermont.—Cooked in butter, garnish with stuffed onions, and artichoke bottoms cover with Madeira sauce.

Cocarde.—Cooked in butter, dressed on artichoke bottoms, place on the tournedos half a tomato and a slice of foie gras, also, slice of truffle, cover with Madeira sauce, garnish with Parisienne potatoes.

Colbert.—Cooked in butter, dress on croûton made with a croquette of chicken preparation, cover with Madeira meat glaze, worked with butter, place a fried egg and slice of truffle on top of tournedos.

Coligny.—Cooked in butter, dress on croûton made of Duchesse potatoes, covered with Provençale sauce mixed with paysanne de Brionne.

Continental.—Grilled, garnish with mushrooms and grilled tomatoes, soufflé potatoes and water-cress, served Maître-d'hôtel butter.

Crécy.—Cooked in butter, garnish with carrots, Madeira half-glaze sauce.

Cussy.—Cooked in butter, garnish with artichoke bottoms filled with mushroom purée, port wine sauce, mixed with cockscombs and kidneys.

Dauphine.—Cooked in butter. Cover with Madeira sauce, garnish with Dauphine potatoes.

Deslignac.—Grilled, garnish Château potatoes, Choron sauce, on top of tournedos.

Dubarry.—Cooked in butter, surround with small cauliflowers covered with Mornay sauce and glazed. Sauce Madeira half-glaze.

Duchesse.—Grilled, dress on potatoes Duchesse croûtons, covered with Château sauce.

Dugléré.—Cooked in butter, dress on croûtons, garnish with whole tomatoes peeled and cooked, chicory and mushrooms, half-glaze sauce.

Duroc.—Same way as **Chasseur,** garnish with dice of tomatoes, and noisette potatoes.

Edesse.—Cooked in butter, cover with Madeira half-glaze mixed with julienne of truffles, cocks combs and kidneys, place round Duchesse potatoes.

G

Falgate.—Cooked in butter, coat both sides with mushrooms purée, wrap in pigs caul grilled slowly, Madeira sauce.

Favorite.—Cooked in butter, dress on croûton, put slice of truffle and foie gras on the tournedos, garnish with asparagus heads, coat with Madeira half-glaze.

Fermière.—Cook in butter, dress and Fermière garnish.

Fleuriste.—Cook in butter, cohered with half-glaze sauce, garnish with halves of tomatoes filled with Jardinière.

Florentine.—Grilled, dress on a bed of spinach leaves, cover with Chateaubriand sauce, garnish with Semolina croquettes.

Forestière.—Cooked in butter, dressed on croûtons, garnish with morels, bacon, and Parmentier potatoes.

Freddy.—Cooked in butter, dress on Anna potato croûtons, place some chicken livers and cockscombs on the tournedos, surround with little bunches of carrots and moulded asparagus heads.

Gabrielle.—Cooked in butter, dress on flat chicken croquette mixed with chopped truffles, garnish the top of tournedos with slices of truffles, alternately with slices of marrowfat, surround with croquette potatoes, and stuffed braised lettuces, Madeira half-glaze sauce.

Givry.—Cooked in butter, garnish with Parmentier potatoes, dice of artichoke bottoms, round of fried onions, covered with Devil sauce with a dash of brandy

Gourmets.—Split the tournedos, stuff it with a piece of foie gras, egg and bread crumbs, cooked in butter, place a slice of truffle on top, garnish with Château potatoes and mushrooms head, Madeira half-glaze sauce.

Grand-Duc.—Cooked in butter, garnish tournedos with a slice of marrowfat and truffles, surround with little bunches of asparagus heads, Périgueux sauce and Madeira.

Grand-Veneur.—(*See* **en Chevreuil**). Serve Grand-Veneur sauce instead of Poivrade sauce.

Helder.—Cooked in butter, place a thread of Béarnaise sauce round the edge of tournedos and dice of tomatoes in the centre, garnish with Parisienne potatoes Veal gravy and Madeira.

Henry IV.—(*See* **Entrecôte Henry IV**).

Ismaïl Bayeldi.—Cooked in butter, dress on slices of cooked egg plant, place half a cooked tomato on the tournedos, surround with pilaw rice, pour over tomatoed thickened gravy.

Italienne.—Cooked in butter, garnish with quarters of artichoke bottoms cooked à l'Italienne, served with Italienne sauce.

Japonaise.—Cooked in butter, dressed on potato croquettes croûtons, cover with half-glaze sauce, garnish with croustades filled with japanese artichokes.

Jetée-Promenade.—Grilled, dress on croûtons, half a grilled tomato filled with Béarnaise sauce placed on the top of tournedos, surround with soufflé potatoes and water-cress.

Jeune-France.—Grilled, garnished with grilled mushrooms and Chatouillard potatoes, place on the tournedos half a grilled tomato containing a fried egg, Bercy sauce.

Judic.—Cooked in butter, cover with Madeira half-glaze, Judic garnish.

Lakmé.—Cooked in butter, place grilled mushroom on top, dress on tartlets filled with broad bean purée, serve with thickened gravy.

Langtry.—Cooked in butter, dress on croûtons, place whole tomato poached in oven on the tournedos and stoned olive and chervil on the tomato, Périgueux sauce.

Lesdiguières.—Grilled, dressed on a large blanched spanish onion, garnish with braised spinach covered with Mornay sauce and glazed.

Lili.—Cooked in butter, dress on Pommes Anna croûtons, place an artichoke bottom garnished with foie gras and slice of truffle on each tournedos, cover, with Périgueux sauce.

Lorette.—Cooked in butter, dress on croûtons, cover with Madeira half-glaze, surround with chicken croquettes alternately with tartlets filled with asparagus heads and sliced truffles.

Lucernoise.—Cooked in butter, dress on croûton, on each tournedos place an artichoke bottom filled with dice of tomatoes and a slice of marrow garnish with croustades containing small croquette potatoes, emptied and refilled with chicken purée.

Lucullus.—Cooked in butter, dress on croûtons, place on the tournedos slice of truffle and a mushroom, surround with cockscombs, kidneys and asparagus heads, pour over, Périgueux sauce.

Lyonnaise.—(*See* **Entrecôte Lyonnaise**).

Mac-Mahon.—Cooked in butter, dressed in cocotte on a bed of potatoes, sauted with chopped onions, cover with meat glaze.

Madeleine.—Cook in butter, garnish with artichoke bottoms filled with Soubise sauce, and timbales of haricot bean purée, alternate.

Majordome.—Marinade the tournedos, cook in oil, coat with half-glaze sauce reduced with the marinade. Serve with lentil purée.

Maréchale.—(*See* **Côte de Mouton Maréchale**).

Marie-Louise.—Cook in butter, dress on round croûtons, coat with half-glaze, garnish with artichoke bottoms filled with onion purée and mushroom purée mixed together.

Marie-Thérèse.—Cook in butter, coat with tomatoed half-glaze, garnish with timbales filled with rizotto and sliced truffle on top.

Marigny.—Cook in butter, coat with madeira half-glaze, garnish with Fondante potatoes alternated with tartlet crusts filled with peas and French beans.

Marion-Delorme.—(*See* **Marie-Louise.**)

Marly.—Cook in butter, coat with madeira half-glaze, garnish with artichoke bottoms filled with carrot balls.

Marquise.—Cook in butter, dress on croûtons, coat with madeira half-glaze sauce. Marquise garnish.

Marseillaise.—Cook in butter, dress on croûtons, coat with Provençale sauce, set on the tournedos a stoned olive surrounded with anchovy fillet, garnish with tomatoes and copeaux potatoes.

Mascotte.—Cook in butter, coat with thickened gravy. Mascotte garnish.

Masséna.—Cook in butter, set on the tournedos an artichoke bottom containing slices of marrow, coat with Périgueux sauce.

Matignon.—Cook in butter, coat with meat glaze and white wine worked with butter and combined with vegetable paysanne, mushrooms and truffles, surround with straw potatoes.

Médicis.—Cook in butter, Médicis garnish, Béarnaise sauce on the tournedos, and Madeira half-glaze round.

G

Melba.—Cook in butter, coat with half-glaze and Port wine reduced, garnish with small tomatoes stuffed with salpicon of chicken, truffles, mushrooms, cohered with velouté and gratin; braised lettuces.

Ménagère.—Cook in butter. Place in a cocotte some French beans, peas, sliced carrot, small onions, salt and butter, moisten with water and cook with sealed lid, dress the tournedos on the vegetables and serve in the cocotte.

Mexicaine.—Cook in butter, dress on grilled mushrooms, filled with dice of tomatoes, garnish with grilled capsicums, tomatoed gravy.

Mignon.—Cook in butter, coat with Madeira half-glaze, set on each tournedos a round quenelle and sliced truffle garnish with artichoke bottoms filled with peas.

Mikado.—Cook in butter, dress on half grilled tomato, coat with Provençale sauce, garnish with Japanese artichokes tossed in butter.

Mirabeau.—(*See* **Entrecôte Mirabeau**).

Mireille.—Cook in butter, dress on croûtons made with Mireille potatoes, coat with Madeira half-glaze.

Mirette.—Cook in butter, coat with meat glaze and white wine reduced and worked with butter, garnish with Mirette potatoes.

Moderne.—Cook in butter, dress on grilled mushrooms, coat with Madeira half-glaze, garnish with croquette potatoes, braised lettuces and tomatoes, Madeira half-glaze sauce.

Moelle.—Grilled, slice of marrow on top, coat with marrow sauce.

Monaco.—Cook in butter, dress on croûtons, coat with Madeira half-glaze, combined with julienne of mushrooms and truffles, set on the tournedos a roundel of ham, a collop of brain on the ham and grilled mushroom to finish.

Montgolfier.—Grilled, garnish with soufflé potatoes, Maître-d'hôtel butter.

Montgomery.—Cook in butter, dress on spinach, mixed with forcemeat and poached in tartlet moulds, decorate with soubise and set a slice of truffle in the middle. Madeira half-glaze sauce.

Montmorency.—Cook in butter, dress on croûtons, coat with white wine reduced with half-glaze, Montmorency garnish.

Montmort.—Cook in butter, dress on croûtons made of fried brioche and stuffed with truffled foie gras purée. Coat with meat glaze, decorate with truffles, surround with Madeira and veal gravy worked with foie gras purée.

Montpensier.—Cook in butter, garnish with artichoke bottoms filled with asparagus heads, cohered with butter, coat with Madeira half-glaze combined with truffles julienne.

Morilles (aux).—Cook in butter, coat with half-glaze, garnish with cooked morels.

Nancy.—Same as **Rossini**, without truffles.

Napolitaine.—Cook in butter, Napolitaine garnish and tomato sauce.

Narbonnaise.—Cook in butter, dress in a cocotte on haricot bean purée, on top set some slices of fried egg plant filled with dice of tomato, coat with Madeira half-glaze.

Nichette.—Cook in butter, garnish with grilled mushrooms filled with small balls of carrots, coat with marrow sauce combined with cockscombs and kidneys.

Niçoise.—Cook in butter, Niçoise garnish, serve with thickened tomatoed gravy.

Ninon.—Cook in butter, dress on Anna potatoes, set on the tournedos a small bouchée filled with asparagus heads and julienne of truffles cohered with butter. Madeira and thickened gravy.

THE COOKERY REPERTORY 135

Opéra.—Cook in butter, dress on tartlet crusts filled with chicken livers cohered with Madeira sauce, coat with half-glaze, surround with asparagus heads.

Orientale.—Cook in butter, dress on croûtons, set on the tournedos a sweet potato croquette, surround with tomatoes, alternate with rizotto " à la Grecque", tomated gravy.

Paloise.—Grilled, Béarnaise sauce with chopped mint, on top, garnish with noisette potatoes. Marrow sauce.

Parisienne.—Cook in butter, coat with Madeira half-glaze. Parisienne garnish.

Parmentier.—Cook in butter, coat with Madeira half-glaze. Garnish with Parmentier potatoes.

Périgourdine.—Same as **Rossini,** without foie gras.

Persane.—Cook in butter, dress on a half grilled tomato, coat with Chateaubriand sauce, garnish with stuffed green capsicums and fried bananas.

Péruvienne.—Grilled, coat with thin tomato sauce, garnish with stuffed oxalis.

Petit-Duc.—Cook in butter, dress on tartlets filled with chicken purée, sauce Madeira half-glaze.

Piémontaise.—Cook in butter, garnish with tartlets filled with rizotto à la Piémontaise, coat with Madeira half-glaze.

Pompadour.—Cook in butter, garnish with artichoke bottoms filled with noisette potatoes, Choron sauce on top of tournedos. Serve with Périgueux sauce.

Portugaise.—Cook in butter, dice of cooked tomatoes on the tournedos, thickened tomatoed gravy.

Princesse.—Cook in butter, garnish with asparagus heads and slices of truffles on the tournedos, white wine, half-glaze sauce.

Provençale.—Cook in butter, Provençale sauce and garnish.

Rachel.—Cook in butter, dress on croûtons, set on the tournedos an artichoke bottom filled with sliced marrow, coat with Bordelaise sauce.

Régence.—Cook in butter, dress on croûtons, Régence garnish.

Renaissance.—Cook in butter, Renaissance garnish, Madeira half-glaze sauce.

Riche.—Cook in butter, set a slice of foie gras and truffle on top, coat with Madeira half-glaze sauce, garnish with artichoke bottoms filled with asparagus heads.

Richemont.—Cook in butter, dress on croûtons, coat with Madeira and thickened gravy combined with paysanne of morels and truffle.

Rivoli.—Cook in butter, dress on Anna potatoes, coat with Périgueux sauce.

Rohan.—Cook in butter, garnish with artichoke bottoms, filled with collops of foie gras, alternate with tartlets filled with sautéd veal kidneys, a cocks comb between, sauce Xérès half-glaze.

Rossini.—Cook in butter, place a foie gras collop on the tournedos and a slice of truffle, coat with Madeira half-glaze.

Roumanille.—Cook in butter, dress on a half grilled tomato, coat with tomatoed Mornay sauce, glaze, garnish with slices of fried egg plant, thickened gravy.

Saint-Florentin.—Cook in butter, Saint-Florentin garnish, coat with white wine Bordelaise sauce.

Saint-Germain.—Cook in butter, Saint-Germain garnish, coat with Béarnaise sauce.

Saint-Gothard.—Grilled, dress on croûtons, set on the tournedos half a grilled tomato filled with Béarnaise sauce, surround with soufflé potatoes.

Saint-Mandé.—Cook in butter, dress on Pomme Macaire croûtons garnish with heaps of green peas, alternated with asparagus heads, white wine thickened gravy.

Sarah Bernhardt.—Cook in butter, dress on croûtons, slice of marrow on the tournedos, coat with Port wine half-glaze sauce. Garnish with tomatoes and braised lettuces.

Sarde.—Cook in butter, Sarde garnish, thin tomato sauce.

Seymour.—Cook in butter, garnish the top of tournedos with an artichoke bottom filled with Béarnaise sauce and dice of truffles, Madeira half-glaze combined with stuffed olives.

Staël.—Cook in butter, dress on round flat chicken croquettes, set on the tournedos a large grilled mushroom filled with mushroom purée, surround with tartlets filled with peas, Madeira half-glaze.

Strasbourgeoise.—Same as **Nancy.**

Sully.—Same as **Judic** with Parisienne potatoes, coat with Madeira sauce, combined with cocks combs and kidneys.

Talleyrand.—Cook in butter, dress on Anna potato croûtons, set on the tournedos an artichoke bottom filled with a foie gras collop, coat with sauce Périgueux.

Tivoli.—Cook in butter, dress on croûton, garnish with grilled mushrooms filled with cocks combs and kidneys cohered with Suprême sauce, asparagus heads. Madeira half-glaze sauce.

Truffes (aux).—Cook in butter, coat with Madeira half-glaze sauce combined with truffles, olive shaped.

Tyrolienne.—(*See* **Entrecôte Tyrolienne**).

Valence.—Cook in butter, garnish with noodle croquettes and Financière garnish added to the Madeira half-glaze.

Valenciennes.—Cook in butter, dress on pilaw rice containing dice of red pimento, coat with white wine half-glaze.

Valentin.—Same as **Portugaise,** add noisette potatoes.

Valentino.—Cook in butter, dress on a croûton made with scooped turnip, blanched, stuffed with semolina, sprinkled with Parmesan ʹand glazed, sauce Madeira half-glaze, reduced soubise on the tournedos.

Valois.—Cook in butter, dress on Anna potato croûtons, coat with white wine half-glaze sauce added with sliced artichoke bottoms.

Vatel.—Cook in butter, dress on Anna potato croûtons, border the tournedos with green pea purée, garnish centre with dice of tomatoes, sprinkle with chopped tarragon, surround with sautéd cèpes and braised chicory, white wine half-glaze sauce.

Ventadour.—Cook in butter, dress on tartlets filled with artichoke purée, slices of truffles and marrow on top, coat with Chateaubriand sauce, surround with noisette potatoes.

Verdi.—Cook in butter, dress on foie gras croûton, coat with Soubise sauce, glaze, garnish with croustades made with potato duchesse and filled with carrot balls, alternate with braised lettuces, Madeira half-glaze sauce.

Vert-Pré.—(*See* **Rognons Vert-Pré**).

Victoria.—Cook in butter, dress on flat chicken croquettes, garnish with tomatoes stuffed with mushroom purée and glazed, Madeira half-glaze sauce.

Villaret.—Grilled, dress on tartlets filled with flageolets purée, grill mushrooms on top, coat with Chateaubriand sauce.

Villemer.—Grilled, dress on croûtons, scooped and filled with soubise purée and chopped truffles, coat with meat glaze, set a slice of truffle on the tournedos, Madeira sauce.

Voisin.—Cook in butter, dress on pomme Anna croûtons, garnish with spinach and chicken forcemeat poached in dariole moulds, thickened tarragon gravy.

Xavier Leroux.—Cook in butter, dress on spinach prepared as above, garnish the top with croustades filled with chicken purée and asparagus heads, surround with noisette potatoes, artichoke bottoms filled with carrot balls, alternate with balls of cooked beetroots.

Zingara.—Cook in butter, Zingara garnish, thickened gravy.

RIS DE VEAU ET D'AGNEAU
LAMB AND VEAL SWEETBREADS

Cooking Process

Blanch the sweetbread in boiling water, trim, lard with fat bacon and braise with aromates and brown veal stock.

Bonne-Maman.—Braised with large vegetable julienne, moisten with veal stock, serve in cocotte, with the reduced braising liquor.

Brighton (*Cold*).—Stud with tongue and truffles, braise, cool, surround with artichoke bottoms filled with jardinière cohered with mayonnaise, chopped aspic.

Broche (à la).—Wrap in oiled paper, cook in front of an open fire, garnish and sauce to taste.

Caisse (en).—Collops of sweetbreads, poach ,dress in " caissettes " garnish with truffles and mushrooms, coat with Suprême sauce.

Cévenole.—Braise, garnish with braised onions, glazed chestnuts and brown bread croûtons, coat with the reduced braising liquor.

Chambellan.—Stud with truffles, braise, glaze, garnish with tartlets made with chicken forcemeat and stuffed with truffles cohered with half-glaze, surround with suprême sauce combined with julienne of truffles.

Champignons.—Braise, garnish and mushroom sauce.

Chartreuse.—(*See* preparation in **Entrées de Gibier**).

Comtesse.—Stud with truffles, braise, glaze, surround with braised lettuces and alternate with large quenelles, coat with reduced braising liquor.

Coquilles.—(*See* preparation in **Entrées Volantes**).

Crépinettes.—(*See* preparation in **Entrées Volantes**).

Cromesquis.—(*See* preparation in **Entrées Volantes**).

Croustades.—(*See* preparation in **Entrées Volantes**).

Demidoff.—Stud with lard and truffles, braise, finish cooking with paysanne of vegetables and slices of truffles and the braising liquor reduced and the fat removed.

Dreux.—Stud with truffles and tongue, braise, finish same as **Côte de Veau à la Dreux**.

Epinards (aux).—Braise, serve with spinach purée, coat with reduced braising liquor.

Escalopes (en).—Same garnishes as for Veal Collops and Côtelettes.

Excelsior.—Stud with truffles, poach in white stock, garnish with quenelles of different colours, 1st. chopped tongue in the forcemeat, 2nd. chopped truffles, 3rd. plain, coat with Soubise sauce combined with julienne of truffles, mushrooms and tongue.

Financière.—Braise, garnish and Financière sauce.

G

Florentine.—Braise, dress on a bed of spinach, reduced braising liquor.

Godard.—Braise, garnish and Godard sauce.

Gourmands (des).—Braise, dress, a thick collop of fresh cooked foie gras on top, surround with asparagus heads, coat with the reduced braising liquor combined with slices of truffles.

Gourmets.—Braise, dress in cocotte with slices of truffles and foie gras, add braising liquor, seal lid with soft paste, serve in cocotte.

Grillé Camargo.—Grilled, dressed in croustade made with brioche paste and filled with peas à la Française and Vichy carrots, slices of grilled ham on top.

Grillé Gismonde.—Grilled, dress in croustade half filled with mushrooms and artichoke bottoms, Chateaubriand sauce.

Grillé Jocelyn.—Grilled, dress on a large potato, cooked, scooped and filled with curried Soubise purée, half a grilled tomato and half pimento on top.

Grillé Saint-Germain.—Grilled, Saint-Germain garnish.

Guizot.—Braise, garnish with tomatoes, stuffed olives and Dauphine potatoes, coat with braising liquor flavoured with chopped mint.

Judic.—Braise, dress on croûtons, garnish with braised lettuces, slices of truffles, coat with Madeira sauce combined with cocks combs and kidneys.

Jus (au).—Braise, serve in cocotte with the reduced braising liquor.

Loubet.—In Chartreuse, garnish top with small cauliflowers coated with Hollandaise sauce, surround with braised lettuces, half-glaze sauce.

Maintenon.—Braise, glaze, dress on croûtons, slices of truffles, surround with Suprême sauce.

Marie-Stuart.—Stud with tongue and truffles, braise, garnish with purée of celeriac, Fleurons.

Montauban.—Braise and glaze, garnish with roundels of white pudding made with chicken forcemeat and truffles, mushroom heads, coat this garnish with Suprême sauce, alternate with croquettes made with rice and tongue.

Montglas.—Braise and glaze, garnish with quarters of truffles and foie gras, reduced braising liquor and half-glaze Madeira.

Montpensier.—Braise. (*See* **Tournedos** same name).

Nesselrode.—Braise, garnish with chestnut purée, reduced braising liquor.

Orloff.—Braise, dress in cocotte with braised celery, julienne of truffles and the reduced braising liquor, seal lid with soft paste.

Papillote.—Collops of sweetbread, braise and treat (same as **Rougets en Papillote**.)

Parisienne.—Stud with truffles and tongue, braise, glaze, Parisienne garnish **(B)**, coat with reduced braising liquor.

Petits Pois (aux).—Braise, glaze, garnish with new peas cohered with butter.

Poulette.—Collops of sweetbreads braised in white stock and coat with Poulette sauce.

Princesse.—Braise, glaze, garnish with artichoke bottoms filled with marrow and coated with Bordelaise sauce, chopped parsley on the marrow, reduced braising liquor.

Quenelles d'Ecrevisses (aux).—Stud with truffles, braise, garnish with crayfish tails cohered with Suprême sauce and crayfish carcases stuffed with chicken forcemeat combined with crayfish cullis, reduced braising liquor.

Rachel.—Braise, glaze, garnish with artichoke bottoms, containing a slice of marrow coated with Bordelaise sauce, chopped parsley on the marrow, reduced braising liquor.

Régence.—Stud with truffles, cook without browning the sweet bread, garnish with Régence **(B)** reduced cooking liquor.

Richelieu (*Cold*).—Operate same as **Bonne-Maman,** add julienne of truffles, cool, remove the fat and serve in the cocotte.

Royale.—Same as **Régence.**

Saint-Cloud.—Stud with truffles, tongue and ham, braise and glaze, Régence garnish.

Suédoise (*Cold*).—Collops of braised sweetbread, cut with a round cutter, coat with horse-radish butter, cover with a slice of tongue same shape, glaze with aspic, dress round a pyramid of vegetable cohered with mayonnaise, shredded lettuces round the dish, heart in middle.

Surcouf.—Braise, dress in timbale, garnish with quarters of artichoke bottoms, carrots, new turnips and asparagus head. Coat with the reduced braising liquor.

Talleyrand.—Collops of sweetbreads, dish in timbale on a Talleyrand garnish, coat with Périgueux sauce.

Timbale Badoise,—Garnish timbale with noodles and ham, dress the collops of sweetbread in a circle, fill the middle with Financière garnish.

Timbale Condé.—Garnish bottom of timbale with tossed mushrooms, coat the collops with truffled chicken forcemeat, poach and dress in a circle, fill centre with slices of truffles cohered with Madeira sauce.

Toulousaine.—Braise in white stock, coat with Suprême sauce, Toulousaine garnish.

Villeroy.—In collops, coat both sides with Villeroy sauce, egg and crumb fry deep fat, dress in a circle, garnish centre with peas or asparagus heads, tomato sauce.

Vol-au-Vent.—Collops of sweetbread with Godard garnish, Régence, Toulousaine, etc., can be served in Timbale if desired.

Volnay.—Braise, glaze, garnish with Soubise on one side and mushroom purée on the other side, reduced braising liquor.

G

Entrees   Volantes   Diverses

ATTEREAUX

Skewers composed of collops of different ingredients, coated with a reduced sauce, egged and crumbed and fried deep fat, served on serviettes with fried parsley.

Génevoise.—Chickens' livers, braised lamb sweetbreads, poached brains, mushrooms, truffles and artichoke bottoms, coated with duxelle sauce, cool, spread with forcemeat and finish as above.

Pahlen.—Lobster tails, mushrooms, truffles, mussels, oysters, coated with Villeroy sauce, finish as above, when fried take off the skewer, replace with a silver one adding a small truffle and rice croquette filled with lobster salpicon, dress on fried bread cushion.

Villeroy.—Sweetbreads, brains, foie gras, cockscombs and kidneys. Extra ingredients: mushrooms, truffles, tongue, ham.

BARQUETTES ET TARTELETTES

Are generally done with short paste and cooked in oven with rice, beans or cherry stones, wrapped in paper and placed in the cavity.

Châtillon.—Garnish with sliced mushrooms cooked with cream, cover with chicken forcemeat, poached in oven.

Diane.—Garnish with collops of partridge fillets and slices of truffles cohered with Salmis sauce, cover with game forcemeat poached in oven.

Filets de Sole.—Garnish with salpicon of fillets of sole, truffles and mushrooms cohered with Normande sauce.

Gauloise.—Garnish with cockscombs and kidneys cohered with meat glaze and butter, cover with chicken forcemeat combined with chopped ham, poached in oven.

Gnocchi.—Garnish with gnocchi cover with Mornay sauce, glaze.

Joinville.—With garnish and Joinville sauce.

Laitances Florentine.—Garnish bottom with spinach, place the poached soft roes on it, coat with Mornay sauce and gratin.

Laitances Parmesan.—Same as above, without the spinach, cover with Parmesan soufflé, cook in oven.

Marly.—Same as **Diane,** pheasant instead of partridge.

Nantua.—With garnish and Nantua sauce.

Ostendaise.—Garnish with oysters cohered with white wine sauce, sprinkle with chopped truffles.

Victoria.—Garnish with lobster, truffles, mushrooms cohered with Victoria sauce. Decorate with truffles and coral.

BOUCHEES

(Are generally made with puff paste.)

Bohémienne.—Small brioches cooked in fluted moulds, scoop and garnish with salpicon of foie gras and truffles, cohered with Madeira sauce.

Diane.—Garnish with salpicon of game and truffles cohered with salmis sauce.

Grand-Duc.—Garnish with julienne of truffles and asparagus heads, cohered with Suprême sauce, are used for garnishes.

Hollandaise.—Garnish with smoked poached salmon, cohered with Hollandaise sauce, poached oysters on top.

Joinville.—Fill with Joinville garnish and sauce.

Marie-Rose.—Shrimp tails, truffles, small quenelles cohered with shrimp sauce, slices of tomatoed forcemeat to form a lid.

Mogador.—Fill with salpicon of tongue, whites of chicken cohered with foie gras Suprême sauce.

Monseigneur.—Garnish bottom with purée of soft roes and truffles, lay a poached roe on it and cover with shrimp sauce, slices of truffles to finish.

Montglas.—Salpicon of foie gras, mushrooms, tongue, truffles cohered with Madeira sauce, finish with sliced truffles.

Nantua.—Fill with Nantua garnish and sauce.

Périgourdine.—Fill with truffle purée cohered with Madeira half-glaze.

Princesse.—Same as **Reine** with asparagus heads.

Reine.—Salpicon of calf's sweatbread or lamb's, white of chicken, mushrooms and truffles cohered with Suprême sauce.

Saint-Hubert.—Fill with game purée, cohered with Salmis sauce.

Stuart.—Fill with minced chicken and mushrooms cohered with Suprême sauce combined with crayfish cullis.

Victoria.—Salpicon of lobster and truffles cohered with Victoria sauce.

BROCHETTES — SKEWERS

Are collops of ingredients on a skewer, alternated with mushrooms, bacon, mint, bay leaves, etc. Coated with duxelle if necessary, rolled in melted butter and crumbs, grilled and served on Maître-d'hôtel butter.

COQUILLES — SHELLS

Make a border with Duchesse potato, brown in oven, coat the bottom with sauce, place the ingredients, fish or meats on the sauce, cover with same sauce and glaze or gratin.

CROMESQUIS

The ingredients are cohered with reduced sauce and yolk of eggs, cooled, made into shapes wrapped in pancake or pig's caul and dipped in batter, fry deep fat.

G

CROQUETTES

Same preparation as cromesquis, shape like a cork, or round and flat, or like cutlets, etc., egg and crumb, fry deep fat. The principal ingredients are lamb, chicken, game, fish, rice, maize, etc., serve on serviette with fried parsley.

CROUSTADES

Generally made with short paste, can be done with potato duchesse, or semolina, or rice well done and cohered with yolk of eggs, let cool on a dish, shape with a round cutter, egg and crumb, fry deep fat and scoop. Croustades are garnished same as tartlets and barquettes.

DARTOIS

Wrap the ingredients in puff paste, can be done with sardines, anchovies, fillets of sole, etc.

FONDANTS

Are croquettes made with purée of ingredients, shaped to taste and finished same as croquettes.

FRITOTS

Collops or pieces of brain, chicken, calves head calves foot, etc., season, add oil, lemon juice, chopped parsley, dry on a cloth, dip in batter, fry deep fat, fried parsley, tomato sauce.

HACHIS ET EMINCES — HASH OR MINCE

Américaine.—Half quantity of minced cooked meat and half cooked potatoes in dice, cohered with tomato sauce, sprinkle with dice of sauté potatoes and chopped parsley.

Bonne-Femme.—Salpicon of chicken and mushrooms cohered with cream, surround with sauté potatoes.

Chicken Hash or Emincé de Volaille.—Mince chicken and cream, dish in timbale.

Corned Beef Hash.—Half potato pulp cooked in oven, crushed with a fork and half quantity of pressed beef mixed with cooked chopped onions, shape into round pellets, cook in clarified butter, each side.

Fermière.—Mince beef, mutton or lamb, mixed with sauce, dress in a border of sliced cooked potatoes, sprinkle with bread crumbs and set to gratin.

Grand'Mère.—Mix 3 parts of hash with one part of mashed potato, cover with potato purée, sprinkle with bread crumbs and grated cheese. Set to gratin.

Gratin.—In a border of duchess potatoes or in shells, finish (same as Fermiere.)

Maintenon.—In a deep dish, mushroom purée, dress in a circle some round flat croquettes of chicken, garnish centre with collops of white chicken, mushrooms and slices of truffles, coat with thin Soubise sauce.

Marianne.—On a bed of spinach in leaves, make a border of mashed potato, garnish centre with hash and set to gratin.

Moussaka.—Hash, gratin and surround with fried egg plant in slices.

Parmentier.—Sauté potatoes underneath a layer of hash and cover with mashed potatoes, sprinkle with crumbs, gratin.

Portefeuille (en).—A layer of Lyonnaise potatoes alternated with minced beef, mutton or lamb, coat with Robert sauce and finish with mashed potatoes, crumbs and gratin.

Portugaise.—Mix the hash with dice of tomato, set to gratin and surround with stuffed tomatoes.

MAZAGRANS

This term is employed to designate all kinds of preparations enclosed between two layers of duchesse potatoes.

RISSOLES

This term is employed to designate all kinds of ingredients enclosed between two layers of puff paste, cooked in deep fat, served on serviette with fried parsley, sauce to taste.

MOUSSE — MOUSSELINE AND SOUFFLE

MOUSSE FROIDE — COLD MOUSSE

Preparation, ingredient required cooked and passed through the sieve, season, work with double cream adding some liquid aspic jelly. The mousses are moulded in large moulds and mousselines in small ones, enough for one person.

MOUSSE CHAUDE — HOT MOUSSE

Raw ingredients pounded and passed through the sieve, work on ice with cream and a little white of egg if necessary, mould and poach.

Mousse de Jambon au Paprika Rose (*Hot*).—With raw ham seasoned with pink paprika, operate same as Hot Mousse.

Mousse de Volaille Périgord (*Hot or Cold*).—With chicken and dice of truffles, operate as above.

SOUFFLE CHAUD — HOT SOUFFLE

Purée of the ingredients raw or cooked, mixed with Béchamel sauce, cohered with yolk of eggs, add white of eggs beaten to a stiff froth.

Soufflé de Volaille à la Reine.—Cooked chicken passed through the sieve, operate same as for hot soufflé, half fill a mould with the soufflé preparation, add salpicon of chicken cohered with Suprême sauce, cover with the soufflé and cook in oven.

PILAW ET RIZOTS — RISOTTO

Preparation of the Rice.—*Chopped onions and rice, fry in butter, moisten with white consomme in the proportion of two parts of liquid to a part of rice, season, add faggot, bring to the boil, and set to cook in oven for 17 minutes. Transfer to another pan as soon as it is cooked and mix in a little butter with a fork.*

Pilaw d'Agneau.—Dice of lamb partly fried with chopped onions, add Curry powder and tomatoed half-glaze, pour in a well of pilaw rice.

Pilaw de Cailles.—Cook some quails, dish them on a bed of pilaw rice combined with meat glaze.

Pilaw de Volaille à l'Orientale.—Cut the fowl in small pieces, fry with chopped onions, moisten with thin half-glaze and tomato sauce, add julienne of red pimento, dish in a well of pilaw rice combined with pimento.

Pilaw de Volaille à la Parisienne.—Fry the chicken pieces in butter, with onion, bay leaf and concasséd tomatoes, add some rice, moisten with white stock and cook 25 minutes. When cooked add a little reduced veal stock, dish in timbale, serve tomato sauce.

Pilaw de Foie de Volaille à la Turque.—Partly fry the chicken livers with chopped onions in butter, moisten with tomatoed half-glaze, dish in a well of pilaw rice.

SUBRICS

Same preparation as croquettes, shaped like macaroons and cook in butter.

TIMBALES

Bontoux.—Half fill a timbale with spaghetti à l'Italienne add quenelles, cockscombs, kidneys, collops of white chicken, sweetbreads cohered with tomated half-glaze.
Milanaise.—Same as above with spaghetti à la Milanaise.

VOL-AU-VENT

Made with puff paste, make the layer of paste about four-fifths of an inch, cut it round the size required, set it on a baking sheet, describe a circle on top with the point of a knife, gild and cook in a rather hot oven. When cooked remove cover and take out the puff paste from the inside, garnish with Banquière, Godard, Financière, eggs, fillets of sole Nantua, Normande, sweetbreads, etc.

GIBIER — GAME

ALOUETTES OU MAUVIETTES — LARKS

Aspic.—(*See* preparation in **Fonds de Cuisine**), bone, stuff, cook and prepare in aspic.
Bonne-Femme.—Cook in butter, in a cocotte, add pieces of bacon and small onions, set alight with brandy, add thickened gravy.
Caisse.—(*See* **Cailles en Caisse**).
Gratin.—Stuff with gratin forcemeat, place them in a deep dish on a layer of forcemeat, coat with Duxelle sauce, sprinkle with crumbs and melted butter, gratin.
Marianne.—Cook in butter, dress in cocotte on a bed of spinach.
Normande.—Sliced apples tossed in butter and placed in the bottom of a cocotte, lay the sautéd larks on the apple and put another layer of apple to finish, add a little cream and finish cooking in the oven.
Paysanne.—Fry in butter with bacon and bay leaves ,add flour, moisten with white white stock, season, add small glazed onions and noisette potatoes.
Père Philippe.—Baked potatoes, scoop enough of the pulp to make room for a lark wrapped in fat bacon and previously tossed in butter, replace the top, placed in greased paper and finish cooking in slow oven.
Piémontaise.—Dish the larks on rizotto à la piémontaise, surround with game half-glaze.
Pithiviers (Pâté de).—Bone the birds, stuff with the inside, brains, and chicken forcemeat, coat them all round with this forcemeat and place them on a layer of pâté paste and cover with another layer, stick together, give it the shape of a pilaw, gild and cook in oven.

BECASSES ET BECASSINES — WOODCOCK AND SNIPE

Alcantara.—Bone the bird, stuff with foie gras and truffles, marinade in port wine for 2 days, cook in casserole, serve on a bed of truffles cooked with port wine, coat with reduced cooking liquor.

Ancienne.—Roast for 10 minutes, cut into joints, take off the skin, chop the carcass and make a sauce with a mirepoix and the bones, add brandy and moisten with veal stock, pass through the tammy cloth or fine strainer, cohere with the intestines and foie gras purée, dress in cocotte, garnish with mushrooms, truffles, cockscombs, surround with heart-shaped croûtons.

Aspic.—(*See* preparation in **Fonds de Cuisine**). Boned and stuffed.

Belle-Vue (*Cold*).—Bone, stuff with gratin forcemeat of game, with a round of foie gras and truffles in the middle, wrap in muslin, poach in veal stock for 20 minutes, cool, coat with brown Chaudfroid sauce, decorate and glaze with aspic jelly, dress and put the heads back after having coated them with same and imitate the eyes with white of egg and truffles, surround with chopped aspic.

Bengalines.—In egg shaped moulds, garnish the bottom with strong game fumet, a collop of woodcock fillet and sliced truffle, cover with snipe mousse, When set unmould and coat with Chaudfroid sauce, decorate, dress in deep dish and cover with aspic jelly.

Carême.—Roasted underdone, remove the suprêmes, cut them in halves lengthwise, coat them with French mustard thinned with lemon juice, dress in timbale, keep warm, prepare a good fumet, add the intestines, strain and coat with the sauce.

Cécilia.—(*See* **Cailles Cécilia**).

Chaudfroid.—(*See* preparation in **Fonds de Cuisine**).

Ecaillère.—Stuff with a preparation of chopped intestines, chicken, mushrooms, bacon, cibols, oysters, salt, paprika, fine Champagne, cook in casserole, swill pan with mushroom cooking liquor, sour cream, anchovy essence, lemon juice, garnish with poached oysters, coat with sauce chopped parsley.

Esclarmonde (*Cold*).—Collops of woodcock fillets coated with mousse of the name and placed on collops of foie gras, decorate ,glaze with aspic, prepare a woodcock mousse and unmould it on a rice cushion, surround with the fillets, chopped aspic.

Flambée.—Cook underdone, carve into joints, swill pan with fine champagne, add the chopped intestines, moisten with the juice of the pressed carcass and game stock, lemon juice and cayenne pepper, work with butter and coat the suprême.

Financière.—Suprêmes, cooked in butter, garnish and sauce Financière.

Grillée.—Split down the back, crumb and grill, dish up and surround with toasts coated with the chopped intestines, salt, pepper and mustard serve with Diable sauce.

Hongroise.—Suprêmes, sprinkle with pink paprika, cook in butter with chopped onions, swill pan with cream and coat the fillets with the sauce.

Impériale.—(*See* **Faisan** same name).

Marivaux (*Cold*).—Remove the suprêmes of a cooked woodcock, stuff the carcass with a mousse of woodcock and foie gras, shape it like a bird, coat the legs and tail with Chaudfroid sauce, replace the colloped fillets alternating with collops of foie gras, decorate with slices of truffles, dress in a deep dish, glaze with aspic and fill the spaces with chopped aspic jelly.

Mousse et Mousseline.—(*See* preparation in **Entrées Volantes**).

Nagornoff.—Suprêmes of woodcock, cook in butter, swill pan with Madeira and woodcock fumet cohered with arrow-root, dress round a mousse of woodcock, collops of foie gras and slice of truffles on each suprême, coat with the sauce.

Salmis (*Hot or Cold*).—(*See* **Perdreaux** in **Entrées de Gibier).**

Sanhard.—(*See* **Grive** same name).

Sautée au Champagne.—Cut into small joints, season, cook in butter for 5 minutes, dress in timbale, swill pan with champagne, add the intestines and chopped carcass, pound in mortar with butter, lemon juice, cayenne pepper, pass through the sieve, warm up and pour on the pieces.

Sautée aux Truffes.—Same as above, with Madeira instead of Champagne, quarters of truffles.

Soufflé Favart.—Roasted underdone, remove the suprêmes and breast bone, fill the carcass with a mousse of woodcock containing the chopped intestines, reshape the bird, poach, collop the suprême and dress them on the mousse, decorate with slices of truffles, coat with half-glaze sauce reduced with woodcock stock.

Souvaroff.—(*See* **Faisan Souvaroff** in **Entrées et Relevés).**

Timbale Diane.—(*See* **Perdreau** same name).

Timbale Metternich.—Dress in timbale, the suprêmes alternated with collops of sauted foie gras, make a cullis with the carcass and fine champagne, work with butter and pour over the pieces.

Timbale Nesselrode.—Same as above, garnish with cooked and glazed chestnuts.

BECS-FIGUES ET BEGUINETTES — FIG PECKERS

These birds are rarely seen in England. All the lark preparations can be applied to them.

CAILLES — QUAILS

Alexandra.—Cook in cocotte garnish with dice of truffles, quarters of artichoke bottoms, cocks combs and kidneys, Madeira sauce.

Alexis.—(*See* **Muscat**). Swill with cream.

Archiduc.—(*See* **Poulet Archiduc** in **Entrées Volantes de Volaille).**

Belle-Vue.—(*See* **Bécasse Froide** same name).

Caisses (*Hot*).—Bone, stuff with truffled gratin forcemeat containing the livers, roll in papers and poach. Serve in caisses. Coat with Duxelle sauce made with game fumet; slices of truffles and mushroom heads on top.

(*Cold*).—(Same as **Belle-Vue**.) Dress in caisses.

Carmen (*Cold*).—Poach in veal stock and white Port wine, cool in the liquor and coat with it. Garnish with pomegranate.

Casserole.—Cook in butter in casserole, swill pan with brandy and game stock.

Cécilia (*Cold*).—In a border mould lined wtih aspic and decorated with truffles, place some quail fillets on collops of foie gras, same shape. Stick together with purée of foie gras, coat with Chaudfroid sauce, decorate with truffles. Set them in the mould and cover with aspic jelly.

Cendre.—Lightly cooked in butter and rolled in meat glaze, wrapped in a thin layer of puff paste (leaving the feet out); make a small hole on top in order to pour in some Périgueux sauce when cooked.

Cerises (*Hot*).—In cocotte, swill with brandy, port, cherry juice and quail fumet. Garnish with stoned cherries.

(*Cold*).—Bone, stuff with foie gras and truffles, wrap in muslin, poach in good stock, Let cool, coat with pink Chaudfroid sauce, glaze with aspic, dress round an ice rock containing cherry juice and stoned cherries.

Chaudfroid.—(*See* preparation in **Fonds de Cuisine**).

Clermont.—(Same as **Souvaroff.**) With morels.

Cocotte.—(Same as **à la Casserole.**) cook in cocotte.

Coings.—Marinade with quince peels and brandy for two days. Cook and serve in cocotte. Swill with marinade liquor, serve with quince jelly.

Dauphinoise (A).—Wrap in a vine leaf, roast and dress in a terrine, garnish with thin slices of ham coated with peas purée.

(**B**).—Cook, dress in a baked potato and coat with Périgueux sauce.

Demidoff.—Cook in a cocotte, finish same as Sweetbread Demidoff.

Diane.—In cocotte, with a garnish of small quenelles, cockscombs and kidneys, cohered with tomated half-glaze, small braised lettuces on the quails.

Dodinette.—Season with salt and spices, wrap in pig's caul containing a " Bordelaise mirepoix " and chopped ham cohered with meat glaze. Serve in a terrine.

Félix.—In cocotte; coat with Archiduc sauce, seal lid with soft paste.

Feuilles de Vigne.—Wrap in a vine leaf and thin slice of fat bacon; roast.

Figaro.—Stuff with truffles, wrap in a piece of gut with a little pale veal glaze; poach in good veal stock, and serve very hot.

Grecque.—Cook in casserole, set them in timbale half filled with " Riz à la Grecque " swill the pan with game stock and coat the quails.

Judic.—Poêle the quails (finish same as **Diane**), without the cockscombs.

Julie.—Split, sprinkle with melted butter, roll in chopped truffles, wrap in pig's caul; grill, a few drops of verjuice on top.

Lucullus.—Bone, stuff with foie gras and truffles, wrap in muslin, braise in brown stock, dress in halves of truffles cooked in champagne, coat with half-glaze reduced with Madeira and the braising liquor.

Mandarine (*Cold*).—Shape the tangerines like a small basket, fill with a mousse of foie gras and quails; arrange the suprêmes of quails on top, and finish with quarters of tangerine; dress on aspic jelly.

Maryland (*Cold*).—Poach, mould with aspic in egg shaped moulds, dress round a pineapple gratiné rock.

Milanaise.—Split as for grilled, coat both sides with Villeroy sauce combined with cheese, egg and crumb, fry deep fat. Serve with Diable sauce.

Minute.—(*See* **Pigeonneaux** same name).

Mousse et Mousseline.—(*See* preparation in **Entrées Volantes**).

Muscats.—Cook in cocotte, swill with curaçao and half-glaze, add Muscat grapes, skinned and stoned.

Nelson.— (*See* **Château Yquem**). Dress in caisse, surround with cocks combs tossed in butter.

Nid (A).—Treat same as **Lucullus.** Dress on artichoke bottoms prepared like a nest, with chestnut purée pushed through a piping bag. Surround with small egg shaped quenelles.

(**B**).—Same preparation, but serve in a nest of straw potatoes, half filled with pancakes; surround with olives, truffles, mushrooms and cockscombs, cohered with thin meat glaze.

G

Normande.—(*See* **Alouettes Normande**). Can be done same as **Sous la Cendre,** but the quail is placed in a scooped apple sprinkled with Calvados, and wrapped in a layer of short paste, baked and served.

Périgourdine.—In cocotte, garnish with dice of truffles and mushrooms.

Pilaw Piémontaise.—Cook in cocotte, dress on Riz pilaw Piémontaise.

Pilaw Roumaine.—Cook in cocotte, dress on rizotto à la Valenciennes.

Pommes d'Or (*Cold*).—Poach, remove the suprêmes, set them in the rinds of small oranges or tangerines and fill with port jelly; dress round a granité prepared with the juice of the fruit used.

Prince Albert.—Same as **Au Nid (B).**

Raisins.—Same as **Muscats,** swill with white wine and verjuice.

Régence.—Bone, stuff, poach, garnish and sauce Régence. In timbale.

Reine Amélie (*Cold*).—Treat as **Maryland,** dress round a granité made with tomatoes.

Richelieu.—In cocotte, swill with Madeira and half-glaze. Add julienne of carrots celery, truffles and onions. Can be served cold in a deep silver dish with the garnish and sauce.

Saint-Hubert.—In cocotte, with a piece of truffle in the interior. Swill with Madeira and game stock, garnish with cockscombs and truffles.

Salvini.—(Same as **Diane.**) With large macaroni stuffed with foie gras and truffles instead of braised lettuces.

Sand.—(Same as **à la Cendre.**) The quail boned and stuffed with foie gras and truffles.

Singapour.—(Same as **Aux Muscats.**) Dices of pineapple instead of Muscat grapes, swill with fruit juice.

Souvaroff.—(Same as **Perdreaux Souvaroff.**)

Timbale Tzarine (*Cold*).—(*See* **Foie Gras** same name).

Turque.—Cook in cocotte, dress on pilaw rice à la Turque.

Vendangeuse (*Cold*).—Set the roasted quails in a small dosser of dry paste, surround with white and black grapes (peeled and pipped); coat with fine champagne aspic jelly.

CANARD SAUVAGE — WILD DUCKS

SARCELLES — TEALS

VANNEAUX — LAPWINGS

PLUVIERS — GOLDEN PLOVER

All these birds are generally served roasted but can be prepared in salmis.

CHEVREUIL — ROEBUCK

Noisettes — Côtelettes — Filets Mignons.

Badoise.—Cook in butter, swill pan with cream, cherry juice and Poivrade sauce, garnish with stoned cherries, coat with the sauce.

Cerises.—Same as above without cream.

Chasseur.—Same as **Côte de Veau Chasseur.**

Conti.—Sauté in oil, drain, dish in a crown, alternate with slices of tongue, garnish centre with lentil purée, swill the pan with white wine and Poivrade sauce and coat with it.

Diane.—Cook in butter, dress in a crown, alternate with game forcemeat croûtons, garnish centre with chestnut purée, coat with Diane sauce.

Genièvre.—Cook in butter, swill with gin, lemon juice, cream and Poivrade sauce, dress in a crown, alternate with croûtons, coat with the sauce, serve with apple sauce.

Hongroise.—Cook in butter, swill with sour cream and Hongroise sauce, dress and coat with sauce.

Minute.—Cook in butter with chopped onion, swill with cognac and Poivrade sauce, work with butter, add lemon juice, dress in a crown, garnish centre with mushrooms tossed in butter, coat the cutlets with sauce.

Napolitaine.—Braise in veal stock, dress in timbale half filled with macaroni à la Napolitaine, coat with the braising liquor.

Nesselrode.—Cook in butter, dress in a circle, garnish centre with chestnut purée, coat with Poivrade sauce.

Pauvre Homme.—Cook in butter, swill with vinegar and marinade, add a few slices of gherkins, thicken with butter and flour.

Romanoff.—Cook in butter, dress in a crown, garnish centre with cèpes à la crème, coat the cutlets with Poivrade sauce, surround with barquettes of cucumber filled with mushroom purée.

Smitanne.—Cook in butter, coat with Smitanne sauce.

Truffles et Champignons.—Cook in butter, dress in a crown, garnish with sauted mushrooms, slices of truffles on the cutlets, Madeira half-glaze sauce.

Valencia.—Cook in butter, dress in a crown, coat with Bigarrade sauce, garnish with quarters of orange, add croûtons of brioches.

Venaison.—Cook in butter, dress in a circle, fill centre with celeriac purée, coat with Venaison sauce.

Villeneuve.—Stiffen in butter, let cool, coat with salpicon of cold game, wrap in pig's caul, finish in oven, dress, serve with game cullis combined with julienne of truffles.

Walkyrie.—Cook in butter, swill with cream and Suprême sauce, dress in a crown, fill centre with Soubise purée, coat the cutlets, grilled mushrooms on top, surround with Berny croquette potatoes.

FAISAN, PHEASANT

(Salmis, Suprêmes et Sautés.)

Archiduc.—(*See* **Suprêmes de Volaille** same name).

Berchoux.—Stuffed Suprêmes, cook in butter, add brandy and lemon juice, dress on barquettes filled with pheasant mousse, poached in oven, half-glaze sauce reduced with pheasant fumet.

Champignons.—Same as **Poulet Sauté** same name.

Châtelaine (*Cold*).—Suprêmes, split in halves, stuff one half with chicken mousse and the other with pheasant mousse, poach, cool, coat the pheasant ones with white sauce and the chicken with brown sauce, decorate, dress in deep dish alternating the colours, glaze with aspic jelly.

Chaudfroid.—(*See* preparation in **Fonds de Cuisine**).

Crème.—(Prepare same as **Poulet Sauté Crème**.)

Gastronome (*Cold*).—Slices of suprêmes coated with Chaudfroid sauce, decorate and dress round a mousse of pheasant, surround with truffles cooked in champagne and glazed with aspic.

Louisette.—Suprêmes coated with Villeroy sauce, crumbed and coloured in clarified butter; dress round a hot mousse, half-glaze sauce reduced with pheasant fumet.

Lucullus.—Suprêmes, stuff with forcemeat, cook in butter, Lucullus garnish and coat Madeira sauce.

Salmis.—(*See* **Salmis de Perdreaux**).

Smitanne.—Suprêmes, cook in butter, swill with sour cream and Smitanne sauce, coat with the sauce.

Soufflé.—(*See* preparation in **Savouries**).

Suc d'Ananas, de Mandarine, etc.—Operate same as **Poulet Sauté**, swill with brandy, juice of the fruit named, and half-glaze sauce, garnish with dice or quarters of the fruit.

GRIVES ET MERLES — THRUSHES AND BLACKBIRDS

Ancienne.—Cook in casserole, swill with brandy and game fumet, garnish with dice of ham, fried bread and juniper berries.

Belle-Vue (*Cold*).—(*See* **Bécasse** same name).

Bonne-Femme.—(*See* **Alouettes** same name).

Caisses (en).—(*See* **Cailles** same name).

Chaudfroid.—(*See* preparation in **Fonds de Cuisine**).

Cherville (*Cold*).—Fillets, coat with Chaudfroid sauce, decorate with truffles, dress in deep dish on a mousse of game, glaze with aspic.

Croûtes (en).—Bone, stuff with a piece of foie gras rolled in gratin forcemeat, poach, glaze with the reduced liquor mixed with half-glaze sauce, dress on fried bread croustade.

Gratin.—(*See* **Alouettes** same name).

Liégeoise.—Cook in casserole, when nearly done, sprinkle with chopped juniper berries, add some fried bread croûtons and serve very hot.

Moderne (*Cold*).—Fillets of thrushes, coat with Chaudfroid sauce, dress in tartlet moulds lined with aspic and filled with mousse of thrushes, decorate and surround with chopped aspic.

Nid (au).—(*See* **Cailles** same name).

Paysanne.—Cook in casserole, dress in rizotto.

Sanhard.—Bone, stuff with forcemeat made with pork liver and pork fat and seasoned with garlic, nutmeg, powdered juniper berries, add brandy, wrap in pig's caul, cook in cocotte, serve as it is.

Sous la Cendre.—(*See* **Cailles** same name).

GROUSES ET GELINOTTES

The best preparation for these birds is roasted, casserole, cocotte, crème, smitanne. They can also be prepared as follows:

Gourmets.—Same preparation with dice of truffles and foie gras.
Grand'Mère.—Cook in cocotte, swill with brandy and game fumet, garnish with dice of fried bread and sauted mushrooms.
Savoy.—Cook in cocotte previously rubbed inside with garlic, and insert a garlic clove inside the bird.

LAPINS, LEVRAUTS, LIEVRES

RABBITS, HARES AND LEVERETS

(*Râbles et Filets.*)

The Râble of a hare means the whole of the back from the root of the neck to the tail, with ribs cut short.

Allemande.—Lard the râble finely and marinade it, roast and swill pan with vinegar and cream, dress on croûtons, coat with sauce.
Badoise.—(*See* **Côtelettes de Chevreuil** same name).
Cerises.—(*See* **Côtelettes de Chevreuil** same name).
Choucroute.—Roast in casserole, serve on braised sauerkraut.
Côtelettes Champignons.—Croquettes shaped like cutlets, garnish with sautéd mushrooms, serve with mushroom sauce.
Côtelettes Diane.—Same as above, garnish with chestnut purée, sauce Diane.
Côtelettes Mirza.—Dress on scooped baked apples filled with red currant jelly.
Côtelettes Morland.—(Same as **Pojarski**) but crumbed with chopped truffles and serve with mushroom purée and Grand-Veneur sauce.
Côtelettes Pojarski.—(*See* **Côte de Veau** same name).
Dampierre.—Fillets studded with truffles and the mignon fillets larded with tongue, set on a buttered dish in the shape of crescents, sprinkle with brandy, poach and dress on a truffled mousse the shape of a truncated cone 2 inches high and the length of a fillet, alternate the fillets, surround the base with glazed chestnuts, glazed onions and mushrooms heads, place a fine glazed truffle in the middle, Poivrade sauce.
Farci Beauval (*Cold*).—Bone the hare leaving the head on, stuff with forcemeat made with the liver, bacon, truffles, the legs and shoulders, egg, spice, salt, pepper, serpolet, add dice of lard and truffles, string and reshape the hare in a terrine, stiffen in the oven and braise with marinade of red wine and glass of brandy for three hours, let cool, clear all impurities, put back in clean terrine, add aspic to the braising liquor and pour over the hare.
Genièvre.—Râble, (same as **Grives Liégeoise**.)
Grand-Veneur.—Râble, cook in casserole, coat with Grand-Veneur sauce, serve chestnut purée and red currant jelly.
Morand.—Râble, cook in casserole, swill pan with Poivrade sauce combined with julienne of lemon zest and truffles.

G

Mornay.—Collops of fillets, cook in butter, large slices of truffles cooked in Madeira, fried round croûtons, mixed. Coat with the cooking liquor reduced with meat glaze and worked with butter. Dress in timbale.

Mortemart.—Collops of hare fillets cooked in butter, alternate with forcemeat croûtons made with hare, slices of truffles on top, dress round a hare mousse combined with mousserons, cèpes and minced oranges, coat with Marsala half-glaze.

Mousse et Mousseline.—(*See* preparation in **Entrées Volantes**).

Navarraise.—Râble, larded, marinaded in red wine, roast on the vegetables from the marinade, reduce the cooking liquor, work it with butter and coat, garnish with grilled mushrooms filled with onions and garlic purée.

Périgourdine.—Stuff the hare with a forcemeat made with the liver, heart and lights, chicken livers, pig's fat, parsley, bread crumbs, cooked onions, truffles and garlic, the lot chopped together and mixed with the blood of the hare, braise with white wine and aromates for two hours, dress, glaze. Périgueux sauce.

Pompadour.—Râble, larded, marinaded and roasted, dress on croûtons, decorate with slices of truffles, garnish with noisette potatoes. Choron sauce.

Raifort et Groseilles.—Râble, larded and roasted, served with red currant jelly, combined with scraped horse-radish, nutmeg, cinnamon and Port wine.

Saint-Hubert.—Râble, larded, marinaded, cook in casserole, coat with Poivrade sauce, surround with grilled mushrooms garnished with game purée.

Sully.—Operate same as **Dampierre** the fillets larded with fat bacon, dress and coat with Poivrade sauce, garnish with celery and lentil purée, set the mignon fillets on the purée, slices of truffles on top ,and a large truffle in the centre.

Vendôme.—Flatten the fillets, stud with truffles, roll round baba moulds well buttered, string and poach, garnish interior with collops of mignon fillets, mushrooms and truffles cohered with Poivrade sauce. Serve with chestnut purée and Poivrade sauce.

ORTOLANS

Aspic. (*See* preparation in **Fonds de Cuisine**).

Brochette.—Set the ortolans on a skewer, alternate with slices of bacon, grilled.

Caisses.—(*See* **Cailles** same name).

Lucullus.—Cook in casserole, dress in a large truffle cooked in Madeira, glaze the ortolan with the reduced liquor, replace the truffle cover.

Mandarine.—(*See* **Cailles** same name).

Marianne.—Cook in cocotte, dress on a layer of spinach, coat with thin glaze.

Questches.—Cut the plums " questches " in halves, remove the stone and cook in oven, place the ortolans wrapped up in vine leaves on the plums, cook four minutes in quick oven, take out the vine leaf and serve on the plums, sprinkle with verjuice.

Rothschild (*Cold*).—Place the roast ortolans in a scooped-out truffle, fill with aspic added with gold leaves, replace the cover and glaze the truffles.

Suc d'Ananas.—(*See* **Cailles** same name).

Sylphides.—Garnish some cassolettes with mousseline forcemeat of ortolans prepared with truffle essence, set to poach in oven, cook the ortolans three minutes, place on the cassolette, coat with meat glaze, nut brown butter and pineapple juice.

Timbale Rothschild (*Cold*).—Timbale in short paste, garnish centre with foie gras purée, cook the ortolans two minutes and place them round the foie gras alternating with truffles cooked in Madeira, fill the timbale with another row, add the liquor from the truffles, place the cover, seal it with soft paste, finish in oven for fifteen minutes, insert some good Madeira aspic, keep two days before serving.

Timbale Tzarine (*Cold*).—(*See* **Cailles** same name).

Vendangeuse.—(*See* **Cailles** same name).

PERDREAUX ET PERDRIX — PARTRIDGES

Alcantara.—(*See* **Bécasse** same name).

Alexis.—(*See* **Cailles** same name).

Bonne-Femme.—(*See* **Alouettes** same name).

Bonne-Maman.—Stuff with foie gras chopped partridges' livers, parsley, chopped truffles and brown crumbs. Cook in cocotte, add a little garlic, slices of truffles and glass of brandy, seal lid with soft paste, serve in the cocotte.

Bourguignonne.—Truss the bird as for an entrée, three parts poêle it and place in cocotte with small glazed onions and cooked mushroom heads, swill pan with red wine, reduce, add game half-glaze, and coat the partridges, complete the cooking for eight minutes and serve.

Carême.—Poêle the bird, dress in cocotte, swill pan with cream and celery, suprême sauce and meat glaze, garnish with braised celery, coat the birds with sauce.

Casserole.—(*See* **Cailles** same name).

Chartreuse (en) (A).—Butter a charlotte mould, decorate with cooked carrots and turnips, alternating the vegetables and completely cover the bottom and sides, stick together with chicken forcemeat, fill cavity with the braised cabbage and pieces of partridges, alternate the layers until the mould is filled, poach in bain-marie, surround with half-glaze sauce reduced with partridge fumet.

(B).—Quicker preparation. Decorate timbale with slices of carrots, bacon and roundels of saucisson, fill with braised cabbages and pieces of partridge, game half-glaze sauce.

Choux.—Same preparations, but the partridges are dressed whole on the braised cabbage.

Couveuse (en).—Cook in cocotte, dress in a nest of straw potatoes, surround with partridge croquettes and egg-shaped truffles, sauce made with Xérès and game stock.

Crapaudine.—(*See* **Pigeon** same name).

Crème.—(*See* **Côtelettes de Chevreuil** same name).

Crépinette.—(*See* preparation in **Entrées d'Abats.**)

Demi-Deuil.—Remove the breast bone, stuff with truffled partridge forcemeat, insert slices of truffles under the fillet, wrap in muslin, poach, dress on croûtons, reduced braising liquor and burned brandy.

Diable.—Split, crumb, and grill, sauce Diable.

Epigrammes.—Fillets cooked in butter, dress, alternating with partridge croquettes, serve with chestnut purée and game half-glaze.

Estouffade (en).—Cook in cocotte, dress on Matignon combined with powder of Juniper berries, burned brandy and game fumet.

Etuvée.—Same as cocotte, swill with Port wine.

G

Fermière.—Cook in cocotte with Fermière garnish.

Grand'Mère.—(*See* **Cailles** same name).

Grenobloise.—Carve into small joints, sauté with garlic, cloves, dice of bacon and croûtons, swill with Madeira and half-glaze, dress and coat with sauce.

Karapanésa.—Cook in cocotte, dress on thick Soubise purée, garnish with kidneys and cockscombs, olives stuffed with foie gras, coat with Madeira half-glaze combined with julienne of truffles.

Kotschoubey.—(*See* **Faisan** same name).

Lautrec.—Grilled, garnish with grilled mushrooms filled with Maître-d'hôtel butter, game stock in bottom of dish.

Marly.—Partly cook in butter, place in cocotte with mousserons tossed in butter, seal lid with soft paste, cook in oven, serve it as it is.

Mousse et Mousselines.—(*See* preparation in **Entrées Volantes**).

Normande.—(*See* **Bécasses, Alouettes** and **Cailles** same name).

Olives.—(*See* **Pigeon** same name).

Périgueux.—(*See* **Faisan** same name).

Polonaise.—(*See* **Poussin** same name).

Prince Victor.—Bone, stuff with partridge forcemeat, poach in game stock, dress on croûton, reduce stock and liaison with arrow-root, coat with it.

Salmis.—Cook partridges, carved in small joints, simmer in a Salmis sauce, dress, add mushroom and truffles, coat with sauce, stuffed croûtons round.

Smitane.—(*See* game treated **Smitane**.)

Soufflé.—(*See* preparation in **Savouries**).

Souvaroff.—(*See* **Faisan** same name in **Entrées et Relevés**).

Suprêmes Magenta.—Cook in butter, let cool, press, coat dôme fashion with partridge soufflé preparation, decorate with slices of truffles, poach in oven, coat with Madeira sauce and truffle essence.

Suprêmes Véron.—Cook in butter, dress in a circle, garnish centre with a mixture of partridge purée and chestnut purée, coat with game half-glaze, surround with croûtons.

VOLAILLE — POULTRY

PIGEONS, PIGEONNEAUX ET POUSSINS

PIGEONS, SQUABS AND CHICKS

Anglaise.—Stuff with bread crumbs, chicken livers chopped and tossed in butter with chopped onions, season, poêle ,and serve with grilled rashers of bacon and gravy.

Bonne-Femme.—Truss, poêle, garnish with glazed onions, mushrooms, cocotte potatoes, gravy.

Bordelaise.—Split in halves, flatten, cook in butter, Bordelaise garnish.

Bressane.—Stuff with rizotto containing dice of chicken livers, poêle, swill pan with Madeira and half-glaze, dress on rizotto, coat with sauce.

Bretonne.—Stuff and insert truffles, poele, garnish with sautéd morels and Collerette potatoes, Madeira half-glaze sauce.

THE COOKERY REPERTORY 155

Casanova.—Split on the back, separate the parts, flatten them, season, mustard, sprinkle with crumbs mixed with chopped ham, parsley and garlic. Grill. Dress on Anna potatoes. Chateaubriand sauce.

Casserole.—Cook in casserole and serve with gravy.

Chartreuse.—(*See* **Chartreuse de Perdreaux**).

Chipolata.—Partly cook in butter, add white wine, half-glaze and brown stock, when cook add Chipolata garnish.

Cocotte (en).—Cook in cocotte with butter, serve with gravy.

Compote.—As above with compote garnish.

Côtelettes en Chaudfroid (*Cold*).—Bone, leave the feet bone, stuff with foie gras and forcemeat, reshape the bird, wrap in muslin, poach, let cool, split in halves, coat with Chaudfroid sauce, decorate with truffles, dress in deep dish on a layer of aspic, coat with aspic jelly.

Côtelettes à la Nesles.—Split in halves, reserve the claws, flatten, season and fry in butter on one side, let cool under pressure. Coat dôme fashion with godiveau combined with gratin forcemeat and chopped truffles, poach in oven, dish in a circle, alternate with collops of veal sweetbreads dipped in egg, crumbed and cooked in butter, garnish centre with mushroooms and sliced fowls' livers tossed in butter and cohered with Madeira sauce.

Côtelettes en Papillotes.—(Prepare as **à la Nesles**,) toss in butter and finish same as "**Rougets en Papillotes.**"

Côtelettes Sévigné.—Half pigeons sauté in butter, let cool, garnish the cut side with salpicon of white chicken meat, mushrooms, and truffles cohered with Allemande sauce. Egg and crumb and cook in clarified butter dish in a circle, garnish centre with asparagus heads, Madeira sauce.

Crapaudine.—Cut the pigeons horizontally in two, from the apex of breast to the wings, open them, flatten, dip in melted butter, roll in bread crumbs and grill. Diable sauce.

Diable.—Split on the back, open, season, butter and crumb, grill. Diable sauce.

Estouffade (en).—Partly cook the pigeons, swill pan with brandy, place in terrine with slices of bacon, surround with collops of mushrooms and small onions partly cooked, add brown stock and the swilling liquor, seal lid with paste, cook three-quarters of an hour, serve in terrine.

Financière.—Poêle, and Financière garnish.

Gauthier.—Split in halves, poach with acidulated butter, dress in a circle, coat with suprême sauce finished with crayfish cullis.

Gelée (en).—Remove breast bones, stuff with truffled forcemeat, poach, cool, dress in deep dish, coat with aspic.

Jacques.—Stuff with gratin forcemeat, poêle, swill pan with white wine, half-glaze and lemon juice, dress in cocotte, coat with sauce.

Laurette (*Cold*).—Make a galantine with boned pigeon, poach, cool, cut in slices, three parts of an inch thick, coat with Chaudfroid sauce. Decorate with pistachios and white of eggs, glaze with aspic.

Minute.—Cut into four pieces, toss in butter with chopped onions, swill with brandy, meat glaze and lemon juice, work in some butter, dress the pieces in a circle, coat with sauce, garnish centre with mushrooms cooked in butter, chopped parsley.

Mousse et Mousseline.—(*See* preparation in **Entrées Volantes).**

Olives.—Poêle, garnish with stoned olives, coat with half-glaze sauce.

G

Paysanne.—(Cook same as **Cocotte,**) when nearly done add blanched dice of bacon and slices of potatoes.

Petits Pois.—Poêle, garnish with petits pois à la Française, coat with half-glaze.

Polonaise.—Stuff with gratin forcemeat, poêle, dress in cocotte; add thickened gravy, chopped eggs, parsley, lemon juice, bread crumbs and nut brown butter on top of birds when serving.

Printanière.—Poêle, surround with new vegetables, coat with half-glaze sauce.

Richelieu — Poêle and Richelieu garnish.

Saint-Charles.—Lard with tongue, braise, garnish with stuffed cépes, coat with reduced braising liquor and lemon juice.

Salmis.—(*See* **Salmis de Perdreau**).

Sauternes.—Poêle, swill pan with Sauternes wine and meat glaze, coat the birds with sauce.

Suprêmes Diplomate.—Fillets, partly cooked in butter, coat with Villeroy combined with chopped mushrooms and herbs, egg and crumb, fry dress in a circle, garnish centre with quenelles of pigeons, truffles and mushroom heads, half-glaze sauce.

Suprêmes Marigny.—Cover the breast with slices of bacon and just cook them, skin the suprêmes and set them on croûtons made of pigeon forcemeat; set in oven a few minutes, dress round a pyramid of peas purée, coat with suprême sauce, finished with pigeon essence.

Suprêmes Saint-Clair.—Poêle the fillets, remove the skin, dress in circle round a pyramid of sautéd cèpes, coat with Soubise sauce, surround with quenelles of pigeon.

Suprémes aux Truffes.—Poêle the fillets, swill with Madeira and half-glaze combined with truffle essence and slices, dress and coat with the sauce.

Sylvain.—Cut into four pieces, season, toss in butter, add sliced cèpes or mousserons sage and thyme, finish cooking and serve.

Valenciennes.—Stuff with gratin forcemeat, collops of foie gras and mushrooms, poêle, swill pan with white wine and tomated half-glaze, dress on riz Valenciennes, slice of ham, heart-shaped on the pigeon.

Viennoise.—Cut in four, season, egg and crumb, fry deep fat, dress, fried parsley and lemon.

Villeroy.—(Treat same as all **Villeroy** preparations.)

POULETS SAUTES — CHICKEN SAUTE

(*How to cut the chicken for sauté.*)

Remove the legs, cut off the claws, cut the tibia above the joint and remove thigh bone, cut pinions at the first joint, remove wings after having cut round a portion of the breast, finally detach the breast bone, cut the carcass in two and trim on both sides.

Cooking Process

Put the pieces in a sauté pan with oil or clarified butter, let them colour quickly, remove the breast and wings before the legs which take longer to cook, in large hotels the legs are cooked separately from the wings and breasts.

Alexandra.—Cook the chicken in butter without colouring, swill with thin soubise and cream, garnish with asparagus heads.

Algérienne.—Sauté, swill with white wine, add dice of tomatoes, garlic and half-glaze.

Annette.—Sauté, swill with Madeira, brandy soubise and thickened gravy, coat, surround with pommes Anna, croûtons and tomated half-glaze.

Anversoise.—Sauté in butter, without colouring, swill with cream and suprême sauce combined with blanched hop shoots and julienne of tongue.

Archiduc.—Sauté, without colouring, swill with sherry, port wine, whisky, cream and velouté combined with brunoise of vegetables and truffles, dress, coat with sauce.

Arlésienne.—Sauté in oil, swill with white wine, garlic, garnish with slices of egg plant and roundels of onions fried in oil, small heaps of concasséd tomatoes.

Armagnac.—Sauté without colouring with raw slices of truffles, swill with brandy, crayfish cullis, lemon juice, work with butter, dress and coat with sauce.

Armenonville.—Sauté, swill with brandy and half-glaze, dress, Armenonville garnish, coat with sauce.

Artois (d').—Sauté, swill with Madeira and meat glaze, add shaped carrots, artichoke bottoms, small glazed onions, finish with butter, dress and pour sauce over.

Bagatelle.—Sauté, swill with Madeira and thick cream, dress and coat, garnish with carrots and asparagus heads.

Bazard.—Sauté, swill with Madeira and half-glaze, add quarters of artichoke bottoms collops of mushrooms, dice of bacon, stoned olives, glazed onions, pour on the pieces.

Beaulieu.—Sauté, swill with white wine and veal stock, garnish with artichoke bottoms, tomatoes, stoned black olives, Cocotte potatoes.

Béhanzin.—Sauté, swill with white wine and thickened gravy, garnish with quarters of " chayottes " coat with sauce.

Belle-Gabrielle.—Sauté without colouring, swill with cream and suprême sauce, coat, sprinkle with chopped truffles, heart shaped croûtons.

Bercy.—Sauté, swill with white wine, meat glaze, lemon juice and chopped shallots, work with butter, add sliced mushrooms and chipolatas, pour on the chicken pieces.

Bergère.—Sauté without colouring the pieces, swill with Madeira and veal stock, reduce, add some cream, garnish with sautéd mushrooms and straw potatoes.

Biarotte.—Sauté in oil, swill with white wine and tomato purée, dress, coat with sauce, garnish with dice of fried egg plant, roundels of fried onions, cèpes tossed in oil, Noisette potatoes, season with paprika.

Blanc.—Sauté in butter, when nearly done add chopped onions and cocks' kidneys, moisten with white wine, reduce ,add cream, simmer for 12 minutes, dress, slices of truffles and crayfish.

Bohémienne.—Sauté in oil, swill with white wine and tomated half-glaze, add garlic and fennel, dress, coat with sauce, garnish with slices of tomato, sweet pimento, glazed onions, separately plain boiled rice.

Boivin.—Sauté with small onions, artichoke bottoms and Cocotte potatoes, swill with consommé, meat glaze, lemon juice, add butter, pour on the pieces.

Bonne-Femme.—Sauté, swill with white wine and thickened gravy, garnish with dice of bacon, small onions, Cocotte potatoes.

Bordelaise.—Sauté, swill with white wine, half-glaze and chopped shallots, garnish with artichoke bottoms in quarters, roundels of fried onions, and sauté potatoes.

G

Bourguignonne.—Sauté, swill with red wine and half-glaze, add garlic, garnish with glazed onions, dice of bacon and mushrooms, chopped parsley.

Bretonne.—Cook in butter without colouring the pieces, add leeks, onions and sliced mushrooms, swill with cream and suprême sauce.

Cacciatora.—(Same as **Chasseur,**) swill with Chianti wine.

Capilotade.—Sauté, swill with white wine and sauce Italienne combined with truffles, coat with sauce.

Catalane.—Sauté in oil, swill with white wine and half-glaze, add collop of mushrooms, glazed onions, cooked chestnuts, chipolatas and dice of tomato, pour the lot on the pieces.

Cecil.—(Same as **Bordelaise,**) swill with tomated half-glaze, halves of tomatoes instead of roundels of onions.

Cèpes.—Sauté in oil, swill with white wine half-glaze, chopped shallots, garnish with sautéd cèpes à la Bordelaise.

Champeaux.—Sauté, swill with white wine veal stock and meat glaze, add butter, garnish with small onions and Cocotte potatoes.

Chandon.—Sauté, swill with champagne, cream and half-glaze, add butter, garnish with cocks combs and kidneys, surround with truffled chicken croquettes.

Chasseur.—Sauté, swill with white wine, brandy, tomated half-glaze, add sliced mushrooms tossed in butter with chopped shallots, sprinkle with chopped parsley.

Côte-d'Azur.—(Same as **Printanière,**) with artichoke bottoms in quarters, asparagus heads and truffles.

Crécy.—Sauté without colouring, swill with cream and suprême sauce combined with Paysanne of carrots.

Curry (au).—Season with Curry, cook in butter and oil, finish cooking in Curry sauce, serve with plain boiled rice.

Cynthia.—Sauté, swill with Curaçao, champagne, lemon juice, chicken glaze, add butter, coat the pieces, surround with oranges, peeled and cut raw in quarters, and grapes skinned and cleared of pips.

Danoise.—Sauté, swill with Madeira and half-glaze, coat the pieces, garnish with stuffed tomatoes, small onions and noisette potatoes.

Dauphine.—Sauté, swill with Périgueux sauce, garnish with Dauphine potatoes.

Demidoff.—Sauté, finish (same as **Ris de Veau** same name.)

Doria.—Sauté, swill with lemon juice and half-glaze, combined with shaped cucumbers cooked in butter.

Durand.—Flour the pieces, sauté in oil, dress in a circle, garnish centre with roundels of fried onions and in the middle of the latter, set a cone made with sliced ham and filled with dice of tomatoes cooked in butter.

Duroc.—(Same as **Chasseur,**) garnish with heaps of dice of tomatoes and Cocotte potatoes.

Ecossaise.—Sauté, swill with Xérès and half-glaze, add salpicon of tongue, truffles and French beans.

Egyptienne.—Sauté in oil, with onions, dice of ham and sliced mushrooms, set the chicken pieces in a cocotte, alternating with the garnish, cover with slices of tomato and complete the cooking, when about to serve add veal stock.

Escurial.—Sauté, swill with white wine and half-glaze, add dice of ham and truffles, sliced mushrooms and stuffed olives, dress in a border of plain cooked rice, surround with small fried eggs.

Espagnole.—Sauté in oil, add pilaff rice combined with dice of capsicums, green peas and slices of poached sausages, set in a terrine and finish in oven for 10 minutes, add small grilled tomatoes.

Estragon.—Saute in butter, swill with white wine, reduce, add tarragon thickened gravy, coat and decorate with tarragon leaves.

Fédora.—Sauté without colouring with raw slices of truffles swill with cream, lemon juice and suprême sauce, finish with crayfish butter and cayenne pepper, dress, coat with sauce, garnish with asparagus heads.

Fenouil.—Saute without colouring, swill with cream, add shaped tuberose fennel partly cooked, finish cooking together, dress the pieces of fennel in a circle, the chicken in the middle, coat with Mornay sauce and set to glaze.

Fermière.—Sauté, swill with thickened gravy, finish cooking in cocotte with Fermière garnish.

Fines Herbes.—Sauté in butter, swill with white wine, veal stock and half-glaze, chopped shallots, finish with butter, chopped parsley, chervil and Tarragon, coat with the sauce.

Forestière.—Sauté in butter, add chopped shallots, and quarters of morel or mushroom, swill with white wine and veal stock, coat with sauce, garnish with Parmentier potatoes, alternate with slices of grilled bacon.

Frou Frou.—Sauté, swill with Madeira and half-glaze, dress in cocotte with quarters of artichoke bottoms and truffles, surround with spinach rissoles.

George Sand.—Sauté without colouring, swill with cream, chicken glaze and crayfish cullis, garnish with crayfish tails, coat, decorate with slices of truffles.

Georgina.—Sauté with spring onions and faggot containing sprig of fennel, swill with Rhine wine and mushroom cooking liquor, reduce, add mushroom heads, chervil and chopped tarragon ,coat the pieces of chicken.

Hermione.—Sauté, swill with white wine and tomated thickened gravy, dress in a circle centre with roundels of fried onions in the middle set a cone of ham, containing asparagus heads, sprinkle with chopped truffles, surround with sliced mushrooms and Collerette potatoes.

Hongroise.—Sauté with paprika and chopped onion, swill with cream and Hongroise sauce, combined with concassed tomatoes, dress in a border of pilaff rice, coat with sauce.

Huîtres.—Saute without colouring, swill with white wine, oyster juice, cream and suprême sauce, garnish with poached oysters.

Indienne.—(*See* **Poulet Sauté au Curry**).

Lapérouse.—Sauté, swill with brandy, cream and mushroom purée, cohere with yolks of eggs, garnish with artichoke bottoms filled with mushroom purée and glazed.

Lathuile.—Sauté with dice of potatoes and artichoke bottoms, when the chicken and vegetables are coloured underneath turn on the other side at one stroke and complete the cooking, set on a dish. Pour nut brown butter on the whole and surround with roundels of fried onions and fried parsley.

Léopold.—Sauté without colouring, swill with white wine, cream and chopped shallots, garnish with braised chicory.

Lyonnaise.—Sauté in butter, when nearly done add minced onions tossed in butter, swill with thickened gravy, coat with sauce, chopped parsley.

Madras.—(*See* **Poulet Stanley**). Without truffles, dress in a scooped cantaloup previously lined with plain cooked rice.

G

Marengo.—Sauté in oil, swill with white wine, add dice of tomato, tomatoed half-glaze, a little garlic, mushroom heads and slices of truffles, garnish round with trussed crayfish, fried eggs and croûtons, chopped parsley.

Marie-Louise.—Sauté, swill with white wine and half-glaze. In a saute pan place some sauté potatoes, dress the chicken on them, add slices of raw truffles, cèpes and potatoes, dress the chicken on them, add slices of raw truffles and cèpes à la Bordelaise, cover with another layer of potatoes, press, set in oven and unmould on a dish, sauce round.

Marigny.—Sauté, swill with white wine and thickened gravy, Marigny garnish.

Marocaine.—Sauté in oil, swill with white wine and half-glaze combined with dice of tomato and garlic, garnish with stuffed marrow, concasséd tomatoes, gombos and chopped onions tossed in butter, noisette potatoes.

Marseillaise.—Same as above without garnish, add green pimento and lemon juice, chopped parsley.

Mascotte.—Sauté, swill with white wine and half-glaze, Mascotte garnish.

Mathilde.—Sauté, when nearly done add chopped onions, swill with champagne and suprême sauce combined with shaped cucumbers blanched and cooked in butter, coat with sauce.

Mexicaine.—Sauté in oil, swill with white wine and tomatoed veal stock, garnish with grilled mushrooms filled with dice of tomatoes and grilled capsicums.

Monselet.—Sauté, swill with Xérès and half-glaze combined with artichoke bottoms and slices of truffles, coat with sauce.

Morilles.—Sauté, when nearly done add morels tossed in butter, finish cooking, swill with brandy and meat glaze and cooking liquor of the morels, finish with butter and coat.

Niçoise.—Sauté in oil, swill with white wine and tomatoed half-glaze. Niçoise garnish.

Normande.—(*See* **Perdreau** same name).

Nouveau Siècle.—Sauté, swill with white wine and half-glaze, add shaped cucumbers cooked in butter under cover, small onions, cèpes, dice of tomato, fried egg plant, Japanese artichokes and Cocotte potatoes. Serve in cocotte all together.

Parmentier.—Sauté, swill with white wine and thickened gravy, garnish with Parmentier potatoes, sprinkle with chopped parsley.

Paysanne.—Sauté, swill with white wine, add paysanne of vegetables, coat with sauce.

Périgord.—Sauté with raw truffles, swill with Madeira and buttered half-glaze, coat the pieces.

Petit-Duc.—Sauté, swill with cream and pale meat glaze, finish with butter, add slices of truffles and morels cooked in butter.

Piémontaise.—Sauté with slices of raw truffles, swill with white wine and pale meat glaze, dress the chicken in a border of riz à la Piémontaise, coat with sauce, chopped parsley, nut brown cooked butter on top.

Portugaise.—Sauté with butter and oil, when nearly done add chopped onion, white wine, dice of tomato, sliced mushrooms, a little garlic, finish cooking, dress, surround with stuffed tomatoes.

Provençale.—Sauté in oil, swill with white wine and Provençale sauce flavoured with chopped basilic, add blanched stoned olives.

Rivoli.—Sauté, swill with Xérès and tomatoed veal stock, garnish with pomme Anna croûtons and slices of truffles.

Romaine.—Sauté in oil, swill with Asti wine and half-glaze, dress on a layer of spinach in leaves.

Rostand.—Sauté, swill with brandy and tomatoed thickened gravy combined with paysanne of vegetables, morels and truffles, coat with sauce.

Saint-James.—Sauté, swill with Madeira and half-glaze, garnish with small heaps of Jardinière.

Saint-Lambert.—Sauté, swill with white wine and mushroom cooking liquor, add purée of vegetables, finish with butter, coat, sprinkle with green peas, small carrot balls and chopped parsley.

Saint-Mandé.—Sauté, swill with veal gravy, dish up and Saint-Mandé garnish.

Samos (au).—Sauté in oil, swill with Samos wine and add dice of tomatoes, coat, garnish with grapes skinned and pipped.

Spatzélis (aux).—Sauté without colouring, swill with cream, garnish with spatzelis tossed in butter.

Stanley.—Cook under cover with minced onions, dress the chicken, add Soubise sauce to the onions, pass through a strainer, add cream, julienne of tongue, mushrooms and truffles, coat, croûtons.

Truffes (aux).—(*See* **Poulet Sauté Périgord**).

Van Dyck.—Sauté without colouration, swill with cream and Suprême sauce, combined with blanched hop sprouts.

Vendéenne.—Sauté without colouring, when nearly done, add small braised onions, swill with white wine and Suprême sauce, chopped parsley, coat.

Verdi.—Sauté, swill with Asti wine and thickened gravy, finish with butter, dress in a border of Piémontaise rice, set a crown of sliced truffles alternated with foie gras on top of the rice, coat the chicken with sauce.

Vichy.—Sauté, swill with veal stock, garnish with carrots Vichy, coat.

Viennoise (A).—Eggs and crumb, cook in butter, dress; lemon juice, and chopped parsley on top, pour nut brown cooked butter over the lot when serving.

   (B).—(Treat same as **Escalope Viennoise**.)

Waterzoï (en).—In marmite, cook the chicken pieces with julienne of celery, leeks and parsley roots, moisten with white consommé, cook and serve in the marmite.

SUPREMES DE VOLAILLE — CHICKEN FILETS

Agnès Sorel.—Poach, and dress on tartlets prepared as follows: line tartlet moulds with mousseline forcemeat, fill with sliced cooked mushrooms, cover with forcemeat and poach, coat with Suprême sauce, decorate with tongue and truffles, surround with a thread of pale meat glaze.

Albuféra.—Stuff, cook under cover in butter, dress on tartlets containing Albuféra forcemeat, coat with sauce same name.

Alexandra.—Poach in butter, slices of truffles on top, coat with Mornay sauce, glaze, garnish with asparagus heads cohered with butter.

Ambassadrice.—Poach, dress, coat with Suprême sauce, garnish with lamb sweetbreads studded with truffles and cooked without colouring, alternate with asparagus heads.

Archiduc.—Poach in butter, dress on croûtons, coat with Archiduc sauce.

Arlésienne.—Season and flour the suprêmes, cook in butter, Arlésienne garnish, tomatoed half-glaze.

Belle-Hélène.—Sauté, dress on croquettes made with asparagus heads and shaped same as suprêmes, sliced truffles on top, thickened gravy, nut brown cooked butter.

Boitelle.—Stuff with mousseline forcemeat combined with purée of mushrooms, poach in butter and lemon juice, dress in a circle, garnish centre with mushrooms, coat with reduced cooking liquor well buttered, chopped parsley.

Champignons (aux) (*A blanc*).—Poach in mushroom cooking liquor, dress in a circle, garnish centre with grooved cooked mushrooms, coat with Suprême sauce. (*A brun*).—Poach in clarified butter, dish, surround with mushrooms and coat with mushroom sauce.

Chimay.—Cook in clarified butter, dress, garnish with morels tossed in butter and asparagus heads cohered with butter, thickened gravy.

Cussy.—Collops of suprême, egg and crumb, cook in butter, dress on artichoke bottoms, put a thick slice of glazed truffle on each collop and a cocks kidney on each slice of truffle, thickened chicken gravy.

Doria.—Egg and crumb, cook in butter, garnish with shaped cucumbers cooked in butter, add lemon juice and nut brown butter when serving.

Dreux.—Insert roundels of truffles and tongue into the suprêmes, poach, dish, surround with cocks combs and kidneys and slices of truffles, coat with suprême sauce.

Ecarlate.—Insert roundels of tongue, poach in butter, dress on flat quenelles of mousseline forcemeat sprinkled with chopped tongue, coat with clear Suprême sauce.

Ecossaise.—Poach, dish and coat with Ecossaise sauce.

Elisabeth.—Poach in butter and lemon juice, dress in a circle, garnish centre with a croûton, set a shell containing oysters on it, coat the chicken with Suprême sauce, slices of truffles on top.

Favorite.—Cook in clarified butter, dish in a crown on tossed slices of foie gras, garnish centre with asparagus heads, serve separately some buttered meat glaze.

Financière.—Stuff with truffled chicken mousseline, poach, dish in a crown on fried croûtons, garnish and Financière sauce.

Florentine.—Poach, dress on a layer of spinach in leaves, coat with Mornay sauce and glaze.

Fonds d'Artichauts.—Cook in butter, dish on a bed of sautés artichoke bottoms, thickened gravy, nut brown butter, parsley.

Georgette.—Dress the poached suprêmes in Georgette potatoes. (*See* **Filets de Sole Georgette**), coat with suprême sauce combined with crayfish cullis, slices of truffles on top.

Henri IV.—Collop the suprêmes, flatten, season and flour, cook in butter, set on artichoke bottoms containing buttered meat glaze, serve Béarnaise sauce separately.

Hongroise.—Season with paprika, cook in butter, swill with cream and Hongroise sauce, dress on pilaff rice containing dice of tomatoes, coat with sauce.

Impériale.—Stud with truffles, cook in butter, swill with Xérès and half-glaze, set on foie gras croûtons, garnish with truffles.

Indienne.—Cook in butter, simmer in Curry sauce, serve in timbale, separately serve plain boiled rice.

Italienne.—Sauté, coat with Italienne sauce combined with artichoke quarters.

Jardinière.—Saute, dress in a circle, centre garnish with Jardinière, thickened gravy and nut brown butter.

Maréchale.—Egg and crumb, cook in clarified butter, Maréchale garnish, thickened gravy and nut brown butter.

Marie-Louise.—Collops of suprême, egg and crumb, cook in butter, set on artichoke bottoms filled with soubised mushroom purée, nut brown butter.

Marie-Thérèse.—Prepare a riz pilaff with dice of chicken, press it in a dôme mould, poach the suprêmes, unmould the rice on a dish, set the chicken round and coat with suprême sauce, alternate with slices of tongue.

Maryland.—Egg and crumb, cook in butter, dish on grilled bacon, Maryland garnish, serve horse-radish sauce separately.

Mireille.—Sauté, Mireille garnish, thickened gravy, nut brown butter.

Montpensier.—Sauté. (*See* **Tournedos** same name).

Orientale.—Sauté, dress on a thick slice of Chow-Chow, coat with Aurore sauce flavoured with saffron, separately serve riz pilaff containing dice of capsicums.

Orly.—(Same as **Filets de Sole Orly.**)

Papillotes (en).—Sauté, finish (same as **Rougets en Papillotes.**)

Paprika.—(*See* **Hongroise**). Without riz pilaff.

Parisienne.—Cook in butter under cover, Parisienne garnish **(B)**.

Périgueux.—Stuff with truffled chicken forcemeat, poach, coat with Périgueux sauce.

Pojarski.—(Treat same as **Côte de Veau** same name.)

Polignac.—Poach, coat with suprême sauce combined with julienne of truffles and mushrooms.

Porto.—Sauté, swill with port wine and Porto sauce, coat.

Princesse.—Stud with truffles, poach, swill with white wine and suprême sauce, dress on croûtons, garnish with asparagus heads and truffles, sauce round.

Régence.—Poach, dish, Régence sauce and garnish.

Richelieu.—Egg and crumb, cook in butter, slices of truffles on top, Maître-d'hôtel butter.

Rimini.—Stud with truffles, poach, set on barquettes filled with mushroom purée, coat with suprême sauce.

Rossini.—Cook in butter, set on collops of foie gras, coat with Madeira sauce combined with slices of truffles.

Talleyrand.—Stuff with godiveau and foie gras purée, dress in timbale on a Talleyrand garnish separate, serve Madeira sauce combined with Julienne of truffles.

Toulousaine.—Poach, dish, garnish and Toulousaine sauce.

Valençay.—Stuff with salpicon of truffles cohered with Allemande sauce, egg and crumb, cook in butter, dress in a circle, garnish centre with mushroom purée, surround with croûtons shaped like cockscombs and stuffed with truffled chicken mousseline.

Valois.—Egg and crumb, cook in butter, dish in a circle, garnish centre with stuffed olives, Valois sauce.

Verneuil.—(Same as **Orly,**) dress in a circle, coat with Colbert sauce, garnish centre with artichoke purée.

Villeroy.—Poach underdone, coat both sides with Villeroy sauce, egg and crumb, fry, dress, fried parsley, Périgueux sauce.

Wolseley.—Stuff with mousseline forcemeat, poach, dress round a fried bread tampon, coat with suprême sauce, small bundle of asparagus between each suprême.

G

Entrées et Relevés

VIANDES — BUTCHERS MEATS

AGNEAU, MOUTON — LAMB, MUTTON

Lamb, Mutton, Barons or pairs of hind quarters of Mutton, Saddles, shoulders, legs, necks of Mutton.

Ballotines.—Boned shoulder, stuffed and braised, the best garnishes for these are: Bonne femme, Boulangère, Bourgeoise, Villageoise.

Note.—Mutton must be roasted underdone, and lamb well done.

Garnishes and sauces suitable for lamb and mutton are the following:

Garnishes	Sauces
Africaine	Tomatoed half-glaze.
Algérienne	Tomatoed half-glaze.
Andalouse	Tomatoed half-glaze.
Anversoise	Thickened gravy.
Belle-Hélène	Half-glaze and Béarnaise.
Bisontine	Half-glaze.
Boulangère	Gravy.
Bouquetière	Half-glaze.
Brabançonne	Half-glaze.
Bréhan	Half-glaze.
Bretonne	Tomatoed thick gravy.
Bristol	Gravy.
Bruxelloise	Gravy.
Châtelaine (A and B)	Half-glaze.
Clamart	Gravy.
Dauphine	Thickened gravy.
Duchesse	Thickened gravy.
Favorite	Half-glaze.
Fermière	Half-glaze.
Flamande	Thickened gravy.
Florian	Half-glaze.
Forestière (A and B)	Half-glaze.
Grecque (boned and stuffed)	Tomatoed half-glaze.
Hongroise	Half-glaze and paprika.
Japonaise	Half-glaze and paprika.
Jardinière	Half-glaze and paprika.
Judic	Tomatoed half-glaze.
Languedocienne	Tomatoed half-glaze.
Macédoine	Half-glaze.
Madeleine	Thickened gravy.
Maillot	Thickened gravy.

Garnishes	*Sauces*
Maraîchère	Thickened gravy.
Marie-Louise (A and B)	Thickened gravy.
Marseillaise (Garlic)	Tomatoed half-glaze.
Mascotte	Half-glaze.
Mexicaine	Pimentoes julienne and tomated half-glaze.
Mirette	Half-glaze.
Moderne	Half-glaze.
Niçoise	Tomatoed half-glaze.
Orientale	Tomatoed half-glaze.
Orléannaise	Thickened gravy.
Orloff	Half-glaze.
Paloise	Half-glaze and Béarnaise.
Panachée	Thickened gravy.
Parmentier	Thickened gravy.
Paysanne	Half-glaze.
Péruvienne	Half-glaze.
Portugaise	Tomatoed half-glaze.
Printanière (A and B)	Half-glaze.
Provençale	Tomatoed half-glaze (garlic).
Renaissance	Half-glaze.
Richelieu	Half-glaze.
Saint-Florentin	Tomatoed half-glaze.
Saint-Mandé	Half-glaze.
Sarde	Tomatoed half-glaze.
Sarladaise	Gravy.
Tourangelle	Thickened gravy.
Viroflay	Thickened gravy.

BŒUF — BEEF

(Ribs, Sirloins, Filets).

Aloyau.—Parts of the beef cut from the haunch to the first ribs.
Contre-Filet.—Bone the upper filet of the sirloin, generally larded and roasted.
Filet.—The undercut of the sirloin, boned, and larded, same garnishes.

Garnishes	*Sauces*
Andalouse	Tomatoed half-glaze.
Arlésienne	Tomatoed half-glaze.
Berrichonne	Thickened gravy.
Bisontine	Half-glaze.
Bouquetière	Half-glaze.
Bourgeoise (Braised)	Half-glaze.
Bréhan	Gravy.
Champignon	Madeira sauce.
Châtelaine (A and B)	Half-glaze.

Garnishes	*Sauces*
Clamart	Gravy.
Dauphine	Thickened gravy.
Dubarry	Half-glaze.
Espagnole	Tomatoed half-glaze.
Financière	Half-glaze.
Flamande	Half-glaze.
Française	Gravy.
Frascati	Half-glaze.
Gastronome	Half-glaze with truffle essence.
Godard	Half-glaze.
Hongroise	Half-glaze and paprika.
Hussarde	Half-glaze and paprika.
Ismaïl Bayeldi	Pimentoes julienne and tomated half-glaze.
Italienne	Italian sauce.
Japonaise	Half-glaze.
Jardinière	Half-glaze.
Judic	Tomatoed half-glaze.
London-House	Half-glaze.

Fillet of beef.

Cut open in halves lengthways, garnish the inside with slices of foie gras and truffles, braise with veal stock and Madeira, glaze and surround with truffles and mushrooms.

Lorette	Half-glaze.
Macédoine	Half-glaze.
Madeleine	Thickened gravy.
Mexicaine	Pimentoes julienne and tomated half-glaze.
Moderne	Half-glaze.
Montmorency	Half-glaze.
Montreuil	Half-glaze.
Nivernaise	Half-glaze.
Orientale	Tomatoed half-glaze.
Parisienne (A and B)	Half-glaze.
Petit-Duc	Meat glaze worked with butter. Madeira sauce.
Portugaise	Tomatoed half-glaze.
Provençale	Tomatoed half-glaze (garlic).
Renaissance	Half-glaze.
Richelieu	Half-glaze.
Saint-Florentin	Tomatoed half-glaze.
Saint-Germain	Half-glaze.
Saint-Mandé	Thickened gravy.
Sarde	Tomatoed half-glaze.
Sous la Cendre (*See Wellington*)	Chasseur.

Garnishes	Sauces
Talleyrand	Périgueux sauce.
Tivoli	Tickened gravy.
Viroflay	Thickened gravy.
Wellington	Half-glaze.

FILET DE BŒUF (Froid) — COLD FILLET OF BEEF

Fillet of beef.

Larded and tossed in butter to a nice brown, after cover same with forcemeat of chicken mixed with Duxelles, wrapped in puff paste, and cook in oven, garnish with tomatoes, braised lettuces, and Chateau potatoes.

Chevet.—Cover with aspic, serve and decorate with aspic.

Coquelin.—In a terrine, carved, covered with **Caille Richelieu** julienne, and a good Madeira aspic.

Mistral.—Cover with aspic, garnish with tomatoes, and decorate with aspic.

Montléry.—Cover with aspic, place on a long dish, surround with timbales of french beans and macédoine of vegetables, cohered with mayonnaise and aspic, also artichoke bottoms, garnished with asparagus tips, mixed with aspic. (Mayonnaise served separate).

Russe.—Served in terrine, cut in slices, cover with aspic and chopped truffles.

Scandinave.—Serve in terrine, cut in slices, reshape the fillet, cover with Madeira aspic, surround with different vegetables.

LANGUES — TONGUES

If salted or pickled, boiled in water, if fresh, braised.

Garnishes are: Alsacienne, Bourgeoise, Flamande, Italienne, Jardinière, Milanaise, Nouilles, Sarde, Tourangelle.

The purées suitable for tongues are: Celery, spinach, cauliflower chestnut, sorrel, peas, potatoes.

The sauces are: Mushrooms, Hachée, Italienne, Madeira, Piquante, Romaine.

PIECES DE BŒUF — BRAISED BEEF

Lard a piece of rump, season and pickle it in brandy and wine for 4 or 5 hours, then dry. After browning in hot fat, moisten with the pickle and brown stock, add bunch of herbs and mushroom peelings, cook in oven. After, pass and reduce sauce, thin glaze.

Bourgeoise.—Same as above with Bourgeoise garnish.

Bourguignonne.—Same as above with garnish of the same name.

Flamande.—Ditto with Flamande garnish.

Mode (à la).—Same as **Bourgeoise** add dice of calves' feet, which have already been cooked with beef. Can also be served cold in a terrine with aspic.

POITRINE, PLATE COTE ET BŒUF BOUILLI
BOILED BEEF

Serve with a garnish of carrots, turnips, leeks, cabbage hearts and boiled potatoes, add horse-radish sauce served separately, hot or cold.

PORC — PORK

(Best Neck, Loin, Shoulder, Fillet.)

Boulangère.—Roasted, garnish Boulangère, gravy.
Choucroute.—Roasted, served with braised sauerkraut and gravy.
Choux de Bruxelles.—Roasted, garnish with Brussel sprouts and gravy.
Choux Rouges.—Roasted, served with braised red cabbage, gravy.
Marmelade de Pommes.—Roasted, apple sauce and gravy.
Paysanne.—Roasted, when half cooked add quarters of potatoes and onions.
Purées Diverses (Various Purées).—Apples, celery, lentils, onions, split peas.
    Sauces: Charcutière, Piquante, Horse-radish and Robert.
Soissonnaise.—Roasted, garnish Soissonnaise, gravy.

JAMBON — HAM

Cooking Process

Hams to be soaked the day before using brush, remove the pelvic bone, boil, then let simmer gently, time 15 minutes to a pound of ham.

Braising Process

Ham to be taken out 15 minutes before done, trim and take away the superfluous fat, then put back in braising pan, sprinkle over Madeira, Sherry, select the wine according to the menu.

Choucroute.—Braise, serve separately, braised sauerkraut and half-glaze Madeira sauce.
Epinards.—Braise, serve separately mashed spinach and half-glaze Madeira sauce.
Froid (Cold).—Cover with aspic, decorate round with chopped aspic and croûtons.
Maillot.—Braise, garnish Maillot, Madeira sauce.
Metternich.—Prepared as **Sous la Cendre**, serve separately slices of foie gras tossed in butter, cover same with slices of truffles also asparagus tips, Madeira sauce.
Mousse and Mousselines.—(*See* preparation), and serve with spinach and peas, etc.
Sous la Cendre.—Bone and stuff with veal forcemeat and whole truffles; tied up and wrapped in a paste, cooked in the oven about the same time as ordinary ham, serve separately mashed spinach and Périgueux sauce.

ZAMPINO — STUFFED LEG OF PORK

In normal times this can be purchased, ready prepared, from Provision Stores ; larded and poached in water for 1½ hours, garnish with sauerkraut, boiled cabbages, broad beans, etc.

COCHON DE LAIT — SUCKING PIGS

Américaine.—Stuff with the following forcemeat: Chopped onions, pigs livers mixed with sausage meat, bread crumbs, eggs and thyme. Cook 2½ hours.

Anglaise.—Stuff with English forcemeat.

Saint-Fortunat.—Sprinkle the interior with brandy, stuff with this forcemeat, chopped onions and barley cooked like **Riz Pilaw**, cook for 25 minutes, pig livers cut in dice and tossed in butter, braised chestnuts, chipolatas and herbs mixed together, season, trussed and cooked in braising pan, dress and serve with apple sauce, red currant with horse-radish and gravy.

VEAU — VEAL

(Best-Neck, Loin, Saddle.)

Agnès Sorel.—Insert tongue and truffles, braise, glaze, garnish like suprêmes of chicken of the same name, serve gravy.

Chartreuse.—Braise, dressed, garnish each side with Chartreuse of vegetables.

Chasseur.—Larded, roasted. (*Separately:*) Sauce Chasseur.

Dreux.—Larded and insert ham, braise, garnish Financière.

Matignon.—Partly braised, cover with Matignon, wrap in crépine, finish cooking in braising stock.

Metternich.—Braise the saddle, then remove the fillets, cut them into regular scallops cover with Béchamel and paprika, reconstruct the saddle and lay slices of truffles between each scallop, cover the whole joint with the sauce, glaze under salamander, serve Riz pilaw separately, and clear braising stock, all grease to be removed.

Nelson.—Prepare as above, cover the fillets with Soubise and place alternately with slices of ham, cover the joint with Parmesan soufflé preparation mixed with purée of truffles, cook and glaze, serve with braising stock.

Orientale.—Prepare same as **Metternich** only cover the fillets with curried Béchamel then cover the joint with tomated Béchamel, glazed surround with braised celery, served separately Riz pilaw and braising stock.

Orloff.—(Prepare same as **Metternich**,) cover the fillets with Soubise purée and mushrooms alternately with truffles, cover with Maintenon sauce, glaze, surround with Orloff garnish, serve with braising gravy.

Paprika.—Larded and seasoned with paprika, braised slowly on chopped onions, dress, surrounded with Hongroise garnish, serve with reduced braising stock mixed with cream.

Piémontaise.—(Same way as **Metternich**,) cover the fillets with Mornay sauce mixed with Piémont truffles, cover with same sauce, serve with rice and brazing liquor.

Renaissance.—Braise, garnish Renaissance, serve with half-glaze.

Romanoff.—(Prepared as **Metternich**,) only cover the fillets with cream sauce mixed with minced cèpes, cover the top with Béchamel sauce finished with crayfish butter, surround the border with braised half fennels, serve braising stock (*separately*).

H

Sicilienne.—Larded, roasted, wrapped with Sicilienne garnish and crépine, sprinkle with bread crumbs and a little melted butter. Served with gravy.

Talleyrand.—Stuffed with truffles, braise, serve with Talleyrand garnish and braising stock.

Tosca.—(Same as **Metternich**,) fill the centre with macaroni mixed with julienne of truffles, reconstruct the saddle them cover with Soubise sauce and glazed under the salamander. Serve braising stock (*separately*).

Turque.—Studded with larding bacon, cook, garnish with egg plant prepared à la Turque, serve braising stock (*separately*).

EPAULE OU POITRINE FARCIE

STUFFED SHOULDER OR BREAST OF VEAL

(*See* **Ballotines**, *at beginning of chapter*)

Farcie.—Boned and stuffed with sausage meat, chives and dry Duxelles, rolled, strung and braised, served with vegetable purée, and braising stock, or with the following garnishes: Boulangère, Bourgeoise, Printanière, etc.

Farcie à l'Anglaise.—Boned, stuffed with English forcemeat and cooked same way as " Epaule farcie ", braise, serve with boiled bacon, and braising stock.

JARRETS ET TENDRONS — KNUCKLES

Bourgeoise.—Browned in butter, then braised, garnish Bourgeoise, and braising stock.

Estragon.—Tossed in butter, moisten with stock to which add a bunch of tarragon, braise, and served with same stock reduced.

Osso Bucco.—Tossed with chopped onions and butter, add tomatoes, and half-glaze with tomato purée, bunch of herbs, braised, dished up and covered with garnish and braising stock.

Printanière.—(Same as **Bourgeoise**,) with Printanière garnish instead.

NOIX DE VEAU ET FRICANDEAU

CUSHION OF VEAL

Bourgeoise.—Braised and garnished Bourgeoise, braising stock.

Briarde.—Larded, braised, garnished with braised stuffed lettuces, serve with new carrots à la crème and braising stock.

Chatham.—Larded, braised, then glazed, serve in timbale with fresh noodles mixed with tongue, then mixed with thin Soubise sauce and slices of mushrooms.

Chicorée.—Braised and served with purée of chicory and braising stock.

Doria.—Braised, cut round the cushion and take out inside, scalop the meat, fill centre with Régence garnish, place the scallops on the garnish and cover with suprême sauce, surround with Duchess potatoes.

Epinards.—Braised, garnished with mashed spinach, serve with braising stock.

Froide.—Braised, cover with the braising stock mixed with aspic, garnish to taste.

Nivernaise.—Braised, garnish Nivernaise, braising stock.

Renaissance.—Braised, garnish Renaissance, braising stock.

Blanquette à l'Ancienne.—Veal or lamb from the shoulder or tendrons cut into pieces, blanched, cool and strain, then cook with white stock, add carrots, onions, bunch of herbs, prepare a white roux and moisten with the stock of the veal, when well boiled, finish the sauce with yolks of eggs and cream, strain the pieces of veal, place in the sauce, add small onions and mushrooms, chopped parsley.

CAPILOTADE

Pieces of chicken trimmed and warmed in half-glazed sauce mixed with braised onions and mushrooms, served in terrine, chopped parsley.

CARBONNADES

Scallops of beef tossed in butter or lard nicely browned, then cooked in a Sauté Dish with finely chopped onion, drop of beer and brown stock mixed with brown roux, add little demerara sugar, cook in the oven for three hours.

CASSOULET

1st.—Haricot beans cooked with onions, carrots, garlic, bunch of herbs, fresh pork rind, blanched and tied together, when half cooked add a piece of the breast of pork and a garlic sausage.

2nd.—Cut into squares shoulder of mutton or goose, fry slowly with chopped onions and garlic, moisten with the bean stock, cook, garnish dish or cocotte with alternate layers of mutton or goose, beans, bacon cut into dice, and slices of sausage, sprinkle with crumbs, and browned in the oven.

CHŒSELS

Oxtails cut in small lengths and sweetbreads partly cooked in hot fat until nicely browned, add pieces of veal, chopped onion, and pieces of beef kidneys, moisten with beer, salt, pepper, bunch of herbs, cook slowly, when nearly done add some sheeps' trotters and mushrooms. Thicken the stock with arrow-root and a little Madeira.

CIVETS — JUGGED HARE

Pieces of hare, lightly fried in butter with onions and minced carrots, add flour, moisten with red wine and brown stock, garlic, and a bunch of herbs, when cooked put the pieces of hare into another saucepan, add small braised onions, dice of bacon, mushrooms, and strain the sauce on the top, before serving thicken the sauce with the blood of the hare.

Civet Mère Jean.—Same as **Civet**, with cream, serve with bread fried in oil, and cèpes à la Provençale.

KARI, CURRIE — CURRY

Lamb or Mutton cut in squares, nicely browned in butter with chopped onions, add dice of apples, moisten with Curry sauce and coconut milk, cook and serve in timbale with plain boiled rice.

DAUBE

Avignonnaise.—Squares of legs of mutton larded with strips of fat bacon, put in a pickle of red wine, oil, sliced carrot and onions, garlic, parsley roots, thyme, bay leaves, garnish the bottom and sides of a braising pan with slices of bacon, place the mutton in layers alternately with onion and bacon, sprinkle with thyme and bay leaf on each layer, bunch of herbs in centre, moisten with the pickle and brown stock, cover with slices of bacon and seal the lid round with a soft paste to keep the steam in, place in the oven and cook gently for five hours. Served in a braising pan.

Provençale.—Pieces of beef larded through with a piece of fat bacon rolled in chopped parsley and crushed garlic, pickled with white wine and brandy, oil, to be cooked in a braising pan, with alternate layers of pieces of beef and fresh pork rind and blanched bacon, carrots, chopped onions, thyme, bay leaf, tomatoes, mushrooms, stoned black olives, and a bunch of herbs, containing dried orange peel, moisten with the pickle, and lemon juice, lid to be sealed with paste, serve in a Daubière pan.

ESTOUFFADE

Fry with onions some pieces of beef, add a piece of garlic and little flour, moisten with red wine and brown stock, bunch of herbs, cook 3 hours, place the pieces in another pan, add some sliced mushrooms, strain the sauce over, and let simmer for 15 minutes.

Nota.—Can also be done with white wine, tomatoes and olives (same name as **Provençale.**) (Meat can be larded).

FOIE GRAS

Aspic (en) (*Cold*).—(*See* preparation in **Fonds de Cuisine**).

Caisses (en).—Large dice of foie gras and truffles, mix lightly with Madeira sauce, serve in cases, place a scallop of foie gras and a slice of truffle on the scallop.

Cocotte (en).—Stud with truffles, fry lightly in butter, add white wine, essence of truffles and veal stock, place in a terrine, with the stock, seal the lid with paste, cook for an hour, serve with Madeira sauce and truffles.

Côtelettes, Croquettes and Cromesquis.—(*See* preparation in **Entrées Volantes**).

Escalopes (en).—Floured, sautéd, garnished with Talleyrand, Godard or Régence, etc.

Financière.—Stud with truffles, lard, cook in Madeira and braising stock, serve with Financiere garnish.

Gastronome (*Cold*).—Trim a foie gras parfait in the shape of an ostrich egg, cover with paprika chaud-froid sauce, decorate according to fancy, and glaze with aspic, placed on a crust shaped like a cushion, cover with chaud-froid of a different colour, surrounded with truffles cooked in Madeira, glaze the lot with aspic.

Mousse et Mousseline.—(*See* preparation in **Entrées Volantes**).

Paprika.—(Same way as **Financière,**) cover with Hongroise sauce. (*Can be served cold in terrine*).

Parfait.—Can be obtained all prepared in the stores.

Périgord.—Stud with truffles, season, pickle with truffles, bay leaf and fine champagne, lard and braise same way as **Financière,** take out when three parts cooked, put back in tureen with truffles all round, strain the stock, thinned with veal gravy, seal lid with paste and cook another 20 minutes, serve in terrine.

Rachel.—Round scallops, dressed on a mousse of foie gras and placed round a Rachel salad on the top place a small bunch of asparagus tips, glaze the lot with aspic.

Sainte-Alliance.—In a tureen surrounded with large truffles, moisten with champagne (dry), poach, and serve in terrine.

Soufflé.—(*See* preparation in **Savouries).**

Souvaroff.—Stud with truffles and lard, poach in butter and Madeira, take out the larding, place in terrine with truffles, strain on it the braising stock thinned with Madeira, seal lid and serve in terrine.

Subrics.—(*See* preparation in **Entrées Volantes).**

Timbale Alsacienne.—In scallops, sautéd, garnish Alsacienne (B).

Timbale Cussy.—In scallops, sautéd, and Cussy garnish.

Timbale Tzarine.—Line a timbale mould with short paste cover the inside with larding bacon, place in the centre a raw seasoned foie gras surrounded with stuffed quails and large truffles, cover the whole with a round slice of fat bacon and close with paste, cook 1½ hours, on withdrawing from the oven when partly cold pour into the timbale some good Madeira aspic jelly.

FRICASSEE

Same way as Blanquette, but the garnish is cooked with the meal.

GOULACHE — GOULASH

Goulache.—Cubes of beef, chopped onions, garlic, paprika, smoked bacon, water put in stew pan and cook slowly, garnish with boiled potatoes.

Hongroise.—Pieces of ribs or shoulder of beef, season with pink paprika and fried with onions, add flour moisten with brown stock, add dice of tomatoes and a little tomatoe purée, cook 2½ hours, when nearly done add some shaped potatoes and serve when cooked.

Tolstoï.—Pieces of ends of fillet of beef, season with salt and paprika, moisten with tomato sauce, add chopped onion partly cooked in butter and pieces of Agoursis, thin with white stock, cook ¾ hour serve in timbale with large potatoes, noisette shaped and steamed.

HARICOT DE MOUTON, NAVARIN, RAGOUT

Cooking Process

Pieces of breast, neck and shoulder of mutton, seasoned and fried with carrots, onions until nicely browned, add a little flour, moisten with thin stock or water, tomato purée, garlic, bunch of herbs, cook about 1½ hours, when cooked transfer the pieces to another pan, add small onions and shaped potatoes, strain the sauce on the lot, finish cooking, serve in timbale.

Haricot de Mouton.—Same process as above, but with haricot beans instead of onions and potatoes.

Navarin Printanière.—Same process with carrots, turnips, onions and potatoes tossed in butter, dish up in timbale with French beans and peas.

Ragoût de Mouton au Riz.—Same process with rice instead of vegetables.

IRISH STEW

Cut the Mutton in pieces, blanch, drain, put to cook with onions, potatoes, celery, and whites of leeks, add a bunch of herbs, when nearly done, transfer the meat into another pan, add small onions and shaped potatoes, strain the liquor and pour over the meat, finish cooking, serve very hot with chopped parsley.

LIEVRE A LA ROYALE — ROYAL JUGGED HARE.

1st.—Line a braising pan with pieces of bacon, place a hare in it, add carrots, 4 onions stuck with cloves, 20 cloves of garlic, 40 shallots, bunch of herbs, moisten with ½ bottle of red wine, and a little vinegar, braise in oven for 5 hours.

2nd.—Then prepare a mince with the heart, lung and liver, 10 cloves of garlic and chopped shallots, take out hare and pick the meat, mix the minced preparation with the braising stock and add the other bottle of wine, strain and pour over the pieces of hare, braise another 2 hours, mix the blood at the last minute before serving.

PAUPIETTES DE VEAU

Are thin slices of veal, seasoned and covered with forcemeat, rolled and tied to keep in shape.

Algérienne.—Stuffed with forcemeat, mixed with chopped pimentoes, braise, serve with Algérienne garnish, tomato sauce with Julienne of green pimentoes.

Anversoise.—Stuffed with chicken forcemeat, and Anversoise garnish tomato sauce.

Belle-Hélène.—Stuffed with forcemeat, braised, dish up and garnish the centre with croquettes made with asparagus tips, slices of truffles on each paupiette, cover with thickened gravy.

Brabançonne.—Stuffed with forcemeat, braise, garnish Brabançonne, thickened gravy.

Champignons.—Stuffed with chicken forcemeat mixed with dry Duxelles, braise, garnish, mushroom sauce.

Fontanges.—Stuffed with forcemeat, braise, dish up, and fill centre with haricot bean purée, surround with flat croquette potatoes.

Hussarde.—Stuffed with forcemeat, braise, garnish with tomatoes à la Hussarde, Duchesse potatoes on each paupiette, serve with braizing stock.

Loose Wiken (*Beef*).—Stuffed with sausage meat, cooked same way as Carbonnades.

Madeleine.—Stuffed with chicken forcemeat, braise, garnish Madeleine, serve with half-glaze mixed with braising liquor.

Marie-Louise.—Same preparation with Marie-Louise garnish (A et B).

Milanaise.—With garnish of the same name.

Napolitaine.—With garnish of the same name.

Portugaise.—With garnish of the same name.

Provençale.—With garnish of the same name.

Renaissance.—With garnish of the same name.

PIES AND PUDDINGS

Beefsteak Pie.—Scallops of beef, season, salt and pepper, nutmeg, add chopped onion and parsley, place round in bottom of a pie dish, fill inside with shaped potatoes, moisten with water, cover with puff paste egg wash, decorate and cook in over 2 hours.

Beefsteak and Kidney Pie.—Same as above with kidneys instead of potatoes.

Beefsteak Pudding.—Same way as for pie, make a pudding paste, 1 lb. flour and ½ lb. shredded suet, salt and water, line a pudding bowl, fill with the meat, moisten with good stock, cover with paste wrapped in serviette and boil 3 or 4 housr.

Steak and·Kidney Pudding.—Same way only sliced kidneys.

Steak and Oysters Pudding.—Same as above, only oysters added.

SAUTES

(Lamb and Veal.)

Aubergines.—Pieces of veal or lamb fried in butter with chopped onion and garlic, add white wine, brown sauce and tomatoes, bunch of herbs, cook in oven for 1½ hour, served in timbale surrounded with slices of fried egg plant.

Catalane.—Same way as above add tomatoes cut in quarters, cooked chestnuts, chipolatas, and stoned olives.

Champignons.—(*See* **Poulet Sauté aux Champignons**).

Chasseur.—(*See* **Poulet Chasseur**).

Fines-Herbes.—(Same as **Aubergines**) without the garnish, chopped parsley.

Indienne.—Fry the pieces in oil, add Curry powder and moisten with thin Curry sauce, serve with plain boiled rice.

Marengo.—(Same process as **Sauté Aubergines**,) the pieces fried in oil, add dice of tomatoes, small glazed onions, mushrooms, and heart shaped croûtons.

Minute Diable.—Small pieces of veal from the cushion, season salt and pepper, tossed quickly in butter, strain, mix with Devil sauce. Croûtons.

Minute Hongroise.—Same as above, season with salt and paprika, thicken with Paprika sauce.

Niçoise.—(Same as **Marengo**,) add **Niçoise** garnish.

Nouilles, Spaghetti, etc.—(Same process as **Sauté aux Aubergines**,) only add noodles, spaghettis, etc., instead of egg plant.

Oranaise.—(Same as **Marengo**,) with dice of tomatoes, shaped Brionnes, blanched and tossed in butter, simmer 15 minutes, serve in timbale, surround with rounds of fried onions.

Portugaise.—(Same as **Marengo**,) with dice of tomatoes.

Printanière.—(Same process as **Aubergines**,) with Printanière garnish.

Provençale.—(Same as **Portugaise**,) with stoned olives and garlic.

TERRINE — GALANTINE — PATE

Galantine (*preparation*).—Skin and bone a fowl or game, season the fillets, marinade with tongue, truffles, lardons, pistachios, brandy and Madeira, prepare a forcemeat with the rest of the meat, veal or pork and lard, season with salt and mixed spices, add the marinade, spread the skin of the bird on a cloth, place a layer of forcemeat, alternately with lardons, tongue, truffles and fillets, sprinkle with pistachios, finish with a layer of forcemeat, wrapped in bacon fat, roll in the shape of a big sausage, boil 90 minutes in a good stock, put to cool under press.

Pâté (*preparation*).—Paste, 1 lb. flour, 4 oz. butter, salt and water, line a mould with this paste, garnish bottom and sides with forcemeat, place a layer of scallops of the meat alternately with lardons until full, cover with slices of fat bacon and place paste on top, egg wash, decorate and cook.

Terrine.—Prepare same way as for the pâté, put in terrine lined with bacon, seal the lid round with paste and cook in a bain-marie in the oven.

CHEVREUIL — ROE BUCK

CERF, DAIM — STAG, FALLOW DEER

(*Is called VENISON.*)

Allemande.—Pickle the saddle after being larded with larding bacon, roast with the pickled vegetables, withdraw the joint, swill the tray with the pickle, reduce, add cream and meat glaze, reduce and strain, serve separate or coat the joint.

Baden-Baden.—Same as **Allemande**, rinse with grame stock, thicken with arrow-root, garnish with pears cut in quarters, cooked with lemon rind and cinnamon. Serve with red currant jelly, thicken the gravy.

Badoise.—Same process as **Allemande,** with stoned cherries.

Beaujeu.—Garnish with artichoke bottoms filled with mashed lentils and chestnuts cooked in consommé, serve Grand-Veneur sauce.

Cerises.—Serve with Poivrade sauce mixed with red currant jelly and stoned cherries.

Créole.—Surrounded with bananas tossed in butter, served with Robert sauce mixed with Poivrade.

Grand-Veneur.—Serve with chestnut purée and Grand-Veneur sauce.

FAISANS — PHEASANTS

Alcantara.—(*See* **Bécasse** of that name in **Entrées Volantes de Gibier).**

Angoumoise.—Stuff the pheasant with chestnuts and truffles, wrapped in chopped fat pork, then roll bird in slices of bacon, roast. Serve with Périgueux sauce.

Bohémienne.—Stuff with small foie gras studded with truffles, cook in a casserole, when serving set alight with brandy.

Carême.—(Same as **À la Crème,**) garnish with braised celery.

Croix de Berny (*Froid*).—Cut of the suprêmes of roast pheasant, garnish the inside with foie gras parfait, cover with foie gras mousse, scallop the suprêmes, reshape the bird, cover with brown Chaud-froid sauce, decorate, then glaze with aspic, dished up, surround with stuffed larks covered with brown Chaud-froid sauce, decorated tongue and truffles, chopped aspic.

Demidoff.—(*See* **Ris de Veau** same name in **Entrées Volantes de Boucherie).**

Géorgienne.—Poach the pheasant in malmsey wine, glass full of green tea, grape juice and orange, fresh walnuts, butter, cook for 40 minutes, add half-glaze sauce to the stock, then reduce same. Cover the pheasant with sauce, serve the rest separately.

Grillé.—(Same as **Grilled Chicken,**) served with Diable sauce.

Gunsbourg.—Stuffed with snipe mousse and truffles, cooked in cocotte, serve with its own stock, add a little cognac and snipe stock.

Kotschoubey.—Cooked in a casserole with raw truffles sliced, served with its own gravy reduced with Madeira and game glaze, also serve brussels sprouts along with pieces of bacon.

Mousse et Mousselines.—(*See* formula in **Entrées Volantes**).

Néva (*Cold*).—(*See* **Poulardes** same name in **Entrées de Volaille**).

Normande.—(*See* **Perdreaux** same name in **Entrées Volantes de Gibier**).

Périgueux.—Stuffed with truffles and fresh pork fat, " Poêler ", serve with Périgueux sauce.

Régence.—Cooked in butter, serve with Régence garnish.

Sainte-Alliance.—Stuff the pheasant with woodcock mousse and truffles, prepare a large fried toast and spread over a forcemeat made with the liver, woodcock intestines, fat bacon, anchovies and truffles, roast the bird on a wire stand, set the prepared croûton underneath so that the juice of the roasted bird falls on it, dish up on the croûton, surround with slices of bitter oranges.

Souvaroff.—Cook in cocotte, when 3 parts done, add dice of truffles and fresh foie gras, cognac and game stock, close lid with paste.

SANGLIERS ET MARCASSINS
BOAR AND YOUNG BOAR

(Cuissot and Selle.)
(Legs and saddles are treated same as Venison.)

A la Mode de Touraine.—Larded, marinade in red wine and vegetables, etc., roast, serve with Grand-Veneur sauce, and French beans.

VOLAILLE — POULTRY

CANARDS ET CANETONS — DUCKS AND DUCKLINGS

(Anglais, Nantais et Rouennais.)

Alsacienne.—(Same as **Choucroute.**)

Anglaise.—Stuffed English way, roast, serve with gravy, apple sauce, sage and onion.

Archiduc.—Stuffed foie gras and truffles, stiffen in oven, wrap in a bladder with brunoise of carrots and truffles, serve with Madeira sauce combined with foie gras purée.

Beaulieu.—Poêler. Set in tureen, surround with stoned black olives, dice of tomatoes, shaped potatoes, serve with Madeira half-glaze sauce.

Bigarade.—Cooked underdone, remove the fillets and slice lengthways. Bigarade sauce.

Bordelaise.—Stuffed with bread crumbs soaked in milk, chopped liver, parsley, stoned olives, mince mushrooms, garlic, egg, salt, pepper, roast, serve with gravy.

Cerises.—(Prepare as **Bigarade,**) with Madeira and veal stock, thickened with arrowroot, add stoned cherries, coat the fillets.

Champagne.—(Same as **Bigarade,**) rinse the pan with champagne and veal stock.

Chemise (en).—Bone the breast, (stuff like **Rouennaise,**) truss, and wrap in a serviette, poach for 45 minutes, take the serviette off and serve in the bladder. Rouennaise sauce.

H

Chipolata.—Braise, garnish with chipolatas.

Choucroute.—Braise, garnish with sauerkraut and plain boiled potatoes.

Dodine au Chambertin.—Rouennais roasted underdone, remove fillets, place them on a dish, cover with slices of truffles and mushrooms, mixed with meat glaze, spread over with a Salmis sauce made with the carcass of the rouennais, serve with noodles.

Ecarlate (*Froid*).—Cut the suprêmes in thin fillets, lengthways, cover each fillet with Chaud-froid sauce, decorate with truffles and glaze with aspic. Dress on a mousse of duck alternately with slices of tongue, spread the same with aspic jelly.

Lambertye (*Froid*).—(*See* **Poulardes Lambertye**).

Lyonnaise.—Braise, garnish with braised onions, and chestnuts cooked in consommé.

Menthe (à la).—Poêler. Serve with thickened gravy and chopped mint.

Molière.—Bone the duck, stuff with forcemeat made of 1 part of foie gras and the other part sausage meat and truffles, rolled up like a galantine, poached in good stock and glaze. Serve with Madeira sauce, and slices of truffles.

Mousse et Mousselines.—(*See* formula in **Entrées Volantes**).

Navets.—Braise in half-glaze, garnish with shaped turnips tossed in butter, and cooked in a braising stock.

Nivernaise.—Braised, served with Nivernaise garnish and braising stock.

Olives.—Same as turnips, olives instead of turnips.

Orange.—Braise same as with turnips, add orange and lemon juice and julienne of zest, surround with quarters of oranges skinned raw.

Petits Pois.—When 3 parts cooked finish it with petits pois **à la Paysanne,** add half-glaze.

Porto.—Cook in casserole, dress, rinse with port wine and veal stock, when serving thicken with the blood of the pressed carcass.

Presse.—Roast duck 20 minutes, serve immediately and treat as follows. Carve the fillets into thin slices and lay them on a warm dish, chop up carcass and press it, add glass full of red wine, drop of brandy, pour this liquor over the fillets, serve very hot, without letting boil.

Rouennaise.—(Stuff like **Rouennaise,**) finish (same **as Presse,**) with foie gras purée added to the sauce.

Saint-Albin (*Cold*).—Coat the fillets, with foie gras forcemeat, and Chaud-froid them with brown sauce, decorate with whites of eggs, tongue and zest of orange, line a dôme shaped mould with aspic, set the fillets round the inside and fill in with duck mousse, dish up on a rice stand, surround with a chopped aspic.

Sévillane (*Cold*).—Bone the breast, stuff with half gratin forcemeat and half mousseline, add tomato purée and dice of foie gras, wrap in a mousseline, poach, slice the suprêmes, reshape and coat with Chaudfroid sauce, glaze with aspic, surround with large olives stuffed with foie gras.

DINDES ET DINDONNEAUX
TURKEYS AND YOUNG TURKEYS

Anglaise.—Poach, (prepare as **Poularde à l'Anglaise.**)

Bouquetière.—Stud the breast, braise, Bouquetière garnish.

Bourgeoise.—Braise, Bourgeoise garnish.

Catalane.—Cut as for fricassée, fry the pieces, rinse the utensil with white wine, add garlic, reduce, moisten with brown sauce, tomato, and stock, faggot, cook 40 minutes, garnish Catalane.

Céleri Braisé.—Poêler, (finish as **Poularde aux Céleris.**)

Cèpes.—Stuffed with forcemeat made of veal, fresh pork, bread crumbs soaked in milk, and pressed, Duxelles of cèpes, salt, pepper, nutmeg, chop and mix the lot, braise until 3 parts done, transfer to another pan with lardons and sautéd cèpes, cover with braising liquor, finish the cooking, dish, with garnish round.

Champignons.—(*See* **Poularde and Poulet** of same name).

Chipolata.—Sauté or braise, chipolata garnish.

Dampierre (*Cold*).—(*See* **Poularde** of the same name).

Estragon.—(*See* **Poularde** of same name).

Financière.—Poêler, garnish and Financière sauce.

Godard.—Braise, garnish and Godard sauce.

Grand'Maman.—Stuff with a preparation of black pudding and cooked chestnuts, roast, serve with gravy.

Jardinière.—Roast, garnish, Jardinière.

Marrons.—Bone the breast, stuff with sausage meat mixed with cooked chestnuts, roast,, serve with gravy.

Navets.—(*See* **Canard** of the same name).

Nivernaise.—(*See* **Canard Nivernaise**).

Parfum des Gourmets.—Bone the breast, stuff with sausage meat, mixed with cubes of foie gras, and truffles, roast, serve with half-glaze combined with large slices of truffles.

Pauvre Homme.—(*See* **Grand'Maman**), without chestnuts.

Petits Pois.—(*See* **Canard**).

Primeurs.—Roast, garnish with spring vegetables, serve with gravy.

Truffes.—(*See* **Poularde Périgord**).

GRAINS ET REINES — SPRING CHICKEN

H

Américaine.—Stuff with American forcemeat, cook in a casserole, dish in cocotte with slices of grilled bacon.

Armenonville.—Cook in cocotte, serve with Armenonville garnish.

Belle-Meunière.—Stuff with truffles, mushrooms, chicken livers, slightly tossed in butter, cook in cocotte, garnish lardons and mushrooms.

Bergère.—Cook in cocotte, garnish with mousserons or mushrooms tossed in butter with lardons.

Bonne-Femme.—Cook in cocotte, garnish with potatoes, lardons, and onions.

Bordelaise.—Cook in cocotte, garnish (same as **Poulet Sauté Bordelaise.**)

Casserole.—Truss in entrée, season, cook in an earthenware saucepan, when serving, clear of all grease and add veal stock, serve in the pan.

Champeaux.—Cook in cocotte, add white wine and half-glaze, garnish with small glazed onions and cocotte potatoes.

Châtelaine.—Cook in cocotte, add white wine and half-glaze, garnish with artichoke quarters, truffles and cocotte potatoes.

Cocotte.—(Same as **Casserole**,) serve in cocotte.

Compote.—Cook in cocotte. (*See* **Pigeons en Compote** in **Entrées Volantes de Volaille**).

Crapaudine.—Split and grill. (*See* **Pigeon** same name in **Entrées Volantes de Volaille**).

Demidoff.—Cook in cocotte. (*See* **Ris de Veau** same name in **Entrées Volantes de Boucherie**).

Estragon.—Cook in cocotte, serve with tarragon gravy.

Falconnet.—Cook in cocotte, garnish with pears, dice of tomatoes, artichoke bottoms, cocotte potatoes, serve with tomatoed half-glaze.

Fermière.—Cook in casserole, Fermière garnish.

Forestière.—Cook in cocotte, Forestière garnish.

Grand'Mère.—Cook in cocotte, garnish with croûtons and dice of mushrooms.

Grillé.—Split, egg and crumbs, grill, serve with Diable sauce.

Jacques.—Stuff with forcemeat, poêler, add red wine and tomatoed veal stock, reduce, butter, and coat.

Katoff.—Split as for grilled, partly cook in oven and finish on the grill, dish up on Pomme Duchesse Galette, serve with gravy.

Limousine.—Stuff with sausage meat combined with dice of sauté mushrooms, cook in cocotte, garnish with lardons and cooked chestnuts, serve with gravy.

Mascotte.—Cook in cocotte, serve with half-glaze and Mascotte garnish.

Matignon.—Stuff with vegetable Paysanne, cook in cocotte, when nearly done cover with Matignon and wrap in crépine, finish cooking in oven, Madeira half-glaze.

Mireille.—Split as for grilled, cook in oven, dish on Mireille potatoes.

Morilles.—Cook in cocotte, garnish with morels tossed in butter, add veal gravy.

Palace.—Split as for grilled, cook in oven, rinse pan with brandy, port, add meat glaze and tarragon, finish with butter, coat with the sauce.

Parmentier.—Cook in cocotte, add white wine and half-glaze, garnish with Parmentier potatoes.

Paysanne.—Cook in cocotte, add white wine and half-glaze, serve with Paysanne garnish.

Primeurs.—Cook in cocotte, garnish Primeurs.

Printanière.—Same with Printanière garnish.

Ravioli.—Same with Ravioli garnish.

Richelieu.—Cook in cocotte, garnish with large julienne of carrots, celery, and truffles, Madeira and veal stock.

Souvaroff.—Cook in cocotte, (finish as **Faisan Souvaroff.**)

POULARDES

Albuféra.—Stuff with rice pilaw, combined with dice of truffles and foie gras, poach and coat with Albuféra sauce, garnish with truffles.

Alexandra.—Lard with tongue and truffles, poach, remove the suprêmes, replace with mousseline forcemeat, reshape the bird, coat with Mornay sauce, glaze; garnish with tartlets filled with asparagus heads, place a scallop of suprême on each, surround with a thread of pale glaze.

Alphonse XIII.—Stuff with pilaw rice combined with ham dice, and truffles, cook with mirepoix, rinse with white wine and Suprême sauce, dress on a layer of rice, coat with the sauce, garnish with quenelles, decorate with truffles, olives and cocks kidneys.

Ambassadrice.—Stud with truffles, cover with Matignon, wrap in muslin, braise, remove suprêmes and breast bones, fill carcass with asparagus heads cohered with butter, slice the suprêmes, reconstruct the bird, coat with Suprême sauce, garnish with lamb sweet breads studded with truffles, braised and glazed, alternately with asparagus heads.

Américaine.—(Same as **Poulet de Grain Américaine.**)

Anglaise (A).—Poach, coat with Suprême sauce, surround base with slices of tongue and heaps of carrots, turnips, celery and peas.

(B).—Poach with water and bacon, dress, surround with pieces of bacon, serve with parsley sauce.

Argenteuil.—Poach, coat with sauce Suprême combined with asparagus purée, garnish with Argenteuil asparagus.

Aumale (d').—Stud with truffles, stuff with mousseline forcemeat, and truffles, braise, garnish with tartlets filled with shaped cucumbers cooked in butter, cooked onions, emptied and filled with tongue and foie gras cohered with Madeira sauce, alternate with Fleurons, serve with braising liquor thickened with arrow-root and flavoured with Madeira wine.

Aurore.—Stuffed with forcemeat combined with tomato purée, poached and coated with Aurore sauce.

Banquière.—Poêle the bird and rinse the pan with half veal stock and half suprême sauce, reduce and garnish Banquière.

Beaufort.—Stuff with foie gras and sausage meat, stud with truffles, braise, dish on a large toast, garnish with lambs' tongues and artichoke bottoms filled with onion purée, serve with braising liquor.

Boïeldieu.—Stuff with chicken mousseline combined with foie gras purée, stud with truffles, poach, add white wine and rich chicken stock, thicken with arrow-root garnish with truffles.

Bouquetière.—Poêle, add Madeira and half-glaze, garnish, Bouquetière.

Cardinal.——Poach, coat with tomatoed Suprême sauce, garnish with stuffed tomatoes.

Carmélite *(Cold)*.—Scallop the suprêmes, coat with Chaud-froid sauce decorated with truffles, fill carcass with crayfish mousseline, dress the scallops on the mousse, alternate with crayfish tails, glaze with aspic.

Céleri.—Poêle and garnish with braised celery, serve with strong gravy.

Champagne *(Cold)*.—(Stuff same as **Louise d'Orléans**,) Poêle, rinse pan with champagne and chicken stock, cool, mix the liquor with chicken aspic, place the chicken in a terrine and fill with the liquid jelly.

Champignons (à blanc).—Poach, coat with Suprême sauce, flavoured with mushroom essence, surround with grooved mushrooms heads.

(A brun).—Poêle, and rinse the pan with mushroom essence, garnish with grooved and cooked mushrooms heads.

Chanoinesse.—(Prepare as **Poularde Soufflée**,) surround with scallops of suprême decorated with sliced truffles, alternate with tartlets, filled with crayfish tails cohered with Suprême sauce.

Châtelaine.—Poêle, rinse pan with white wine, and veal stock, garnish Châtelaine (B)

H

Chevalière.—Suprêmes larded with truffles and tongue, trim the small fillets; insert thin slices of truffle and draw the ends together to form a ring, poach with mushroom stock, remove the legs, bone them to within a third of an inch of the joint, stuff with Godiveau, and trim in such a manner as to imitate a small duck, poach in stock, prepare a croûton the shape of a pyramid, surround base with 4 large quenelles, place the legs and suprêmes on them, and arrange small heaps of cockscombs and kidneys and white mushrooms, between the legs and the suprêmes, pierce the croûtons with an Attlet, garnished with truffles, cocks combs and a large mushroom, cover with Suprême sauce.

Chimay.—Stuff with noodles mixed with dice of foie gras, poêler, dish and cover with the stock thickened, sprinkle on top, with raw noodles tossed in butter.

Chipolata.—Poêler, place in a terrine, garnish with glazed onions, chipolata, chestnuts, dice of bacon.

Chivry.—Poached, cover with Chivry sauce, garnish with tarlets filled with macédoine of vegetables, mixed with cream.

Coq-en-Pâte.—Stuff with truffles and foie gras, brown in oven, let cool, wrap in puff paste, finish cooking in oven, make small chimney to pour Périgueux sauce during the cooking process.

Cussy.—Braise, serve with Cussy garnish and Madeira half-glaze.

Dampierre (*Cold*).—Stuff the Poularde raw, with mousseline forcemeat, poach, cool, strain, cover with Chaud-froid sauce made with almond milk, garnish with small mousses of tongue and foie gras, glaze with aspic.

Demi-Deuil.—Stuff with chicken mousseline, stud with truffles, poach, and cover with Suprême sauce, and slices of truffles.

Demidoff.—Poêler, (finish same way as **Ris de Veau Demidoff.**)

Derby.—Stuff same way as Albuféra, poêler, garnish with truffles cooked in champagne, and croûtons garnished with slices of foie gras tossed in butter, served with a thickened gravy.

Devonshire.—Bone the breast, fill with chicken forcemeat and sausage meat, in the middle set a cooked calf tongue, sewn up with string larded, poached and strained, make an insertion round the breast, detach the stuffing with a knife and cut off the pieces consisting of the breast stuffing and tongue, dish the carcass on a low cushion, cut breast lengthway in halves, re-slice each half and reconstruct the bird, cover with Suprême sauce mixed with brunoise of tongue, garnish with artichoke bottoms, stuff with mashed peas.

Diva.—Stuff with pilaw rice mixed with foie gras and truffles, poêler, and cover with Hongroise sauce, surround with small heaps of cucumber mixed with cream.

Dreux.—Stuff with truffles and tongue, poach, cover with Suprême sauce, Régence garnish (B).

Duchesse.—Poach, remove the suprême, scallop, stuff the carcass with barley and asparagus heads, mixed with chicken glaze, dish up on a border of same preparation with chicken scalloped on the carcass and on the border, alternately with small bunches of asparagus heads, cover with braising stock, reduced, and thicken with arrow-root.

Duroc.—Stuff with foie gras forcemeat mixed with julienne of tongue and truffles, poêler, slices of truffles on the breast; serve with Madeira sauce.

Ecarlate (*Cold*).—Stuff like Dampierre, insert a tongue in the interior, cover with white Chaud-froid sauce, decorate with truffles and tongue, glaze with aspic.

Ecossaise.—Stuff with forcemeat mixed with large brunoise poach, cover with Ecossaise sauce, serve with French beans mixed with cream.

Edouard VII.—Stuff like Diva, cover with Suprême sauce flavoured with Curry and mixed with dice of pimentoes of red capsicums, serve cucumbers mixed with cream.

Elysée.—Stuff with chicken mousseline and foie gras purée, stuff with truffles, poach, surround with Régence garnish, Suprême sauce.

Escuriale.—Stuff with pilaw rice, ham dice and mushrooms, and fried eggs, serve with half-glaze sauce.

Espagnole.—Stuff with pilaw rice mixed with dice of pimentoes and Chiches peas, poêle, dress, cover with thickened gravy, garnish with grilled tomatoes and rounds of onions fried in oil.

Estragon.—Poêler, decorate breast with blanched tarragon leaves, cover with thickened gravy, flavoured with tarragon essence.

Favorite.—Stuff with chicken mousseline mixed with foie gras purée and truffles, poach, cover with Suprême sauce, garnish with cockscombs kidneys and slices of truffles.

Fermière.—Poêler, serve with Madeira sauce and Fermière garnish.

Financiere.—Poêler. Financiere garnish and Madeira sauce.

Gastronome.—Stuff with morels, tossed in butter, poêler, dress, surround with heaps of truffles and chestnuts, alternately with cockscombs, serve with half-glaze sauce flavoured with champagne and truffles essence.

Géraldine.—Poêler with vegetables, moisten with Saint-Marceaux wine and veal stock, dress, cover with cooking liquor reduced with Velouté, surround with small marrows, tomatoes and egg plants stuffed à la Grecque.

Godard.—Braise, garnish and Godard sauce.

Grammont.—Poach, remove the suprêmes and the bones of the breast, fill cavity with lark fillets, grooved mushroom heads, cockscombs and kidneys, cohere the lot with Béchamel sauce and truffle essence, slice the fillets, cover with Supreme sauce, sprinkle with parmesan cheese and, set to glaze.

Grand-Hôtel.—Cut the bird as for Sauté, cook in butter under cover, set the pieces in a cocotte with raw truffles cut in thick slices, rinse the pan with white wine and chicken stock, and pour over the chicken, serve in the cocotte.

Grecque.—Stuff with rice à la Grecque, cook and serve with the thickened gravy.

Gros Sel.—Poach, garnish with onions and carrots, serve with cooking liquor, and a sauce boat of kitchen salt.

Héloïse.—Poach, remove the suprêmes and the breast bone, fill carcass with chicken mousseline and truffles, replace the fillets, decorate with hard boiled eggs, the whites cover with buttered paper and poach, coat with Suprême sauce.

Hollandaise.—Poach, surround with plain steamed shaped potatoes, serve with Hollandaise sauce.

Hongroise.—Poêler, cover with Hongroise sauce, serve with pilaw rice, mixed with dice of tomatoes.

Huîtres.—Poach, cover with Suprême sauce mixed with oysters.

Impératrice.—Poach, cover with Suprême sauce, mixed with chicken purée, surround with calves' brains cut in dice and lamb sweetbreads alternately with small braisef onions.

Indienne.—Poach, cover with Curry sauce, serve with plain boiled rice separate.

Infante.—Poach, cover with Suprême sauce mixed with mushroom purée, garnish with grilled tomatoes.

Isabelle de France.—Stuffed with rizotto mixed with crayfish tails and truffles, poached in white wine and white stock, cover with Suprême sauce, surround with black truffles cooked in champagne and dressed in hollowed croûtons.

Ivoire.—Poach, serve with Suprême sauce and cèpes with cream.

Lady Curzon.—(Stuff same as **Diva**,) poach, cover with Italian sauce flavoured with Curry, serve shaped cucumbers cooked with cream.

Lambertye (*Cold*).—Poach, remove the suprêmes, and slice them lengthways, cover with white Chaud-froid sauce, decorate with truffles, fill carcass with chicken mousse and foie gras, reshape the bird and glaze with aspic.

Languedocienne.—Poêler, serve with thickened chicken stock, flavour with Madeira, and Languedocienne cream, then garnish.

Louise d'Orléans.—Stuff with a foie gras studded with truffles and marinaded in brandy and Madeira, brown in oven, cover with slices of truffles, lard, and wrap in paste, cook, and serve, hot or cold.

Louisiane.—Stuff with maize, mixed with dice of pimentoes, poêler, garnish with pilaw rice, fried bananas, and tartlets filled with sweet corn, serve Madeira sauce.

Lucullus.—Stuff with chicken mousseline and truffles, braise, dish and surround with truffles cooked in champagne, cockscombs, cover with half-glaze and cooking stock reduced with truffle essence.

Maintenon.—Studded with truffles and tongue, braised in white stock, cover with Suprême sauce, surround with quenelles, heads of mushrooms and artichoke bottoms filled with slices of truffles, cover with Mornay sauce and brown.

Maison d'Or.—Poêler, rinse with Madeira, half-glaze and thickened stock, strain, dish up the chicken surround with a garnish of cockscombs, kidneys, mushrooms, quenelles, truffles, add scallops of foie gras, at the last moment cover with the sauce.

Mancini.—Poach, remove suprêmes and breast bone, fill carcass with macaroni mixed with dice of foie gras and julienne of truffles, replace the fillets sliced lengthways, alternately with slices of truffles covered with Mornay sauce, glazed.

Maraîchère.—Poach, in terrine, surround with Maraîchère garnish, add Madeira and half-glaze, seal the lid with thin paste, serve in the terrine.

Maréchale.—Stuff with scallops of sweetbread, brains and mushrooms mixed with Suprême sauce, poach, cover with Suprême sauce, Maréchale garnish.

Marguerite de Savoie.—Stuff with larks, tossed in butter, with white truffles, braised with white wine and veal stock, dress on a croûton of bread, surround with small rounds sprinkled with cheese and glaze, cover with thickened gravy, serve in timbale of white truffles cooked in butter and consommé.

Marie-Louise.—Stuff with pilaw rice, sliced mushrooms and truffles, mixed with Soubise sauce, poached, cover with Suprême sauce, garnish with braised lettuces, and artichoke bottoms, filled with mushroom purée and Soubise sauce.

Ménagère.—Poach with carrots, onions and potatoes, serve in a terrine with the vegetables and cooking liquor.

Métropole.—Poach, garnish with artichoke bottoms, small onions and mushrooms, coat with Suprême sauce, surround with heart shaped croûtons.

Monte-Carlo.—Poach, cover with half Suprême sauce and half Aurore sauce, garnish the white side with tomato quenelles, and the pink side with white quenelles.

Montfermeil.—Poêler, rince with white wine and veal stock, garnish with carrots, turnips small onions, peas, Château potatoes, serve in a terrine.

Montglas.—Poêler, cover with Madeira half-glaze combined with julienne of truffles, tongue, ham, and mushrooms.

Montmorency.—Stud with truffles, braise in half-glaze and Madeira, dress and cover with the sauce and Montmorency garnish.

Nantua.—Poach, cover with Suprême sauce combined with crayfish cullis, decorate with slices of truffles, garnish with crayfish tails and quenelles.

Néva (*Cold*).—(Stuff and poach same as **Dampierre**,) with the addition of dice of foie gras and truffles, in the forcemeat, cover with white Chaud-froid sauce, surrounded with shaped Russian salad.

Niçoise.—Poêler, rinse with Madeira, and tomated veal stock, Niçoise garnish with black olives instead of potatoes, cover with sauce.

Normande.—Poach, cover with Suprême sauce, garnish with carrots, turnips, potatoes, and leeks, plainly cooked.

Nouilles.—Stuff with noodles, mixed with grated cheese, cream, dice of foie gras and truffles, poach, cover with Mornay sauce, glazed.

Œufs d'Or.—Poached, cover with Suprême sauce, surround with hard-boiled eggs stuffed with chicken purée, egg and bread crumbs, fried slices of truffles and rounds of potatoes.

Orientale.—Stuff with pilaw rice and saffron, poach, remove the fillets and breast bone, cover the rise with Aurore sauce, replace the suprêmes, sliced lengthways, cover with the same sauce, garnish with quarters of Brionnes, cooked in butter.

Paramé.—Wrapped in matignon and mousseline, poêler, dress, garnish with carrots and lettuces, served with thickened gravy.

Parisienne.—Poach, cover with Suprême sauce, decorate with rounds of truffles and tongue, Parisienne garnish, border the dish with a thread of pale glaze.

Parisienne (*Cold*).—(Same as **Lambertye**,) add quenelles of chicken to the mousse, garnish same as **Néva**.

Patti Adelina.—(Stuff as **Diva**) poached, dress on a low croûton, cover with paprika Suprême sauce, garnish with artichoke bottoms, filled with a large truffle rolled in meat glaze.

Paysanne.—Poach, dress in terrine, rinse with white wine and half-glaze, Paysanne garnish.

Périgord.—Stuff with raw truffles, mixed with fresh pork fat, poêler gently, rinse pan with Madeira and half-glaze, dish in terrine, sauce over.

Périgourdine.—Same as above, add cubes of foie gras, poach and cover with Suprême sauce, flavoured with essence of truffles.

Petite Mariée.—Poach, cover with Suprême sauce, garnish with bunches of carrots and peas, and Noisette potatoes.

Piémontaise.—Stuff with Piémontaise rice, poêler, dress in terrine, sauce Madeira and half-glaze.

Poincaré.—Braise in veal stock, reduce the liquor of the stock, add crayfish in velouté, cream and cover with sauce, serve with Coquillettes mixed with cream, butter and cheese (grated), mixed with crayfish tails and slices of truffles, decorate with cockscombs.

Polignac.—Poach, remove suprêmes, and breast bones, fill carcass wtih chicken mousseline and julienne of chicken and truffles, cook in slow oven, replace the fillets alternately with slices of truffles covered with Suprême sauce mixed with mushroom purée and truffles and julienne of mushrooms.

Portugaise.—Stuff with pilaw rice and dice of tomatoes, poêler, cover with Portugaise sauce, garnish with stuffed tomatoes.

Princesse.—Poach, cover with Suprême sauce, mixed with green asparagus purée, garnish with croustades of Duchesse potatoes, filled with green asparagus purée and round quenelles on top.

Princesse Hélène.—(Same as **Diva,**) dress, cover with Suprême sauce, garnish with spinach subrics, and slices of white truffles.

Printanière.—Poêler, rinse with white wine and half-glaze, dress in terrine, cover add Printanière garnish, seal lid with soft paste, finish in the oven.

Régence.—Stuff with mousseline of chicken and crayfish purée, Régence garnish (B), cover with Suprême sauce.

Reine.—Poach, cover with Suprême sauce, surround with timbales of chicken purée.

Reine Anne.—Poêler, remove suprêmes, and breast bone, fill inside with macaroni mixed with foie gras and truffles, cover with Mornay sauce and glaze, dress on a croûton, garnish with tartlets, filled with cockscombs and kidneys, mixed with Suprême sauce, alternately with shells filled with truffles, serve Suprême sauce with truffle essence.

Reine Blanche.—Stuff with chicken mousseline, mixed with dice of tongue and truffles, poach, serve with cockscombs and kidneys, truffles and mushroom heads mixed with Suprême sauce.

Reine Margot.—Stuff with chicken mousseline mixed with almond purée, poach, cover with Suprême sauce made with almond milk, garnish with quenelles flavoured with pistachios and alternate with crayfish quenelles.

Reine Marguerite.—Poach, remove the suprêmes, slice them in thin scallops, fill inside with cheese soufflé, place the scallops on top alternately with soufflé preparation, surround with buttered paper to keep it in shape, cook in oven, serve with Suprême sauce, mixed with white truffles in slices.

Renaissance.—Poach, cover with Suprême sauce, Renaissance garnish.

Riz.—Poach dress on pilaw rice, with Suprême sauce.

Rose de Mai (*Cold*).—Scallops of suprêmes, covered with Chaud-froid sauce, décorate with truffles, glazed with aspic, and placed on barquettes filled with tomato mousse, the carcass is treated the same, Chaud-froid sauce and filled with tomato mousse, decorated with truffles, and whites of eggs, glaze the lot with aspic, dish on mould of rice, surround with suprêmes.

Rose Marie (*Cold*).—(Same as **Rose de Mai,**) with ham mousse instead of tomato, cover the suprêmes and carcass with paprika Suprême sauce.

Rossini.—Poêler, rinse with Madeira and half-glaze, dress in terrine, garnish with slices of foie gras, and quarters of truffles, seal lid with thin paste, finish in the oven, serve in terrine.

Russe.—Poach, cover with Suprême sauce, mixed with beetroot juice, garnish with braised fennels.

Sainte-Alliance.—Stuff with truffles cooked in Madeira, poêler, rinse with truffles cooking stock, and chicken stock, serve with collops of foie gras, ortolans and the cooking liquor.

(*This poularde must be served quickly and in the dining room*).

Saint-Cyr (*Cold*).—(Prepare same as **Rose de Mai,**) with foie gras mousse instead of tomato, cover the carcass with brown Chaudfroid sauce and the fillets with white, place half a stuffed lark on each suprême.

Santa-Lucia.—(Stuff same as **Sainte-Alliance,**) braise in Marsala wine and veal stock, dress, garnish with gnoki alternately with sauted collops of foie gras.

Sicilienne.—Poach, remove the suprêmes and breast bones, fill the inside with spaghetti mixed with dice of truffles, mushrooms, cockscombs and kidneys, wrap the pieces in pig's caul, sprinkle with crumbs and melted butter, place in the oven to colour, surround with tartlet crusts, filled with a slice of suprême covered with foie gras, and surmounted with a slice of truffles, serve chicken glaze with butter separately.

Soufflée.—Poach, raise the suprêmes, suppress breast bone and fill chicken with foie gras mousseline, mixed with scallops of truffles and supremes, reconstruct the bird, smooth its surface, and poach in the oven, serve with Suprême sauce.

Souvaroff.—(*See* **Pheasant** same name).

Stanley.—Stuff with pilaw rice mixed with julienne of mushrooms, truffles and tongue, poach, finish (same as **Poulet sauté Stanley.**)

Sylvana.—Stuff with sautéd mushrooms, poêler, dress in terrine with peas cooked à la Française, add a bunch of mint leaves, seal lid with paste, finish in the oven, serve in terrine, with chicken gravy separate.

Talleyrand.—Poêler, remove suprêmes, cut them in large dice, suppress the breast bone, stuff the carcass with a Talleyrand garnish mixed with suprême dice, cover with chicken mousseline, decorate with slices of truffles, poach, dress, serve with half-glaze flavoured with essence of truffles.

Tivoli.—Poêler, rinse with white wine, lemon juice and veal stock, garnish with large mushrooms filled with cockscombs and kidneys, cover with Suprême sauce alternately with small bundles of asparagus heads.

Tosca.—Stuff with pilaw rice, poêler, rinse with Madeira and thin half-glaze, add butter on croûton, surround with braised fennels, serve with the sauce.

Toscane.—(Same as **Diva**) but stuffed with noodles, mixed with foie gras, dice of truffles.

Toulousaine.—Poach, garnish and Toulousaine sauce.

Trianon.—Poach, cover with Suprême sauce, mixed with foie gras purée, garnish with large quenelles stuffed with foie gras of different colours, (*green*) parsley; (*red*) chopped tongue; (*black*) chopped truffles, pierce the chicken with an " Attlet, " garnish with a grooved mushroom, large truffle and a red quenelle.

Valenciennes.—Poêler, dressed on rizotto mixed with dice of ham, place a crown of grilled bacon upon the rizotto, serve with tomated Suprême sauce.

Vénitienne.—Poach, cover with Suprême sauce, garnish with grooved mushrooms, scallops of veal brains, cockscombs.

Vert Pre.—Poach, cover with Suprême sauce finished with Printanière butter, surrounded with peas, French beans, asparagus heads mixed with butter.

Vichy.—Poach, cover with Suprême sauce, finish with purée of carrots, garnish with tartlets crusts, filled with Vichy carrots.

Victoria.—(Stuff same as **Souvaroff,**) and three parts poêler it, put in into a cocotte with dice of potatoes, complete cooking in the oven.

Vierge.—Poach, cover with Suprême sauce, garnish with scallops of sweetbread and veal brains alternately with cockscombs.

Villars.—Poach, cover with Suprême sauce, garnish with lamb sweetbreads, cocks kidneys and mushrooms, alternately with slices of tongue.

Washington.—Stuff with sweet corn or green maize, poêler, rinse with whisky, brandy, port and Suprême sauce, cover and serve in a timbale of maize mixed with cream.

Wladimir.—Poach, cover with Béarnaise and Suprême sauce, mixed together, also julienne of celery, carrots and truffles, decorate with tarragon leaves and chervil.

OIE — GOOSE

Is generally roasted and stuffed English way or any other forcemeat with apple sauce and gravy. Can be prepared same way as Ducks.

PINTADE — GUINEA FOWL

(Same preparation as pheasants.)

Rôtis — Roast

Agneau et Mouton (Lamb and Mutton).—Baron or pair of hind quarters of Mutton, Neck, Shoulders, Legs, Saddle.

Beef.—Ribs, Sirloin, Fillet.

Gibier (Game).—Woodcocks. Snipes. Wild ducks. Black-game. Pheasant. Grouses. Hares. Larks. Blackbirds. Ortolans. Partridges. Plovers. Lapwings. Sandpipers. Teals. Widgeons. Fig peckers.

Pork.—Leg. Loin. Sucking pig.

Veal.—Leg of Veal. Loin. Fillet. Cushion.

Volaille (Poultry).—Ducks. Ducklings. Aylesbury. Nantais. Rouennais. Turkeys. Geese. Pigeons. Guinea fowl. Poulardes. Spring chickens. Poussins.

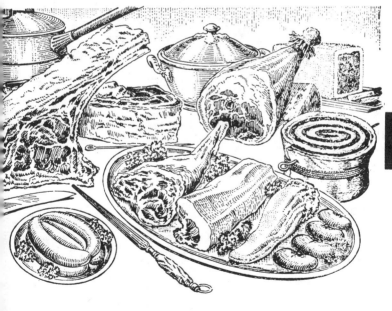

H

Salades—Salads

SIMPLE SALADS

Beetroots. White dandelions. Celery. Chicory. Endives. Red cabbage. Cucumber. Water Cress. Lettuces. Corn salad. Potato. Salsify (leaves). Tomato.

Seasoning.—Olive oil and vinegar, cream and vinegar, egg seasoning, mustard with cream, mayonnaise.

SALADES COMPOSEES — COMPOUND SALADS

Aïda.—Curly chicory, tomatoes and sliced artichoke bottoms, julienne of green pimentoes and whites of hard boiled eggs, cover with hard yolks, passed through the sieve, vinaigrette with mustard.

Alice.—Large apple, scooped and fill with small balls of green apples, red currants, and sliced almonds, thicken with cream and lemon juice.

Allemande.—Half apples, half potatoes, dice of gherkins, and fillets of herrings, onions and chopped parsley, egg vinaigrette, and decorate with beetroot.

Alsacienne.—(Same as **Allemande,**) with slices of truffles, and walnuts, instead of herrings and gherkins.

Américaine.—Slices of tomatoes and potatoes, julienne of celery, onions and hard boiled eggs, vinaigrette.

Andalouse.—Quarters of tomatoes, julienne of sweet pimentoes plain boiled rice, crushed garlic, onions and chopped parsley, Vinaigrette sauce.

Augustin.—Long lettuce, french beans, tomatoes in quarters, hard boiled egg, peas, mayonnaise with Worcester sauce.

Bagatelle.—Julienne of carrots and mushrooms, asparagus tips, and vinaigrette.

Bagration.—Julienne of celery and chicken and artichoke bottoms, macaroni and tomatoes, decorate with truffles, eggs and chopped parsley, mayonnaise sauce.

Béatrice.—Julienne of white of chicken, truffles, potatoes, asparagus tips, sauce mayonnaise with mustard.

Beaucaire.—Julienne of celery, ham, chicory, apples, parsley, chervil, and chopped tarragon on top, decorate round with potatoes and beetroot. Mayonnaise sauce.

Belles de Nuit.—Slices of truffles and crayfish, oil and vinegar, pepper from the mill.

Canaille.—Tomatoes cut in quarters, asparagus heads, bananas, rice, julienne of celery. Sour cream.

Caprice.—Julienne of tongue, ham, truffles, chicory, chicken, artichoke bottoms, vinaigrette with mustard.

Caprice de Reine.—Chicory, apples, julienne of truffles and celery, Mayonnaise sauce.

Carmen.—Red poivrons grilled and peeled, dice of chicken, peas and rice, vinaigrette with mustard and chopped tarragon.

Cendrillon.—Julienne of celeriac, truffles and artichoke bottoms, potatoes and apples, asparagus tips, vinaigrette.

Châtelaine.—Hard boiled eggs, truffles, artichoke bottoms, potatoes, vinaigrette with chopped tarragon.

Chicago.—Tomatoes cut in quarters, asparagus tips, french beans, slices of foie gras, julienne of carrots and mushrooms. Mayonnaise.

Crémone.—Japanese artichokes, tomatoes, fillets of Anchovies, vinaigrette with mustard.

Créole.—Small melons, take inside out, cut in dice, salt and ginger, rice mixed with acidulated cream, replace in melon, serve surrounded with crushed ice.

Cressonnière.—Slices of potatoes, and water cress leaves, sprinkle with ɪparsley, chervil and hard boiled eggs.

Dalila.—Bananas, apples, julienne of celery. Mayonnaise.

Danicheff.—Asparagus tips, celeriac, potatoes, artichoke bottoms, mushrooms. Mayonnaise. Decorate with crayfish, truffles and eggs.

Délices.—(*See* **Japonaise (C).**)

Demi-Deuil.—Julienne truffles and potatoes, and border round with slices of each, cream with mustard.

Egyptienne.—Rice, add salpicon of chicken livers, ham, mushrooms, artichoke bottoms, peas, tomatoes, red pimentoes.

Eléonora.—Hearts of long lettuces, surround with artichoke bottoms, garnish with poached eggs, and asparagus tips. Mayonnaise sauce.

Espagnole.—French beans and quarters of tomatoes, decorate with pimentoes, slices of onions and mushrooms.

Estrées (d').—Julienne of raw truffles, celery, Mayonnaise with mustard and cayenne.

Eve.—Prepare apples (same as for **Alice,**) garnish with apples, bananas, pineapple, cream, lemon juice and salt.

Fanchette.—Julienne of chicken, raw mushrooms, chicory and truffles, vinaigrette·

Favorite.—Crayfish tails, slices of white truffles, asparagus tips, seasoned with lemon juice, olive oil, salt and pepper, celery and chopped parsley.

Florida.—Lettuces and quarters of oranges, seasoned with acidulated cream.

Francillon.—Mussels, potatoes, cooked in Chablis wine, cover with truffles, vinaigrette. Mussels should be bearded.

Gauloise (A).—Truffles, potatoes, celery and mushrooms, Mayonnaise sauce.

(B).—Long lettuce, julienne of fresh walnuts, Mayonnaise with cream.

Gobelins (des).—Celeriac cooked, and potatoes ,artichoke bottoms and raw mushrooms, truffles and asparagus tips. Mayonnaise with lemon juice and chopped tarragon.

Grande Duchesse.—French beans, julienne of potatoes and celery. Mayonnaise.

Hermine.—Julienne of chicken, celery hearts, chicory, potatoes and Mayonnaise.

Hollandaise.—Smoked salmon in dice, potatoes, caviar of Berg-op-Zoom, onions and cibols chopped, lemon juice and oil.

Hongroise.—Julienne of cabbage, partly boiled bacon, potatoes, lemon juice, oil and scraped horse-radish.

Impériale.—French beans, carrots, apples and truffles cut in julienne, vinaigrette and chopped parsley.

Indienne.—Rice, asparagus tips, julienne of sweet pimentoes, dice of apples, and curry cream.

I

Irma.—Cucumbers, asparagus tips, french beans, pieces of cauliflower, mixed with mayonnaise, flavour with tarragon and chervil, dressed dome shape, sprinkle with julienne of lettuces and mustard and cress, decorate with nasturtium flowers, border round with pink radishes.

Isabelle.—Truffles, celery, raw mushrooms, potatoes and artichoke bottoms, vinaigrette with chopped chervil.

Italienne.—Vegetable salad with dice of salami and fillets of anchovies, Mayonnaise sauce.

Japonaise (A).—(*See* **Salade Francillon).**

    (B).—Dice of fillets of herrings, slices of truffles, oysters, potatoes, seasoned and dished separately, chopped herbs on top.

    (C).—Dice of tomatoes, seasoned with sugar, salt and lemon juice, dice of pineapple, soaked in lemon and orange juice, dress the fruits on lettuce leaves, acidulated cream.

Javanaise.—Quarters of oranges, the rind of oranges cut in julienne, acidulated cream and scraped horse-radish.

Jockey-Club.—Asparagus heads, julienne of raw truffles, seasoned separately, with oil and vinegar, mixed with mayonnaise.

Lakmé.—Dice of red poivrons and tomatoes, rice, chopped onions, vinaigrette with Curry.

Lapérouse.—Tomatoes, dice of ham, french beans, artichoke bottoms, onions, sour cream.

Légumes (de).—Dice of potatoes, french beans, peas, cauliflower, vinaigrette with chopped parsley.

Lords (des).—Lettuces leaves, quarters of oranges, julienne zest of oranges, walnuts and almonds, acidulated cream.

Lorette.—Corn salad, celery and beetroot, vinaigrette.

Louisette.—Long lettuce, tomatoes, muscat grapes, oil and vinegar.

Manon.—Lettuces, quarters of grape fruit, lemon juice, pepper from the mill and vinaigrette.

Maraîchère.—Rampion, salsify leaves, celeriac, decorate with potatoes and beetroots, mustard sauce with cream and horse-radish.

Marie Stuart.—Julienne of celery and lettuces, vinaigrette, decorate with eggs and truffles.

Mariette.—Julienne of cooked carrots, orange zest and quarters, vinaigrette.

Mascotte.—Asparagus tips, plovers' eggs, cocks' kidneys, crayfish tails and slices of truffles, mustard with cream.

Mercédès.—Julienne of celery and beetroot, tomatoes, endives, dressed in bouquets, season, vinegar, walnut oil, parsley and yolk of eggs passed through the sieve.

Midinette.—Julienne of apples, chicken, celery, and Gruyère cheese, mayonnaise thinned with vinaigrette.

Mignon.—Shrimp and dice of artichoke bottoms, surrounded with slices of truffles, mayonnaise with cream, cayenne.

Mignonne.—Dice of truffles, artichoke, celeriac, potatoes, and asparagus heads, season and dish up separately, mayonnaise in the centre.

Mignonnette.—Vegetables cut in large brunoise, mayonnaise.

Mikado (A).—Oysters poached, rice, dice of green and red poivrons, vinaigrette with mustard.

(B).—Japanese artichokes, julienne of celery, dice of potatoes, mayonnaise.

(C).—Japanese artichokes, french beans, tomatoes sliced, and long lettuce, mixed with Gribiche sauce.

Mimosa..—Half lettuce hearts, garnish quarters of oranges, grapes and bananas, cream and lemon juice.

Monégasque.—Rounds of potatoes, blanched nonats, quarters of artichoke bottoms, tomatoes, and black olives, season with salt, pepper, mustard, anchovy paste, olive oil and lemon juice.

Monte-Carlo.—Dice of pineapple and oranges, grains of pomegranate, lemon juice and cream, dressed in tangerine skins, served on crushed ice, hearts of lettuce between each tangerine.

Monte-Cristo.—Dice of lobster, truffles, potatoes, hard boiled eggs, dished up separately, hearts of lettuce in the centre, mayonnaise with mustard.

Montfermeil.—Salsify, artichoke bottoms, potatoes, julienne of whites of eggs, mix with vinaigrette, sprinkle with whites of eggs passed through the sieve, chopped parsley.

Montmorency.—Julienne of celery, cherries, cream with scraped horse-radish and lemon juice.

Moscovite.—Salade Russe in a parfait mould, dished, surrounded with tartlets, filled with half caviar and half sigui purée (smoked eel).

Mousmé.—(*See* **Montmorency**).

Muguette.—Curly endives, russet apples, julienne of celery, tomatoes, cerneaux, mayonnaise, surrounded with pink radishes and chervil leaves.

Nelusko.—Julienne of beetroots, potatoes shaped like an olive, asparagus heads, mayonnaise thinned with Robert sauce.

Niçoise.—French beans, tomatoes quarters, potatoes, decorate with fillets of anchovies, olives and capers. Vinaigrette sauce.

Ninon.—Lettuce, quarters of oranges, season with orange and lemon juice, salt and olive oil.

Noël (de).—White dandelions, corn salad, julienne of celery and truffles, dressed in bouquets, vinaigrette.

Noémi.—Dice of roast poussins, crayfishes tails, hearts of lettuces, season with cream and crayfish cullis, salt, pepper and lemon juice, sprinkle with shreds of chervil.

Nonnes (des).—Cooked rice, julienne of chicken mixed with vinaigrette and mustard, sprinkle with chopped truffles.

Nouvelle Japonaise.—Lettuce leaves, quarters of walnuts, julienne of almonds and rounds of bananas, sour cream served separate.

Opéra.—Julienne of chicken, tongue and celery, truffles, asparagus heads dressed separately, surrounded with cocks' kidneys, rounds of gherkins, thin mayonnaise.

Orientale.—Rice and tomatoes, tossed in oil and garlic, dice of red poivrons, french beans, vinaigrette with fillets of anchovies.

Palois.—Asparagus heads, artichoke in quarters, julienne of celeriac, vinaigrette with mustard.

Parisienne.—In a mould lined with clear Aspic and decorated with slices of lobster tail and truffles, filled with vegetables salad combined with dice of lobster, mixed with mayonnaise and a little melted Aspic to set it.

Paulette.—Julienne of celery, potatoes, raw truffles and french beans, mayonnaise.

Piémontaise.—Potatoes and minced truffles, decorate with fillets of anchovies, vinaigrette.

Poisson.—Mix together different sorts of fish, season with mayonnaise or vinaigrette, surround with tomatoes, and vegetable salad, lettuces, etc.

Polonaise.—Dice of carrots, turnips, beetroots, cucumbers gherkins, potatoes, hard boiled eggs, fillets of herrings, vinaigrette, parsley and tarragon.

Provençale.—Artichoke in quarters, tomatoes and black olives, vinaigrette with anchovy purée, garlic and chopped basilic.

Rachel.—Julienne of celery, truffles, artichoke bottoms and potatoes, asparagus tips, and thin mayonnaise.

Régence.—Raw truffles, cocks' kidneys, julienne of celery, asparagus heads, lemon juice, oil salt and pepper.

Réjane.—Asparagus heads, dice of potatoes, julienne of truffles and vinaigrette.

Russe.—Carrots, turnips, french beans, peas, truffles and mushrooms, tongue and ham, lobster, gherkins, fillets of anchovies, capers, coated with mayonnaise, decorate with beetroot, eggs, caviar, etc.

Saint Jean.—Asparagus heads, french beans, peas, artichoke bottoms, cucumbers, chervil, mayonnaise, surrounded with rounds of hard boiled eggs and gherkins, tarragon leaves.

Saint Sylvestre.—Julienne of celeriac, artichokes, mushrooms, truffles, whites of eggs, decorate with potatoes, and truffles, mayonnaise with chopped walnuts.

Sicilienne.—Dice of russet apples, celeriac, tomatoes, and artichoke bottoms, mayonnaise.

Tanagra.—Julienne of celery, tomatoes, bananas, mixed with sour cream.

Tosca.—Dice of chicken, white truffles, celery, and parmesan cheese, mayonnaise with anchovy essence, thinned with mustard vinaigrette.

Tourangelle.—Julienne of potatoes, french beans, flageolets beans, mayonnaise with cream, and chopped tarragon.

Tredern.—Crayfish tails, poached oysters, asparagus heads and raw truffles, mayonnaise with cullis of crayfish.

Truffes (aux).—Raw truffles, seasoned with hard boiled eggs, salt, black pepper, lemon juice and olive oil.

Victoria.—Dice of lobster tail, truffles, cucumbers and asparagus heads, mayonnaise mixed with the creamy part of the lobster and coral purée.

Viennoise.—Julienne of chicory, tongue, gherkins, truffles and endives, sprinkle with paprika, vinaigrette.

Vigneronne.—Hearts of lettuce, skinned and stoned grapes. (*Separate*): Sour cream and lemon juice.

Waldorf.—Dice of celeriac, russet apples, halved peeled walnuts, thin mayonnaise.

Windsor.—Julienne of celery, raw truffles, chicken, tongue, piccallilis, mushrooms, mayonnaise, border with raiponces.

Yam Yam.—French beans, slices of cucumbers, julienne of celeriac, quarters of lettuces, vinaigrette.

SALADES AMERICAINES — AMERICAN SALADS

Ainsée.—Long lettuce, chicory, alligator pears, grape fruit, hazel nuts, (serve separate) vinaigrette, with chopped cibols.

Alexandra.—Grape fruit, pears, apples, celery, muscatel grapes in halves, oranges surrounded with lettuces, mayonnaise, with chopped walnuts.

Algonquin.—Lettuces cut in halves, dressed on grape fruit and pears, sprinkle with julienne of green pimentoes, vinaigrette, mixed with chopped whites of eggs.

Alice.—Dice of pineapple, lettuces, quarters of grape fruit, sprinkle with hazel nuts, grilled and chopped, olive oil and lemon juice, salt and peper.

Allan.—Lettuce leaves, julienne of celery, apples, sweet pimentoes, serve with mayonnaise mixed with tomato purée.

Alma.—Hearts of lettuces cut in halves, quarters of grape fruit and alligator pears, serve with vinaigrette.

Arlésienne.—Sliced potatoes, tomatoes, asparagus heads, egg plants cut in julienne, sprinkle with sliced almonds, cream sauce, with scraped horse-radish.

Beach.—Empty half grape fruit, garnish interior with lettuce leaves, replace quarters of grape fruit, decorate with cherries soaked in maraschino, season with grape fruit juice, oil, salt and pepper.

Bellevue.—Endives, celery, brussels sprouts, chicory, white dandelions, curried mayonnaise.

Bismarck.—Lettuce hearts and red cabbage in julienne, vinaigrette with scraped horse-radish.

Bombay.—Lettuce leaves, mangoes, red pimentoes and rice, vinaigrette.

Brésilienne.—Celery, dice of apples, sprinkle with crushed brazil nuts, serve with guava jelly, thinned with vinegar.

Bruxelles.—White dandelions, and chicory with vinaigrette.

Chiffonnade.—Lettuces, celery in julienne, chicory, endives, tomatoes, watercress, hard boiled eggs, and beetroot, vinaigrette with chopped cibols.

Danicheff.—Asparagus heads, potatoes, celeriac, artichoke bottoms, mushroooms, thin mayonnaise, decorate with crayfish tails, eggs and truffles.

Delmonico.—Celeriac and apples in dice, mayonnaise thinned with cream.

Fantaisie.—Celery, apples, pineapple, julienne of lettuces, vinaigrette with mint.

Fédora.—Hearts of lettuces, apples, oranges, julienne of lettuces, mayonnaise.

Figaro.—Julienne of tongue, rounds of beetroots, celery, lettuces, and fillets of anchovies, mayonnaise with dice of tomatoes.

Florentine.—Long lettuces, celery, green pimentoes, blanched spinach leaves and water cress, vinaigrette.

Florida.—Quarters of grape fruit, pineapple, celery, bananas, apples, mixed with mayonnaise and served in banana skins.

Fushimi.—White dandelions and alligator pears, mushrooms cut in julienne, red poivrons, french beans, decorated with grapes, vinaigrette.

Gadski.—Long lettuce cut in halves, alligator pears in slices, dressed with dice of apples, pimentoes, truffies, white grapes, vinaigrette with crushed walnuts.

Globe.—Apples, pineapple, grape fruit, tangerines in quarters, vinaigrette with crushed olives.

Gracia.—Celeriac in julienne, apples, pimentoes, green and red cut in dice, mayonnaise.

Harvey.—Lettuces, endives, water cress, serve with black currants and vinaigrette.

Havanaise.—Lettuces, shrimps, asparagus heads, mayonnaise thinned with cucumber purée.

Hélène.—Green pimentoes, truffles, asparagus heads, tangerines, vinaigrette with brandy.

Impératrice.—Oranges cut in halves, and emptied, fill with julienne of long lettuces, quarters of grape fruit, red pimentoes, and pineapple, vinaigrette with whisky.

Indienne.—Alligator pears, in dice, apples and grape fruit celery, and red poivrons, cooked chestnuts, pineapple, green pimentoes in julienne, mayonnaise thinned with mangoes.

Japonaise.—White dandelions, grape fruit, pineapple, mayonnaise with chopped parsley.

Jeannette.—Water cress, cauliflower, french beans, parsley, vinaigrette.

Lehr.—Artichoke bottoms, chicory, beetroots, vinaigrette with Robert sauce.

Lorenzo.—Celeriac, beetroots, lettuces ,endives, chicory, pears, and hard boiled eggs, mayonnaise with cream.

Louise.—Lettuce leaves, serve one leaf to each guest on a plate, garnish with stoned malaga raisin, grape fruit and crushed walnuts.

Louisiana.—Tomatoes, bananas, blood oranges, tomatoe sauce with cream.

Marquise.—Lettuces, tomatoes, celeriac in julienne, brazil nuts, tomato sauce, mixed with whipped cream.

Mexicaine.—Celeriac, cold chicken in julienne, pimentoes, hard boiled eggs, cibols or onions, endives, rhubarb in julienne, vinaigrette with saffron.

Miami.—Lettuce hearts, tangerines, tomatoes, lemon slices, vinaigrette.

Mikael.—Long lettuces, pineapple, pears, raspberries, mint and tarragon, vinaigrette.

Milliken.—Dice of truffles, rice, red pimentoes, tarragon, grape fruit juice, vinaigrette, served on large lettuce leaves.

Millionnaire.—Long lettuce hearts, truffles, pears, sliced almonds, mayonnaise with truffle essence.

Mona Lisa.—Hearts of lettuces cut in halves, apples, julienne of truffles, mayonnaise thinned with Ketchup.

Nantaise.—Cucumbers, water cress, tomatoes, french beans, Tartar sauce with cibols.

Néva.—Lettuces, chicory, beetroots in julienne, truffles and endives in the centre, vinaigrette.

Ninon.—Apples, pineapple, lettuces, shrimps, small gribouis cooked in water, mayonnaise and scraped horse-radish.

Olga.—Celeraic in julienne, potatoes, truffles, apples, artichoke bottoms.

Olinda.—Oranges cut in halves, emptied, fill with orange quarters, grape fruit, apples, celery and pimentoed mayonnaise.

Orientale.—Endives, tomatoes, pimentoes, vinaigrette with crushed walnut tossed in butter.

Orleans.—Grape fruit, white and black grapes cut in halves, pineapple, bananas, oranges in quarters, pears, served on large lettuce leaves, surround with lemon slices, salt, pepper, cayenne and oil.

Otto.—Long lettuce, pineapple, apples, oranges in quarters, black grapes, melon in slices, mayonnaise.

Oxford.—Truffles, whites of chicken in dice, whites of eggs, gherkins, dressed on large lettuce leaves covered with slices of tomatoes, vinaigrette with chopped tarragon.

Régent.—Celery, pears, potatoes, asparagus heads, raw truffles in julienne, vinaigrette mixed with foie gras purée.

Riviera.—Tangerines in quarters, celeriac, apples, strawberries, lettuces, pineapple, mayonnaise with chopped pimentoes.

Rochelle.—Celeriac in dice, pineapple, apples, radishes, vinaigrette with nutmeg.

Roosevelt.—Artichoke bottoms in slices, apples, lettuces, crushed walnuts, white dandelions, fruit and petals of nasturtiums, mayonnaise with sweet corn.

Rossini.—Long lettuces in julienne, celery, curly endives, white dandelions, water cress and vinaigrette.

Saint-Pierre.—Julienne of truffles, artichoke bottoms, beetroots, chicory, vinaigrette with chopped mint.

Saint-Régis.—Pineapple, grape fruit, celery, potatoes, asparagus heads, vinaigrette with cream.

Salisbury.—Chicory, white dandelions, celery, endives, hard boiled eggs, tarragon, chopped olives, vinaigrette with beetroot juice.

Scotch.—Hard boiled eggs, with salmon, potatoes, truffles, lettuces in julienne, mayonnaise with Curry powder.

Séville.—Lettuce hearts, grape fruit, oranges in quarters, vinaigrette.

Sherrywise.—Long lettuce, beetroots, cherries, hazel nuts, vinaigrette with cinnamon.

Tosca.—Julienne of chicken, tongue, beetroots, artichoke bottoms, whites of eggs, mayonnaise with black grape juice.

Turquoise.—Endives, tomatoes, red pimentoes, celery, mayonnaise.

Vénitienne.—Celery, olives, truffles in dice, oranges in quarters, chicken livers cooked in butter, passed through the sieve, and mixed with green mayonnaise sauce.

Vicomte.—Asparagus heads, tongue, green pimentoes, truffles, celery, tomato sauce with reduced vinegar.

Waldorf.—Celery, apples, bananas, walnuts, mayonnaise.

Windsor.—Large apples, cut in halves, and scooped out, fill centre with dice of apples and pineapple, mixed with mayonnaise, served in lettuce leaves, surrounded with slices of tomatoes, mayonnaise.

Yolande.—Celery, carrots in julienne, apples, beetroots, vinaigrette with mint.

I

Vegetables and Farinaceous Products

VEGETABLES

ARTICHAUTS — GLOBE ARTICHOKES

Barigoule.—Trimmed and blanched, remove the centre of the artichokes, fill with Duxelles preparation combined with chopped ham and herbs, braise them with white wine, dress the artichoke with brown sauce made from the liquor.

Beignets Colbert.—The bottoms of small artichoke filled with forcemeat and duxelles, place them two by two on a skewer, dip them in batter and fry in deep fat. Colbert sauce.

Boulangère.—Stuffed with sausage meat, covered with a paste and cook in the oven about 1½ hours, serve.

Cavour.—Shape like eggs, cook in white consommé, strained, dip them in melted butter and roll in grated cheese. Cooked in a gratin dish, pour over some melted butter mixed with chopped egg and anchovy essence.

Clamart.—In a cocotte, with new carrots and peas, bunch of mixed herbs, add a little salt water and butter. Serve in the cocotte.

Cromesquis and Croquettes.—(*See* preparation in **Entrées Volantes**).

Cussy.—Cooked bottoms, garnish with foie gras purée and truffles, coated with Villeroy sauce, Madeira sauce served separate.

Diétrich.—Artichoke in quarters, blanched, tossed in butter with chopped onion, add little Velouté sauce, dished in a border of rizotto, pour over reduced liquor.

Favorite.—Bottoms cooked in a blanc, garnish with asparagus tips, cover with Mornay sauce, glaze, slices of truffles on top.

Florentine.—Bottoms of artichokes cooked in a " blanc ", garnish with spinach leaves, covered with Mornay sauce. Glaze.

Grand-Duc.—Cut in heart shapes, cooked in salt water ,cover with cream sauce, sprinkle with grated cheese, glaze, garnish with asparagus tips and slices of truffles.

Gratin.—Dished in a gratin dish, cover with Mornay sauce, sprinkle with cheese and glaze.

Hollandaise.—Take off the outer leaves, cut artichoke half of their height, cook in salt water, serve with butter sauce or Hollandaise sauce.

Italienne.—Cut in quarters, blanch, lay in the bottom of a braised dish, add a little white wine, reduce the stock, add brown sauce covered with Italian sauce.

Juive.—Small artichokes stuffed with bread crumbs, chopped mint, garlic, salt and pepper, cooked in a frying pan until crisp add a little water at the last moment.

Lucullus.—Cook the bottoms and cover with Madeira sauce and chopped truffles.

Lyonnaise.—Cut in quarters, braise like Italienne, dress on fried onions, reduce stock and add little butter, pour over artichokes, chopped parsley on top.

Maraîchère.—Cut in heart shapes, place in a cocotte, with chopped onions, whites of leeks, tomatoes, garlic, cooked in oil, lay the artichokes with new potatoes on this preparation, season to taste, add white wine sprinkled over with sorrel and spinach, close the cocotte and cook in oven.

Paysanne.—Cut in quarters, blanched, toss with bacon, onions and potatoes, cover with white consommé, bunch of mixed herbs, cook quickly until nearly dry.

Provençale.—Small artichokes trimmed and tossed in hot oil, cooked in a cocotte with new peas and lettuces, season with salt and pepper, cook in their own juice.

Purée (en).—Cook bottoms, then pass through a sieve, thicken with cream and season to taste.

Stanley.—Small bottoms, onions and slices of raw ham, cooked with white wine, add a thin Béchamel sauce, cover with stock reduced.

Vinaigrette.—(Same as for **Hollandaise,**) served cold, with Vinaigrette sauce.

ASPERGES — ASPARAGUS

Preparation and Way of Cooking

Scrape, wash, and put in bundles, cook in salt water from 18 to 20 minutes, serve with sauce Hollandaise, Mousseuse, Mousseline or melted butter.

Flamande.—Served with sauce made of hard yolk of eggs mixed with melted butter.

Froide.—Dressed on serviette, serve with Vinaigrette sauce.

Gratin.—Dished in rows, cover the heads with Mornay sauce, cover the rest of the asparagus with buttered paper, sprinkle the heads with grated cheese, glaze.

Italienne.—(Same as **Milanaise,**) without the eggs.

Milanaise.—Dished in rows, sprinkle the heads with grated cheese, pour over some nut brown butter, surround with fried eggs cut with pastry cutter.

Mornay.—(*See* Gratin).

Pointes d'Asperges (*Green asparagus heads, or spruce*).—Cut 2 in. long, tied into small bundles, cooked in boiling salt water, then removed into cold water.

Pointes au Beurre.—Cooked and strained, season with salt and sugar, add melted butter.

Pointes à la Crème.—Same as above, only add thick cream around the asparagus.

Pointes Royales.—Asparagus heads and julienne of truffles, thicken with Allemande sauce. Dressed in a timbale.

Polonaise.—Dished in rows, sprinkle with hard boiled eggs and parsley chopped, pour over some bread crumbs tossed in butter nicely browned.

Sibérienne.—Cold, served on crushed ice, Mayonnaise sauce, serve separate.

AUBERGINES — EGG-PLANT

Andalouse.—Cut in thick slices, scoop the centre out, stuff with tomatoes, pimentoes, and chopped ham, pour round half-glaze and tomato sauce.

Châtelaine.—Cut in two, length ways, fry and scoop the centre out, garnish with chopped chicken, tongue, truffles and mushrooms, thicken with Allemande sauce, sprinkle over with chopped truffles, sauce demi-glace.

Crème (à la).—Cut in rounds, cook in butter thicken with cream sauce.

Egyptienne.—Cut length ways, chisel the centre, fry, take out the pulp and chop it, also add chopped onion, cooked in oil refill the skins with this preparation, sprinkle over little oil, dish up with slices of round tomatoes tossed in butter and chopped parsley.

J

Farcie.—Cut in halves, lengthways, stuffed with tomatoes and gratin stuffing, sprinkle with bread crumbs and melted butter, demi-glaze sauce with tomato.

Frite.—Peeled, then cut in thin round slices, floured and fried in deep fat.

Gratin.—(*See* **Farcie**).

Grillées à la Provinciale.—Cut in halves lengthways, sprinkle with oil, seasoned, grilled over a slow fire, dish up and pour over nut brown butter combine with crumbs, and little garlic.

Italienne.—Same as **Farcie**, surround with Italienne sauce.

Nîmoise.—Cut in halves, fried in oil, garnish with tomatoes, and dice of poivrons, garlic and parsley.

Orientale.—Peeled, divide in six slices lengthways, fry, reform the plant stuffing the slices with gratin farce, sprinkle with oil and finish cooking in oven, serve either hot or cold.

Provençale.—(Same as **Farcie**,) with larger quantity of tomatoes, surrounded with thin tomato sauce.

Sautée à la Niçoise.—Peel, cut in round slices, flour and toss in oil, toss separately poivrons slices of tomatoes and garlic, mix together and sprinkle with fines herbes.

Soufflée.—(Operate same as **Egyptienne**,) and fill the skins with soufflée preparation made of the pulp, mixed with parmesan soufflé.

Turque (à la).—Fill the skins with the pulp mixed with chopped mutton, rice and dry duxelles, thicken with good half-glaze sauce, sprinkle with bread crumbs, surround with thin tomato sauce.

BLETTES

The leaves are cooked like spinach and the stalks like cardons and salsifis.

BROCOLI

(Prepared same as cauliflowers.)

CARDONS — CARDOONS

Cooking Process

Cut the white stalks 3 in. long, rub with lemon, withdraw the fibrous part from the heart, cook in a " blanc ", with chopped veal fat, time 2 hours.

Crème (à la).—Strained, warmed in butter, covered with cream sauce.

Demi-Glace.—Same as above in butter, demi-glaze sauce poured over.

Gratin.—Cover with Mornay sauce, sprinkle with grated cheese, and glaze.

Italienne.—Cover with Italienne sauce.

Jus (au).—With buttered veal stock.

Milanaise.—(Same as **Asparagus Milanaise**.)

Moelle (à la).—Garnish with slices of marrow, cover with marrow sauce.

Moelle Gratinée.—Same as above with grated parmesan, glaze.

Polonaise.—(Same as for **Asparagus Polonaise**.)

CAROTTES — CARROTS

Cooking Process

Turn the carrots in the shape of olives if they are old or trim them whole if new ones, cook them in salt water, sugar and butter until almost entirely evaporated so that the carrots have a brilliant appearance.

Crème (à la).—Prepared as above, add cream when reduced to the desired consistency.
Purée.—Carrots cooked as above and pass through the sieve, add butter and cream.
Vichy.—Cut in slices, cook with Vichy water if possible, dish up in timbale, sprinkle with chopped parsley.

CELERI — CELERY

Cooking Process

Cut the sticks about 8 in. long, clean the roots well and take away the stringy parts, soak them in water containing lemon, then bunch them, after braise them, when cooked divide them in halves, lengthways and double up each section, can be served the same as Cardons.

CELERI-RAVE — CELERIAC

Cooking Process

Peel and turn in crescent shape, blanch and finish cooking in butter, used for garnishing.

CEPES, MORILLES, ORONGES

Bordelaise.—Scallop the cepes, toss in boiling oil, salt and pepper, add chopped shallots and parsley, lemon juice added.
Crème.—Scallop, cook in butter with chopped onion, add thick cream, season, reduce.
Gratin.—Same as above, grated cheese on top, gratin.
Gribouis.—Dried cèpes, soaked in water, after cook in butter, Smitanne sauce.
Provençale.—(Same as **Bordelaise**) with chopped garlic.
Ranini.—Cèpes with cream, add slices of fresh truffles during cooking process.
Toulousaine.—Sliced, tossed in butter, oil, onions and shallots, garlic and dice of ham and tomatoes, toast.
Tourangelle.—Cooked whole in butter, add onions, shallots, garlic, and chopped parsley, thicken with meat glaze.

CHAMPIGNONS — MUSHROOMS

Crème.—(*See* **Cèpes**).
Croûte (en).—Mushrooms with cream, dished in bread croustades.
Farcis.—Cook the heads in butter, season, garnish the centre with Duxelles gratin.
Grillés.—Heads of meadow mushrooms, oiled, seasoned and grilled.
Grillés Bourguignonne.—Same as above with snail butter preparation.
Périgourdine.—(Same as **Bordelaise**,) sprinkle with chopped truffle.
Purée (en.).—Peel, wash, and pass quickly through the sieve, cook in butter cream and Béchamel sauce.
Sautés.—Scallop, toss in oil and butter, season with salt and pepper, add chopped parsley.
Tartelettes (en).—Meadow mushrooms, sliced and treated same as cèpes à la Crème, dished up in tartlets.
Tournés ou Cannelés.—Heads turned or grooved with a pointed knife, cook in water, salt, butter and lemon juice for 5 minutes, use for garnishing.

CHAYOTTES AND BRIONNES — CHOW-CHOW

(*See preparation of Cardons and Cucumbers.*)

CHICOREE — ENDIVES

Wash, blanch, chop and braise with Béchamel sauce, 2 hours. Can be prepared same as spinach.

CHOUX — CABBAGE

Anglaise.—Green cabbage, cook in salt water, strain, press between two plates, cut in shapes.
Choucroute (Sauerkraut).—Use fresh if possible, put in braising pan lined with bacon, add carrots, onions, cloves, bunch of mixed herbs, juniper berries, peppercorns in a canvas bag, moisten with white consommé and white wine, cook slowly from 4 to 5 hours.
Braisés.—Wash and blanch, then strain, braise with carrots and onions, bunch of herbs, moisten with white consommé.
Farcis.—Blanch the leaves, strain and place on a serviette the larger ones, put 4 or 5 smaller ones on it, place in the centre some forcemeat in the shape of a ball, roll in fat bacon, put to braise with fat consommé for an hour.
Flamande.—Red cabbage, cut into quarters, take out the stumps, sliced in julienne, season and cook in terrine with butter and vinegar, when 3 parts cooked add dice of apples and sugar.
Limousine.—Same preparation as above, moisten with consommé add pieces of raw chestnuts, and pork dripping.
Sou-Fassum.—Blanch the cabbage whole, take out the inner leaves, stuff with the following preparation. Sausage meat, cabbage leaves, bacon cut in dice, onions, tomatoes, cooked rice, peas and a little garlic, reconstruct the cabbage, tie it and braise with stock, 3 to 4 hours.

Valencienne.—(Same as **Flamande,**) with chipolata.
Vivaraise.—(Same as **Sou-Fassum**) without rice and peas, braise with stock.
Westphalienne.—(Same as **Flamande,**) add chopped onion tossed in butter, moisten
with red wine and vinegar.

CHOUX DE BRUXELLES — BRUSSELS SPROUTS

Anglaise.—Cook in salt water, strain well, serve on strainer or timbale.
Beurre (au).—Cook, toss in frying pan with butter.
Crème.—Cooked, chopped and seasoned, add a little cream.
Bonne-Femme.—Lightly cooked, seasoned and finish with butter in the oven.
Gratin.—Cook, dressed in a gratin dish, cover with Mornay sauce, grated cheese,
glaze.
Limousine.—Cook, toss in butter with pieces of cooked chestnuts.
Milanaise.—(*See* **Cauliflower** same name).
Polonaise.—(*See* above).
Purée (en).—Pass through a sieve, finish with butter and cream.

CHOUX-FLEURS — CAULIFLOWERS

Cooking Process

*Trim and wash in water containing lemon, then cook in salt water, served with either of the
following sauces: Bâtarde, Melted Butter, Hollandaise, Mousseline and Cream.*

Anglaise.—Cook in salt water with a few green leaves left round.
Dubarry.—Small cauliflowers, gratined and placed on artichoke bottoms.
Fritot (en).—Small bouquet of cauliflowers partly cooked, dipped in butter and
fried in deep fat. Tomato sauce served separate.
Gratin.—Cooked, toss in butter, dress on gratin dish, cover with Mornay sauce,
sprinkle with grated cheese, glazed.
Italienne.—Bouquet of cauliflowers dressed on a gratin dish, covered with Italienne
sauce combined with tomatoes, sprinkle with cheese and bread crumbs, gratined.
Milanaise.—Put cauliflower on a buttered dish, sprinkle with cheese, pour round little
melted butter, gratined, and pour over some nut brown butter.
Polonaise.—Dressed cauliflower on buttered dish, sprinkle with chopped parsley
and hard boiled eggs, and bread crumbs, browned in butter.
Purée (en).—Pass through a sieve, finish with butter and cream.

CHOUX DE MER — SEA KALE

Trim, tie in bundles, cooked in salt water, same process as Cardons.

CONCOMBRES — CUCUMBERS

Crème.—Cut and shape like olives, blanch, and cook in cream until the desired
consistency is obtained.
Farcis.—Peel, cut in rounds or lengthways, take out centre, blanch and stuff with
duxelles and chicken forcemeat.
Glacés.—Cut olive shapes, blanch, cook in salt water and butter, reduce until dry,
serve as garnish.

J

COURGETTES — BABY MARROW

Anglaise.—Peel, cut in pieces, cook in salt water, serve with melted butter, Hollandaise, etc.

Crème.—Cooked, strained, toss in butter and coat with cream.

Farcies.—Cut and partly cook, stuff with duxelles, gratin in oven.

Frites.—(*See* **Aubergines** of the same name).

Ménagère.—Cut in halves lengthways, hollow and chop the interior, mix with same (preparation as **Choux à la Vivaraise,** braise in white stock.)

Provençale.—(*See* **Aubergines** same name).

CROSNES DU JAPON OU STACHYS

JAPANESE ARTICHOKES

Cooking Process

Blanched in water and a little carbonate of soda, wash and cook in a blanc, like cardons.

Beignets.—(Same preparation as for **Croquettes,**) dip in batter and fry in deep fat.

Crème.—Cooked, tossed in butter, add cream, reduce, serve in a timbale.

Croquettes (en).—Cook, thicken with Allemande sauce, shape in croquettes, egg and crumbs, fry in deep fat.

Gratin.—(*See* **Cauliflower** same name).

Milanaise.—(*See* **Caulflower** same name).

Polonaise.—(*See* **Cauliflower** same name).

Purée (en).—Cook, pass through a sieve, season and finish with butter and cream.

Sautés.—Cook, strain and toss in hot butter.

Velouté (au).—Cook, strain, thicken with Velouté sauce.

ENDIVES — CHICORY

Cooking Process

Wash, lay in a buttered pan, salt and lemon juice, butter, cover hermetically, cook for half an hour.

Notice.—*It is' not necessary to put water to cook the chicory as they contain sufficient water to cook them.*

Ardennaise.—Proceed as above, when partly cooked add chopped ham and dice of bacon. Omit lemon.

Crème (à la).—Cook and finish with cream.

Jus (au).—Cook, finish with thickened veal gravy.

Mornay.—Cook, cover with Mornay sauce, sprinkle with cheese and glaze.

Naturel.—Cook, serve in timbale with reduced stock.

EPINARDS — SPINACH

Cooking Process

Thoroughly wash, cook in salt water, well strained, chop or pass through a sieve, for epinards en branches take out the stalks before cooking.

Anglaise.—In leaves, strained, serve in timbale without cooling.

Crème.—In purée, add cream, season, dish up in timbale.

Croûtons (aux).—As above with croûtons round it.

Fleurons (aux).—As above with fleurons.

Garniture (pour).—Half chicken forcemeat, mixed with half spinach purée and poach.

Gratin (au).—Dress in a gratin dish, sprinkle with grated cheese and nut brown butter, glaze.

Œufs (aux).—(Same as **Crème,**) surround with quarters of hard boiled eggs.

Soufflé.—Mix half spinach purée and half Béchamel sauce, thicken with yolk of eggs, season with pepper and salt, nutmeg, beat the whites to a firm froth, mix and put in a soufflé dish, cook about 10 minutes.

Subrics.—Mixed with reduced Béchamel and eggs, salt and pepper, nutmegs, cook in clarified butter like drop scones, dish in timbale, cream sauce separate.

Viroflay.—Wrapped subrics in blanched spinach leaves, dressed in a gratin dish, cover with Mornay sauce, sprinkle with grated cheese, gratined.

FENOUIL TUBEREUX — TUBEROUS FENNEL

(Cook in salt water, treat like Cardons.)

FEVES — BROAD BEANS

Cooking Process

Shelled, boiled in salt water, containing a bunch of savoury. Skin before serving.

Anglaise (à l').—Cook as above, serve with fresh butter.

Beurre (au).—Cook, toss in butter and season.

Crème (à la).—Cook, finish with cream.

Lard (au).—Chopped onions tossed in butter, add pieces of bacon, and a little flour, moisten with white stock, put the beans in the sauce and cook for 10 minutes.

Purée (en).—Cook, pass through the sieve, finish with butter and cream.

GOMBOS — RAMIA OR RAMIES

Cooking Process
(Trim and partly boil in salt water, strain.)

J

Crème (à la).—Toss in butter, finish with cream.

Etuvée (à l').—Chopped onions partly cooked in butter, add pieces of bacon and the gombos blanched, moisten with veal stock.

Farcis.—Hollow, and stuff with Duxelles, braise with veal stock.

Garniture (pour).—Blanch, cook in butter with tomatoes.

Janina.—Blanched onions, tossed in sheeps-tail fat, add tomatoes and dice of raw mutton, moisten with a little water, cook slowly, and well season.

Turque.—(Same preparation as **Janina,**) the ingredients tossed in oil instead of sheeps tail fat.

JETS DE HOUBLON — HOP SPROUTS

Cooking Process

Prepare as asparagus heads, wash and cook in water containing lemon, can be done with butter, cream, Velouté, etc., or with poached eggs and croûtons.

HARICOTS BLANCS — HARICOTS BEAN

Cooking Process

Soak for 12 hours, after boil in water slowly, add salt when half cooked, also onion, clove, carrots and a bunch of mixed herbs.

Américaine.—Cooked with a piece of bacon, cut in dice, mix together with tomato sauce.

Beurre (au).—Strain, season, thicken with fresh butter, add chopped parsley.

Boston Beans.—Small white beans, cook in earthenware terrine with bacon, treacle and salt. Serve in timbale with slices of the cooked bacon, add chopped parsley.

Bretonne.—Strain, season, thicken with Bretonne sauce, parsley.

Gratin.—Mix with fat gravy, pour in a gratin dish, sprinkle with bread crumbs, put a little melted butter on top, gratin.

Lyonnaise.—With butter and onions à la Lyonnaise.

Purée (en).—Pass through a sieve, finish with butter and cream.

Purée Bretonne.—Add Bretonne sauce to the purée.

Purée Musard.—Flageolet purée.

HARICOTS FLAGEOLETS

(*Same process as Haricot blancs.*)

HARICOTS ROUGES — RED BEANS

Same process as Haricots blancs with the addition of red wine and bacon cut in dices.

HARICOTS VERTS — FRENCH BEANS

Cooking Process

To be cooked quickly in salt boiling water, then strain, do not cool them if possible

Allemande.—Lightly blanched, chopped onion cooked in butter with a little flour, moisten with white consommé, finish cooking the beans in this sauce.

Anglaise.—Boil, season, strain and add a little butter.

Panachés.—Half flageolets and half french beans, and add little butter, serve.

Purée (en).—Pass through the sieve, add a little flageolet purée if possible, finish with butter and cream.

Tourangelle.—Lightly blanched, and finish cooking in a thin Béchamel sauce, add garlic and chopped parsley.

LAITUES — LETTUCES

Cooking Process

Wash, parboil and cool, well press, then tie together, braise them with white consommé when cooked strain and cut the lettuces in two or four, double them up, dress in a timbale cover with thick gravy, demi-glace, etc. Croûtons or fleurons placed round.

Crème (à la).—(*See* **Chicorée** same name).
Farcies.—Stuff the lettuces with Duxelles mixed with chicken forcemeat.
Grecque.—Stuff with riz à la Grecque, cover with thick veal gravy.

LENTILLES — LENTILS

(*Same process as Haricots Blancs.*)

MAIS — MAIZE

Cooking Process

Cook whole with the leaves in salt water and lemons, serve on a serviette, melted butter separate.

Crème (à la).—Sweet corn is generally used in Europe, pour in a pan, reduce and add butter and cream, season with salt and sugar, serve in timbale.
Croquettes.—(*See* formula type in **Entrées Volantes**).

MARRONS — CHESTNUTS

Cooking Process

Split open the shells of the chestnuts put them in the oven for 5 minutes, to be shelled while very hot.

Braisés.—Place them in a Sauté pan, moisten with veal stock, when cooked strain the stock and reduce to a glaze.
Etuvés.—Put them to cook with white consommé and a few stalks of celery.
Purée (en). As above pass through a sieve, finish with butter and cream.

NAVETS — TURNIPS

(*Same preparation as Carrots.*)

TURNIP TOPS

(*Prepare same as Green Cabbage.*)

OIGNONS — ONIONS

Farcis.—Small Spanish onions, parboil them, empty and stuff with vegetables Duxelles, combined with onions or rice, soufflé of spinach, tomato or chicory, etc.

Frits.—Cut in thin rounds, separate the rings, season, then flour, fry in deep fat.

Glacés (à blanc).—Small onions, peeled, moisten with white consommé add a little butter, cook, and reduce the stock to a glaze.

Glacés (à brun).—Small onions, peel, add sugar and cook slowly with butter, moisten with brown stock. Reduce the stock to a glaze.

Lyonnaise.—Peel, cut thin slices, cook slowly in butter.

OSEILLE — SORREL

Cooking Process

Pick and wash well, then cook gently in butter, strain, mix with ' Roux Blond " or pale brown sauce, braise, pass through the sieve, thicken with yolk of eggs, finish with butter and cream, add strong veal gravy on the top.

OXALIS

Wash, boil in salt water, prepare with cream, stuff gratin or purée, etc.

PATATES DOUCES — SWEET POTATOES

Same preparation as potatoes, or can be baked in the oven, sauté, duchesse, or purée, etc

Lavigerie.—Cook in oven, scoop, mix pulp with chestnut purée, and stuff.

PETITS POIS — PEAS

Cooking Process
English Way — A l'Anglaise

Cook quickly in boiling salt water, strain, and serve with a pat of fresh butter on top.

French Way — A la Française

Freshly shelled peas, cooked with small new onions, and shredded lettuces, add butter, sugar and salt, cover with a little water, and cook quickly.

Beurre.—Cook English way, strain, add fresh butter.

Bonne-Femme.—Cook French way, add pieces of cooked bacon, serve in a cocotte.

Etuvée.—Cook French way, serve in earthenware cocotte.

Flamande.—Half quantity of new carrots, cooked same as for glaze and half petits pois à l'Anglaise.

Garniture (purée pour).—Three parts of purée of peas and one part of chicken forcemeat.

Menthe (à la).—Cook English way with a bunch of mint, serve with mint leaves on the top.

Paysanne.—Cook French way, add paysanne of vegetables.

Purée.—Cook English way, pass through a sieve, finish with butter and cream.

  Note.—The peas called **Mange-tout** or " eat all " can be prepared the same way as the peas.

PIMENTS DOUX — POIVRONS DOUX
CAPSICUM OR PIMENTOES

Farcis.—Grill to take off skins, fill with pilaw rice, braise with veal stock.
Garniture (pour).—Grilled to take skins off, braise and use as wanted.
Purée (en).—Red pimentoes, braised with rice, pass through the sieve add butter.
Vivaraise.—Stuff with Vivaraise stuffing, combined with poivrons dice, without the bacon.

POMMES DE TERRE — POTATOES

Algérienne.—Purée of sweet potatoes, mixed with chestnut purée, thicken with yolk of eggs, shape as quoits, egg and breadcrumbs, fry in clarified butter.
Allemande.—Sautées potatoes cut in thick rounds and well buttered.
Allumette.—Cut matches shape, fry in deep fat, add pinch of salt.
Alphonse.—Cook in their jackets, peel, slice, and add Maître-d'hôtel butter, season, sprinkle with grated cheese and glaze.
Alsacienne.—New potatoes cooked in butter with bacon and small onions, chopped parsley.
Ambassadeur.—(*See* **Pommes Voisin**).
Anglaise.—Shape, cook in a steamer, and season.
Anna.—Cut them in cylinder shape, slice in rounds, well wash and dry on a cloth, set them in layers in a special pan with clarified butter, cook in the oven, when half done turn over to colour both sides. For garnishing use dariole moulds.
Arlie.—Baked in oven, empty interior, mix the potato with chopped cibols, butter and cream and refill the skins, sprinkle with grated cheese and gratin.
Bataille.—Cut in dice, fry in deep fat.
Bénédictine.—Cut spiral shape with machine, fry in deep fat.
Berny.—Potato croquettes combined with chopped truffles, shape like an apricot, egg and roll in sliced almonds, fry, deep fat.
Berrichonne.—Turn and cook in consommé with chopped onions, bacon and chopped parsley.
Biarritz.—Mash to a purée, add dice of ham, poivrons and herbs.
Bignon.—Shape like small boxes, fill with sausage meat, sprinkle with a little crumbs and cook in oven, Madeira sauce.
Bohémienne.—Peel, cook in the oven, scoop out the centre, fill with sausage meat, finish cooking in the oven.
Bonne-Femme.—**Pommes Cocotte,** cook with braised onions.
Bordelaise.—**Parmentier Potatoes,** add little garlic chopped.
Boulangère.—Sliced onions and potatoes, cook in butter, add the potatoes after, season, moisten with a little consommé, cook in the oven.
Bretonne.—Cut in large dice, cooked in consommé with onions, little chopped garlic and dice of tomatoes.
Brune.—Cook in water, peel, chop, then toss in butter, must be well fried and crisp.
Brioches.—**Pommes Duchesse** shaped like brioches.
Bussy.—**Pommes Lorette** with truffles and chopped parsley.
Byron.—**Pommes Macaire,** hollow the top, sprinkle with Chester cheese, cover with cream.

Cendrillon.—Shape raw like a sabot, egg and bread crumbs, fry in deep fat fill with the crushed pulp mixed with cream.

Chambéry.—(*See* **Pommes Savoyarde**).

Chamonix.—**Dauphin Potatoes** with cheese.

Champignol.—**Pommes Fondantes.** with cheese and glazed.

Château.—Shape like a large olive, blanched, roasted nice brown colour, in butter.

Chatouillard.—Cut in ribbons, cooked the same way as **Pommes Soufflées.**

Cheven.—Cut in thin julienne, fry very dry.

Chips.—Slices very thin, fry in deep fat, dry and golden colour.

Cocotte.—Turn **Château** shape but smaller, cook same way.

Collerette.—Cylinder shape, cut them with a special knife which grooves them, fry like **Chip Potatoes.**

Colombine.—Sliced raw, sauté add julienne of pimentoes.

Copeaux.—Cut in ribbons, fry in deep fat, very dry.

Crème.—Cook in water, peel, slice, moisten with milk, add butter and salt, cook, add cream when serving.

Cretan.—**Pommes Fondantes** with powdered thyme.

Croquettes.—(*See* **Pommes Duchesse**), shape as you fancy, egg and bread crumb, fry in deep fat.

Darphin.—Cut in julienne, cook same way as **Anna Potatoes.**

Dauphine.—One part choux paste without sugar, two parts **Duchesse Potatoes**, shape as corks, egg and bread crumbs or fry like Beignets soufflés.

Dauphinoise.—Cut in raw slices, cook in oven with milk and grated gruyère cheese.

Delmonico.—Cut in raw dice, cooked as à la crème, brown with bread crumbs, without cheese.

Duchesse.—Cook as purée, thicken with yolks of eggs.

Elisabeth.—**Pommes Dauphine,** stuffed with spinach.

Farcies.—Peel, scoop, fill with forcemeat, braise in the ordinary way.

Flamande.—Turn as **Château Potatoes,** cook with small onions, carrots, in white consommé.

Fondantes (A).—**Château Potatoes,** cooked in a covered pan, with a little white consommé.

(B).—Mashed baked potatoes buttered, season, squeeze in a serviette in the shape of a oval ball, place in a buttered tin, browned in the oven.

Four (au).—Large potatoes, baked in the oven, served in their skins.

Frites.—(*See* **Pommes Pont-Neuf**).

Galette.—**Duchesse Potatoes,** shaped like small flat scones.

Gastronome.—Shape like corks, blanched and cooked in butter, after roll in meat glaze and chopped truffles.

Gaufrettes.—Cut with a special cutter, fry in deep fat, golden colour.

Gratinées (A).—Mashed potatoes well buttered, put into a gratin dish, sprinkle with cheese and browned.

(B).—Baked potatoes, split in halves lengthways, take out the pulp, crush with fork add a little butter, season, refill the shells, sprinkle with grated cheese and brown.

Grillées.—Slices half inch thick, butter and grill.

Hongroise.—Chopped onions cooked in butter with paprika, add dice of tomatoes and large rounds of potatoes, moisten with consommé, cook and reduce, add chopped parsley.

Idéale.—**Pommes Darphin,** with julienne of truffles.

Irlandaise.—Cut in ribbons, cooked in a steamer.

Jacquette.—Wash, and cut the skin round, cook in a steamer.

Jetée-Promenade.—**Pommes Darphin** with julienne of artichoke and truffles.

Julienne.—Cut in julienne and fry in deep fat.

Lard (au).—Cut in quarters, cook with bacon and small braised onions, moisten with consommé and chopped parsley.

Liard (en).—Cut and shape like a cork, slice and fry in deep fat.

Lorette.—**Pommes Dauphine,** cigar shaped.

Loulou.—(*See* **Gaufrettes**).

Lyonnaise.—Sauté potatoes, mixed with onions à la Lyonnaise.

Macaire.—Mashed baked potatoes pulp, seasoned, buttered, cooked with clarified butter in a **Pommes Anna** mould.

Maire.—Same as **A la Crème.**

Maître-d'Hotel.—**Pommes à la Creme** with chopped parsley.

Marquise.—**Pommes Duchesse,** mixed with reduced tomato sauce, made same way as **Pommes Galette.**

Ménagère.—**Pommes Gratinées (B),** add dice of raw ham and chopped onions, cooked in butter.

Menthe.—Same as **Anglaise,** add leaves of mint.

Mignonnette.—Cut double the size of **Pommes Allumettes,** cook the same way.

Mireille.—**Anna Potatoes,** mixed with artichoke bottoms, and slices of truffles.

Mirette.—Cut in dice, cook in butter, add julienne of truffles, and roll in meat glaze, sprinkle with grated cheese, brown.

Monselet.—Raw potatoes cut in thick rounds, cook in butter, dish like a crown, garnish the centre with sliced mushrooms tossed, add truffles, finish with butter and milk.

Mongolienne.—Half **Pommes Cocotte,** half Japanese artichoke, tossed and mix together.

Mousseline.—Mashed potatoes with whipped cream.

Nana.—**Pommes Darphin,** cook in dariole mould.

Nature.—(*See* **Pommes à l'Anglaise**).

Nid (au) (A).—**Pommes Soufflées,** dressed in a nest made with straw potatoes, in a special nest mould (basket), fry in deep fat.

(B).—In the same nest fill with **Pommes Parisienne.**

Noisette.—Cut the potatoes with a round scoop cutter the size of a hazel nut, cooked the same as **Château Potatoes.**

Normande.—Sliced and cooked with onions and whites of leeks tossed in butter, add a little flour with milk, season, place in gratin dish, brown.

O'Brien.—**Pommes Brune,** add chopped pimentoes.

Ortiz.—As above, treat raw.

Paille.—Cut in large julienne, fried in deep fat.

Panama.—Cook raw in butter, press together.

Parisienne.—**Pommes Noisette,** rolled in meat glaze, larger size.

Parmentier.—Cut in cubes $\frac{1}{2}''$ size cook in clarified butter.

Paysanne.—Sliced thickly, cook in butter with consommé, garlic shredded sorrel, and chervil.

Persillées.—**Pommes à l'Anglaise,** season, roll in melted butter, chopped parsley.

Pont-Neuf.—Cut in shape of a ruler and fry in deep fat.

J

Provençale.—**Pommes Sautées** with chopped garlic.

Purée.—Cut in quarters, cook in salted water 18 to 20 minutes, strain. pass through sieve, season, butter and cream.

Quelin.—Large **Noisette Potatoes,** cook in water or steam, same as **Persillées.**

Rissolées.—Same as **Château,** well browned.

Robe de Chambre.—Wash and cook in steamer with skins.

Robert.—**Pommes Macaire,** add cibols and eggs.

Rosette.—**Duchesse Potatoes** in rose shape, put on a buttered gratin dish, sprinkle with clarified butter.

Roxelane.—Soufflé preparation mixed with mashed potatoes, dressed in headless brioches which have been hollowed out, cook in oven.

Royale.—**Pommes Croquettes,** add chopped ham, roll in egg and vermicelli, fry in deep fat.

Sablées.—Cut raw in dice, toss in butter, add bread crumbs when nearly cooked.

Sautées.—Cooked in their jackets, peel, cut in slices, toss in butter until nicely browned.

Savoyarde.—Same as Boulangère mixed with tossed squares of bacon. grated cheese on top. Cook in oven.

Schneider.—Same as **A la Crème.** Moisten with consommé and meat glaze, butter and chopped parsley.

Soufflées.—Trimmed square, cut one eighth of an inch thick, put in a moderately hot fat until partly cooked, strain, then plunge into them another clean hot fat to effect the puffing. Let dry and strain.

Surprise.—Baked potatoes with skins on, when cooked scoop out through small aperture, crush potato, season, add cream and butter and refill.

Suzette.—Trim in the shape of an egg, treat as **Farcies.**

Vapeur.—(*See* **Anglaise).**

Villa des Fleurs.—Same as **Delmonico** with cheese.

Voisin.—**Anna Potatoes** with grated cheese.

PUREES

Argenteuil	White asparagus.
Clamart	Of green peas.
Condé	Of red beans.
Conti	Of lentils.
Crécy	Of carrots and rice.
Dubarry	Of cauliflower.
Esaü	Of lentils.
Favorite	Of french beans.
Freneuse	Of turnips.
Musarde	Of flageolets.
Palestine	½ Jerusalem artichoke and ½ potatoes
Parmentier	Of potatoes.
Rachel	Of artichokes bottoms.
Saint-Germain	Of peas.
Saxonne	Of turnips, potatoes and onions.
Soubise	Of onions.
Vichy	Of carrots.

RIZ — RICE

Cooking Process

(A).—Nature. *Cook 17 minutes in plenty of boiling salt water, cool and strain.*

(B).—Pilaw. *Chopped onion fried in butter, add carolina rice, moisten with white consommé, twice the quantity of rice, season, add small bunch of herbs, cover with buttered paper, cook 17 minutes in the oven, after, transfer to another pan, add butter.*

Créole.—Rice pilaw, add sliced mushrooms, dice of pimentoes and tomatoes.

Croquettes.—(*See* preparation in **Entrees Volantes**).

Egyptienne.—Rice pilaw. Add salpicon of chicken's livers, ham and mushrooms.

Grecque.—Rice pilaw. Cook with sausage meat, divided into small portion, add petits pois à la Française, and dice of red capsicums, or pimentoes.

Indienne.—Patna rice cooked in boiling water for 15 minutes, strain and dry on a serviette and kept warm in the oven.

Parisienne.—Rice pilaw. Add dice of mushrooms, mixed with tomato sauce and grated cheese.

Rizotto Italienne.—Rice pilaw. Add grated gruyère or parmesan, buttered and finished with white consommé.

Rizotto Milanaise.—Same as above, coloured with saffron water and raw mushrooms and tomatoes.

Rizotto Piémontaise.—Same as **Milanaise** without saffron, add slices of pimentoes and truffles.

Saint Denis.—Same as **Parisienne,** add meat glaze instead of tomato.

Turque.—Same as **Milanaise** without mushrooms or cheese.

Valenciennes.—Rice pilaw. Add dice of raw ham, pimentoes, tomatoes and green peas.

SALSIFIS ET SCORSONERES
SALSIFY OR OYSTER PLANT

Cooking Process

(Wash, scrape and cook in a blanc like Cardons.)

Crème.—Cook, strain, cut into lengths, dished in timbale cover with cream sauce.

Fines Herbes.—Same as **Sautés.**

Frits.—Cook, strain, cut two inches in length, dip in batter and fry in deep fat.

Gratin.—Same as **Crème,** coated with Mornay sauce, sprinkle with grated cheese and browned.

Polonaise.—Same as **Cauliflower** of the same name.

Sautés.—Cook, strain, toss in hot butter, add chopped parsley.

J

TOMATES — TOMATOES

Ancienne.—Stuffed with vegetable duxelles, add dice of ham and chopped parsley, Madeira sauce.

Carmélite.—Cut the top off, fill with mousseline of sole mixed with Oursins purée and dice of hard boiled eggs, place the top back, and cook slowly in oven.

Concassées.—Peeled, cut in halves, remove the seeds, chopped and cooked with chopped onions in butter, season.

Farcies.—Cut the tomatoes near the stem side, scoop out with a pommes noisette scooper, season, stuff with vegetables duxelles, sprinkle with bread crumbs on top and a little melted butter, brown in the oven, demi-glace sauce.

Hussarde.—Stuff with salpicon of pimentoes, mushrooms, tongue, gherkins, thicken with Béchamel sauce.

Italienne.—Stuff with rizotto Italienne add meat glaze.

Ménagère.—Stuff like **Choux Vivaraise.**

Navarraise.—Stuff with chicken mousseline mixed with dice of chicken and truffles.

Portugaise.—Stuff with rice mixed with chopped tomatoes.

Provençale.—Cut in halves, season, sprinkle with bread crumbs, parsley and chopped garlic mixed together, pour a little oil over, cook in oven.

Rivoli (*Cold*). Stuff with tomato mousse, in the middle place a cocks' kidney, cover with Aspic.

Sautées.—Peel, cut in thick slices, season, little flour and tossed in butter.

Soufflé.—(*See* preparation in **Savoury**).

TOPINAMBOURS

(Jerusalem Artichokes.)

Anglaise.—(*See* **Potatoes** same name).

Frits.—(*See* **Chip Potatoes**).

Purée.—(*See* **Purée de Pommes**).

TRUFFES — TRUFFLES

Cendre (sous la).—Clean some nice large truffles, season, moisten with fine champagne, wrapped in a paste, cook in the oven for 25 minutes.

Champagne.—Clean, season, cook with Mirepoix and champagne in a covered pan, dress in small silver casseroles, reduce the champagne, add a strong veal gravy, strain and pour over the truffle.

Crème.—Peel cut in thick slices, season, set alight with fine champagne, reduce, add cream and butter.

Porto.—Same as **Champagne,** cook with Port wine.

Rêve d'Amour.—Cook in champagne with small bunch of herbs for 25 minutes, left to cool in the stock for 24 hours before serving.

Serviette.—Same as **Champagne,** only cooked in Madeira, dish in timbale, placed in the middle of a folded serviette.

PATES ALIMENTAIRES — FARINACEOUS PRODUCTS

CANNELONI

Paste and Farce for Ravioli, roll and·cut the paste in squares, poach the paste, cook and let drain, spread the Farce, after roll up, place them side by side in a gratin dish buttered and sprinkle with grated cheese, add a little veal stock, cook.

GNOKI OR GNOCCHI

Gnoki (A).—Choux paste with cheese in a piping bag, cut in short lengths and let drop in boiling water, poach, strain, cover with Mornay sauce, and browned.

(B).—One quart milk, 3 oz. butter, salt and nutmeg, when boiling add 8 ozs. semolina, cook 20 minutes, add 2 yolk of eggs, cool on a buttered tin, cut in round shapes.

(C).—Potato pulp, mixed with equal quantity of chicken forcemeat, make some balls, poach in salt water.

Notice.—Gnokis can be cooked as au gratin with veal gravy and Béchamel sauce, etc.

LASAGNE

(Are large noodles done the same way.)

MACARONI AND SPAGHETTI

Cooking Process

Cook in boiling salt water, poach slowly from 15 to 18 minutes for the macaroni and 10 to 12 for the spaghettis.

Anchois.—Same as **Italienne** with anchovy purée.

Bolonaise.—Same as **Italienne** with slices of fillet of beef, cooked with chopped onions veal stock and a bunch of herbs.

Génoise.—Same way as **Gratin,** add mushrooms.

Gratin.—Same as **Italienne.** add Mornay sauce, sprinkle with grated cheese and bread crumbs, browned.

Italienne.—Cook, strain, season, add butter, cream and grated cheese mix together.

Jus.—Cook, into short lengths and simmer gently in veal gravy.

Milanaise.—Same as **Napolitaine,** add Milanaise garnish.

Napolitaine.—Same as **Italienne,** add tomatoes in dice and tomato sauce.

Niçoise.—Same as **Italienne,** add chopped onions cooked in oil, garlic and tomatoes.

Sicilienne.—Same as **Italienne,** add onions chopped and cooked, also chicken liver purée, thicken with Velouté.

NOUILLES — NOODLES

Cooking Process

Cook for 2 minutes in boiling salt water, cool, strain, and serve in same manner as Macaroni.

Pâte à Nouilles (Noodles Paste).—One pound flour, 5 eggs and 2 yolks, salt, moisten as ordinary paste, leave to stand a couple of hours before cutting.

J

POLENTA

Maize flour.   Mix in boiling water and cook 25 minutes, stirring occasionally, add butter and grated cheese, serve in timbale or cool in buttered dish, then cut and toss in butter.

RAVIOLI

Cooking Process

Poached in boiling salt water, strain, then place on a serviette to dry, cover the bottom of a timbale with good veal stock mixed with tomatoes, lay alternating layers of raviolis, cheese and stock, finishing with grated cheese, then browned.

Farce à Ravioli.—Braised beef, brain and chopped spinach, season and moisten with good veal stock.

Pâte à Ravioli.—One pound flour, 2 eggs, salt, 1 oz butter, made into paste, roll into a thin layer, and stamped out with cutter, garnish the centre with little balls of stuffing, moisten the side and fold, poach in salt water.

SPATZELLI

Cooking Process

Poached in boiling water, press the preparation through a colander, strain, cool, serve like macaroni.

Pâte (Paste).—8ozs. flour, 5 eggs, salt and nutmeg, dilute with water, not too thick.

Entremets — Sweets

CREAMS

Anglaise.—16 yolks of eggs, 1 lb. sugar. Beat well together. Add 1 quart boiling milk. Vanilla. Cook slowly until thick.

Beurre.—16 yolks, 1 lb. sugar. Beat and cook in bain-marie. Let cool. Mix 1 lb. butter. Flavour, coffee, chocolate, etc.

Chantilly.—Whipped cream. Sugar. Flavour to taste.

Frangipane.—1 lb. sugar. Work in gradually 8 eggs and 16 yolks. Add 10 ounces of flour and 5 pints of milk. Boil a few minutes. Vanilla.

Meringue.—8 whites of eggs. Beat stiff. Mix 16 ounces castor sugar. Vanilla.

Meringue Italienne.—8 whites of eggs. Beaten stiff. Work in slowly 16 ounces sugar cook to Grand Boulet *i.e.* hard ball grade.

Pâtissière.—12 yolks, work with 1 lb. of sugar. Add 4 ounces of flour. Mix in 1 quart of milk. Let boil. Vanilla.

Renversée.—1 quart of milk, 4 eggs, 8 yolks, 16 ounces of sugar. Vanilla.

PASTES

Amandes (d').—1 lb. ground almond, 1 lb. castor sugar. Mixed with 4 white of eggs.

Baba (à).—1 lb. flour, 7 eggs, salt, 1 ounce sugar, 1 pint milk, 1 ounce yeast, 4 ounces sultanas and currants.

Beignets.—(*See* **Pâte à Frire**). Add sugar and brandy.

Biscuits à la Cuiller.—1 lb. sugar, work in 24 yolks. Mix 1 lb. flour and 24 whites stiffly beaten.

Biscuit Savoie.—1 lb. sugar, work in 16 yolks. Mix in 8 ounces potato flour and 16 white of eggs stiffly beaten.

Brioche.—1 lb. flour, ½ ounce salt, 1 ounce sugar, 7 eggs. Work in 12 ounces butter. Add ½ ounce yeast made into dough with a little flour and water. Let rise all night.

Brisée.—1 lb. flour, 10 ounces butter. Water.

Choux.—1 lb. butter, 2 pints water, salt, 3 ounces sugar. When boiling mix in 1 lb. flour, add gradually about 16 eggs.

Crêpes (à).—1 lb. flour, 3 ounces sugar, salt, 12 eggs, 3 pints of milk. Flavour to taste.

Dumplings (à).—1 lb. flour, 10 ounces suet, salt water.

Feuilletage.—1 lb. flour, salt, water, mix to the consistency of the butter used. Roll flat. Add 1 lb. butter. Give 6 turns, 2 at a time, set in cool place for ten minutes between each two turns.

Foncer (à).—(*See* **Pâte Brisée**).

Frire (à).—1 lb. flour, salt, a tablespoonful of oil, 1 egg, half-glass beer, water, 4 white of eggs whipped to a firm froth.

Galette.—Feuilletage with 12 ounces of butter to a pound of flour and give 5 turns only.

Génoise.—1 lb. sugar, 16 eggs whipped on slow fire. Add 1 lb. flour and 1 lb. melted butter. Vanilla.

K

Pannequets (Pancakes).—(*See* **Crêpes**).
Profiteroles.—(*See* **Pâte à Choux**). Without sugar.
Savarin.—(*See* **Pâte à Baba**). Less fruits.
Sucrée.—1 lb. flour, 8 ounces butter, 6 yolk of eggs, milk. Flavouring.

SWEET SAUCES

Abricot.—Purée of fresh apricots thinned with 18° syrup.
Anglaise.—(*See* **Crème Anglaise**).
Cerises.—$\frac{1}{2}$ cherries and $\frac{1}{2}$ red currant jelly flavoured with kirsch.
Chocolat.—$\frac{1}{2}$ lb. chocolate or cocoa dissolved in water, sugar and vanilla to taste. Add cream and a little butter.
Fraises.—Strawberry jam thinned with syrup, kirsch.
Framboises.—Raspberry jam thinned with syrup, flavoured with kirsch.
Groseilles.—Red currant dissolved, kirsch.
Noisette.—Crème anglaise, mix with powder of aveline toffee.
Orange.—Marmelade orange and apricot purée dissolved, flavour curaçao.
Sabayon.—8 ounces sugar, 6 yolk of eggs, 1 glass of white wine. Whip on slow fire until frothy and thick. Flavour to taste.
Sirop.—Sugar cook to light caramel, dissolve with water.

ENTREMETS

BAVAROIS (Cold)

Formula (A).—*16 ounces sugar work with 16 yolks, add quart of milk cook like a custard, add 1 oz. gelatine, vanilla, let cool and mix in 1 quart whipped cream.*

Formula (B).—*1 quart fruit purée, 1 quart syrup at 30°, lemon juice, 2 oz. gelatine, mix in 1 qt. whipped cream.*

Clermont.—Same as **Bavarois (A)**, add chestnut purée and pieces of marrons glacés.
Diplomate.—Line mould with **Bavarois (A)**. Fill interior, firstly with a layer of Bavarois flavoured chocolate, preparation (A). Let set. Continue the operation with another layer of preparation (B), flavoured with strawberry purée. Let set. Repeat until mould is full.
Diplomate aux Fruits.—Preparation (B), unmould on Génoise garnish round with same fruit as the one used for the Bavaroise.
Figaro.—Mould lined with preparation (B), flavoured with strawberry purée. Interior filled with interposed layers of preparation (A). One flavoured vanilla the other chocolate. Operate as for **Diplomate.**
Marquise Alice.—Bavarois praliné garnish with finger biscuits soaked with Anisette. When unmould, coat with whipped cream, decorate with streaks of red currant jelly.
My Queen.—Mould lined with preparation (A). Interior filled with preparation (B). Strawberries, mixed with strawberries macerated in kirsch.
Normande.—Preparation (B) with apples and dice of apples.

Religieuse.—Mould lined with preparation (A). Interior filled with Bavarois flavoured chocolate.

Rubané.—Mould filled with interposed layers of different flavours and colours.

Tivoli aux Fraises.—Mould lined with kirsch jelly. Filled with preparation (A), mixed with wild strawberries. Dish up. Garnish round with jelly.

BEIGNETS (Hot)

Fruits et Fleurs.—Dip fruit or flower in pâte à beignets and fry in deep fat.

Soufflés.—Pâte à choux cooked in deep fat. Can be filled with Chantilly cream, jelly, marmalade, etc.

Viennois.—Brioche paste, red currant jelly inside, let rise and fry in deep fat, roll in sugar.

BLANC-MANGER (Cold)

Formula (A).—*1 lb. sweet almonds pounded with a glass of water. Strain the liquid mix it with 8 oz. of sugar and 1 oz. of gelatine. Flavour to taste. Can be made with fruits, liqueurs, or like ribbonned Bavarois.*

Formula (B).—*One quart boiling milk, 4 oz. sugar. Stir in 4 oz. of cornflour diluted with a little cold milk. Let boil 2 minutes. Flavour to taste.*

CHARLOTTES (Hot)

Pommes (de).—Line in a well buttered mould some oblong slices of bread. Fill the interior with quarters of apples partly cooked in butter. Cook in oven. Dish up. Pour apricot sauce over.

Portugaise.—Génoise cooked in charlotte mould. Cut in slices. Garnish with orange cream. Reform cake. Decorate with meringue. Sprinkle with sugar. Glaze in oven.

CHARLOTTES (Cold)

Arlequine (à l').—Mould lined with oblong pieces of génoise iced in different colours. Garnish interior with Bavarois of different colours cut in dice and fill with Bavarois cream. Unmould on Génoise. Ice the top and decorate with fruits.

Carmen.—Mould lined with wafers. Garnish with two parts of marmelade of tomatoes and one of red pimentoes mixed with ginger dice, 3 lemon juice, syrup at 32°, 10 sheets of gelatine, 1 qt. whipped cream.

Chantilly.—Mould lined with finger biscuits, filled up with whipped cream.

Colinette.—Mould lined with small meringues, garnished whipped cream flavoured vanilla.

Montreuil.—Mould lined with finger biscuits, garnished Bavarois au kirsch.

K

Napolitaine.—Génoise cooked in charlotte mould. Scoop out the middle. Fill up with whipped cream mixed chestnut purée. Decorate cream and fruits.

Opéra.—Mould lined with wafers. Filled with preparation (A) of Bavarois mixed with chestnut purée and dice of glacé fruits macerated in maraschino.

Plombières.—Mould lined with finger biscuits. Filled Plombières ice cream.

Renaissance.—Same as **Arlequine.** Iced white and pink. Filled with Bavarois (A), mixed with dice of strawberries, peaches, apricot macerated in kirsch. On top slice of pineapple decorated with candied fruits.

Russe.—Mould lined with finger biscuits. Filled with preparation (A) of Bavarois.

CREMES (Cold)

Baisers de Vierge.—Meringues filled with whipped cream mixed with crystallised white violets and roses. Veil with spun sugar.

Bordelaise.—Stewed prunes purée mixed with whipped cream. Vanilla.

Brise de Printemps.—Whipped cream flavoured with violet, served in glasses.

Caprice.—Whipped cream, mixed with broken pieces of meringues.

Caramel.—Mould lined with caramel sugar, filled with crème renversée preparation. Cook in oven in bain-marie.

Chantilly aux Fruits.—Whipped cream mixed with fruit purée required.

Florentine.—Same as **Caramel** cream mixed with ground almond toffee. When cool decorate with whipped cream flavoured kirsch sprinkled with chopped pistachios.

Mont-Blanc.—Whipped cream mixed with chestnut purée.

Mont-Blanc aux Fraises.—Whipped cream mixed with wild strawberries. Dish up like a pyramid. Surround the base with large strawberries rolled in castor sugar.

Mont-Blanc Mère Jean.—Savarin soaked in kirsch syrup, covered with chestnut purée in vermicelli. Centre garnish with whipped cream.

Mont-Rose.—Same as **Charlotte Plombières.** Decorate with whipped cream mixed with raspberry purée

Mousse Monte-Carlo.—Whipped cream mixed with pieces of dry meringues, flavoured tangerine.

Nid.—Chestnut purée in a nest mould. Centre filled with imitation eggs in whipped cream.

Opéra.—Caramel cream cooked in border mould. Centre filled with crème Caprice. Surround outside with large strawberries macerated in kirsch.

Viennoise.—Crème renversée flavoured caramel.

CREMES (Hot)

Custard-Pudding.—Crème renversée cooked in pie dish. Serve hot.

Frites.—1 lb. flour, 8 oz. sugar, pinch of salt, 24 yolks, 8 eggs, 2 qts. milk, 4 oz. butter. Let cool on buttered dish. Cut in shapes, egg and crumb or dip in batter. Fry in deep fat.

Meringuée.—Crème Régence in a border mould. Centre filled with candied fruits macerated in kirsch. Decorate with meringue italienne, brown in oven. Serve separately sauce Anglaise flavoured orange.

Œufs à la Neige.—Take some meringue with a spoon, shape like an egg, poached in sugared and vanilla flavoured milk, make custard with the milk.

Petits Pots à la Crème.—Crème Caramel cooked in special dishes, flavoured to taste.

Régence.—8 ozs. biscuits soaked in a quart of milk, pass through sieve, add 8 eggs, 10 yolks, 10 ozs. sugar pinch of salt, cook in charlotte mould. Unmould. Base surrounded with apricot compote one cherry on each, Apricot sauce over.

CREPES — PANCAKES

(*See* **Pâtes à Crêpes.**)

Couvent (du).—Cook on one side, sprinkle the other with dice of pears, cover with batter, cook in oven. Serve very hot.

Gelée de Groseilles.—Cook. Spread red currant jelly and roll up.

Georgette.—Same as **Couvent,** pineapple soaked in kirsch instead of pears.

Gil-Blas.—Spread pancake with this preparation: 4 ozs. of butter worked with 4 ozs. of sugar and aveline powder.

Jeannette.—Same as **Gil-Blas,** flavoured maraschino.

Normande.—Same as **Couvent,** apples instead of pears.

Parisienne.—Add cream and powdered biscuits to the batter.

Paysanne.—Batter flavoured with essence of orange blossom.

Russe.—Same as **Parisienne,** flavoured with kümmel.

Suzette.—Same as **Gil-Blas,** flavoured with curaçao and tangerine.

CROQUETTES

Fruits (de).—Dice of fruits bound together with frangipane, egg and crumbed. Fry in deep fat.

Riz (de).—Rice cooked in milk bounded with yolk of eggs. Let cool. Shape. Egg and crumbed. Fry, Sauces: red currant, raspberry, apricot, etc., serve immediately.

CROUTES

Fruits (aux).—Slices of brioche sprinkled with sugar, glaze then put fruit compote on each slice, sauce over with apricot sauce flavoured with kirsch (*Cold*).

Joinville.—Slices of savarin soaked with kirsch, dish up like a crown alternate with slices of pineapple, decorate with chocolate drops, garnish centre with whipped cream, apricot round.

Lyonnaise.—Slices of brioches spread over with chestnut purée, coat with reduced apricot jam, sprinkle with grilled sliced almonds. Dish up like a crown, fill centre with marrons glacés.

Madère.—Slices of brioche. Dish up. Fill centre with macédoine of fruits sultanas raisins, currants. Coat with apricot sauce flavoured Madeira.

Maréchale.—Same as **Normande.** Centre garnish with salpicon of pineapple, raisins, cherries, orange peels, pears cooked in pink syrup. Coat over with apple jelly.

K

Mexicaine.—Slices of genoise glazed with Condé praline. Fill centre with ice cream **Plombières.**

Normande.—Slices of brioche coated with apple marmelade, dish up in crown. Apple poached in pink syrup on top, sauce over with apple jelly, flavoured with kirsch.

Pain Doré.—Slices of bread soaked in sweetened milk flavoured Vanilla. Dip in beaten eggs. Cook each side in clarified butter. Sprinkle with vanilla sugar.

Parisienne.—Same as **Normande**, with pineapple and all sorts of fruits.

Victoria.—Same as **Madère** with cherries and marrons glacés.

GELEES

Formula (A).—1 *calves foot to each quart of water, bring to the boil skim carefully, cook 7 hours. To each quart of liquid add 8 ozs. sugar, 1 lemon juice and orange zest. Clarify.*

Formula (B).—1 *quart water, 2 ozs. gélatine, 8 ozs sugar, lemon and orange juices and zests. Clarify.*

Fruits (aux).—Add to the jelly the juice of the fruit required.

Liqueurs (aux).—Add the flavour required to the jelly.

Marbrée.—Russian jelly of different colours. (*See* **Russe**).

Miss Helyett.—Jelly with raspberry and kirsch flavours. Decorate with whipped cream and compote of raspberry.

Moscovite.—Jelly slightly iced.

Rothschild.—Jelly with gold leaves and flavour with champagne.

Rubanée.—Alternated layers of jelly of different colours and flavours.

Russe.—Whip the jelly when nearly cold. Flavour and colour to taste.

Suédoise.—Garnish the jelly with different sorts of fruits.

OMELETTES ET RUCHES

Célestine.—Make a small omelette with marmalade in centre. Make another one larger, spread jam on it. Place the small omelette on the jam, roll both together and turn on dish, sprinkle with sugar, glaze with red iron.

Cerises.—Operate like **Novégienne**, ½ raspberry ice cream, and ½ cherry ice, surround with cherries in brandy. Pour kirsch all round and light as Xmas pudding.

Confiture.—Omelette with jam inside, glaze the top with hot iron.

Elisabeth.—Operate like **Norvégienne**. Vanilla ice cream sprinkle with candied violets. Veil with spun sugar.

Islandaise.—Operate like **Norvegienne** with round genoise, ice cream to taste. Cover with meringue italienne. Place on top some dry meringue tartlets and fill with rum, set alight when serving.

Mandarines.—Same as **Norvégienne** with tangerine ice cream.

Milord.—Same process with pears and vanilla ice cream.

Napolitaine.—Same process as **Islandaise** with vanilla and strawberry ice cream, garnish with marrons glacés. Cherries in tartlets.

Noël.—Omelette flavoured with rum. Garnish inside with mince meat. Set alight.

Norvegienne.—Génoise oval-shaped on dish same shape. Heap some ice cream to taste. Cover well with meringue italienne or preparation omelette soufflé. Decorate, quickly in oven.

Ruche Edouard VII.—Same as **Norvégienne** round génoise, strawberry ice cream with dice of peaches. Decorate, in shape of beehive. Brown in oven.

Ruche George V.— Same as above. Vanilla ice cream instead of strawberry.

Soufflée.—8 ozs. sugar, work with 6 yolk of eggs, flavour to taste, mix with 6 white of eggs beaten to a stiff froth. Shape on a dish like an omelette, decorate and glaze in oven.

Surprise.—As **Norvégienne.**

Sylphes (des).—Savarin soaked in maraschino syrup. Centre filled with strawberry mousse, cover with meringue, decorate and glaze in oven.

POUDINGS — PUDDINGS

Albert.—1 lb. butter, 1 lb. sugar, 16 yolks, 1 lb. flour, 16 whites beaten stiff, 1 lb. candied cherries, cut in dice, madeira.

Allemande.—1 lb. butter, 12 oz. sugar, 8 yolks, 4 oz. chopped almonds, 6 oz. bread crumbs, 4 lemons zest, and juice, 6 white of eggs, beat. Serve with syrup.

Américaine.—Same as **Plum-Pudding**, pound it, and pass through sieve, cook as plum-pudding, Rum sauce.

Anglaise.—1 lb. sugar, 1 lb. raisins and fruits, 1 lb. suet, 1 lb. bread crumbs, 3 apples chopped up, spices. Rum, 6 eggs ½ flour, custard sauce, Rum.

Apple-Pudding.—Line a pudding basin with suet paste, fill with apples, cloves, sugar, cover with paste. Boil or steam.

Aremberg (*Cold*).—Bavarois au kirsch, with dice of pears, decorate bottom of mould with candied fruits and biscuits soaked in kirsch.

Bread-and-Butter.—Slices of bread and butter in a pie dish, Sultanas and currants, fill dish with custard preparation.

Brésilien.—Tapioca pudding cooked in caramelled mould.

Cabinet.—Pieces of finger biscuits in a buttered charlotte mould, mixed peel, sultanas, and currants, fill with custard preparation, custard sauce, flavour vanilla.

Cermont (*Cold*).—Bavarois flavoured with Rum and chestnut purée, pieces of marrons glacés.

Chevreuse.—Semolina pudding with mixed peel and fruit soaked in kirsch.

Diplomate.—Cabinet pudding cold, with fresh fruits.

Ecossaise.—1 lb. bread crumbs soaked in milk, 2 oz. raisins, 2 oz. orange peel, lemon, citron, 3 eggs, 4 oz. suet, 4 oz. flour, apricot syrup. madeira.

Eva Pudding.—12 oz. bread crumbs, 6 oz. sugar, 6 oz. suet, 6 oz. raisin, 6 oz. chopped apples, 5 eggs, spices, salt, sauce apple syrup.

Malakoff (*Cold*).—Bavarois vanilla, with biscuits soaked in liquor, mince, almonds, currants, sultanas, orange peel in dice.

Mince Meat.—8 oz. suet, 8 oz. cooked fillet of beef, in dice, 8 oz. raisins, 8 oz. currants, 8 oz. sultanas, 8 oz. mixed peels, 4 oz. apples, spices; brandy, madeira, rum, mix well and put in jars.

Moelle.—Marrow and suet melted in bain-marie, work with sugar, bread crumbs soaked in milk, yolk of eggs, mixed peels, currants, sultanas, Sabayon sauce flavoured rum.

Nesselrode (*Cold*).—Crème anglaise with mixed peels, sultanas, currants, chestnuts purée, mix with equal quantity of whipped cream, moulded and put to freeze, dish up and surround with marrons glaces.

Nouilles.—Same as **Tapioca** with noodles.

Plum-Pudding.—8 oz. currants, 12 oz. raisins, 12 oz. sultanas, 4 oz. mixed peels, 4 oz. chopped apples, 2 oz. lemons, 1 oz. mixed spices, 8 ozs bread crumbs, 9 oz. castor sugar, 8 oz. flour, 12 oz. suet, 6 eggs, 4 yolks, sherry, stout, brandy, mix well, boil 4 hours.

Rice.—Same as **Tapioca.**

Riz à la Crème.—Cook rice, flavoured to taste ,mix with whipped cream.

Rizzio.—Same as **Diplomate** with macaroons soaked in kirsch.

Rolly Polly Pudding.—Roll flat and square some suet paste, spread jam on it, roll up, boil in pudding cloth.

Sagou.—Same as **Tapioca.**

Semoule.—With Semolina.

Soufflé (A).—4 oz. butter, 4 oz. sugar, 2 oz. flour, 2 oz. corn flour,$\frac{1}{2}$ pt. milk, 5 yolks, 5 whites, whites to be beaten to stiff froth, put milk butter and sugar to boil, flavour to taste, add flour, mixed to stiff paste, let cool, mix yolks and then the whites. Butter mould and sugar it, cook in bain-marie.

(B).—4 oz. butter, 4 oz. sugar, 1 oz. corn flour, 4 yolks, cooked in bain-marie, let cool, mix 4 whites whipped to a stiff froth.

Soufflé Bananas.—Add dice of pineapples. (Same as above).

Soufflé au Citron.—Same as above flavoured with lemon zest and juice.

Soufflé à l'Indienne.—Add ginger powder and dice of candied ginger. (Same as above).

Soufflé aux Liqueurs.—Flavour with liqueur to taste.

Soufflé Maltais.—Flavour with orange zest and juice.

Soufflé aux Marrons.—With chestnut purée and pieces of marrons glacés. Apricot sauce.

Soufflé Montmorency.—With cherries soaked in kirsch.

Soufflé Pineapple.—Add dice of pineapples. (Same as above).

Soufflé Régence.—In a mould lined with caramel.

Soufflé à la Reine.—In a savarin mould, fill centre with candied fruit soaked in kirsch, Apricot sauce.

Soufflé Royale.—Line mould with slices of swiss roll, Apricot sauce.

Soufflé Sans-Souci.—With currants and dice of cooked apples.

Soufflé Saxon.—Flavour vanilla custard sauce.

Soufflé Vésuvienne.—With raisins and tomato jam, in a savarin mould, serve with rum in the centre. Set alight.

Suédois.—Same as bread and butter with mixed candied fruits cup ut.

Tapioca à l'Anglaise.—1 qt. milk, 4 oz sugar, 2 oz. tapioca, 2 eggs, boil milk, add tapioca. When cooked mix eggs, flavour, cook in pie dish in bain-marie.

Tapioca Soufflé.—1 qt. milk, 2 oz. sugar, 1 oz. butter, 4 oz. tapioca, 1 oz. cornflour, 5 whites of eggs whip to a firm froth.

Vermicelle.—With vermicelli and flavour vanilla.

Viennoise.—12 oz. butter, 8 oz. sugar, 8 oz. brown bread crumbs, 1 oz. chocolate, 1 oz. chopped almonds, zest of a lemon, 1 oz. mixed fruit, mix 10 yolks and 2 eggs, 10 whites to be whipped to a stiff froth, cook like a soufflé.

RIZ — RICE

Condé.—1 lb. rice, 8 oz. sugar, 2 qts. milk, 16 yolks, 4 ozs. butter, flavour to taste. Bring rice to the boil, cook in milk, sugar and butter, pinch of salt, cooked in oven 30 minutes, add the yolks.

Fédérale.—Riz **Impératrice** in charlotte mould, decorate bottom with red currant jelly.

Impératrice.—Prepare rice as for Condé without the yolks, add salpicon of mixed fruits soaked in kirsch and maraskino, mix with Bavarois preparation, set jelly in bottom of mould and fill with mixture.

Maltais.—Riz **Impératrice**, flavour orange, decorate quarters of orange.

Palerme.—Riz **Impératrice** in savarin mould coated with jelly of red fruits, fill centre with whipped cream and strawberries.

Sicilienne.—Border mould with riz **Impératrice**. decorate with candied fruits, garnish with strawberry ice.

SOUFFLES

Formula (A).—*Crème pâtissière, yolk of eggs, mix the whites whipped in a firm froth.*
Formula (B).—*Sugar, cooked to breaking point and purée of fruits in the proportion of 5 of purée to 4 of sugar, mix with white of eggs to a firm froth...*

Aïda (B).—Flavour orange, add fresh fruits soaked in curaçao.

Amandes (A).—With almonds, milk.

Ananas (B).—With pineapple cubes, flavour kirsch.

Arlequin (A).—Half vanilla, half chocolate.

Avelines (A).—With avelines, milk.

Bananes (aux) (B).—With dice of bananas, flavour kirsch.

Camargo.—Half avelines soufflé and half tangerine, between each layer put finger biscuits soaked in curaçao.

Cambacérès.—Vanilla ice on creamy rice, cover with praline soufflé, flavour kirsch

Cavaliera.—On a piece of génoise, ⅓ strawberry ice, ⅓ pineapple, ⅓ kirsch, cover with (A), flavoured chocolate.

Cerises (B).—With stoned cherries and purée of Raspberry, flavour kirsch.

Chocolate (A).—Flavour, chocolate vanilla.

Citron (B).—Flavour lemon.

Elisabeth (A).—Garnish with pieces of macaroons soaked in kirsch, and candied violets, flavour vanilla, veil with spun sugar.

Fraise (B).—Flavour kirsch.

Grand Succès.—On a piece of génoise, put a piece of stale bread supporting a small recipient containing cherries soaked in kirsch, surround the stand with strawberry ice cream, cover with omelette soufflé mixture, set the cherries alight when serving.

Hilda (B).—Flavour lemon, split strawberries covered with raspberry purée

Idéal (A).—With avelines toffee, garnish interior with macaroons soaked in liquor.

Javanais (A).—Tea in place of milk, add chopped pistachios.

Liqueurs (aux) (A) or (B).—Flavour: Anisette, Chartreuse, Curaçao, Absinthe, Rum, etc.

Lucullus (B).—Soufflé with purée of fruits, fill the centre of a savarin, flavour kirsch, surround savarin with buttered paper, to cook the soufflé.

Mandarine (B).—Flavour tangerine, and dice of tangerines.

Mercédès (A).—Flavour vanilla, kirsch and maraschino, garnish with salpicon of mixed fruits soaked in liquor.

Moka (A).—Flavour coffee.

Montmorency.—Same as cherries.

K

Montmorency (A).—Flavour cherry, brandy, add cherries soaked in fine champagne.

Moscovite (B).—Flavour curaçao and strawberries.

Nassau.—Orange soufflé, cooked in scooped oranges.

Nougat.—(*See* **Praliné**).

Oriental.—Moka with granulated chocolate.

Orléans (A).—All pieces of Rheims biscuits, soak in cream of peaches and kirsch, dice of cherries and angelica.

Palais (du) (A).—Bottom garnished with apples cooked in butter. Flavour kirsch and vanilla.

Palmyre (A).—Flavour vanilla, add pieces of biscuits soaked in kirsch and anisette.

Paulette (A).—Flavour vanilla and strawberry.

Poires (B).—Same with pears in dice.

Pommes (B).—Flavour kirsch.

Praliné (A).—Flavour vanilla and pralin.

Printanière (A).—Flavour vanilla, interior Macédoine of fresh fruit.

Rachel (A).—Half vanilla, half pistachios.

Rothschild (A).—Flavour eau-de-vie aux paillettes d'or de Dantzig, add fresh fruit soaked in same liquor, decorate with pineapple and strawberries.

Royale.—Same as last, flavour kirsch and candied fruits.

Shokileff (A).—Praline and flavour Anisette, add biscuits soaked in Anisette and Bar-le-Duc red currants.

Sicilien (A).—Flavour orange, praline, add sliced oranges.

Vanilla (A).—Flavour vanilla.

Violettes.—With candied violettes, decorate crystalized violets.

DIVERS

Eaton Mess (*Cold*).—Fresh strawberries crushed with a fork, mix with equal quantity of whipped cream, decorate.

Eugénie à l'Italienne (*Cold*).—fruit Peel, mince, soaked in maraschino, dish on vanilla ice cream, decorate with whipped cream, sprinkle with candied violettes.

Flamri (*Cold*).—Boil ½ bottle of white wine, ½ qt. water, add 8 oz. semolina, cook 20 minutes, add 10 oz. sugar and pinch salt, 2 eggs and 6 whites whipped to a stiff froth, cook in a buttered mould, cover with a fresh fruit purée to taste.

Ile Flottante (*Cold*).—Biscuits de Savoie split in slices, soaked in kirsch and maraschino, spread with apricot jam, almonds and currants, reform biscuits, cover with whipped cream, decorate and sprinkle with pistachioes and currants, dish up and pour round vanilla custard.

Junket-Milk (*Cold*).—1 qt. milk warmed to blood heat, add 2 oz. sugar, 2 tea spoonfuls of essence of Rennett, flavour to taste, set to cool without disturbing. Serve very cold.

Macédoine de Fruits Rafraîchis.—Salpicon of fruits, dish in timbale with heavy syrup, flavour with kirsch and maraskino lightly iced.

Melon frappé.—Cut the top of a melon, take the inside out with a spoon, sprinkle with liquor, refill with melon ice and the pulp, serve on a block of ice.

Melon à l'Orientale.—Same as **Melon Frappé,** with wild strawberries instead of ice, flavour with kirsch.

Melon Surprise.—Same as above with macédoine of fruits and purée of wild strawberries.

Œufs à la Neige Moulés.—Œufs à la neige in a border mould, cover with custard, add a few gélatine sheets in the custard.

Œufs à la Neige Réjane.—Œufs neige piped round shapes, poach in milk, when cold place two by two, half apricot on top, cover with thick custard.

Œufs à la Religieuse.—Fresh eggs poached in vanilla milk, place them in a flan croûte with praliné inside croûte. Pour over some cream custard, cook in a slow oven.

Tarte de Fruits à l'Anglaise.—Fruit required in a pie dish, sugar and water, cover with puff or short paste.

FRUITS

Aiglon.—Peaches, Apricots, Nectarines.—Poached in syrup dressed on Vanilla ice, sprinkle with crystalised violets, veiled with spun sugar.

Alexandra (*Cold*).—Same as **Aiglon,** fruits covered with strawberry purée sprinkled with white and pink roses, veil.

Alma (*Cold*).—Pears.—Poached in Port wine, sprinkle with grilled almond powder, decorate with whipped cream.

Almina (*Cold*).—Tangerines.—Take the inside out, fill with Bavarois flavour with kirsch and candied violets.

Andalouse (*Hot*).—Apricots, Pineapple, Peaches, Apples, Pears.—Poached, dressed on vanilla rice, cover and decorate with Italian meringue, colour pink, syrup of fruit.

Aurore (*Cold*).—Apricots, Nectarines, Peaches.—Dress on strawberry mousse

Belle Dijonnaise.—Strawberries, Peaches, Nectarines, Pears.—Dressed on blackcurrant ice, flavoured with fine champagne, cover fruit with blackcurrant purée flavoured with cream de cassis, sprinkle with soaked blackcurrant in fine champagne

Beurre (*Hot*).—Apples.—Scoop the middle out, cook in oven with butter and vanilla syrup, cover with buttered Apricot sauce.

Bonne-Femme (*Hot*).—Apples.—Scoop the middle out, fill inside with butter and sugar, cut skin round the centre of the apple, bake in oven.

Bourdaloue (*Hot*).—Apricots, Bananas, Nectarines, Peaches, Pears, Apples.—Dished up in halves, cover with vanilla frangipane, sprinkle with crushed macaroons and melted butter, glaze.

Cardinal (A) (*Cold*).—Strawberries, Peaches, Pears.—Poached, dressed on vanilla ice, covered with Raspberry purée. Sprinkle with sliced grilled almonds.

(B) (*Hot*).—Pears, Apples.—Divide in quarters, poached in syrup, after reduce the syrup and add crème de cassis, sprinkle with fresh walnuts chopped.

Carignan (*Cold*).—Pears, Peaches, Apples.—Poached, scooped, filled in with chocolate ice cream, dressed on Génoise covered with fondant, flavour vanilla.

Champagne.—Pears, Peaches, Nectarines, Strawberries.—Poached, covered with granité au champagne.

Château-Laffitte (*Cold*).—Peaches in halves, poached in wine and sugar, leave to cool, reduce syrup with raspberry and red currant jelly, cover the fruit with syrup.

Châtelaine (*Hot*).—Apples, same as **Au Beurre,** fill centre with cherries cut in squares and apricot purée, cover with thin frangipane, sprinkle with crushed macaroons and biscuits, and glaze.

K

Chevreuse (*Hot*).—Poached apples, dressed on semolina croquette composition, fill the centre with mixed fruit and raisins put together with apricot purée, decorate with meringue in pyramid shape. Sprinkle with pistachioes.

Colbert (*Hot*).—Apricots, poached, take stone out, fill with rice, egg-and-bread crumb, fried in deep fat. Apricot sauce.

Compote (*Hot or Cold*).—All kinds of fruits peeled and poached in light syrup, flavour to taste.

Condé (*Hot*).—Apricots, Pineapple, Bananas, Peaches, Pears, Apples.—Poached and dress on rice, coat with fruit syrup.

Côte d'Azur.—Oranges and Tangerines. Cut the orange in basket shape, fill with macédoine fruits, flavour curaçao, cover with fruit ice.

Créole (*Hot*).—Apricot, Pineapple.—Dressed on vanilla rice, or in a pineapple, coat Apricot sauce and rum.

Créole (*Cold*).—Strawberries soaked in kirsch and maraschino, dressed on thin slices of pineapple.

Cussy.—Apricots, Peaches, Nectarines.—Split in halves, dressed on macaroons stuffed with salpicon of fruit and apricot purée, cover with Italian meringue, brown in slow oven. Apricot sauce flavour kirsch.

Dame Blanche (*Cold*).—Peaches.—Poached, dressed on Vanilla ice, covered with thin slices of pineapple, decorate with whipped cream.

Diable (*Hot*).—Peaches, Apricots, Pears, Apples.—Poached, cover with crème Chantilly, add kirsch and set alight.

Eve.—Apples scooped, fill with vanilla soufflé, cherries soaked in kirsch, and biscuits soaked in anisette.

Favorite (*Hot*).—Pineapple, Apricots, Peaches, Pears, Apples.—Poached, let cool cover with frangipane, then egg and bread crumbs and fry in deep fat.

Félicie (*Cold*).—Apricots, Peaches, Pears, Apples.—Poached, dressed on Viennoise cream, cover with crème Chantilly, sprinkle with crushed pink pralines.

Femina (*Cold*).—All sorts of fruits, soaked in curaçao, dressed on orange ice

Feu d'Enfer.—All sorts of fruits, poached, add liqueur to taste and set alight.

Feu Follet (*Hot*).—Same as **Feu d'Enfer.**

Fool (*Cold*).—All sorts of fruits, cooked in syrup, pass through sieve, mix with whipped cream.

Fraisette des Bois.—Pears, Peaches, Nectarines.—Poached, dressed and covered with wild strawberry purée, serve very cold.

Friande.—Peaches, Apricots, Nectarines.—Poached, set alight with kirsch, dressed on pineapple slices, surrounded with raspberries decorated with lemon ice and strawberry purée separate.

Georgette (*Cold*).—Salpicon of fruits, soaked in kirsch and maraschino mix with pineapple Bavarois, dressed in scooped pineapple.

Gratiné (*Hot*).—Apricots, Apples.—Poached in quarters, dressed on marmalade of apples, cover with Condé pralin, sprinkle with sugar and glaze.

Hélène (*Cold*).—Pears, Apples.—Poached dressed on vanilla ice and candied violets, serve with hot chocolate sauce.

Infante.—Oranges, Tangerines.—Fill orange skins with strawberry ice, cover with orange soufflé, glaze quickly.

Irène (*Cold*).—Apples scooped, fill with vanilla ice, mixed with dice of stewed prunes, cover with meringue, flavour with kirsch and glaze.

Jeanne d'Arc.—Peaches, Pears, Apples, Strawberries.—Dressed on a white mousse flavoured maraschino, cover with mousse, veil.

Joséphine.—Pears, Apples.—Poached, dress round Impératrice rice, decorate with pistachioes cream, beehive shape, stuff the pears with same cream and cover with strawberry purée.

Jubilée (*Hot*).—Cherries, stoned and poached, dressed in small timbales, reduce the syrup, thicken with arrow-root, add kirsch and set alight.

Lerina (*Cold*).—Srawberries soaked in Lerina liquor, mix with melon pulp, dress in scooped melon.

Lombardi (*Cold*).—Apricots, Bananas, Nectarines, Pears, Apples.—Dressed on rice Impératrice, decorate whipped cream, flavour maraschino.

Louise (*Cold*).—Apricots, Nectarines, Peaches.—Stoned and poached, fill inside with different ices.

Maintenon (*Hot*).—Peaches.—Sponge cake cut in half, garnish with salpicon of fruits and grilled almonds, reform biscuits and cover with meringue Italienne, glaze in oven, surround with half peaches, syrup flavoured with kirsch.

Maltaise (*Cold*).—All sorts of fruits, dressed on border of rice, garnished with salpicon of orange peel, orange sauce with curaçao.

Marguerite (*Cold*).—Wild strawberries soaked in kirsch and maraschino, mix with grenadine sorbet, decorate whipped cream, flavour maraschino.

Mariette.—Pears, Apples.—Poached, dressed on chestnut purée, cover with apricot sauce, flavour Rum.

Marquise (*Cold*).—Strawberries, soaked in kirsch, and rolled in castor sugar, dressed on whipped cream, mixed with strawberry purée.

Mary Garden (*Cold*).—Pears.—poached, dressed on Melba sauce with candied cherries, decorate with whipped cream.

Melba (*Cold*).—Strawberries, Nectarines, Peaches, Pears.—Dressed on vanilla ice, cover with raspberry purée.

Meringue (*Hot*).—Apricots, Bananas, Nectarines, Peaches, Apples.—Dressed on rice, cover and decorate with meringue, spots of red currant jelly to decorate.

Mireille.—Same as **Mistral,** use the almonds of the fruits, flavour vanilla sprinkle with violets and jasmin.

Mistral.—Peaches, Apricots, Nectarines.—Sprinkle with castor sugar, cover with wild strawberry purée, add fresh almonds, cover with whipped cream and vanilla.

Montreuil (*Cold*).—Peaches, poached, dressed on vanilla ice cream, half the fruit covered with raspberry purée and the other half covered with apricot purée.

Moscovite (*Hot*).—Apples poached, and scooped, fill inside with soufflé made of fruit purée, flavour kümmel.

Nina (*Cold*).—Strawberries, same as **Marguerite,** pineapple Sorbet instead of grenadine.

Ninon (*Cold*).—Pineapple, Strawberries.—In timbale, vanilla ice, scoop out centre, pineapple slices dressed on ice, garnish the centre with wild strawberries in a pyramid, cover with raspberry purée, sprinkle with chopped pistachioes.

Norvégienne (*Cold*).—Oranges, Tangerines, Bananas.—Scooped, fill inside with ice of the fruit, cover with meringue Italienne flavoured with rum and glazed.

Palikare (*Hot*).—Oranges, Tangerines.—Scoop out fruit and fill with rice, dressed upside down, round pyramid of rice, decorate with quarters of oranges, cover with tangerine syrup.

K

Parisienne (*Hot*).—Pears, Apples.—Poached, cut in halves, dressed on Génoise, soaked with kirsch, and dress on rice vanilla flavoured, decorate with meringue, glaze, surround base with cherries, pears, glazed with apricot syrup well reduced.

Petit-Duc (*Cold*).—Peaches, Pears.—Poached, scoop, fill with walnut praliné mixed with cream, dressed on vanilla ice, cover with red Bar-le-Duc jam.

Portugaise (*Hot*).—Apples. Same as **Moscovite**, fill with salpicon of orange peel, macaroons, currants, sultanas, thicken with frangipane, flavour curaçao, dress on semolina, cook in oven, cover with red currant jelly, with julienne of orange peel.

Printanière (*Cold*).—All sorts of fruits, poached, dressed on red currant jelly, cover with whipped cream, flavour violets.

Religieuse (*Cold*).—Pears, poached in halves, dished in timbale, cover Bavarois chocolate, keep in cool place.

Rêve de Bébé (*Cold*).—Pineapple, strawberries.—Thin slices of pineapple soaked in kirsch, and wild strawberries in maraschino, dressed on layers of pineapple placed in a scooped pineapple, whipped cream between each layer, place on Génoise, decorate.

Richelieu (*Cold*).—Pears compote dressed in quarter on a Flamri border, cover with whipped cream, mix with frangipane and crushed macaroons, decorated, apricot sauce with kirsch.

Ritz (*Cold*).—Strawberries, covered with Chantilly, mix with half purée of strawberries and half purée of raspberries.

Romanoff (*Cold*).—Strawberries soaked in curaçao, covered and decorated with whipped cream.

Rose Chéri (*Cold*).—Peaches, nectarines.—Poached, dressed on pineapple ice, cover with custard, flavour with champagne, sprinkle with crystalized rose leaves.

Rose Pompon (*Cold*).—Nectarines, peaches.—Stoned and poached, fill with vanilla ice dressed on raspberry ice, cover with whipped cream, veil of pink sugar.

Royale (*Cold*).—Pineapple, scooped, fill with macédoine of fresh fruits soaked in kirsch, dressed, surround base with peaches and strawberries.

Rubané (*Cold*).—Oranges, tangerines.—Scoop fruit out and fill skin with gelée or Bavarois of different colours and flavour to taste, when cool cut in quarters.

Sarah Bernhardt (*Cold*).—Strawberries, Peaches.—Poached, dressed on pineapple ice, covered with mousse of strawberries and curaçao.

Sultane (*Cold*).—Nectarines, Peaches.—Poached, dressed on pistachio ice, browned in the oven, dressed on pyramid of rice mixed with frangipane and pistachioes, place fruit cut in halves round, sprinkle with chopped pistachioes, syrup sauce with buttered fresh almond milk.

Sultane (*Cold*).—Nectarines, Peaches.—Poached, dressed on pistachio ice, covered with syrup flavour with essence of roses, veil.

Surprise (*Hot*).—Oranges, Tangerines.—Fill inside with soufflé of fruit cook in oven.

Tredern (*Cold*).—Bananas cut in halves, fill the skins with purée of bananas mixed with Bavarois, place on it half banana poached, and cover with apricot sauce, decorate with fruit.

Trianon.—Peaches, Apricots, Nectarines, pears.—Poached, dressed on vanilla mousse mixed with pieces of macaroons soaked in liquor of noyaux, cover fruit with purée of wild strawberries.

Valérie (*Cold*).—Cherries, gooseberry ice in tartlets, cover with meringue italienne. Place on stoned cherries poached in red sweet wine, brown in oven, coat cherries with red currant jelly, sprinkle with chopped pistachioes.

Vanilla (*Cold*).—All kinds of fruits, poached in vanilla syrup.

Vin (*Cold*).—All kinds of fruits poached in different wine.

Virginie (*Cold*).—Same as **Georgette** with Bavarois and strawberries.

Wilhelmine (*Cold*).—Strawberries, soaked in kirsch, orange and sugar, whipped cream vanilla.

Zelma Kuntz (*Cold*).—Strawberries cooled in timbale, cover and decorate with raspberry purée, sprinkle with avelines pralin.

ICE CREAMS

Compositions

Biscuit.—12 yolk of eggs, 1 lb. sugar, 8 oz. meringue italienne, 1 qt. whipped cream, garnish and flavour to taste.

Bombe.—32 yolks, 1 qt. syrup at 28°, 3 pts. whipped cream. Flavour to taste.

Crème.—10 yolks, 10 oz. sugar, 1 qt. milk, flavour to taste.

Fruits.—1 qt. fruits purée, 1 qt. syrup 18° to 22°.

Granités.—Syrup of fruits at 14°, flavour to taste.

Liqueurs.—Ice, fruits and cream, flavour to taste.

Marquise.—Kirsch syrup at 17° add whipped cream mixed with strawberry and pineapple purée.

Mousse.—Syrup at 35°, add same quantity of fruit purée, and double whipped cream.

Parfait.—Same as **Bombe**, mould in parfait moulds.

Punch.—Syrup at 22°, thinned to 17° with white wine or champagne, add peel of oranges and lemons, infuse, reduce to 18°, when iced add meringue italienne, liquor when serving.

Sorbets.—Same as punch, but thinned to 15° with liquor, wine or fresh fruit juices, add meringue Italienne, serve in glasses.

Spooms.—Same as **Sorbets** with double quantity of meringue.

BISCUITS

(Dressed in paper cases, interposed layers.)

Bénédictine.—One layer strawberry, one Bénédictine, one violet.

Excelsior.—1st Vanilla, 2nd raspberry mixed with biscuits soaked in maraschino 3rd pistachioes.

Maire.—Vanilla, between 2 Palmer biscuits.

Marquise.—1st Vanilla, 2nd strawberry, 3rd vanilla, 4th strawberry.

Mont-Blanc.—1st Rum, 2nd chestnuts, 3rd vanilla.

K

Napolitaine.—1st Vanilla, 2nd strawberry, 3rd pistachioes.

Princesse.—Praline, sprinkle sliced and grilled almonds, decorate with vanilla and tangerine.

Sigurd.—1st Strawberry, 2nd pistachioes.

Tortoni.—1st Vanilla, 2nd pistachioes.

BOMBES

(Dressed in Conical Moulds.)

Aboukir.—Lined pistachioes, interior bombe pralinée with pistachioes.

Abricotine.—Lined apricots, interior bombe kirsch, and layers of apricot jam.

Africaine.—Lined chocolate, interior bombe vanilla.

Aïda.—Lined strawberries, interior bombe kirsch.

Aiglon.—Lined strawberries, interior bombe chartreuse.

Alaska.—(*See* **Omelette Soufflée**).

Alhambra.—Lined vanilla, interior strawberry bombe, surround base with strawberries soaked in kirsch.

Alméria.—Lined anisette, interior grenadine.

Alsacienne.—Lined pistachioes, interior half vanilla, half bombe chocolate.

Américaine.—Lined strawberries, interior bombe tangerine, decorate pistachioes.

Andalouse.—Lined apricot, interior bombe vanilla.

Archiduc.—Lined strawberries, interior bombe pralinée vanilla.

Batavia.—Lined pineapple, interior bombe strawberries, and dice of ginger.

Bernoise.—Parfait anisette with salpicon of fruits, soaked in same liquor, decorated with fruits.

Bourdaloue.—Lined vanilla, interior bombe anisette, decorate with violets.

Brésilienne.—Lined pineapple, interior bombe vanilla and rum, pineapple dice.

Camargo.—Lined coffee, interior bombe vanilla.

Cardinal.—Lined red currant and raspberries, interior bombe vanilla, with red rose leaves.

Carnot.—Lined raspberries, interior bombe maraschino, vanilla Custard sauce.

Ceylan.—Lined coffee, interior bombe rum.

Chateaubriand.—Same as **Andalouse.**

Clarence.—Lined pineapple, interior bombe violets.

Columbia.—Lined kirsch, interior bombe with pears, decorate with candied cherries.

Comtesse Sarah.—Lined vanilla and kirsch, interior kümmel mousse with crystalized red and white rose leaves.

Coppélia.—Lined coffee, interior bombe pralinée.

Créole.—Lined pineapple, interior bombe strawberries and pineapple.

Cressane.—Lined vanilla, interior bombe pears, with quarters of pears.

Cyclamen.—Lined pistachioes, interior bombe kirsch and cyclamen leaves.

Cyrano.—Lined praline, interior bombe cherries, flavoured kirsch.

Czarine.—Lined vanilla, interior bombe kummel, decorate candied violets.

Dame Blanche.—Lined vanilla, interior bombe with fresh almond milk.

Danicheff (A).—Lined coffee, interior bombe kirsch.

(**B**).—Lined coffee, interior bombe pralinée.

Délicieuse.—Lined peaches, interior bombe fine champagne.

Diable Rose.—Lined strawberries, interior bombe kirsch with candied cherries.

Diplomate.—Lined. vanilla interior bombe maraschino and candied fruits.

Duchesse.—Lined pineapple, interior bombe pears, flavoured kirsch.

Espagnole.—Lined coffee, interior bombe vanilla pralinée.

Esperanza.—Lined orange, interior bombe kirsch and pralinée, add red Bar-le Duc currants. Decorate vanilla ice.

Falstaff.—Lined pralinée, interior bombe strawberry.

Fanchon.—Lined pralinée, interior bombe kirsch, add coffee drops (*sweets*).

Fanfreluche.—Lined vanilla, interior bombe tangerine.

Fedora.—Lined orange, interior bombe pralinée.

Fellah.—Lined pistachioes, interior bombe oranges.

Florentine.—Lined raspberry, interior bombe pralinee.

Formosa.—Lined vanilla, interior bombe strawberry, add large fresh strawberries.

Francillon.—Lined coffee, interior bombe fine champagne.

Frou-Frou.—Lined vanilla, interior bombe rum and candied fruits.

Gabrielle.—Lined peaches, interior bombe vanilla.

Georgette.—Lined pralinée, interior bombe kirsch.

Gismonde.—Lined pralinée, interior bombe anisette and Bar-le-Duc white currants.

Gladstone.—Lined ginger, interior bombe flavoured gin and dice of ginger and angelica.

Grand Duc.—Lined oranges, interior bombe Bénédictine.

Grande Duchesse.—Lined pears, interior bombe chartreuse.

Havanaise.—Lined coffee, interior bombe vanilla and rum.

Hilda.—Lined avelines, interior bombe chartreuse and pralinée avelines.

Hollandaise.—Lined oranges, interior bombe curaçao.

Jaffa.—Lined pralinée, interior bombe curaçao.

Jamaïque.—Lined pineapple flavoured rum, interior bombe orange.

Japonaise.—Lined peaches, interior mousse tea.

Javanaise.—Lined coffee, interior bombe chocolate.

Jeanne d'Arc.—Lined vanilla, interior bombe chocolate pralinée.

Jocelyn.—Lined peaches, interior bombe maraschino.

Joséphine.—Lined coffee, interior bombe pistachioes.

Jubilée.—Bombe vanilla (*Separate*): serve brandy cherries (set alight).

Léopold.—Lined vanilla, interior wild strawberries bombe flavoured kirsch.

Madeleine.—Lined almonds, interior bombe vanilla and kirsch with candied fruits

Madrilène.—Lined coffee praliné, interior vanilla.

Maltaise.—Lined blood oranges, interior whipped cream flavoured tangerine.

Maréchale.—Lined strawberry, interior one layer pistachioes, one vanilla and orange.

Margot.—Lined almond, interior bombe pistachioes, decorate vanilla.

Marie-Louise.—Lined chocolate, interior bombe vanilla.

Marquise.—Lined apricot, interior bombe champagne.

Mascotte.—Lined peaches, interior bombe kirsch.

Mathilde.—Lined coffee, interior bombe apricots.

Médicis.—Lined cognac, interior bombe raspberries.

Ménélik.—Lined tangerine, interior bombe rum.

K

Méphisto.—Lined apricots, interior bombe rum and curaçao.

Mercédès.—Lined apricots, interior bombe chartreuse.

Mignon.—Lined apricots, interior bombe hazelnuts pralinée.

Mikali.—Lined pineapple, interior bombe kirsch, with red Bar-le-Duc currants.

Mireille.—Lined red currants, interior strawberry bombe flavour kirsch maraschino.

Miss Helyett.—Lined raspberry, interior bombe vanilla.

Mogador.—Lined coffee, interior bombe kirsch.

Moldave.—Lined pineapple, interior bombe curaçao.

Mont-Carlo.—Lined tangerine, interior mousse tangerine pralinée.

Montmorency.—Lined vanilla, interior mousse kirsch and vanilla with candied cherries.

Moscovite.—Lined kümmel, interior bombe bitter almonds and candied fruits.

Mousseline.—Lined strawberry, interior whipped cream and strawberry purée.

Nabob.—Lined pralinée, interior bombe fine champagne and candied fruits.

Nelusko.—Lined pralinée, interior chocolate.

Néron.—Lined vanilla caramel, interior mousse vanilla and chocolate drops, unmould on slice of sponge cake, coat and decorate with meringue Italienne, on top put coupe in pastry, coated with reduced apricot, rum in the coupe, set alight when serving.

Nesselrode.—Lined chestnut, interior bombe vanilla.

Odessa.—Lined apricots, interior bombe strawberry.

Odette.—Lined vanilla, interior bombe pralinée.

Orientale.—Lined ginger, interior bombe pistachioes.

Otéro.—Lined apricots, interior bombe blackcurrants.

Othello.—Lined pralinée, interior bombe peaches.

Parisienne.—Lined strawberry, interior bombe walnuts.

Patricienne.—Lined vanilla, interior bombe hazelnuts and Bar-le-Duc red currants.

Pompadour.—Lined asparagus, interior bombe grenadine.

Printanière.—Lined strawberry, interior mousse strawberry and fruits.

Prophète.—Lined strawberry, interior bombe pineapple.

Reine.—Lined vanilla, interior bombe vanilla and pieces of marrons glacés.

Richelieu.—Lined rum, interior bombe coffee, sprinkle coffee drops (*sweets*) when serving.

Rosette.—Lined vanilla, interior whipped cream and fresh red currants.

Royale.—Lined kirsch, interior bombe pralinée chocolate.

Russe.—Lined vanilla, interior whipped cream and purée marrons glacés.

Saint-Laud.—Lined raspberry, interior half bombe melon, half whipped cream.

Santiago.—Lined cognac, interior bombe pistachioes.

Selika.—Lined pralinée, interior bombe curaçao.

Sicilienne.—Lined lemon, interior bombe vanilla pralinée, decorate grilled almonds.

Skobeleff.—Lined Vodka, interior whipped cream flavoured kümmel.

Strogoff.—Lined peaches, interior bombe champagne.

Succès.—Lined apricots, interior whipped cream flavoured kirsch and apricot dice.

Sultane.—Lined chocolate, interior bombe pralinée.

Suzanne.—Lined rum, coloured pink, interior bombe vanilla and Bar-le-Duc red currants.

Tortoni.—Lined pralinée, interior bombe café and coffee drops (*sweets*).

Tosca.—Lined apricots, interior bombe maraschino, and fruits, decorate lemon ice.

Trocadéro.—Lined orange, dice of orange peels, interior layers of whipped cream and slices of génoise soaked in curaçao and sprinkled with dice of orange peel.

Tutti Frutti.—Lined strawberry, interior bombe lemons and dice of candied fruits.

Tzigane.—Lined pralinée, interior bombe pistachioes sliced grilled almonds.

Valençay.—Lined vanilla pralinée, interior, layer of whipped cream flavoured kirsch and layer apricot jam.

Vénitienne.—Lined half vanilla, half strawberry, interior bombe maraschino.

Victoria.—Lined strawberry, interior glace Plombières.

Westphalienne.—Lined pumpernickel, interior whipped cream and fresh walnuts.

Zamora.—Lined coffee, interior, bombe curaçao.

COUPES

Alexandra.—Macédoine fruits in glasses, cover with strawberry ice.

Andalouse.—Orange quarter soaked in maraschino, cover with lemon ice cream.

Antigny.—Garnish strawberr ice half a peach on it, veil with spun sugar.

Bébé.—Garnish half raspberry ice and half pineapple, add fresh strawberries, decorate whipped cream and violets.

Brésilienne.—Dice of pineapple soaked in maraschino, cover with lemon ice.

Clo-Clo.—Garnish with pieces of marrons glacés maraschino flavour and vanilla ice, whole marrons glacés on top, decorate whipped cream with purée of strawberries.

Coucher de Soleil.—Strawberry mousse, flavoured Grand Marnier liquor, thinned with cream.

Dame Blanche.—Garnish almond's milk ice, $\frac{1}{2}$ peach upside down, fill cavity with Bar-le-duc white currants, decorate lemon ice.

Denise.—Garnish coffee ice, sprinkle liquor, bonbon, decorate whipped cream.

Edna May.—Garnish vanilla ice and compote cherries, cover and decorate whipped cream and raspberry purée.

Elisabeth.—Garnish poached cherries soaked in kirsch and cherry brandy, cover and decorate with whipped cream, sprinkle with cinnamon and spices.

Emma Calvé.—Garnish vanilla ice pralinée, compote of cherries flavoured kirsch, coat with raspberry purée.

Eugénie.—Same as **Clo-Clo,** cover and decorate Chantilly, sprinkle candied violets.

Favorite.—Garnish vanilla ice, border with pineapple ice and middle with whipped cream and strawberry purée.

Germaine.—Garnish vanilla ice, cherries soaked in kirsch, cover with chestnuts in vermicelli, border whipped cream.

Gressac.—Garnish vanilla ice, 3 small macaroons soaked with kirsch, — peach upside down, fill cavity with Bar-le-Duc red currant, border with whipped cream.

Jacques.—Garnish with macédoine fruits soaked in kirsch, half lemon half strawberry, nice grape in middle.

K

Jamaïque.—Pineapple dice, soaked in rum, cover coffee ice, sprinkle coffee drops (*sweets*).

Malmaison.—Vanilla ice with muscats grapes, veil with spun sugar.

Mexicaine.—Tangerine ice with dice of pineapple.

Mireille.—Half vanilla ice, half red currant cream ice, stoned nectarines in middle, fill cavity with white Bar-le-Duc currants, decorate whipped cream.

Monte-Cristo.—Macédoine fruits soaked in kirsch, cover pistachio ice.

Montmorency.—Cherries in brandy, cover vanilla ice.

Niçoise.—Macédoine fruits flavoured curaçao, cover orange ice.

Petit Duc.—Garnish vanilla ice, half peach, coat with Bar-le-Duc currants, border lemon ice.

Royale.—Macédoine fruits soaked in kirsch, cover with vanilla ice.

Sans-Gêne.—Vanilla ice, Bar-le-Duc currants on it, cover and decorate whipped cream.

Savoy.—Macédoine fruits flavoured anisette, cover half coffee ice, half violet ice.

Silésienne.—Pieces of marrons glacés soaked in kirsch, cover vanilla ice, decorate whipped cream.

Suzette.—Same as **Clo-Clo**, decorate whipped cream, flavour kirsch.

Thaïs.—Macédoine fruits and pieces of marrons glacées, flavour kirsch, cover vanilla ice, decorate whipped cream.

Tutti-Frutti.--Garnish in layers, salpicon of fruits flavoured kirsch, strawberry ice, pineapple ice and lemon ice.

Vénus.—Vanilla ice, one small peach, strawberry on top of peach, decorate whipped cream.

Verdoot.—Vanilla ice, half peach, cover same ice, border strawberries and raspberries, coat fruits with quince jelly, sprinkle candied violets.

Victoria.—Macédoine fruits soaked in fine champagne, cover half strawberry, half pistachio ice.

GLACES DIVERSES — ICES

Carmen.—One third raspberry, one third coffee and one third vanilla.

Comtesse Marie.—Lined strawberry, interior vanilla.

Dame Jeanne.—Lined vanilla, interior whipped cream flavour kirsch, add dice of pineapple and red Bar-le-Duc currants.

Etoile du Berger.—In a star shaped mould, lined raspberry, interior mousse Bénédictine, dressed on a spun sugar layer.

Etoile du Chemineau.—In a heart shaped mould, whipped cream and macaroons flavoured kirsch, set in crushed ice to freeze, unmould, surround with nice strawberries coated with wild strawberry purée, decorate with pulled sugar and spun sugar.

Fleurette.—Garnish square mould with layers of strawberry ice and pineapple, decorate lemon ice.

Francillon.—Lined coffee ice, interior ice fine champagne.

Gourmets.—Lined vanilla pralinee ice, interior layer of chestnut ice rum-flavoured, and vanilla whipped cream, sprinkle with grilled almonds.

Iles (des).—Lined vanilla, interior pineapple ice.

Madeleine.—Garnish vanilla ice, and candied fruits soaked kirsch.

Mandarines Givrées.—Fill tangerine skin with fruit ice put to freeze in refrigerator.

Mandarines aux Perles des Alpes.—Same as above with chartreuse bonbons.

Meringues glacées.—Fill two shells of dried meringue with ice required.

Moulées.—In mould of different shapes fruits, pears, apricots, etc.

Plombières.—Vanilla ice, with apricot marmelade and candied fruits soaked in kirsch.

Wafer.—Between two flat biscuits put any ice required.

K

Savouries

Anchois.—Anchovy fillet on canapé. (*Hot*).

Anges à Cheval.—Bearded oysters, wrapped in thin slices of bacon—skewered and grilled—serve on toast.

Baron (*Croûtes*).—Bacon, grilled mushrooms, marrow.

Beurreck à la Turque.—Gruyère cheese wrapped in nouille paste, egg and crumbs, fry.

Cadogan (*Canapé*).—Oysters Florentine.

Champignons (*Canapé*).—English mushrooms. Grilled.

Champignons sous Cloche (Mushrooms).—Filled with Maître-d'Hôtel butter, cook slowly in special utensil glass.

Charlemagne (*Canapé*).—Shrimps with curry.

Charles V.—In barquettes, soft roes, cover with cheese soufflé, cook in oven.

Croque-Monsieur (*Croûtes*).—Slices of cooked ham placed between two slices of gruyère cheese, and then between two thin slices of plain bread, cut with round cutter, and fried both sides in clarified butter.

Derby (*Croûtes*).—Garnish ham purée, half pickled walnut on top.

Diablotin (*Canapé*).—Garnish small gnoki, sprinkle with cheese, glazed.

Diane (*Croûtes*).—Chicken livers wrapped in bacon on skewer, grilled.

Ecossais (*Canapé*).—Garnished scrambled eggs, anchovy fillet in middle.

Epicure (*Canapé*).—Mixed half roquefort cheese, ⅓ butter, ⅓ dry walnuts, chopped up.

Eureka (*In barquettes*).—Garnish with mushroom souffle and in centre anchovy fillet.

Favorite (*In tartlets*).—Parmesan soufflé, dice of truffles and crayfish tails.

Fédora (*Canapé*).—Grilled mushrooms, bacon, stuffed olive.

Florentine (*In tartlets*).—Spinach in leaves, parmesan soufflé and anchovy purée.

Gourmets (des) (*Canapé*).—Chopped ham, season with mustard butter.

Haddock (*Canapé*).—Fillets of haddocks, cooked in butter.

Hollandaise (*Canapé*).—Chopped haddock and slices of hard boiled egg.

Indienne (*Bouchées*).—Garnish curried shrimps and chutney.

Ivanhoë (*Croûtes*).—Puree of haddocks cooked in cream, small grilled mushroom on top.

Kippers or Bloaters (*Canapé*).—Grilled fillets of kipper or bloater.

Laitances (*Toast*).—Soft roes, poached and peppered cayenne.

Lucifer.—Poached oysters, rolled in English mustard, egg, and crumbs, fry deep fat.

Marquise (*In tartlets*).—Coat sides with gnoki paste, fill centre with Mornay sauce, cayenne pepper.

Méphisto (*In barquettes*).—Soft roes, sauce Diable.

Moelle (*Toast*).—Slices of marrow poached.

Nina (*Canapé*).—Grilled mushrooms, ½ grilled tomato, ½ pickled walnut.

Omelette Savoury.—Small omelette with parsley.

Paillettes au Parmesan.—Puff paste with parmesan cut in small sticks and cooked, cayenne pepper.

Quiche Lorraine.—In boat shape or pomponette moulds, make thin pastry, bottom, fill with chopped ham, yolk of eggs, cream, and parmesan cheese, cook in oven.

Quo Vadis (*Canapé*).—Soft roes, and grilled mushrooms.

Radjah (*Croûtes*).—Ham purée with curry, cover with chutney.

Raglan (*In tartlets*).—Smoked herring roe puree, cover with haddock souffle.

Ritchie (*Canapé*).—Chopped haddock cooked in cream sprinkle with cheese, glaze.

Royale (*Croûtes*).—Border chicken farce, fill centre with chicken purée, gratin.

Sardines (*Toast*).—Skinned and boned sardines, cayenne pepper.

Scotch Woodcock (*Toast*).—Scrambled eggs and anchovy fillets.

Soufflé Champignons.—Add mushroom purée to the soufflé preparation.

Soufflé Florentine.—Soufflé with spinach purée.

Soufflé Haddock.—With haddock puree, cook in dariole mould or souffle dish.

Soufflé Parmesan.—Soufflé with grated parmesan.

Soufflé (*Preparations*).—Reduce white sauce, season with yolk of eggs mixed with white of eggs beaten to a firm froth.

Spratts (*Toast*).—Same as **Sardines.**

Tosca (*In tartlets*).—Garnish crayfish cooked American style, cover soufflé parmesan.

Vendôme (*In tartlets*).—Cèpes bordelaise chopped, dice marrow, hard boiled egg, bread crumbs, lemon juice, meat glaze, mix the lot, warm in oven, slice of marrow on top.

Venise (*Bâtons*).—Macaroni poached, cut 3 inches long fill inside with gruyère cheese, egg and crumbs fry deep fat (cayenne).

Welsh Rarebit (*Toast*).—Melt cheddar cheese with cream and beer, glaze salamander.

Windsor (*Croûtes*).—Ham paste cover with grilled mushrooms.

L

Printed and bound in Great Britain by
Biddles Ltd, Guildford and King's Lynn

A — Fonds de cuisine
Fundamental elements of cookery

B — Garnitures et Sauces
Garnishes and Sauces

C — Hors-d'œuvre

D — Potages—Soups

E — Œufs—Eggs

F — Poissons—Fish

G — Entrées d'Abats, Entrées Volantes
Entrées of Abats, Poultry and Game

H — Entrées, Relevés, Rôtis
Relevés and Entrées of Butchers' Meat

I — Salades—Salads

J — Légumes et Pâtes Alimentaires
Vegetables and Farinaceous Products

K — Entremets—Sweets

L — Savouries